The Middle School

Edited by

Louis G. Romano
Michigan State University
Nicholas P. Georgiady
Miami University ■ Ohio
James E. Heald
Northern Illinois University

The Middle School

Selected Readings on an Emerging School Program

Professional-Technical Series

Nelson-Hall Company

ISBN: 0-911012-82-6

Library of Congress Catalog Card Number: 72-97847

Copyright © 1973 by Louis G. Romano, Nicholas P. Georgiady, and James E. Heald

Manufactured in the United States of America

Contents

Part IV. The Middle School Multipurpose Plant

Preface

Within this decade there has been a rapidly growing interest in the school organization called the "middle school." The genesis of this educational unit has been in the widespread dissatisfaction with the "junior" high school and a strong desire to fashion a program truly relevant to the nature and needs of the later elementary and early adolescent youth. The literature varies in identifying the scope of such a program expressed in familiar grade level terms. Some writers include grades 5–8 while others limit it to grades 6–8. There appears to be general agreement that it should not include grade 9. However, the importance of the middle school lies not in the grade levels covered but rather in its philosophy and provisions for recognizing and meeting the truly unique needs of the youth it seeks to serve.

The collection of readings included in this volume have been carefully selected to provide boards of education, administrators, and teachers with greater insights into the rationale for the development of a middle school. These readings are conveniently grouped into five major areas and represent those problems to be dealt with when the formation of a middle school is under consideration.

Part I attempts to give the reader an understanding of the purposes and philosophy of the middle school. This growing school organization must be based upon a program of learnings planned for the transescent which follows the program of learnings from the elementary school and precedes the program of learnings for the high school. Planning the middle school must move toward a program which meets the educational needs of the "middle-schooler," more appropriately called the transescent. The transescent is a child who is considered a pre-adolescent or early adolescent and finds himself in a unique group so far as growth and development are concerned. In this state of development there are marked differences among these young people in growth rate, weight, height, interests, sexual maturity, social maturity, mental maturity, and academic skills. Furthermore, the transescent is found by some experts in child development to be more precocious and more complex than his parents were at that chronological age.[1]

In Part II, the reader examines some of the thinking related to the evolving growth patterns and changes as related to the transescent.

Part III includes readings related to planning a curriculum or program of learnings which has meaning for the middle school child. The curriculum becomes the means by which the school attempts to help the middle school child gain the needed understandings, attitudes, and skills which our society believes are essential. These readings should present the reader with curricular strategies which point out that the program of learnings should bridge the elementary and secondary programs, but be significantly different.

Presented in Part IV are innovative ideas and plans suggested by outstanding educators and architects for the middle school for tomorrow. Today the shape and atmosphere of the school plant are changing drastically to meet the educational needs of the particular group of students to be educated. Some of the basic concepts in modern architecture such as "open," "flexible," and "simple" are now part of any design in the middle school building.

Part V points out many of the questions raised by educators when one considers a change in school organization. These questions must be examined and studied if the educator is to conceive a school to answer the emotional, social, physical, and intellectual needs of the transescent.

The compilation of the readings included in this volume represents the thinking of outstanding people in education, psychology, architecture, and other fields who are vitally concerned with the growth of the middle school and the program of learnings for the transescent. The editors wish to express their appreciation to the authors and publishers who graciously gave their permission to reproduce their copyrighted materials in this book.

Note

1. Robert J. Havinghurst, "Lost Innocence—Modern Junior High School Youth," *Bulletin of the National Association of Secondary Principals,* April 1965, p. 2.

Part I

Introducing
the Middle School

For a society that is living in an accelerated tempo, where man has been launched into one new age after another before he has time to adapt to the previous one, the concept of change is no longer a premise, it is a truism. The pre-adolescents and teenagers of today are not even questioning this assertion; for them it is a natural and continuous living experience.

In the new social context, the essential problem that confronts education is not to acquire and accumulate knowledge. Neither is it to learn how to learn. Of foremost importance, it is to learn how to become a full-functioning self as an individual, as a citizen of one's country, and as a citizen of the world.

From this perspective, the aims of education are manifold. The schools should attempt to:

1. Develop the individual so that he can demonstrate abilities to change and to adapt to the rapid evolution of technology and science.
2. Create adequate conditions so that the individual will be able to develop a strong personality, be able to gather and coordinate coherently the multiplicity of information that will assail him from all sides.
3. Provide the individual with intellectual capacities to master the technological and economical conditionings that surround him rather than become subject to them.
4. Teach the individual active participation processes, the necessity and fruitfulness of dialogue, how to elaborate new ways of thinking, and how to engage in community actions.

The implementation of this philosophy calls for an objective review of the present paternalistic conception of the school and learning activities within it. One must look forward to transforming the actual pedagogical relationship that limits students in their formative years and confines them to a round of purposeless tasks in a school environment in which they are bored with dull courses. Growing into maturity, the transescents experience the need to test their potentiality and assert their individuality. Thus, when they lack recognized means and environment to do so and are confined to fixed and imposed activities, they soon become utterly apathetic and begin to consider schooling as

3

something to be completed—the sooner the better. Furthermore, if one considers that school attendance is, at minimum, a 12 to 13 year span of duration, such a state of affairs is a concealed but real institutionalized alienation process in which people subjected to it are unable to realize and define themselves. Quite to the contrary, education should define itself as a means to encourage freedom and an exploratory and creative pattern of life.

The middle school concept of school organization for pre-adolescents is designed to meet the challenge by presenting the learner with schooling experiences that are relevant to his needs and interests, to his maturity, and to his goals at a particular time in his development. Functionally and structurally different from the organization of the junior high school, the middle school in its conception seeks to serve more effectively the intellectual, emotional, social, and physical needs of the 10-14 year old child of today. Rather than a new graded structure, it offers a new philosophical outlook that places emphasis on the development of each pupil's experiences based on the understanding that individual differences necessitate different pacing of learning in that stage of development.

Truly, a school organization for the middle grades is not new in the American system of education. The early decades of the twentieth century witnessed the emergence of the intermediate school followed by the growth of the junior high grouping, the 12-15 year olds. An innovation at that time, the purpose of such an organization was to provide schooling in an environment that would serve a bridge function between childhood and adolescence.

Today, although the theory underlying the junior high school is worthy of consideration, educational leaders are questioning whether in practice it still does perform the function for which it was intended. The major contentions are that while we are educating a new and different generation of students, junior high schools have become miniature, watered-down versions of the senior high school, and therefore are failing to meet the individual needs of the students in their transition period. Indeed, moving into the junior school level activities (such as interscholastic athletic competition, sophisticated social activities, and instructional programs and methods of the senior high school) is not really providing adequate education for the pre-adolescent. In this age span he needs small group participation and intramural activities that permit him to explore and assess his world. Similarly, exposing him to subject matter that does not affect him, arouse him, or involve him directly is not contributing to the emergence and the development of his personality and skills. The middle school on the contrary needs to focus on individual freedom and opportunities so that the pupil becomes aware, receptive to feelings and experiences, conscious of himself, and able to develop a sense of purpose and commitment.

This book of selected readings is evidence of the growing interest among thinkers for the development and implementation of an adequate philosophy of education predicated on the knowledge of individual needs. This section seeks to acquaint the readers with a number of viewpoints and features distinguishing the middle school from the junior high school organization. Historical trends in the development of schools for the transescent are traced to identify the matters of cardinal concerns when implementing the desired changes. A rationale and philosophical bases are spelled out on the postulate that a new structural organization might offer greater opportunities to reorganize teaching-learning experiences in such a manner as to present the preadolescent with more appropriate education. It is a shrewd and more global conception about learning experiences that is emerging. It attempts to systematize the present scientific information about child and adolescent growth so that it is consistent with the needs of this post-modern, societal generation of pupils.

Use of the above points can be made in discussions and study leading to the development of a middle school program for a given community. Certainly, the particular interpretation made of these characteristics and their implementation will be the product of the individuals involved and the nature of the community they represent. While there is a great deal more to be said with regard to the above and to other aspects of the nature of the transescent and the school program most appropriate for him, it is important to note that generally, the middle school should reflect the transitional nature of the child at this age and provide a truly transitional program to fit the situation. It is important both from the standpoint of bridging the gap from the elementary school to the secondary school as well as from the transitional or altering nature of the developing transescent himself.

1

Stanley G. Sanders

Challenge of the Middle School

Rapid acceptance of the junior high school has occurred within the life span of present leaders of our profession. This movement was led by men who were respected and have become revered. For the past two or three decades, school officials, in the vast majority, have accepted this as the preferred grade organization.

Within the past two or three years, small but significant numbers of school districts have been investigating and organizing intermediate schools, middle schools, or junior high schools with grades other than the accepted seven through nine. They have adopted their new patterns, not as second best substitutes for the junior high school, but as something better, something designed to overcome observed weaknesses of the older organization.

The junior high school was adopted during a period when much lip service was given to the scientific approach. One might assume, therefore, that its acceptance came as a result of convincing research. Such was not the case. A number of early studies attempted to compare academic achievement of groups of students from the new junior high schools with that of comparable groups from traditional eight-year elementary schools. Although a few of the studies showed superior achievement by students from the traditional schools, and even fewer found superior achievement by students of the new junior high schools, the most typical finding was "no significant difference."

From *The Educational Forum* (January, 1968): 191–97.   Reprinted by permission of Kappa Delta Pi, an Honor Society in Education.

Junior high school proponents began to take satisfaction from the fact that their students did "as well" on tests of "fundamentals" while spending substantially less time on the study of them.

More subjective evaluations did show that the new junior high schools seemed to have more advantageous effects upon the development of students and were deemed preferable by majorities of teachers, administrators, parents, and pupils.

Factors Influencing Acceptance of the Junior High School

In the nineteenth century the eight-grade elementary school and the four-year secondary school had become the dominant pattern. In the 1890s, President Charles W. Eliot of Harvard criticized that existing arrangements as being wasteful of time. Other leaders, particularly those who served on a series of national committees to study the problem, supported his contention that six years was long enough for provision of the elementary education. By about 1910, schools began to be formed which adopted the six-year secondary plan, but which dealt in a practical way with the extreme age range between grades seven and twelve by putting half the grades in a junior high school and half in a senior high school. At the same time, shocking studies of dropouts called attention to the need for programs which better met the needs of many youngsters in grades seven through nine. A change in the handling of these students was hastened after publication of Hall's classic *Adolescence*,[1] which looked upon the young adolescent as a "new breed" passing through a period of ferment and upheaval. Changes in educational philosophy, under the leadership of Dewey, demanded reform and reaction against the traditional school, and adoption of the junior high school became a "thing to do," a dramatic and progressive way to demonstrate a determination to eliminate the weaknesses of the schools of the past.

Some observers have interpreted the growth of the junior high school as merely an expedient solution to a housing problem. It has been common for districts to change the grade alignment of the schools when enrollments in the existing grades have outgrown the buildings, or when the buildings have become obsolete. However, a need for new buildings does not necessarily require a new grade combination. Officials of a school district have some choice between alternative solutions to their housing problems.

TABLE I. ORGANIZATION PLANS OTHER THAN 8-4 AND 6-3-3[2]

Organization Patterns	Years Advocated	Advocates and Occurrence
6-6	About 1900 by early reorganization committees	Always common in smaller communities as a substitute for 6-3-3
7-5	Existed in early 1900s.	Prevalent in the South where seven-year elementary schools were common
6-2-4	Late 1800s	Constantly common through the years
6-4-4	1940s	Leading advocate—Koos. Much recommended, seldom adopted
4-4-4	1950s	Leading advocate—Woodring. Receiving more attention in the 1960s
5-3-4	1950s	Most common in Texas and some cities of the Northeast. Now receiving support as more than an expedient

Proponents of the junior high school were influenced by factors which were many, varied, complex, and interrelated. However, all of these factors and conditions were based on, or reinforced by, one dominant and continuing theme—the desire to provide a better education to students in the period of transition between childhood and youth.

Challenges by Other Grade Combinations

The 7-8-9 junior high school has been challenged by various individuals who maintained that other grade combinations were equally or more desirable. Table I summarizes the various reorganized grade plans which have received support.

In 1965, two publications called national attention to a growing interest in the "middle" or "intermediate" school.[3] These schools, by definition, include one or more grades from the elementary school (below grade seven) and one or more grades previously found in the junior high school. It is not uncommon for districts to begin considering the 4-4-4 plan because of the symmetry of the equitable distribution of grades into three divisions. However, in many cases it is decided that fifth graders do not fit into the more advanced school, so that a majority of these schools are composed of grades six, seven, and eight.

There has been no complete, official survey to show the prevalence of schools of this type. Cuff reported on a survey which included returns from all states, but some of which were described as being "unofficial," "probably incomplete," or "indefinite." For the purpose of that survey, a middle school was defined as including grades six and seven and not extending below grade four or above grade eight. He found 499 middle schools in 446 public school districts in 29 states, during the school year 1965-66.[4]

Some of these schools adopted their particular grade patterns because of unique enrollment and housing problems. Most claim that their decisions also were influenced by the possibility of offering to children in grades five and/or six certain special programs, facilities, and faculties usually available only in the junior high school. Implicit in this recommendation is the assumption that this generation's fifth or sixth graders are *ready* for experiences similar to those which were deemed appropriate only at the seventh-grade level in the past.

The Ninth-Grade Problem

Most of those who have adopted the middle school plan also are seeking solutions to some problems involved with having the ninth grade in the junior high school.

Rigid state and college requirements have demanded four years of "Carnegie Credits" for admission to college or in some instances for high school graduation. Vocational education programs which are supported by federal aid have traditionally been four-year programs, beginning with ninth grade. These factors have limited the ability of school officials to provide flexible programs of study for the ninth grade. Once the program has allocated staff, facilities, and time to the ninth grade, schedules for seventh and eighth grades are automatically structured and limited in many schools. In other schools this problem has been met by planning one type of program for the seventh and eighth grade years and a distinctly different one for the ninth grade, even though all three are supposed to comprise one unified school. "For all practical purposes we frequently find that the ninth grade is attached to our building for quarters and rations only."[5] In their extensive study of the Carnegie Unit and its effects, Tompkins and Gaumnitz found it to be used more extensively and to be emphasized more restrictively in the East and South and less in the North Central and Northwest regions.[6] It is interesting to note that the middle school is appearing more frequently in the former two regions, where the problem of ninth-grade credits has been less satisfactorily solved.

Proponents of the junior high school stressed as one of its chief advantages the separation of ninth graders from older students in the senior high school. The freshmen obviously lacked the development and interests which patterned the social and extracurricular activities of the high school. However, today's youngsters, for better or worse, are far more precocious and sophisticated in these areas than were those of past generations. School officials and parent groups have battled, often in vain, against the tendency for the junior high school to become a little high school. If the school ignored the demand of the ninth-grade students for evening activities, dating, and wider contacts through interscholastic activities, large numbers of the more mature students turned to non-school related groups having less stringent controls. School activities, and consequently the school itself, tended to be viewed as juvenile, "square," "out"! Often school administrators and parents surrendered to the demands of these more mature students and allowed more advanced activities to develop; activities which then aroused opposition because they were inappropriate for a majority of seventh- and eighth-graders. In some cases, behavior problems in the ninth grade have been so severe as to occasion demand for its separation from the earlier grades. *Newsweek* described this issue as considered by a special panel recommending a new organization for New York City.

> "Middle school students," said the report, "would begin their exposure to secondary education earlier, yet not be subjected to the undesirable peer models provided by so many ninth graders." This was a polite way of calling attention to the extraordinary discipline problems that prevail in many of New York's junior highs.[7]

Obviously, it may be undesirable for ninth-graders to be closely associated with more mature eleventh- and twelfth-graders. The administrative staff of one school district has recommended a four-year high school, but with arrangements for appropriate distinctions between the ninth and tenth grades, on the one hand, and the eleventh and twelfth grades, on the other hand. These arrangements would, in effect, call for a school-within-a-school organization.[8]

Changing Developmental Patterns of Children and Youth

Junior high schools were organized in order to meet the peculiar needs of youngsters in the age range where they must make the transition from childhood to adolescence. The needs and characteristics of this group differ from those of children in the lower elementary grades and also from those of adolescents in the senior high school. For the past two generations educators have operated on the premise that the young people in grades seven, eight, and nine constituted this transitional group. Assuming that the decisions to combine these particular grades were wise decisions, the question now arises as to whether or not the conditions which made this desirable at the time remain unchanged in this generation. There is evidence to indicate that the youngsters in these grades today differ from the children who comprised the same grades one and two generations ago. They differ in chronological age. They differ in physical growth and development, as children not only are bigger and heavier today, but they mature at earlier ages. They certainly differ strikingly in social development. It is also very possible that they differ in mental development. Publishers of standardized tests have found that their national norms must be revised every three or four years, if they are to be appropriate for students enrolled in our improved educational programs. It is possible that today's sixth-graders are equivalent to yesterday's seventh-graders in age, size, physical maturity, and social development, and also in intellectual development, and that today's eighth-graders are similarly equivalent to yesterday's ninth-graders.

Two recent research projects have attempted to compare the appropriateness of the middle or intermediate school containing grades six, seven, and eight with that of the junior high school containing grades seven, eight, and nine. Each of the two studies was based upon premise that, while many factors will influence the determination of the graded organization of schools, serious consideration should be given to the characteristics and needs of the children or youth who would make up the student bodies of the schools. Each then sought to determine which group, grades six through eight, or grades seven through nine, constituted a more compatible or more homogeneous group.

In 1963, Dacus completed a study which compared the social maturity, emotional maturity, physical maturity, and opposite-sex choices of students in the respective grades, selecting his sample from one school district. In attempting to identify the more compatible group, Dacus obtained measures of the four characteristics, and then examined the significance of differences between measures of central tendency for successive grades. He found that ninth-graders were more similar to tenth-graders in the characteristics measured than they were to eighth-graders. Also, sixth-grade subjects were slightly more similar to seventh-graders than they were to fifth-graders, but this finding was influenced almost entirely by measurements of the female half of the sample. It should be pointed out that differences were comparatively slight, and that the author was very cautious in the conclusions which he drew from the findings. Furthermore, it must be remembered that the study was based upon subjects from a single school district, and that there was no evidence that the findings would be the same in other districts.[9]

Another study attempted to determine whether there was greater intellectual homogeneity within a student body composed of grades seven through nine or one composed of grades six through eight. The raw score distributions for the original nationally representative norming samples were reconstructed for three intelligence or academic aptitude tests, four achievement test batteries, and one reading survey test. The nine batteries, with their various subtests, provided forty-nine measures of various aspects of mental ability or educational achievement. For each of the forty-nine measures, variances for the two grade combinations were compared to see which was the larger. The primary finding was that differences in variances were too small to be deemed educationally significant, and that one grade combination could not be considered inferior to the other in this respect. Where differences in mental or educational development did exist, they tended to favor slightly the grade combination six through eight as being more homogeneous than grades seven through nine. Not surprisingly, variances between grades were shown to be much smaller than variances within grades, showing that no combination of grades can remove the need to provide for very substantial differences in intellectual development within each grade.[10]

Tradition and the Proponents of the Junior High School

In 1932, Spaulding, Frederick, and Koos carried out an extensive national survey of secondary education designed to determine "the existing forms of American secondary school organization with the greatest promise." After analyzing data from representative schools having different major types of organization, they identified certain characteristics which were likely to promote an effective organization. Among these desirable characteristics was "adoption of grade combinations which free the school from a traditional pattern."[11] In the early 1930s the junior high school composed of grades seven through nine was a combination which departed from the traditional. Today, the junior high school is no longer an innovation. In fact, the junior high school is no longer a departure from the traditional. It is the traditional.

Most of today's educational leaders "grew up" during a period when forward-looking innovators led the movement away from the traditional organizational pattern and toward the adoption of junior high schools as an improvement upon the previous educational program. During that period, opposition to the junior high school amounted to opposition to improvement. Failure to respect the new institution amounted to lack of respect for its proponents. It is natural for many of today's educators to be defensive when this revered institution, which bears the label "modern," is attacked or when its basic form is questioned.

However, the early proponents themselves might well be leading the reexamination of the structure if they were alive and active today. Certainly they would not object to the questioning of the existing pattern merely because it is "approved."

It is doubtful if the most extensive study of the characteristics of preadolescents or early adolescents could ever result in unanimous agreement that one combination of grades is inherently superior for all schools. However, failure to examine their development and blind acceptance of one pattern could result in programs which are inappropriate in many, many schools.

Notes

1. G. Stanley Hall, *Adolescence*, Vols. I and II (New York: D. Appleton & Co., 1904).

2. Stanley G. Sanders, *Differences in Mental and Educational Development from Grades Six Through Nine and Implications for Junior High School Organization* (Iowa City: The University of Iowa, 1960, unpublished doctoral dissertation), p. 68.

3. Judith Murphy, *Middle Schools* (New York: Educational Facilities Laboratories, 1965), and "Middle Schools," *Educational Research Service Circular,* No. 3, 1965 (Published by the American Association of School Administrators and the Research Division of the National Education Association).

4. William A. Cuff, "Middle Schools on the March," *The Bulletin of the National Association of Secondary School Principals,* 51:316:82–83 (February, 1967).

5. Alvin Howard, "Which Grades in Junior High School?" *The Clearing House,* 33:7:405 (March, 1959).

6. Ellworth Tompkins and Walter Gaumnitz, "The Carnegie Unit: Its Origin, Status and Trends," *NAASP Bulletin,* 48:288:19 (January, 1964).

7. "Remaking the City Schools," *Newsweek,* 63:21:100 (May 25, 1964).

8. Administrative and Supervisory Staffs, *A Plan for Reorganization of the Clear Creek Schools* (League City, Texas: Clear Creek Independent School District, 1965, mimeographed).

9. W. Pence Dacus, *A Study of the Grade Organizational Structure of the Junior High School as Measured by Social Maturity, Emotional Maturity, Physical Maturity* and *Opposite-Sex Choices* (Houston, Texas: University of Houston, 1963, unpublished Ed.D. dissertation); also Dacus, *A Grade Structure for the Early Adolescent Years* (Houston, Texas: Bureau of Educational Research and Services, University of Houston, 1963).

10. Sanders, *op. cit.*

11. F.T. Spaulding, O.I. Frederick, and L.V. Koos, *The Reorganization of Secondary Education,* National Survey of Secondary Education Monograph No. 5, U.S. Office of Education Bulletin No. 17, 1932.

2

William M. Alexander &
Ronald P. Kealy

From Junior High School
to Middle School

We in American education are witnessing a major reorganization of the middle years of our educational ladder. The middle school movement is reaching almost bandwagon proportions and it seems inevitable that the remaining junior high schools soon will be challenged to change to middle schools or at least to adopt some of the middle school concepts. A recent survey (1967-8) by the authors identified some 1101 operating middle schools—"schools which combine into one organization and facility certain school years (usually grades 5-8 or 6-8) which have in the past usually been separated in elementary and secondary schools under such plans as the 6-3-3, 6-2-4, and 6-6."[1]—Of the sample of these school randomly selected for further study, almost fifty percent had been developed during the years of 1965 and 1966; only ten percent existed prior to 1960. Although the survey has not been repeated to include all of the middle schools established in the 1967-8, 1968-9, and 1969-70 school years (the most recent data that could be obtained from some states for the 1967-8 survey was from 1966-7 state directories) there is every indication that the increase in number of these schools has been at least as great during these years as it was in the years included in the survey. The numerous publications about the middle school, its popularity as a topic for workshops and conferences, and continuous correspondence to the authors from those interested in information and assistance

From *The High School Journal* (December, 1969): 151-63.

regarding the planning and operation of middle schools are all indicators that the middle school movement is indeed a burgeoning one.

Middle Schools vs. Junior High Schools

It is interesting to note the similarity in the rationale of the emergent middle school and the basic concepts underlying the junior high school movement earlier in the century. A review of statements of rationale of numerous middle schools suggests three principal lines of justification:

1. To provide a program especially adapted to the wide range of individual differences and special needs of the "in-between-ager."

2. To create a school ladder arrangement that promotes continuity of education from school entrance to exit.

3. To facilitate through a new organization, the introduction of needed innovations in curriculum and instruction.[2]

The basic concepts underlying the junior high school idea which were stressed by various planning groups around the turn of the century are reviewed by Gruhn and Douglass as follows:

> ... (1) better provision for the needs of young adolescents; (2) better provision for exploration by the pupils of their interests and abilities; (3) better individualization in the instructional program; and (4) better articulation between elementary and secondary education.[3]

The rationales are interchangeable!

If the program of the junior high school had achieved its goals as originally stated, there would be little need for change except perhaps for a reorganization by years to accommodate earlier maturing children. Unfortunately, the initial movement toward the junior high school was, in actuality, an attempt to alleviate the crowded conditions in existing school organizations caused by the post-World War I population boom. This was accomplished by removing the two upper grades from the eight-year elementary school and taking the ninth grade from the high school. This expediently created junior high school conveniently inherited the Carnegie Unit requirements, schedule, departmentalization and extra-curricular activities of the senior high school, a program designed for full-blown adolescents. It subsequently became staffed predominantly by teachers who had been prepared to teach in the senior high school. The original goals of the junior high school were overlooked in the urgency of alleviating administrative problems.

A great percentage of the middle schools surveyed, like the junior high schools, had been established to alleviate current administrative problems including crowded conditions in other school organizations and the need to desegregate school systems. In the same 8-4 situations the obvious solution to overcrowding in the elementary school was to remove the top three or four grades, thereby creating a 6-8 or 5-8 middle school. In the 6-3-3 organization the ninth grade can be moved into the high school and the top one or two grades of the frequently overcrowded elementary school can be moved in with grades seven and eight, again forming a middle school. The middle school also presents an opportunity to get children out of segregated neighborhood elementary schools one or two years earlier.

Criteria for a Middle School Curriculum

If the middle school, as intended by its proponents, is to serve the specialized needs of the transescent learner, its curriculum should include certain characteristics. The authors and their colleagues proposed elsewhere[4] the following criteria for a middle school curriculum:

Is the curriculum balanced? The successful middle school cannot focus only on the area of *organized knowledge* as has most often been the case in predecessor organizations. The authors feel that two other general areas are at least as important as organized knowledge—*personal development* and *continued learning skills.* Broad and varied learning opportunities should be provided in each of these three major components of the curriculum for the total school population. Also, the school facility and schedule should accommodate each of these aspects of the curriculum. Another dimension of balance is that which deals with the individual's own program. Each transescent learner should have the opportunity to have appropriate learning experiences in each of the three components and sufficient guidance and counseling to assure a balance of experiences in accordance with his individual needs.

Is continuity provided? The middle school curriculum should be designed to provide continuity in both the total school program and in each student's program. This involves articulating for smooth transition from school to school, year to year, and level to level. Some form of continuous progress should be maintained to allow individual students to progress at their own rates and an efficient planning and evaluation system utilized to assure the optimum progression of each student.

Is the curriculum plan flexible? Flexibility is an important key to the success of a middle school program—flexibility to accommodate the wide range of individual differences and the characteristic ambivalence of the transescent learner. Interdisciplinary and/or subject area teams which are free to develop their own schedules within alloted blocks of time can be effective approaches to such flexibility. Learning resources and space should be available when they are needed and teachers should be encouraged to experiment and to use new content, materials, and methods as they are made available.

Is curriculum individualization provided? The middle school must in particular attend to the wide range of individual differences among transescent learners. Along with the provision for a continuum of progress, self-direction and independent study should be emphasized. The student, along with his teacher-counselor, should cooperatively evaluate his progress and plan for experiences that are most appropriate for his individual needs and interests. The reporting of his progress should be in non-competitive terms, indicating his level of achievement with regard to his goals and not as compared to other students.

Are the Middle Schools Really Different?

How do operating middle schools stack up against the above mentioned criteria? Unfortunately, the results of the 1967-8 survey indicated that relatively few of the middle schools operating at that time had curricula that differed significantly from their predecessor organizations. Most were middle schools by grade level grouping only, their program descriptions reflecting little concern for middle school rationale. Several findings from the survey testify to the discrepancies between middle school theory and middle school practice:

1. The reason most often given for the establishment of these schools was "to eliminate crowded conditions in other schools."

2. The schools reporting as an aim of their middle school establishment "to remedy the weaknesses of the junior high school" had programs which did not differ markedly from typical junior high

school programs in regard to such items as interscholastic athletics, departmentalized organization, and curriculum opportunities in general.

3. More than half of the schools including grade five maintained at this grade the typical elementary self-contained classroom arrangement.

4. About three-fourths or more of the schools used the junior high school's departmentalized organization for grades seven and eight.

5. A relatively low number of these schools had an extensive offering of exploratory electives at any level; grades five and six commonly had a dearth of electives.

6. Relatively few schools used the back-to-back and other team teaching plans at any grade level.

7. Large group, small group instructional procedures were used in a relatively small number of schools.

8. Schedules with five to seven daily periods, uniform in length, were utilized in more than seventy percent of the schools; less than five percent used any type of modular schedule.

9. Sharing of faculty and program opportunities to promote articulation between the middle school and other schools was almost nonexistent.

10. Some twenty percent provided scheduled independent study time, but relatively few schools had seminars and individually planned programs of independent study at any grade level.

11. Almost ninety percent of the schools used the traditional A–E marking system.

We certainly would hope and rather believe from our recent observations that the middle schools established since the 1967-8 survey have made an attempt to decrease this middle school theory-practice gap. In spite of the often extraneous but most always necessary reasons for its establishment, educators agree that the emergent middle school should serve as an opportunity to institute the changes in program necessary to serve the educationally neglected transescent learner. As Gordon Vars points out:

> Any shake-up of an established pattern provides an excellent opportunity to make fundamental improvements. Whether we regard the change from the junior high to the middle school as a revolution, a reformation, or a colossal mistake, let us seize this golden opportunity to make a fresh

approach toward the goals we have always held for schools for young adolescents, however they are organized and whatever they are called.[5]

The middle school will go the way of the junior high school, a path toward which it seems already to be moving, unless those involved in the reorganization plan and prepare carefully, designing the program on the basis of the nature of the transescent learner. There is still time, we believe, for middle schools to achieve their promise—but much more care is needed. The following section suggests some critical steps in changing from a junior high school to a middle school.

Some Critical Steps from Junior High to Middle School

Once the decision to move from junior high to middle school is made, the first critical matter of facilities is usually already determined. Hopefully there is still time to work with the school architect in designing the new facility for a middle school population and program, or at least for making essential alterations in the building to be inherited by the middle school. Whatever the situation, there are other critical steps that may be influenced by plans for the facility but must be taken regardless of whether the facility is a new plant yet to be planned fully, an old plant to be adapted, or an old plant to be used as is. It is with some of these essential steps that this section is concerned.

Selecting a Staff

The appointment of the principal of the middle school-to-be is needed as long in advance as possible of the actual opening of the new school. He or she will need to direct all of the other steps and could use to great advantage a full year devoted completely to them. Prior experience in teaching and school leadership roles at the middle school years, perhaps in both elementary and junior high organizations, would be useful for the principal, although even more critical are an informed vision as to the potential of the middle school organization and a high competence in curriculum development, group leadership, and human relations.

As the principal-to-be undertakes his new role, priorities will have to be set to get staffing, program development, administrative and instructional organization, interpretation, and other critical tasks in proper prospective and relationship. The authors' observation of middle schools in operation indicate that staffing is of highest priority and should be undertaken at least on a skeleton basis before other decisions can be made. Yet there is the paradoxical reality that staffing patterns must be based at least in part on some assumptions as to program and organization of the new school. We regard the following assumptions as tenable:

1. At least three functions, program-wise, must be cared for, with some person appointed to a leadership role (the title varying in accordance with local job definitions, salary schedules, etc.) for each: (a) The coordination of curriculum planning, instructional organization, cooperative teaching, and related activities; (b) the organization and management of counseling of students, student activities, student records, and related matters; (c) the development and management of learning resources and spaces—library, audiovisual, independent study centers, and others. These persons should be freed to work with the principal as long in advance as possible.

2. The curriculum plan will include provisions for three central components: (a) the personal development of the transescent; (b) continued learning skills; and (c) organized knowledge. Staffing of the school should reflect attention to each of these components.

3. Instructional organization will be one uniquely adapted to a middle school population; specifically it will be neither the self-contained nor departmentalized organization respectively associated in the past with the elementary school and junior high. Ideally, the middle school teacher would be able to teach in either of these past organizations but would prefer to work in a cooperative organization in which he is at times a generalist and at others a specialist.

On the basis of these assumptions the principal-to-be can begin to staff his school. First of all, he could organize his coordinating, steering group by selecting the curriculum coordinator, the pupil services coordinator, and learning resources coordinator indicated by the first assumption. These four persons could operate as the nucleus of a planning group that would be steadily enlarged as other staff members can be employed and brought in for such planning activities as possible.

Such an enlarging staff needs opportunities to identify itself, of course, and the principal will have to arrange for such meetings as possible during the school year(s) prior to opening the new school, and for as much summer time for as many staff members as possible to plan and work together. At least a six-weeks workshop for the new middle school staff has been found effective in a number of school districts.

Focusing on the Transescent

A focus on the transescent—his nature, needs, and program—is suggested as a central emphasis in most activities of the nucleus staff. This focus can permeate planning through such means as the following:

1. *The critical test in staffing.* Obviously mere expression of interest in teaching transescents is no guarantee that the teacher applicant will really perform well, but we would question assignment of any teacher to a middle school who is known to be primarily interested in another level. The traditional practice of assigning high school teacher applicants to the junior high school to await high school opening can be utilized in the middle school with the same undesirable results as have been true of the junior high. Instead, in the large school system teachers would be encouraged to apply for transfer or assignment to the middle school only if this is their preferred level. Similarly teachers in the junior high who prefer to work with ninth grade and other adolescents would be encouraged to transfer to the high school or other junior high schools.

In addition to expressed interest, other indicators are available to the principal as to an applicant's qualifications for the middle school: What experience and what quality of experience has he had with teaching children of middle school age? What college or inservice education has he had regarding human growth and development, especially at the period from childhood to adolescence? What is his interest in continuing study related to middle school education?

2. *Planning the personal development component of the curriculum.* The emerging middle schools generally provide some type of pupil organization which results in many teachers, usually the members of interdisciplinary teams, or perhaps all teachers, serving as teacher-counselors for particular home base groups or other groups of advisees. Accordingly teacher selection and assignment would need to include consideration of the teacher's preparation for and possible competence in this role. Full utilization of the home base group

concept would place major responsibility on the teacher-counselor for working with the individual advisee's program planning and also for working with the group in analysis of issues in the school and community which have imbedded in them the opportunity for consideration and development of values.

For the transescent an especially critical aspect of the personal development area is that of health and physical education. This period of his changing body needs to be paralleled with a program of physical education to help him develop adequate physical coordination and skill and also physical activites of a recreational nature. At the same time he needs health education to help him understand himself and his continuing development. Staffing and program planning for the new middle school needs to include adequate attention to these areas. Although not all middle schools have shaken off the adolescent paraphernalia of interscholastic athletics, many have and the newly-emerging ones hope to. Surely there are better ways of providing for physical development and recreational interests of all middle schoolers than the use of varsity-type competition; intramural athletics can involve far larger numbers and avoid the associated difficulties of interscholastics.

Personal development for the transescent also involves the development of interests which will add variety and even depth to his school experience. Various patterns of special interest opportunities need to be planned perhaps to include arrangements for utilizing sponsors or leaders from the faculty and the community. For example, many interests may be tapped or stimulated through some of the short-term exploratory experiences customarily available, but more on a course basis, in the junior high school, such as art, dance, dramatics, foreign language, home arts, industrial arts, journalism, music, typing, and various types of school and community work projects. Interests aroused or identified in the short term experiences can be further served and deepened by year-long laboratory courses. In addition, a variety of special interest clubs, classes, or centers may be provided through some scheduling arrangement that gives each student a chance without enforcing uniform participation.

3. *Involvement of the transescent and his family.* Increasingly the planners of emergent middle schools are involving the pupils themselves and their parents in planning the middle school program. Communication is especially vital during the months prior to opening the

new organization so that the children concerned and their parents may understand the nature of the middle school program and the expectations as to what can be done for children through the new organization. Data can also be collected as to parents' and children's expectations and aspirations for the new program. Inventories of parent volunteers for various tasks to be done and resources to be supplied can also be taken. In time plans for teacher-parent conferences about individual children become critical.

Providing for Continued Learning Skills

The nucleus planning group should early make some plans as to the continuation of instruction in the learning skills already introduced in the elementary school and as to additional skills to be taught in the middle school. Too early crystallization of plans for specific types of remedial reading, for example, would be avoided, but plans would be made for diagnosing reading skills and arranging for individualized and other types of reading instruction as indicated. Probably a first step is the identification of the whole range of learning skills to be taught, including reading, listening, asking questions, interviewing, viewing films and television, using library tools and resources, observing the natural and social environment, organizing information, generalizing, evaluating, and problem solving. Subsequent alternative plans are needed as to which skills will be taught in every learning situation and how; which will be taught in specialized instructional centers, and by whom; and when and how independent study will be introduced.

All of these questions will concern the entire faculty, and it is not suggested that detailed plans and schedules be made before the total staff is employed and assembled. Certainly the pre-school workshop is not too early, however, for making such plans. Much of the unique contribution of the middle school may well be made in the learning skills component of the curriculum, so largely neglected except from a remedial standpoint in the junior high school. The success of the middle school in helping learners become both skilled and interested in the processes of learning can be reflected in the lower dropout rates and more satisfying school careers of adolescents and youth continuing in high school and college.

Planning for the Major Curriculum Areas

All middle schools known to the authors have central in their curriculum plan the basic areas of language arts, social studies, science, and mathematics. Most include some provision, frequently on an exploratory or elective basis, for the fine and practical arts, and many include instruction in the foreign languages. The planning group will need to consider what fields of knowledge are to be involved in the curriculum of each middle school student and how instruction in these fields is to be provided. The authors are inclined to hope that organized knowledge from the arts and humanities fields will be included in the basic knowledge component of the curriculum in addition to the usual four areas or perhaps as a planned part of these areas.

An instructional organization of seemingly growing popularity in the newly-emerging middle schools that have been more carefully planned, is that of a cooperative, interdisciplinary team pattern. The pattern some schools follow is that of a four-member team, whose members represent some specialized competence in the four fields of language arts, social studies, science and mathematics. Each team member serves as the person responsible for planning the program of his home-base group and counseling initially individual students therein, and also represents his particular curriculum area in team planning. The instructional program for the four home-base groups is planned by the team with appropriate provision for large group, small group, and individualized instruction, and for utilization of the special competences of the team members. Typically each home base group has about 25 members, so that the total instructional group planned for and taught by the team is about 100.

If some such organization is hoped for, the staffing patterns must include the indicated numbers of teachers representing specialization in the curriculum areas concerned and also possessing competencies required for such home base organization and team teaching. The latter competencies likely have to be developed, so that initial selection may simply have to involve enough discussion of these possibilities to eliminate teachers strongly prejudiced against such instructional organization.

Planning for Experimentation and Evaluation

"Flexibility" is a popular and critical word in middle school education, but it is difficult to advise the middle school planning group on ways and means of insuring flexibility. Hopefully the middle school staff will be composed of flexible people, for this is probably the first prerequisite. Certainly scheduling patterns which force inflexibility can be avoided; for example, large blocks of time assigned to teaching teams and their instructional groups can be arranged flexibly by the teams, whereas schoolwide uniform period schedules virtually prohibit flexibility in the use of time.

Even more important than provisions for flexibility is the spirit of informed experimentation which needs to dominate the middle school. The principal and staff need to see innovation as a way of keeping the school experimenting with programs and procedures that seem promising for the education of transescents. Staff organization that encourages even the newcomer to try out his ideas must be sought. The school coordinators need to be regarded as persons who are resourceful in identifying innovation, not as those whose permission must be sought to innovate. Mistakes have to be tolerated, and experiments undertaken that do not have the support of prior research.

Experimentation cannot long continue successfully, however, unless it is accompanied by evaluation. The entire middle school concept may need to be evaluated in operation by long-term comparative studies such as the authors and their colleagues have proposed elsewhere.[6] Designs may also be set for evaluating individual innovations by use of before-and-after data and other means. Not to be overlooked is the continuing subjective judgments of students, teachers, and parents, which should be highly important data for continued planning and evaluation of the program and specific aspects of middle school operation.

To make possible such experimentation and evaluation, the initial planning group will do well to set up many opportunities for continued staff planning. The pre-school workshop may need to be an annual affair. Some type of schoolwide planning group should be meeting weekly to review progress and problems in connection with original plans and their modifications. Teaching teams must have a time and place to plan and evaluate their instruction. Student involvement in school planning and evaluation necessitates some type of student council or other organization, as well as means whereby home base groups can discuss issues and needs in the school. Finally, the principal should be helped to play a particularly vital role in working with the elementary and high school leadership for understanding and articulation, with parent representatives and community groups in interpreting the middle school and getting data for the staff planning group, and with school district leadership in gaining support for the middle school program.

Notes

1. William M. Alexander and others, *The Emergent Middle School,* 2nd., enl. ed. (New York: Holt, Rinehart & Winston, 1969), Ch. 9.

2. *Ibid.,* p. 11.

3. William T. Gruhn and Harl R. Douglass, *The Modern Junior High School* (New York: Ronald Press Company, 1956), p. 15.

4. Alexander and others, *op. cit.,* Ch. 4.

5. Gordon F. Vars, "Junior High School or Middle Schools? Which is Best for the Education of Young Adolescents?" *The High School Journal* (December 1966), p. 113.

6. See Alexander and others, *op. cit.,* Ch. 7.

3

Clayton E. Buell

An Educational Rationale for the Middle School

In the literature proposing the middle school as part of a 4-4-4 grade organization, there is a distressing paucity of *educational* reasons presented for the establishment of such a school. Yet in the literature the elements of such a rationale do exist. In this article some of the background and research will be reviewed.

The school for pupils between elementary school and high school should care for pupils in transition. This concept is accepted by proponents of the junior high school consisting of grades seven, eight, and nine, and by proponents of the middle school consisting of grades five, six, seven, and eight. But there is no agreement on the age at which pupils are "in transition."

The junior high school people would include in their school the pupils who have left childhood, who have reached puberty, but who have not yet reached late adolescence. However, the middle school adherents wish to include in that school the pupils who have left childhood, who are in the preadolescent stage, but who have not reached adolescence.

Both schools are alike in that they claim to serve pupils whose characteristics are different from pupils who populate either elementary schools or high school. Both recognize that the intermediate school should serve pupils who are in a stage of development that is

---

From *The Clearing House* (December, 1967): 242–44.

unique and who should therefore be given a unique school environment.

Arguments for the Middle School

What arguments are given for the middle school? Alexander and Williams[1] have summarized some of the advantages of the middle school; they note certain weaknesses in many junior high schools and therefore recommend a change.

Another argument for the creation of a middle school is based on the present-day need for specialized knowledge. The Brown-Bridgewater Project[2] stresses the necessity for bringing enriched knowledge to pupils at an earlier age than before.

The middle school has an advantage over the elementary school in that there is a fast-diminishing or nonexistent supply of teachers in self-contained classrooms who can teach effectively all the complexities of modern developments in science and in mathematics, who can teach modern foreign language properly with the proper pronunciation that younger children copy so readily, and who do not have difficulty in keeping up with modern developments in the teaching of English through the linguistics approach.

Another "claimed advantage of the Middle School is the availability of both specialized teachers and specialized facilities not existent in the small elementary school," according to the same report.[3]

The new middle school will benefit from the Hawthorne effect and the halo effect that usually accompany the natural interest in an accepted new proposal.

The establishment of a new type of school organization will furnish an incentive and a natural reason for setting up staff development activities that are of value in improving the capabilities of the faculty, whereas a traditional organization would present a greater problem for a similar inservice program.

An additional argument sometimes presented for the middle school claims that integration of the races will be increased in grades five and six of a middle school, as stated in the so-called Allen Report.[4] Note, however, that by the same token, integration will be decreased in grades seven and eight of a middle school.

When Are Pupils in Transition?

At what time of life are children actually "in transition"? At what time do they need a different school? A case has been made for the junior high school and another case for the middle school. Because much has already been written about the junior high school, this article will not repeat those claims. Rather, research that makes a point for an intermediate school of grades five, six, seven, and eight will be selected and quoted.

The experimental work of Stolz and Stolz[5] from 1932 to 1937 indicates that there are several stages through which children develop. Definite indicators in the form of changes in the rate of growth show progress from one of these stages to the next. Stolz and Stolz show that changes in the rate of growth in height can be taken as an indicator of growth in several other skeletal measures, in weight, in muscular strength, and in certain phases of growth of internal organs and body functions.

According to Meek[6] the first stage, the onset of preadolescence, is indicated by the beginning of a rapid growth rate, as the pituitary gland markedly increases in production of growth hormones. The beginning of the second stage is indicated by a falling off of the rate of growth, while the child continues to grow at an even rate. The onset of the third stage is indicated by puberty, when the gonads have matured to the point where their hormones are flowing at a pronounced rate and the growth rate decreases rapidly as new hormones begin to flow. During the fourth stage the pituitary growth hormone is significantly decreased or neutralized and the growth rate slacks off to almost zero and adolescence begins.

The transitional period between the beginning of the first stage and adolescence usually takes about three and a half or four years. For the child this is a time of confusion, of emerging new characteristics and needs, of wide differences among individuals. This is the span of life called preadolescence.

The intermediate school is advocated for the preadolescent. The pupil who enters this school has started on a growth pattern that makes a somewhat different person of him. As he leaves the school his adult-type body has largely taken shape and characteristics and potentials have largely been determined as he passes into adolescence. After this point (the beginning of adolescence) the individual has the task of becoming acquainted with his new adult-type body and of developing it, now that the violent changing typical of preadolescence has ended. This is, then, the time for the high school to begin, according to those who recommend the middle school.

At what age do these changes take place? The growth curve varies considerably among individuals of the same sex and between sexes. Girls reach these different stages approximately two years before boys, although some girls have completed the preadolescent cycle before others have started on it.

The studies of Stolz and Stolz were conducted in 1932 and 1937. Today the cycle occurs earlier in life due to better nutrition, vitamins, and reduced infection from disease. Experts disagree on how much earlier children mature, but an average figure seems to be about nine months to one year.

Taking into consideration both the differences between boys and girls and the earlier maturation of children today, the four grades that will care for the maximum number of both boys and girls throughout their four-year period of preadolescence, according to Daniel A. Prescott,[7] are grades five, six, seven, and eight.

The characteristics of the child are quite different from those of the adolescent, and the characteristics of the preadolescent who is in the transitional stage between childhood and adolescence are different from them both.

Some characteristics of the preadolescent are listed here, as given by a study committee in Montgomery County, Maryland.[8]

(1) The child in transition is experiencing a general reorientation to adults and to his peer group.
(2) The childish personality structure is giving way to a more mature personality structure.
(3) The preadolescent is restless.
(4) The preadolescent is characterized by mood instability.
(5) The preadolescent is a study in ambivalence between sophistication and childishness.

Surprisingly enough, these are the same characteristics that have been attributed to the junior high school children of grades seven, eight, and nine, in the literature that makes a case for that school.

Some Unanswered Questions

The elements of this rationale for the middle school exist in the literature. It is in conflict with that generally accepted by junior high school people. Which is correct? Or is neither entirely correct?

Some questions remain unanswered, and should be explored. Most of all, educators must find the relationship between physical changes and the type of schooling needed. Should the school for pupils in transition exist at the beginning stages of change, or should pupils enter the school after changes have been in effect for a time? Should it end before pupils in their adolescence have found their new roles?

Junior high school people and middle school people must learn many more facts and conduct much more research if they are to resolve that dilemma.

Notes

1. William M. Alexander and Emmett I. Williams, "Schools for the Middle School Years," *Educational Leadership,* 23 (Dec. 1965):217–223.

2. *Brown-Bridgewater Project,* Providence, R.I.: Brown University. No date given, p. 16.

3. Ibid., p. 19.

4. *Desegregating the Public Schools of New York City,* New York: The Institute of Urban Studies, Teachers College, Columbia University, 1964, pp. 14–16.

5. Herbert Howell Stolz and Lois Meek Stolz, *Somatic Development of Adolescent Boys,* New York: The Macmillan Company, 1951.

6. Lois H. Meek (chairman), *The Personal-Social Development of Boys and Girls with Implications for Secondary School Education,* New York: Progressive Education Association, 1940.

7. This estimate was given orally in answer to a direct question. Dr. Prescott is Professor Emeritus and former Director, Institute for Child Study, University of Maryland.

8. The subcommittee was composed of Dr. Samuel Goodman, Chairman, Dr. Richard Ahlberg, and Mr. William Porter. The report from the superintendent to Members of the Board of Education of Montgomery County Public Schools, Rockville, Maryland, is dated November 22, 1965.

4

H. Edgar Pray &
John A. McNamara

Transition to Middle School

For almost seven years the Van Antwerp Junior High of Niskay-una, New York, has been organized as a grade 6-7-8 school. Within this framework the patterns and procedures of operation have passed through several stages. As we look toward the construction of a second building and the possible inclusion of grade 5 in a middle school organization, some patterns of experience have developed which we have accepted as premises and which may be useful to others:

(1) A change in a pattern of organization must reflect that change in the manner in which the school system functions. For example, if we place grade 9 in a four-year high school arrangement, then we must modify our procedures to recognize the fact that this grade is no longer a part of a junior high, and that the special needs of these students are being met elsewhere. Likewise, the inclusion of grades 5 and 6 in a four-year middle school should not simply reproduce a junior high school pattern two years sooner. This point seems obvious, but so often it is neglected.

(2) Teachers in grades 5 and 6 need to be specialists in subject disciplines. It is not reasonable to expect a teacher to develop the background of content and method in at least four subject disciplines to the level of adequacy attainable when fewer disciplines are required. Typically, we expect teachers of these grades to attend modern mathematics workshops, study and develop newer approaches to

From *The Clearing House* (March, 1967): 407–09.

science, become knowledgeable in linguistics and semantics, show sophistication in relation to the newer anthropological and sociological approaches to social studies, and on Tuesday afternoons attend the seminar on health education!

(3) While paying attention to the need for competence in subject disciplines, we must not lose sight of the "child-centered" philosophy so well championed over the years by the elementary school. Some ways must be found to off-set the possible depersonalized aspects of a departmental pattern.

(4) Our primary task is to find ways to concentrate on the really important number in education—one. How do we in fact meet individual needs for self-instruction, self-expression, and self-growth in relation to the child's environment?

Educational Patterns

Traditionally the typical high school was a departmental, vertical type of organization. On the other hand, the elementary school tended to be organized horizontally, with one teacher primarily responsible for the learnings in language arts, social studies, mathematics, and science. We believe that our function at the junior high or middle school level is to meld these two philosophies with a balance of emphasis on the subject and the child.

Graphically, these patterns can be shown in the following way:

A.   High School Vertical

Language Arts	Mathematics	Science	Social Science

B.   Elementary Horizontal

Language Arts	Mathematics	Science	Social Science

C.   Junior High or Middle School
                         Vertical–Horizontal

Language Arts	Mathematics	Science	Social Science

In Niskayuna

The Vertical, Departmental Organization.

Presently in grades 6, 7, and 8 each teacher has responsibilities in only one subject field and at a given grade level. This allows the teacher time to be thoroughly conversant with the materials and methods of his field. He does not need to spread himself thinly over several fields of learning and dissipate his energies in a desperate attempt to keep up with the rapidly expanding and changing content of more than one discipline.

In each of the departmental areas the teacher meets the subject-matter colleagues at least once a week on built-in time before the beginning of the formal school day. In addition, a subject area coordinator within the building works with the teacher in planning, providing curriculum materials, demonstrating and making available a myriad of other services meant to strengthen the teacher's competency and security in his own field.

The Horizontal, Team Organization.

The elementary school's emphasis on the child's needs is felt in this phase of the pattern. Four teachers—one in English, social studies, mathematics, and science—form an academic teaching team which meets the same student groups. Another built-in time is offered to these teachers so that they can plan cooperatively for the needs of the youngsters they teach. It should be noted that this is not the usual type of subject-matter team. Rather, it is an attempt to offset the possible depersonalized aspects of the departmental pattern, by bringing the teachers of the same students together to look at these children and their total educational program.

Team planning sessions for teachers take place two to three periods a week, at a time when a given team of students attends physical education classes. In addition, entire teams of students are assigned to study pools supervised by lay study-hall aides. This takes place two periods a week in grades 7 and 8, and four and one-half periods a week in grade 6. At these times team teachers are encouraged to draw off pupils from this study pool for individual or small-group instruction.

Some advantages derived from this horizontal teaming are:

(1) Teachers tend to know each other better.

(2) Teachers know students better, for they share information about youngsters.

(3) A guidance counselor sits with a teaching team during planning sessions on a regular basis. Never before have our guidance and teaching staff and children been so closely related. Also, as the needs arise, the psychologist, speech teacher, principals, reading specialist, and parents meet with teaching teams on this built-in time.

(4) During study pool periods each team teacher may draw off the pupils he wants for individual or small group teaching. These are regularly assigned teaching periods when, perhaps, some of the most important teaching and learning take place. Often students take the initiative in this scheduling.

(5) All kinds of flexibility in scheduling are possible. Teachers may plan long or short periods, schedule field trips, engage in large or small group instruction. None of this is predetermined for the year. Rather, a given scheduling can be for a period, or a day, or a week, or as long as it serves the needs of the teachers and pupils.

(6) Ordinarily, house plans try to break large enrollments into more manageable groupings. We feel no need for a house pattern because our nine teams (three at each grade level) reduce the 1140 pupil enrollment to a little more than 125 students per team.

These educational patterns have emerged in our school because we feel they are a good way to focus on the individual, the critical point on which we will succeed or fail. Within our present structure we are developing programs for independent study and self instruction, as well as working with ungraded class situations.

Therefore, what patterns might we establish for a grade 5-8 middle school? We should retain more of the elementary school flavor in grade 5 and possibly grade 6 because the children are younger at this level and need to be with one teacher for longer periods of time. Consequently, we would suggest the following arrangements:

In grades 7 and 8, horizontal-vertical, four-teacher teams as previously described.

In grade 6, four teacher teams with extra time and effort given to the articulated, sequential development of basic skills in language arts including reading. As needs arise, some two and three teacher teams described below may be appropriate.

In grade 5, two and three teacher teams in a combined studies pattern.

Example of 3-teacher team:
 Teacher A—English, Reading
 Teacher B—Social Studies, Reading
 Teacher C—Mathematics, Science
Example of 2-teacher team:
 Teacher A—English, Social Studies, Reading
 Teacher B—Mathematics, Science, Reading

Finally, a transition to middle school is more effectively accomplished when we understand that its objectives and methods of implementation do not resemble high school, nor elementary, nor even junior high school, but a distinct and unique educational institution appropriate for youngsters of this age and maturity.

5

Pearl Brod

The Middle School: Trends toward Its Adoption

The middle school evolved out of the familiar concept of a transitional school, clothed in a different organizational pattern. The 5-3-4 or 4-4-4 middle school organizational plan has served as a practical solution to the pressing building needs. At the same time, theorists have seen in the middle school educational advantages over the traditional junior high school. The following is offered as a fairly comprehensive, generalized list of the advantages claimed for the middle school:

(1) It gives this unit a status of its own, rather than a "junior" classification.

(2) It facilitates the introduction in grades 5 and 6 of some specialization and team teaching in staff patterns.

(3) It also facilitates the reorganization of teacher education which is sorely needed to provide teachers competent for the middle school; since existing patterns of neither the elementary nor the secondary teacher training programs would suffice, a new pattern must be developed.

(4) Developmentally, children in grades 6-8 are probably more alike than children in grades 7-9.

(5) Since they are undergoing the common experience of adolescence, 6th-8th graders should have special attention, special teachers, and special programs, which the middle school permits.

From *The Clearing House* (February, 1966): 331-33.

(6) It provides an opportunity for gradual change from the self-contained classroom to complete departmentalization.

(7) Additional facilities and specialists can be made available to all children one year earlier.

(8) It permits the organization of a program with emphasis upon a continuation and enrichment of basic education in the fundamentals.

(9) It facilitates extending guidance services into the elementary grades.

(10) It helps to slow down the "growing up" process from K–8 because the oldest group is removed from each level.

(11) It puts children from the entire district together one year earlier, aiding sociologically.

(12) Physical unification of grades 9–12 permits better coordination of courses for the senior high school.

(13) It eliminates the possibility of some students and parents not being aware of the importance of the ninth grade as part of the senior high school record, particularly in terms of college admission.

(14) It eliminates the need for special programs and facilities for one grade and eliminates the problems created by the fact that the ninth grade is functionally a part of the senior high school.

(15) It reduces duplication of expensive equipment and facilities for the one grade. The funds can be spent on facilities beneficial to all grades.

(16) It provides both present and future flexibility in building planning, particularly when it comes to changing school population.

However, to the administrators and teachers who must work with this plan, the vital question is: How is it working out in practice? When a school system as large as that of New York City undertakes a change to a 4-4-4 organization, the question becomes even more pertinent.

We can assume that any system contemplating an organizational change seeks information from systems functioning under the plan being considered. If we assume that the ultimate decision is influenced by reports, the rate of growth of the new plan can then be considered an indirect indicator of its success in practice. A direct indicator would be the experience of administrators in functioning middle schools.

The middle school concept is an undercurrent that appears to be gaining momentum. It may become a major educational development in our times. The extent of its popularity is difficult to judge because the literature is sparse and research is virtually nonexistent. However, if the explorations I have made are an indicator, the middle school appears to be growing at a phenomenal rate.

Educational Research Service made a survey of patterns of grade organizations for the 1963–64 school year. Of the 344 school systems reported, only 5, or 1 per cent, followed a 5-3-4 organizational plan. It was interesting to note that seven systems reported that they were considering a change to a 5-3-4 or 4-4-4 plan. The school systems contemplating the change were greater in number than the total of those reported as utilizing this plan.

The 50 state departments of education as well as more than 5,000 school districts throughout the country were contacted by me. From direct responses, repeated references, and school directories, information was obtained relative to the organizational structure of almost 40 per cent of the nation's school systems. Of these, 10 per cent either were functioning on a 5-3-4 or 4-4-4 plan or were in the process of changing to one of these plans. Another 1 per cent reported that they were considering the middle school organizational plan or were seriously interested in it.

At least 45 of the 50 states have one or more middle schools in operation. However, the majority of the middle schools are concentrated in about 18 states, located at the four axial points of the country: east, west, north, and south.

The southern center is Texas, one of the pioneers in implementing the middle school organizational plan. Of the 201 school districts in Texas which responded, 92 reported that they operated on a 5-3-4 or 4-4-4 plan, 7 stated that they were in the process of changing to one of these plans, and 2 were contemplating such a change. It is extremely unlikely that this ratio exists throughout the state. However, it is indicative of the widespread popularity of the middle school organizational plan in Texas. Included in the southern area concentration of the middle schools is Louisiana, where one or more can be found in 15 per cent of the parishes.

The northern area includes Ohio, Illinois, Michigan, and Wisconsin.

Although the Middle Schools in Highland Park and Glencoe in Illinois and at Saginaw, Michigan, are widely known, Ohio appears to have the largest concentration of middle schools.

In the west, Washington appears to be the leader. There are many middle schools in operation in the state and there is also considerable interest throughout the state in this type of organization. Oregon is not far behind in this movement. California must be included in this western area because numerous middle schools can be found in that state. However, it is difficult to evaluate the trend in California because the school districts are undergoing statewide changes in administrative and organizational patterns.

The largest area of concentration lies in the east. From New Hampshire to Delaware, there has been a growing interest in the middle school. In terms of experience, Massachusetts appears to be the leader in this sector, with Connecticut close behind. However, interest is widespread throughout the area and New York appears to be taking the lead in the rate of development of new middle schools.

According to the data, there is no question that the middle school is "catching on," especially in specific geographical areas. But how is it working out in practice? From the comments accompanying many of the responses, it would appear that it is a resounding success. Only a handful of administrators who have had experience with the middle school commented negatively. The overwhelming majority of the comments ranged from cautious optimism to enthusiastic endorsements.

Perhaps more meaningful are the comments from individuals who have experienced the middle school organization by accident of housing needs. They have no commitment that might bias their opinion. The instances of systems planning to return to the middle school because of their past experiences are extremely impressive.

The advantages offered by the middle school have made this organizational plan attractive to school planners. This is reflected in the extremely rapid growth in popularity of this concept. The data I have accumulated suggest that the middle school is no longer a theoretical concept. It has come into reality, and the advantages claimed for it are passing the test of practical application. It is rapidly becoming an important aspect of the American educational scene.

6

Ann Grooms

The Middle School and Other Innovations

I like to talk about the middle school as a school of change. Now the term "change" tends to raise apprehension among those most likely to be affected. History is replete with records of how institutions and even whole societies have either resisted change or have been unable to cope with it.

The steam engine gave way to the gasoline engine in the late 1880's as a propulsion device for personal conveyances, and within our lifetimes the gasoline engine may well be replaced by the zinc-air battery for passenger cars. Rather than refusing to acknowledge that the gasoline engine is a prime contribution to the air pollution problem, automobile manufacturers are engaging in massive research to find alternative power sources. Those automobile makers who refuse to recognize the requirement for nonair-polluting engines will go the way of nineteenth-century buggy-makers who discounted the transportation innovation of the period—the automobile.

Education is well known for its resistance to change. Peter Drucker, the management lecturer and author, speaks of education as being one of the last strongholds of the handcrafts. He says that teaching has changed but little since the days of the Greeks. A recent study by Powell and Roberson shows that 66 percent of classroom talking is done by teachers. Education under such circumstances must be assumed as being the process of transferring knowledge from the head of the instructor into the head of the student, a process not unlike that

From *NASSP Bulletin* (May, 1967): 158–66.

of a pump lifting water from a well into a pail. The inadequacy of the teacher function under such circumstances is highlighted by the revelation that available technical knowledge has doubled since 1950.

A professional friend of mine was recently called upon to address a management association concerning the nature of change. He cited the following as an example of how tenaciously people resist change:

> A research director who was retiring from his position with a well-known chemical corporation was asked to make a study of the products that were introduced into the corporation's line during his tenure as research director, so that the conditions which stimulate invention and inquiry among the scientific staff could be better understood. The director found that some 90 percent of the products or processes originally conceived as innovations were turned down at least once by management personnel.

Writers seeking to make change more palatable to those in authority positions suggest that the new not depart too far from the old. You will find that the middle school presented here departs significantly from current practices.

Maturity of Students

Having talked about change and change factors, I want now to look at a particular group of students in our public schools whom I feel need a changed system of education. I'm talking about the children in the 10- to 14-year-old age group. The rate of maturation of this group has been increasing rapidly in recent years. Students in the 1960's are much more mature than their parents were at similar ages.

The junior high school was conceived of a generation ago as providing an easier transition between the elementary and high school, thus increasing the latter's holding power. The school was intended for relatively unsophisticated students living in an unsophisticated society. Education was assumed to be the responsibility of the school, with teachers standing in the same relationship toward imparting knowledge to the student as the parents stand relative to providing food, shelter, and clothing. Decisions as to what is to be learned, when it is to be learned, and what resources are to be utilized were all prerogatives of the school.

The unsophisticated student might accept such learning conditions, especially if he is imbued with the Horatio Alger idea that to work hard is to succeed. But the 10- to 14-year-old of 1967 is quite likely not to accept those conditions. Modern communication affords him access to information that was foreign to his parents, even in their high school or college years. Technology is making feasible events that were beyond the imagination of his parents in their school days. Yet, the student today is afforded many of the same educational experiences his parents had. Recently visiting a school, I heard a teacher extolling the beauty of a famous landmark of India with the same eloquence, I am sure, that was used in extolling the landmark's virtues some 35 years before. The reaction of the students was obvious, inasmuch as this particular architectural gem has been periodically displayed on television and through other communication media.

Organization

Recognizing that the 10- to 14-year-old student differs from his counterpart of a generation ago, what type of school organization would serve him best—the school containing grades 5 through 8, grades 6 through 8, grades 7 and 8, or grades 7 through 9? We have seen within the last 50 years a proliferation of grade arrangements. The arrangements have all been based upon the premise that educational experiences can be neatly packaged into single-year programs and that the single programs somehow can be integrated into a total package without an integrator being involved. Hence, it really hasn't made too much difference how the organization was structured. Advocates of a given grade arrangement are hard-pressed in many instances to identify the differences among elementary, intermediate, middle, and junior high school programs.

I would say that none of the foregoing arrangements are adequate for the education of the 10- to 14-year-old student. I am going to identify a different approach to the education of these students. For lack of a better description, I have chosen to call the approach "middle school," but I assure you that the middle school discussed here will differ significantly from the institution usually identified by that term.

Authorities have written much in recent years regarding the inadequacy of the junior high school in satisfying the educational requirements of older children and preadolescent students. Such critics as the eminent American anthropologist Margaret Mead evoke images of dull, uninteresting, and unchallenging programs for students of all abilities. We are led to conclude that students are underachievers, that social rather than intellectual facets of school programs are most esteemed by students, that inquiry and experimentation are not encouraged, and that school years for the 10- to 14-year-old are to be endured and passed through as rapidly as possible.

The middle school, then, must provide a solution to the problem of a dull, uninteresting, and unchallenging program. The task is complicated by the need to afford equal opportunity to all students. The Fox Lane Middle School of Mount Kisco, New York, eloquently expresses a fundamental tenet of middle school education: This school is dedicated to each pupil who enters—that each may discover his own talents for learning, for growth, and for service.

Before a large commercial enterprise introduces a product into its merchandise line, a careful study is made of conditions affecting its probable marketing success. Part of the market investigation includes a survey of what qualities potential consumers want in the product and an analysis of how well existing products are meeting market requirements. I went through a similar type of analytical process in developing middle school ideas.

Middle School Planning

Surveys, including one conducted for an educational foundation in 1966, show that parents and educators are ready to accept educational change. Analyses of existing education for the 10- to 14-year-olds stress the junior high school's capability in providing a smooth transition for the student from an elementary to a senior high school program without significant loss in program continuity.

Planning for the middle school must

- emphasize the worth of the individual student
- enable students to begin to accept responsibility for their own learning
- recognize student involvement with change
- provide for opportunities to participate in decision-making

- prepare for formulation of learning situations most conducive to student growth
- establish growth criteria and a program for acquiring data on growth which can be measured quantitatively.

Does this list disappoint you? Did you expect novel planning for the middle school? A little consideration will show why the foregoing elements are necessary. Any school seriously striving to provide an adequate educational program for the 10- to 14-year-old student will involve these planning elements. The difference between our middle school and other schools is not in the planning elements but in their interpretation and implementation.

Consideration of planning for student responsibility provides an example. Since schools have taken away the authority of the student relative to decision-making in the areas of what will be studied, when, and how, it should come as no surprise that the student feels he has delegated his responsibility for learning to the school. When the student experiences learning difficulties, does it seem unnatural that he hold the school responsible? I don't think so.

Middle school returns to the student his responsibility for learning. School activities support student programs. During the student's early years at middle school, he shares in the development of his learning program with professional-staff planning predominating. As the student develops decision-making and analytical thinking capabilities and skill in selecting learning goals, he assumes increasing responsibility for determining his educational program.

Education of 10- to 14-year-old students requires a professional who is a generalist in his given discipline and who possesses skill and knowledge in learning theory, social psychology, and public relations. The elementary school utilizes the generalist who is a scientist, mathematician, social scientist, and communications expert at various times throughout the day. The junior high school requires a subject rather than a discipline generalist. That is to say, a professional may teach the same material several times during his daily duty tour. The middle school professional always operates within his discipline, but student interactions are likely to cover a wide spectrum of his expertise.

The professional staff is composed of a team of teachers—a learning coordinator, a teacher counselor, and discipline generalists for science, mathematics, social science and language arts. Each teaching team joins with a student team of 90 to 110 of the 10- to 14-year-old students in a nongraded structural arrangement, to form a student-professional team. A single discipline generalist supports the team for his particular discipline. Thus, the professional must possess expertise across the total spectrum of his discipline.

Evaluating Middle School Programs

How should the middle school be evaluated? The proposed national assessment of education would be a poor approach to evaluation. Middle school students should perform satisfactorily on tests, but the present standardized achievements are "antique instruments."

The middle school must foster the student's rate of growth with respect to a given discipline, not in the absolute quantity of growth. Only as the student improves his growth rates can he hope to keep abreast of the mountain of information descending upon him today.

A challenge to the NASSP is to develop or to cause the development of measuring devices for student growth rates and criteria for measuring student effectiveness based upon growth rates per expenditure of resources.

7

Ray Budde

(5)-6-7-8, The Middle School of the Future

How to best house children and youth for educational purposes is a continuing problem in American education. The problem is intensified by a growing population which somehow never seems to provide the "right" number of pupils for the existing spaces in the "right" buildings. In the hurry of planning from one year to the next, decisions such as these are made:

"Let's place that extra class from Foster Elementary School in that vacant corner room at Lincoln Junior High. All the other elementaries will be able to take care of their own for another year."

"Our eighth and ninth graders will take up all the room in the old high school building. This year we'll drop the seventh back to elementary."

"We just can't handle all four top grades at Central High School. Let's drop the ninth grade down and make a three year junior high. Most of the other towns in our area seem to be happy with this arrangement."

Why Not Where

Most of the decisions on what grades should be housed together seem to hinge around tradition, or worse yet what spaces are available, rather than what age groups live and learn together best. The real questions which should be answered are: Why should tenth, eleventh,

From *Michigan Journal of Secondary Education* (Fall, 1964): 43–51.

and twelfth graders or ninth through twelfth graders be placed in one building? Why should all the seventh, eighth, and ninth graders from a wide area be gathered together under one roof in a building called a junior high school? What is the rationale behind placing kindergarten and the six grades in an elementary school?

True, a school system must face the problem of growing numbers. Fortunately most superintendents and school board members are becoming conditioned to the idea of growth—and realize they must look ahead—two, three, five, and even ten years. Assuming a long-range view is taken, a rationale for grouping students for educational purposes can be worked out. Then, future building plans can be tailored to this plan to achieve the desired vertical grade organization for the system.

The Present "Best Answer"

No one wants to be accused of acting without thinking. The next best thing to developing one's own rationale for grouping grades is to look around and see what the "other fellow" has done to solve this problem. One will readily discover that the popular solution seems to be to work toward an 7-8-9 junior high school. This, of course, would mean an elementary school, K–6, and a three year high school, grades ten, eleven, and twelve. Two of the largest groups of junior high principals are those who already have 7-8-9 junior high schools and those who wished they had 7-8-9 junior high schools.

It takes no more than a casual glance at the literature to discover the bias toward the 7-8-9 junior high school. A good example here is Bulletin 1963, No. 32 of the Office of Education. This bulletin is entitled "The Junior High School, 1959–60."[1] And what is its sub-title? A Survey of Grades 7-8-9 in Junior and Junior-Senior High Schools." Most of those who write about the junior high seem to bind "7-8-9" and "junior high" together. This, incidentally, includes the present writer in a doctoral dissertation a number of years ago.

Are the assumptions and "functions" on which the 7-8-9 junior high is based still valid? Are these ideas—many of them over a half century old—still pertinent to school organization in the 1960's and 1970's? Are there any new research studies which indicate a new direction is needed? Do the educational realities support the continued dominance of the 7-8-9 junior high school as the middle school to be or the middle school to become?

The (5)-6-7-8 Unit, A Better Answer

For the 1960's and 1970's, the 7-8-9 junior high school is no longer a defensible unit of vertical school organization. It has made its contribution; it has had its day. The 6-7-8 or the 5-6-7-8 middle school is a better answer for grouping students between elementary school and the four year high school. Let us look at five educational realities which support these contentions.

Educational Reality Number One: The philosophic basis for the 7-8-9 junior high school is no longer valid. The foundation ideas on which the 7-8-9 junior high school is based were originally formulated by L. V. Koos and Thomas H. Briggs in 1920. The ideas were revised and restated as "functions" in 1947 by William T. Gruhn and Harl R. Douglass.[2]

a. One argument for making the ninth grade a part of the junior high was that this would bring about a reduction in drop-outs. When this was proposed over forty years ago, there were large numbers of boys and girls quitting school at the end of the eighth grade. Placing the ninth grade with the seventh and eighth grade did result in a reduction of the number of drop-outs. But what about the drop-out problem today? The major concerns are elsewhere at other levels: How can we keep students from dropping out of high school? How can we encourage many able high school graduates to continue their education? How can the rate of attrition from freshman level to senior level in college be decreased? And interestingly enough, we wonder if some kind of pre-school educational experience might not reduce the drop-out rate in high school. The 7-8-9 junior high, although it has differentiated its curriculum to assist the potential drop-out, no longer has a distinct specific role that would justify a ninth grade being a part of an intermediate unit.

b. Vocational education was one of the original tasks of the 7-8-9 junior high school. With more and more students staying in school for longer and longer periods of time and with societal pressures pushing the age upward at which a person assumes his first full-time job, this function, too, is placed further up the educational ladder.

The role of the junior high has not disappeared but is considerably blunted from what it was several generations ago.

c. One of the original dreams of the 7-8-9 junior high unit was that its existence would enable guidance services to be extended to a lower age group. This function is no longer distinctive for a 7-8-9 junior high or, as a matter of fact, for secondary schools. Visiting teachers are now a part of many elementary programs. With federal assistance, a person can now be trained to give guidance services at the elementary level.

d. One of the continuing functions of the 7-8-9 junior high school is helping the young person understand himself and to develop his powers and his personality during the difficult years of adolescence. One research study has found that a number of the basic developmental tasks such as learning an appropriate sex role, achieving emotional independence of parents and other adults, and getting along with age-mates are accomplished by the age of thirteen!

> "The very high correlations at ages thirteen, sixteen show quite conclusively that the level of achievement on these particular tasks is practically fixed by age thirteen. Therefore, the period from ten to thirteen years seem the crucial period for adolescent changes and development in personality and socialization patterns in these subjects . . . it appears that other adolescent changes may well forerun the physiological changes . . . these correlations hint that (the latency period) and the early adolescent years are the time when permanent patterns are being formed and socializing influences are most effective."[3]

On the basis of this study, ten to thirteen year olds should be grouped together to accomplish the "guidance function" and the "socialization function" of the junior high school. This would mean a middle school of 5-6-7-8 with the ninth grade being a part of the senior high school.

e. Other so-called "functions" of the 7-8-9 junior high school have never been particularly and distinctly junior high school functions. "Integration" is a goal of a fifth grade teacher or a senior high math teacher as well as being a goal for a junior high teacher. The kindergarten teacher feels perfectly at home accomplishing the "exploration" function. "Differentiation," certainly, is not something particular to any grade level. "Articulation" is something which is accomplished by everyone in a school system working together.

Educational Reality Number Two: Many 7-8-9 junior high schools have become JUNIOR high schools. Lacking a sound philosophic base, it is not surprising that many 7-8-9 junior high schools have found their place in the educational sun by becoming JUNIOR high schools in the true, literal sense of the word. How many of our 7-8-9 junior high schools have a varsity-type interscholastic athletic program at "center stage" in the school's life? How many 7-8-9 junior high schools have marching bands, cheerleaders, and night athletic contests with the majority of students being relegated to the role of spectator at the school's most important events? How many 7-8-9 junior high schools have frozen their seventh and eighth grade offerings because the ninth grade program had to follow the time and credit pattern set by the senior high school? How many 7-8-9 junior high schools have built into their students the merry-go-round of mixed-up ends and means caused by a high-school-type marking system? How many ninth graders graduate into tenth grade through formal and informal "rites" (awards assembly, ninth grade graduation dance, etc)—again aping a portion of the senior high school program? Space does not permit the complete list of questions, the answers to which would certainly indicate that many 7-8-9 junior high schools are not playing any truly distinctive role in the vertical organization of their school systems.

Educational Reality Number Three: Growth and research studies support placing ninth graders in senior high school. Present ninth graders are growing up in an entirely different world from the one in which previous generations of ninth graders lived. Most children's diseases have been conquered or the harmful results considerably lessened. Better nutrition with the added boost of vitamins have made for improved health and growth. The pace of living in the fast-changing society of the '60's furnishes a much more stimulating environment for young people than the "roaring twenties" or the "dying thirties." The importance of some of these factors come to light in a number of research findings.

a. "(Their) most interesting findings have to do with a striking secular trend over the last fifty years ... boys in the United States, both white and Negro, are 6 to 8 per cent taller and 12 to 15 per cent heavier than boys were half a century ago."[4] In a study of adolescent girls today as compared with twenty-four years ago, another researcher found no striking difference in motor abilities but did find that present day girls were significantly taller and heavier.[5] Insurance company statistics also bear out the fact that teenagers are taller and heavier than they were in previous generations.

b. One study of the attitudes and interests of ninth graders indicates that today's ninth graders are more mature and grown-up in other ways. "One fact is outstanding in our results. In the more recent tests, boys and girls in the ninth grade marked items in such a way as to indicate greater maturity and greater social sophistication ... Fourteen year olds of 1953 and 1959 were more studious, more broadly in the contemporary scene, more tolerant in their social attitudes, and more inclined to value controlled behavior and disapprove ... irresponsible behavior in others than were the fourteen year olds of 1935 ... (Today's fourteen year old) shows greater maturity of heterosexual interests, seems to have a more serious purpose in life, and is more tolerant toward social issues."[6] This seeming greater maturity was seen viewing a wider age span by D. B. Harris in his work.[7]

c. The study by Havighurst (already mentioned with reference to the functions of the 7-8-9 junior high school) indicated that many of the developmental tasks of adolescence are already accomplished by the start of ninth grade.

From these studies, there seems to be strong evidence to support placing today's ninth graders with older adolescents rather than with younger boys and girls.

Educational Reality Number Four: A four year high school is an inherently stronger unit of vertical organization than is a three year high school. The following are organizational advantages of the four year high school over the three year high school:

a. Guidance of student in choice of at least three years (and sometimes three and a half years) of high school courses is under the control of the high school staff.

b. All classes in grades nine through twelve have to meet a certain number of minutes per week if students are to be granted units of credit. Having a four year high school means that this "system" is all under one roof.

c. Many colleges are now asking for recommendations from high school principals at the end of a student's junior year. Judgments can be based on three rather than two year's knowledge of the student.

d. Occupational information and counseling are clearly the province of the high school if grades nine through twelve are housed in one building—again one set of counselors, one library, and one administration.

e. A strong intramural program can be maintained through eighth grade. Interscholastic sports with varsity teams can begin with ninth grade. (The intramural program can be continued in either type of high school.) More ninth graders will be involved in interscholastic sports because the better eighth graders are not available to be placed on teams. Again, another system, the athletic "system," is under the coaching staff which is located in one building and which is under one athletic director and one principal.

Educational Reality Number Five: Later elementary teachers can no longer be asked to teach all subjects. With the explosion of knowledge in many fields, there has been a downward spiraling of advanced concepts into the elementary curriculum. It seems that every last person who is writing curriculum for the elementary school is taking Bruner seriously. ". . . any idea can be represented honestly and usefully in the thought forms of children of school age, and that these first representations can later be made more powerful and precise the more easily by virtue of this early learning."[8] Mathematics furnishes us with perhaps the most dramatic example. "Sets" used to be a part of college mathematics. In some of the new programs, "sets" are introduced in kindergarten!

Here is what is presently being required of a later elementary classroom teacher:

a. She must be able to teach a mathematics which is totally different from the math she was taught (and the math she was taught to teach).

b. She must learn to teach some advanced notions in science, using the inductive or discovery technique. As a by-product, she must teach her charges how to become problem-solvers.

c. She must learn what the new social studies, based on "culture areas," is all about.
d. Before long, she will be teaching sentence patterns from a language arts book which has been written from the linguistics point of view.
e. For thirty minutes each day, she is supposed to do her bit for the national fitness program through use of a more sophisticated physical education and physical education testing program.
f. In many instances she has responsibility for teaching or following up on the teaching of a foreign language.
g. In addition, she may have to shoulder major responsibility in a number of the enrichment areas such as art and music.

Not only does the later elementary teacher have more lesson plans to prepare, but she must take it on herself to learn new interpretations of every basic field in which she is teaching! This is virtually impossible for any one person to do well. The only solution lies in some form of team teaching or departmentalization. This kind of organization for teaching can best take place in a secondary school. Teachers of these grades, five and six, in an intermediate school would still be elementary-certified teachers, but they would be able to concentrate their teaching in two or three areas in which they would have a strong interest and background.

Educational reality number five, then, provides justification for the lower grades of a middle school whose top grade would be eight.

The Need to Organize

Not all the answers are in so far as what the (5)-6-7-8 school should be like. Some systems have realized the advantages of this kind of school after "falling into" the plan because of shifts in enrollment. A number of schools have been built around ideas which could be the heart of a philosophy of the new intermediate school.

The present writer has ideas and opinions which might serve as grist for a sequel to this article. But perhaps some sharing should be done by schools presently using this form of school organization. Those interested in this type of middle school should be encouraged to organize on a state-wide basis or even nationally.

In Summary

Those making decisions on housing of pupils for educational purposes should seek to develop an intelligent rationale on which to build a sound vertical grade organization. Five "educational realities" have been presented to support the contention that, in the 1960's and 1970's, the 7-8-9 junior high school is no longer a defensible unit of school organization. The necessary effort should be made to develop the (5)-6-7-8 intermediate school into the truly distinctive middle school of the future.

Notes

1. Grace S. Wright and Edith S. Greer, "The Junior High School, 1959-60." Office of Education Bulletin 1963, no. 32, U.S. Gov. Printing Office.

2. See p. 13 of *Junior High School Facts—A Graphic Analysis* by Walter Gaumnitz. Misc. No. 21 U.S. Dept. of Health, Education, and Welfare. U.S. Gov. Printing Office.

3. Aileen Schoeppe and Robert J. Havighurst, "A Validation of Development and Adjustment Hypotheses of Adolescence." Quotation from p. 243 of *The Adolescent—A Book of Readings* edited by J. Seidman. Holt, Rinehart, and Winston 1953, 1960.

4. Harold C. Stuart, "Normal Growth and Development During Adolescence." Quoting a study by Meredith and Meredith on p. 115 of *The Adolescent—A Book of Readings* by Jerome Seidman. Revised 1960. Holt, Rinehart and Winston.

5. H.E. Meleny, "Motor performance of adolescent girls today as compared with those of twenty-four years ago." MA Thesis, University of California, 1959.

6. Mary C. Jones, "A comparison of attitudes and interests of ninth grade students over two decades," *J. of Educa. Psychol.* LI, No. 4 (1960), p. 178.

7. D.B. Harris, "Sex differences in the life problems and interests in adolescents, 1935-1957." *Child Development* 1959, 30, 453-460.

8. Jerome S. Bruner, *The Process of Education,* Vintage books # V234, 1963, p. 33.

8

Jack E. Blackburn

Middle Schools: Dreams and Realities

> All movements, however different in doctrine and aspiration, draw their early adherents from the same types of humanity; they all appeal to the same types of mind.
>
> Eric Hoffer, *The True Believer*

My ninth grade English teacher asked each of her students to write a story entitled "Man on the Moon." I remember this assignment well because of the exciting possibility that man might someday reach the moon; a place far, far away.

This experience flashed through my mind as I sat watching Neil Armstrong and Edwin Aldrin descend from the lunar module Eagle and take giant steps on the moon. The exciting hypothesis hundreds of school students have dreamed about had come true.

Many equally imaginative goals and dreams have been explored and recorded by educators. One such aim began to emerge at the turn of the present century. The question—how can we best provide for the schooling of early adolescents? In Ohio and California in the early 1900's schoolmen began to take giant steps to find answers to the question by establishing junior high schools. The movement caught on, and by the 1960's over 7,000 separate junior high schools were in operation.

Because we cherish the dream of providing the best educational opportunities for all youth, we are still searching for better ways of

From *The High School Journal* (December, 1969): 145-50.

designing school experiences for our young people. The search for better, more humanistic educational purposes and practices has led to a re-examination of the question: how can we best provide for the schooling of pre and early adolescents?

Some educators hold that the junior high school is no longer a valid concept. They say that the evidence is in that this school has not proven to be a good plan. Others say there is a need to reorganize the graded structure from about grade 5 to grade 8. These educators hypothesize that a "middle school" which provides for a system of education planned for the 10 to 14 year old age group is a better plan than the junior high school.

Alvin W. Howard feels that "Most of the diverse reasons which gave rise to the junior high school either no longer exist or are much changed . . ." and that ". . . the junior high school was conceived and grew not because of any strong and proven educational values but more as an expendient, an effort to remedy supposed weaknesses of the 8-4 system."[1] Other critics are more concerned with what the junior high school has become rather than with the purposes advocated by its supporters.

Certain scholars such as Margaret Mead point out that the junior high school concept was conceived prior to insights we have today about pre and early adolescence.

Despite these criticisms, junior high school proponents claim that through the years the underlying, modern purpose of the junior high school has become to provide a program of education designed for early adolescence. Innovations in these schools have been implemented to provide a better program suited to the underlying purpose.

Leaders in the middle school movement also accept the concept of accommodating a particular age grouping as essential to the middle school program. Yet, as with many other proposals, there are differing opinions concerning the middle school.

The differences can be seen in the table on page 59. The table is a representative listing of goals, functions, reasons, and essentials as perceived by writers, practitioners, and researchers in middle school education. The statement of aims set forth by William Alexander and his associates are goals accepted by these authors. The reasons stated in the second column are based upon the perceptions of 110 middle school principals as explanations of why their middle schools were established. (Numbers in parentheses following these reasons indicate

REPRESENTATIVE AIMS, REASONS AND FEATURES OF MIDDLE SCHOOL PROGRAMS

Aims as accepted in The Emergent Middle School[2]	Reasons as Perceived by 110 Middle School Principals[3]	Features Summarized by the *NEA Research Bulletin*[4]
To serve the educational needs of the "in-between-agers" in a school bridging the elementary school for childhood and the high school for adolescence.	To provide a program specifically designed for students in this age group. (2)	A span of at least three grades to allow for the gradual transition from elementary to high school instructional practices.
To provide optimum individualization of curriculum and instruction for a population characterized by great variability.	To provide more specialization in grades 5 and/or 6. (4)	Required special courses, taught in departmentalized form such as industrial arts, home economics, foreign language . . . .
In relation to the foregoing aims, to plan, implement, evaluate, and modify, in a continuing curriculum development program, a curriculum which includes provision for:	To try out various innovations. (7)	Guidance program as a distinct entity to fill the special needs of this age group.
(a) a planned sequence of concepts in the general education areas; (b) major emphasis on the interests and skills for continued learning; (c) a balanced program of exploratory experiences and other activities and services for personal development; and (d) appropriate attention to the development of values.	To use plans that have been successful in other school systems. (9)	Limited attention to interschool sports and activities.
To promote continuous progress through and smooth articulation between the several phases and levels of the total educational program.	To better bridge the elementary and the high school. (3)	Emerging departmental structure in each higher grade to effect gradual transition from the self-contained classroom to the departmentalized high school.
To facilitate the optimum use of personnel and facilities available for continuing improvement of schooling.	To eliminate crowded conditions in other schools. (I)	Flexible approaches to instruction–team teaching, flexible scheduling . . .
	To move grade 9 into the high school. (5)	Faculty with both elementary and secondary certification.
	To remedy the weaknesses of the junior high school. (6)	
	To utilize a new school building. (8)	
	To aid desegregation. (10)	

their rank order as reported by the principals.) According to the NEA Research Bulletin, the statements in Column 3 are features which must be part of a functioning middle school. The order in which some of the statements originally were listed has been altered to point up similarities and differences in the statements.

A preliminary look at available data indicates that the middle school hypothesis cannot be supported yet. This conclusion is partially based upon an analysis of the aims, functions, and reasons of the program as perceived by varying groups. A close look at these perceptual views upon which practitioners base their decisions indicates that some of the views are incompatible with each other. For example, in the table above, as well as in a majority of statements on middle schools, the major purpose for having such schools is to serve educational needs of a particular group. Yet, principals gave as their number one reason for establishing middle schools, "to eliminate crowded conditions in other schools." Some of the listed statements support and condemn at the same time certain practices of junior high schools. "Correcting weaknesses of the junior high school" has been commonly cited as a reason for implementing middle schools. Statements included in the table indicate that some of these so-called weaknesses are already built into the operational stage of the middle school movement—limited attention to interschool sports and activities, faculty with both elementary and secondary certification, providing more specialization in middle school grades. An oft-voiced criticism of the junior high school idea is that it is in actuality a junior version of the senior high school. Looking at the evidence in the table, an interesting observation is that the articulation aim of the middle school caters to senior high school. Such purposes lead one to ask "what is so differ-contained classroom to departmentalization. One can also see that another aim is to push downward the specialization function of the senior high school. Such purposes leads one to ask "what is so different in these aims from the criticisms leveled at those junior high schools which emulate senior high schools?"

Middle school education makes sense when it is conceived as contributing to the continuing education of the person. This concept is consistent with the idea that each level of the educational structure complements the other and that each unit within the structure helps in the continuing development of wholeness for each child.

Middle school advocates agree with the general notion that a child's schooling should help in his total development. Research indicates generally that middle schools presently are not oriented toward unity in human development and learning. By and large the same old diet of a departmentalized, subject matter emphasis dominates the curriculum. There is little if any attention paid in the reorganization of middle schools to bringing relevance or pertinence into the "required" curriculum. Beginning at the fifth grade level departmental plans predominate the organizational structure of the school. In grade 8, according to the USOE survey, subject areas in the curriculum are overwhelmingly departmentalized. Does our experience and research evidence tell us that such practices are the more promising means of helping to develop unity of the self?

A small survey of the new middle school organization was conducted by Dr. Warren Buford in 1965.[5] He found that some middle schools were organized in hopes that innovative ideas such as independent studies, teaching teams, flexible scheduling and free exploratory time might be actualized. This reason along with the possibilities for its implementation has much potential for contributing to the goal of wholeness for the person. Research reports indicate that in reality few of the national, innovative instructional trends are being employed in reorganized middle schools.

The present status of the reorganized middle school movement seems to be summed up in the following conclusions:

> The survey data clearly confirm the existence of a recent and current movement toward a different grade organization of the school ladder. They also indicate that the new middle school organizations in general fail to provide a program and instructional organization differing very much from those in the predecessor schools, especially in the grade 7-9 junior high school. Obviously, critical evaluation of the emerging middle schools is needed to determine what improvements they are making and can make over prior organizations.[6]
>
> The reports received from the principals of schools in the survey often reveal that in a great many of the schools the middle school concept has not yet been fully implemented. The full implementation is hampered by such factors as financial problems, the inflexibility of instructional facilities,

lack of specialized teacher preparation and/or orientation
and size of school (too large or too small).[7]

The reorganized middle school movement, including a reorganization of junior high schools, is an attempt to provide a better educational setting in which young people can be helped in their continuous
process of becoming adequate, human persons. Right now, the practices in most middle schools fall short of this goal.

What is being done presently seems to be not as significant as the
fact that interested educators are trying to provide for a better educational setting for young people. Their attempts not only affect the
middle school age child, but all school youth.

In closing, I would like to make one final observation. We know a
great deal today about human behavior. We know about the influence
of perception, self-concept, involvement, and relevance upon behavior. It would seem that the success of such an endeavor as the
reorganization of middle schools would depend to a large degree upon
teachers' behaviors. How committed are they to the reorganization?
How involved have they been in desiring and planning for reorganization? How have their perceptions been "stretched" or clarified concerning the person in middle schools and the purposes of middle
schools?

If we truly want to reach our goals—dreams—for better and better
educational settings for our youth, why not start with the persons
involved. Their beliefs will determine dreams and realities.

Notes

1. Alvin W. Howard, *Teaching in Middle Schools* (Scranton: International Textbook Company, 1968), pp. 1-2.

2. William M. Alexander and others, *The Emergent Middle School*
(New York: Holt, Rinehart and Winston, Inc., 1969), p. 19.

3. William M. Alexander, U.S. Department of Health, Education,
and Welfare Project No. 7-D-026, *A Survey of Organizational Patterns of Reorganized Middle Schools*, p. 16.

4. "Middle Schools in Theory and Fact," *NEA Research Bulletin*,
Volume 47, Number 2, May 1969, p. 49.

5. Warren M. Buford, *A Survey of Middle Schools*. (An unpublished paper.)

6. Alexander, *op. cit.*, p. 2.

7. "Middle Schools," *op. cit.*, pp. 49-50.

9

J. H. Hull

Are Junior High Schools the Answer?

The junior high school, in my opinion, may be America's greatest educational blunder. It probably serves some children in some communities well. In others it fails perhaps in the way it is operated in a particular situation. One of its chief weaknesses is the bland assumption that anything called a junior high school is the answer to all problems of early adolescent education. Junior high schools in practice are not what people dream about when they are organizing them; besides, they are expensive. They are not easy to put together and there are always loose ends.

In the first place, a junior high school is not a standard institution. It initially was an administrative device for controlling children in large groups rather than an organized effort to improve instruction. Some are called junior high schools and are only two-year institutions. They vary greatly in operation. Some are truly middle schools instead of junior high schools. To really say much, one has to be talking about a specific school. The criticism of being too general may apply to what follows, for there are not many objective facts to go on for either side of this argument.

Tests, research, experimentation, and evaluative devices of a so-called objective design lack sufficient comprehensiveness to match

From *Educational Leadership* (December, 1965):213–16. Reprinted with permission of the Association for Supervision and Curriculum Development and J. H. Hull. Copyright © by the Association for Supervision and Curriculum Development.

subjective judgment in measuring the value of anything as comprehensive as a junior high school program.

The seventh, eighth, and ninth grades are far from appropriate
devices for grouping students together. Take a look at a group of
seventh graders and at a group of ninth graders separately. If they
have anything in common, it is that they are boys and girls with two
eyes, two arms, and two legs; but there the similarity ends. Seventh-
and ninth-grade interests are not the same, and their growth and
development are so far apart that they literally live in different worlds.

Many times one can observe maturing eighth-grade boys and girls
completely drop their seventh-grade friends with whom they have
been very chummy for several years until this physical change completely altered their interests and objectives. Maturing ninth-grade
boys and girls have usually outgrown their former seventh-grade
friends, and the seventh-grade friends lose interest in them, also. To
single out these youngsters and house them together in the same
school appears to some to be illogical and poor educational design.
Ninth-grade students have much more in common with high school
students than they do with seventh graders.

A four-year high school transcript is much more meaningful than a
three-year transcript of a three-year senior high school. Colleges
prefer four-year transcripts.

High schools do not like to give full credit for junior high school
subjects such as foreign language or typing. In fact they usually prefer
not to give full credit even when the junior high school is a part of
their own system.

Both high schools and colleges have much more confidence in a
ninth-grade curriculum from the four-year high school. One reason for
this may be that there is still no real source of training for the junior
high school teacher. This makes most junior high school teachers
either converted elementary teachers or high school teachers who too
often are waiting for a senior high school job. This does not improve
the morale of junior high school teachers or long-range thinking by the
faculty.

Progress and Mobility

Today's society is fast moving. Subjects that once were studied in
college are now studied in high school, and the elementary school

teaches subjects that once were taught in high school. The trend is toward departmentalized upper elementary grades, semi-departmentalization, or what are coming to be called middle schools, including sixth, seventh, and eighth grades with the ninth grade back in the four-year high school where it belongs. The turnover in today's mobile population results in a two-year school being unstable and losing its identity. Every year the student body is 66 percent to 75 percent new. This gives pupils little chance to develop morale or anything else of a positive nature under these conditions.

In my opinion, the current trend to departmentalize the upper grades may be good. At least, this seems to fit the development patterns of some students better. Such an arrangement necessitates only one transition instead of two between schools to be achieved, and it tends to produce an institution that is sounder administratively and educationally. The seventh grader is not left dangling. Yet we must not ever assume that such a program is any easier to organize just because it is called upper elementary or intermediate. The problems still exist.

A subject formerly taught only in high school, such as science, which is now a standard elementary school subject, justifies the specialists who are being imported into elementary teaching, and one gradual change to high school rather than two changes make the arrangement worth while. How many teachers a day should young adolescents be expected to meet, and how many students should teachers be expected to teach per day is the key question.

The competitive athletics program that develops into too big a pattern of little high schools does not get out of hand in an elementary school setup. Such an arrangement would reduce the huge outlay for junior high gymnasiums and the whole competitive athletic show that the junior high school tries to carry. We have more important places for tax funds, and schools cannot be expected to do everything.

Anyone who has taught in a senior high school following a junior high that apes the high school knows the blasé junior high school student from the less sophisticated, or normal student who came up by way of the elementary school. It takes no great insight to spot such students immediately, but it does take a lot more know-how to get them to learn and take their schooling seriously.

The typical junior high school in the past decade has improved greatly in discipline, in curriculum, in organization, in counseling effort, and in attempting to be a responsible institution. However, it is still up against a lot of built-in problems that would not have to be overcome if we would avoid such an organizational pattern in the first place.

Teachers Make Schools

It is time parents, educators, and college professors went back to the fundamental truth that fancy organizations do not make good schools for young adolescents. Good schools are made by good teachers, regardless of level or organizational pattern. After a certain point, the fewer the number of students per day the teacher meets the better the job he is able to do with the ones he does work with. What is that number? We limit educationally handicapped classes to eleven. This is recognition of the problem and would improve the quality of education in the regular classes.

Simple, uncomplex organizations give students better relations and better contacts and better understanding between student and teacher. This is what we should be working toward. This is where elementary education excels.

The complex junior high with its huge enrollment, its frequent class changes, its teachers meeting 150 students a day, and its students being jostled about among all these strangers every forty minutes all day long is too often a six- or seven-ring circus instead of an educational institution.

Many parents with whom I talk do not want their children in one of these monstrosities. "It's difficult enough," they say, "to bring up children without adding all the problems a junior high school can provide a parent to cope with in addition to his child's normal early adolescent problems."

The junior high is one of America's educational blunders that was gone into for reasons that were not educationally sound. Because the existing system is not perfect and needs improvement is no sign that whatever is devised to overcome it (in this case the junior high school) is as good as or better than the thing it replaced. Why did many school systems never make the change? Neither is it a sign that the educational program could not have been improved better within the original organizational pattern, difficult though it may be, with the same effort and resources that were put into the junior high school movement.

A Service, Not a Product

The pattern of organization of the industrial revolution that produced a division of labor and specialized operations for the manufacturing of material things should not necessarily be applied to the design of educational services for early adolescents.

The fact is that there is mounting evidence that such an organization could possibly be all wrong because the raw materials upon which the services are applied are so unlike, so non-standard, and lack the uniformity of the raw materials for manufacturing a product. Nor can children be made uniform. We want intelligent, productive citizens, not sausages, when we complete the combined efforts of home, school and community in developing our future citizens.

We want to develop and recognize the variabilities of our future citizens. Mass production education will perhaps tend to develop the likenesses we want, but perhaps it may fail the recognition that is needed in the development of diversity. It is possible the junior high school can be made to meet this test, or any other kind of organization, if the right goals are set up to achieve it supported by adequate resources. Yet some educators still prefer to work toward the idea of taking a more gradual, less sophisticated step in the upper elementary school as a transition to the high school program. This is not an argument for holding children back, it is an argument for a little less pushing, less aping of the high school, and more appropriate tailoring of the program to the particular students.

10

John J. Hunt,
Lyle L. Berg & Donald Doyle

The Continuing Trend toward Middle School Organizational Patterns

Numerous articles have appeared in professional journals recently pertaining to the organizational pattern of the traditional junior high school housing grades seven, eight, and nine as opposed to the more recent attendance center, the middle school, which typically houses students from grades five through eight. Woodring, in an article entitled "The New Intermediate School,"[1] stated that the traditional 6-3-3 administrative plan with the junior high school (grades 7–9) as the attendance center is on its way out.

There are many definitions of junior high schools including those of approximately sixty years ago when the seven, eight, nine attendance center came into vogue in the United States. However, not all junior high schools are comprised of grades seven, eight, and nine; in fact, patterns such as six, seven, and eight; five, six, seven, and eight; and seven and eight are called junior high schools in some locales. The recent emphasis on the pre-adolescent has raised serious questions about the relevancy and suitability of the junior high instructional program offered to such youth.

The movement toward the middle school, which usually begins with grades five or six and does not extend past grade eight, continues to gain momentum. Dr. William Cuff[2] reported that twenty-nine states

From *Journal of Secondary Education* (April, 1970): 170–73.

were operating a total of four-hundred ninety-nine middle schools in the 1965–66 school year.

Dr. William Alexander[3] reported that a total of one-thousand, one-hundred one middle schools were in operation in thirty-seven of the fifty states in the 1967–68 school year.

To update the available information pertaining to numbers of middle schools operating in the United States, a survey of the fifty states was conducted during the spring of 1968 at the University of Montana, Missoula. The purpose of this survey was to locate and identify the states and the city locations of middle schools. A letter was forwarded to each of the Superintendents of Public Instruction of the fifty states. The following working definition of a middle school was used as a guide line: "Usually beginning with the 5th or 6th grade and not extending past grade 8." All fifty State Superintendents of Public Instruction were asked to forward a listing of the schools in their particular states by category; that is, grade organizational patterns of five, six, seven, eight; organizational patterns of six, seven, eight; and organizational patterns of seven, eight, with the location of the schools and the approximate enrollment in each middle school. The returned information varied considerably; therefore, enrollment figures and city locations are not included in this summary of the survey. Nor was there any attempt made to analyze any of the instructional programs being offered in the identified middle school attendance centers. One clear result of the survey indicates that the middle school continues to gain momentum.

A total of 48 of the 50 state instruction offices replied to the questionnaire. Five of the replying states indicated no middle schools in operation. Seven states are absent from the operating middle school totals listed on the accompanying table; even though the researchers have knowledge of attendance centers operating in at least one of these states which fit the formulated description of middle schools.

Some states indicated a beginning movement in the direction of the middle school organization; however, these individual school figures were not supplied to the researchers. Arizona listed ten districts as containing middle schools but did not list separate schools by name nor location. Illinois reported three districts operating middle schools, but did not list separate schools nor locations. Oklahoma replied that a "few" middle schools are in operation. West Virginia supplied a

Rank	Name of State	5-6-7-8	6-7-8	7-8	Total
1	Texas	55	183	192	430
2	Massachusetts	23	38	59	120
3	New Jersey	32	47	39	118
4	Wisconsin	16	26	71	113
5½	Missouri	5	7	89	101
5½	New York	38	63	—	101
7	Michigan	27	63	—	90
8	Virginia	16	23	47	86
9	Indiana	—	20	62	82
10	Maine	18	30	23	71
11	Georgia	9	10	39	58
12	North Carolina	12	18	22	52
13	Connecticut	21	19	9	49
14	Iowa	10	18	13	41
15	Washington	5	13	20	38
16	Alabama	10	7	20	37
17	Pennsylvania	5	30	1	36
18	Kentucky	7	11	17	35
19	Louisiana	5	10	19	34
20	California	28	—	—	28
22	North Dakota	1	—	25	26
22	Oregon	16	10	—	26
22	Rhode Island	9	6	11	26
24	Kansas	1	6	16	23
25	Colorado	7	13	—	20
26	Maryland	6	11	1	18
27½	Arkansas	2	7	6	15
27½	South Carolina	8	5	2	15
29	Florida	13	—	—	13
30	South Dakota	—	2	8	10
31	Alaska	1	3	5	9
32½	Hawaii	—	1	4	5
32½	New Hampshire	4	—	1	5
34½	Delaware	4	—	—	4
34½	Utah	—	4	—	4
36	Wyoming	3	—	—	3
37½	Minnesota	2	—	—	2
37½	Nebraska	1	1	—	2
	Totals	420	705	821	1946

number representing "junior high schools" but furnished no grade designation.

The results of the survey were made on the basis of information from thirty-eight of the fifty states. Three middle school categories were specifically designated:

1. Grades five through eight
2. Grades six through eight
3. Seven and eight

Separate middle schools in the third category, grades seven and eight, totaled eight-hundred twenty-one for the most popular organizational pattern reported; with category two, grades six, seven, and eight, second in popularity with a total of seven-hundred five middle schools operating; and category one, grades five, six, seven, and eight, in third place with a total of four-hundred twenty schools. New Mexico listed a total of fifteen middle schools operating in five, six, seven, and eight organizational patterns. The fifteen schools from New Mexico were not included in the first category or in the second category summarizations as the researchers were unable to identify the correct placement for these middle schools.

A further analysis of the returns indicated that Texas was by far the leader in the middle school movement in terms of number of operating schools; a total of four-hundred thirty, which represents twenty-two percent of the total middle schools reported in the thirty-eight states covered in this survey. The remainder of the thirty-seven states were categorized into middle school operations ranging from 1–19, 20–39, 40–59, 60–79, 80–99, and 100–119.

States reporting as having between 1 and 19 operating middle schools, six per cent of the total number reported in this survey, include Alaska, Arkansas, Delaware, Florida, Hawaii, Maryland, Minnesota, Nebraska, New Hampshire, New Mexico, South Carolina, South Dakota, Utah, and Wyoming.

Eleven states reported between 20 and 39 operating middle schools which comprises eighteen per cent of the total middle schools reported. These states include Alabama, California, Colorado, Kansas, Kentucky, Louisiana, North Dakota, Oregon, Pennsylvania, Rhode Island, and Washington.

Four states reported having between 40 and 59 middle schools, or ten per cent of the total number of middle schools. These four states include Connecticut, Georgia, Iowa, and North Carolina.

Maine was the only state reporting between 60 and 79 middle schools. This represents four per cent of the total return.

Five states, including Massachusetts, Missouri, New Jersey, New York and Wisconsin reported between 100 and 119 middle schools in each state. This represents twenty-eight per cent of the total number of middle schools reported.

The percentages quoted in the preceding paragraph were rounded to the nearest per cent. The number of middle schools by state may be found in the accompanying table.

There are approximately 6,500 junior high schools in operation in the United States. Available information indicated that these junior high schools are primarily for grades seven, eight, and nine; however, "the number of middle schools is presently increasing, accompanied by a decrease in the number of junior high schools."[4] Cuff, 1965–66 school year, found four-hundred ninety-nine middle schools in twenty-nine states, and Alexander, 1967–68 school year, located one-thousand one-hundred one middle schools in thirty-seven states. The 1968–69 school year survey contained in this report, identified one-thousand one-hundred forty-six middle schools* in thirty-eight states. It is apparent from these three studies that a definite trend from the traditional seven, eight, and nine junior high school to some lower combination of grades which do not include grade nine is under way.

Notes

1. Paul Woodring, "The New Intermediate School," *Saturday Review,* October 16, 1965.

2. William Cuff, "Middle Schools on the March," *National Secondary School Principals Bulletin,* February, 1967, p. 83.

3. William Alexander, "The New School in the Middle," *Phi Delta Kappan,* February, 1969, p. 356.

4. William Cuff, "Middle Schools on the March," *National Secondary School Principals Bulletin,* February, 1967, p. 84.

* Does not include New Mexico, Arizona, Illinois, Oklahoma, and West Virginia which reported middle schools in general terms which did not specifically conform to the guidelines established in the request letter.

11

Nicholas P. Georgiady,
Jack D. Riegle & Louis G. Romano

What Are the Characteristics
of the Middle School?

The unrest in our public schools today is the result of a number of factors. Certainly one of these is the concern for the relevance or lack of it for students who view society and see little reflection in education of the changing nature of society. Among the significant and notable efforts to reshape education in light of present societal conditions is the movement towards the middle school concept. Despite its recency on the educational scene, the middle school has been receiving increased attention and growing adoption. The National Education Association in its on-going research studies reports[1] that "over 1000 middle schools [are] estimated to be operating in this country." Further substantiation is provided by Alexander[2] indicating that 1101 schools were reported as operating middle school programs.

The inevitable question which arises at this point is why is this strong trend underway and, concomitantly, why has the junior high school which has held sway for more than a half century no longer viewed as being appropriate for education at this age level. In seeking answers to these questions, a review of the history of the junior high school discloses two major reasons for its failure to fulfill its early promise. First, it has failed to adequately recognize and provide for the early adolescent or transescent child as he is today. Secondly, it will be seen that the traditional junior high school program displays a serious lack of relevance to the true nature of the society in which these transescents must live. "Transescence is defined as that period in an individual's development beginning prior to the onset of puberty and continuing through early adolescence. It is characterized by

73

changes in physical development, social interaction, and intellectual functions."[3]

Let us consider each of these general characteristics in order.

1. As we observe the ways in which the child grows and develops, we cannot help but note that the physical maturation of children, particularly in the years from 11 to 14, has been considerably accelerated. Improved diet and upgraded health care have seen to this. As a result, children today are larger, stronger, and in many ways more mature physically than children of the same ages in previous generations.

2. Along with these physical changes, and perhaps more significant for educators, we also note socio-psychological differences between transescent children of today and those of previous generations. Increased travel by families contributes to this, such travel taking place both within this country and abroad as well. Coupled with this, the more numerous cultural and informational resources provided by the mass media are a factor. Books are available in quantities never present before. The paperback revolution exemplifies this impact. Reading material and the information, ideas, and stimulation that these provide contribute to the intellectual development of children to a considerable degree. Along with this and certainly not to be ignored is the impact on the transescent created by the widespread and considerable viewing of television programs. Studies by Witty[4] and others conducted over a period of years have yielded ample data which indicate that the time spent by children and youth in such viewing is a factor of major scope in their environment. It is not uncommon for many young individuals to spend as much and often more time viewing television than is spent in formal study in school.

3. Growing recognition is being accorded the basic principle of education which stresses the importance of providing differentiated educational treatment of young people at varied maturity levels. This leads to consideration of the differences inherent in transescents as against younger and older children and follows with an examination of the kinds of educational programs called for by such identified developmental characteristics.

In light of the above and in an effort to provide general guidelines for use by educators in considering the middle school approach and in planning its implementation, the authors have reveiwed the literature dealing with this concept, have carried on discussions with leading practitioners and theoreticians in the field, and have noted their own perceptions and observations growing out of active involvement in middle school programs in varied communities. Their findings have been organized in logical sequence below for study and consideration by those interested in the movement.

Eighteen Characteristics of the Middle School

Characteristics
Continuous Progress

What and Why
The middle school program should feature a nongraded organization that allows students to progress at their own individual rate regardless of chronological age. Individual differences are at the most pronounced stage during the transescent years of human development. Chronological groups tend to ignore the span of individual differences.

Explanation
The curriculum built on continuous progress is typically composed of sequenced achievement levels or units of work. As a student completes a unit of work in a subject he moves on to the next unit. This plan utilizes programmed and semi-programmed instructional materials, along with teacher-made units.

Multi-material approach

What and Why
The middle school program should offer to students a wide range of easy accessible instructional materials, a number of explanations and a choice of approaches to a topic. Classroom activities should be planned around a multi-material approach rather than a basic textbook organization.

Explanation
Maturity levels, interest areas, and student backgrounds vary greatly at this age and these variables need to be considered when materi-

als are selected. The middle school age youngster has a range biologically and physiologi-
cally anywhere from seven years old to 19
years old. Their cognitive development, according to Piaget, progresses through different
levels, too. (Limiting factors include environment, physical development, experiences, and
emotions.) The middle school youngster is one
of two stages: preparation for and organization
of concrete operations and the period of formal operations. These students have short attention spans. Variation in approach and variable materials should be available in the school
program to meet the various needs and abilities of the youngsters and to help the teachers
retain the interest of the youngsters.

Flexible Schedules

What and Why
The middle school should provide a schedule
that encourages the investment of time based
on educational needs rather than standardized
time periods. The schedule should be employed as a teaching aid rather than a control
device. The rigid block schedule provides little
opportunity to develop a program to a special
situation or to a particular student.

Explanation
Movement should be permissive and free
rather than dominated by the teacher. Variation of classes and the length of class time as
well as variety of group size will help a student
become capable of assuming responsibility for
his own learning.

Social Experiences

What and Why
The program should provide experiences appropriate for the transescent youth and should
not emulate the social experiences of the se-

nior high school. Social activities that emulate high school programs are inappropriate for middle school students. The stages of their social development are diverse and the question of immaturity is pertinent in the planning of activities for this age level.

Explanation

The preadolescent and early adolescent undergo changes which affect the self-concept. The youngster is in an in-between world, separate from the family and the rest of the adult world. This is a time of sensitivity and acute perception, a crucial time in preparation for adulthood. This is the age of sex-role identification. The youngsters model themselves after a same-sex adult and seek support from the same-sex peer group. The youngster needs to be accepted by the peer group. The attitudes of the group affect the judgment of the individual child. There is the necessity for developing many social skills—especially those regarding the opposite sex. There are dramatic changes in activity: dancing, slang, kidding, practical joke give and take, etc. Common areas should be provided in the building for social interaction among small groups.

Physical Experiences and Intramural Activities

What and Why

The middle school curricular and co-curricular programs should provide physical activities based solely on the needs of the students. Involvement in the program as a participant rather than as a spectator is critical for students. A broad range of intramural experiences that provide physical activity for all students should be provided to supplement the physical education classes, which should center their activity upon helping students understand and use their bodies. The middle school should feature intramural activities rather than inter-scholastic activities.

Explanation

Activities that emulate the high school program are inappropriate for the middle school. The stages of their physical development are diverse and the question of immaturity is pertinent in planning activities for this age level. The wide range of physical, emotional, social development found in youngsters of middle school age strongly suggests a diverse program. The child's body is rapidly developing. The relationship of attitude and physical skill must be considered in planning physical activities consistent with the concern for growth toward independence in learning. The emphasis should be upon the development of fundamental skills as well as using these skills in a variety of activities. Intramural activity involves maximum participation, whereas interscholastic activity provides minimum involvement. There is no sound educational reason for interscholastic athletics. Too often they serve merely as public entertainment and encourage an overemphasis on specialization at the expense of the majority of the student body.

Team Teaching

What and Why

The middle school program should be organized in part around team teaching patterns that allow students to interact with a variety of teachers in a wide range of subject areas. Team teaching is intended to bring to students a variety of resource persons.

Explanation

Team teaching provides an opportunity for teacher talents to reach greater numbers of students and for teacher weaknesses to be minimized. This organizational pattern requires teacher planning time and an individualized student program if it is to function most effectively.

Planned Gradualism

What and Why

The middle school should provide experiences that assist early adolescents in making the transition from childhood dependence to adult independence, thereby helping them to bridge the gap between elementary school and high school.

Explanation

The transition period is marked by new physical phenomena in boys and girls which bring about the need for learning to manage their bodies and erotic sensations without embarrassment. Awareness of new concepts of self and new problems of social behavior and the need for developing many social skills is relevant. There is a responsibility to help the rapidly developing person assert his right to make many more decisions about his own behavior, his social life, management of money, choice of friends, in general, to make adult, independent decisions. The transition involves a movement away from a dependence upon what can be perceived in the immediate environment to a level of hypothesizing and dealing with abstractions. There is an establishment of a level of adult-like thought and a desire to test ideas in school as well as social situations.

Exploratory and Enrichment Studies

What and Why

The program should be broad enough to meet the individual interests of the students for which it was designed. It should widen the range of educational training a student experiences rather than specialize his training. There is a need for variety in the curriculum.

Elective courses should be a part of the program of every student during his years in the middle school.

Explanation

Levels of retention are increased when students learn by "doing" and understanding is more complete when viewed from a wide range of experiences. Time should be spent enriching the student's concept of himself and the world around him, rather than learning subject matter in the traditional form. A student should be allowed to investigate his interests on school time, and to progress on his own as he is ready.

Guidance Services

What and Why

The middle school program should include both group and individual guidance services for all students. Highly individualized help that is of a personal nature is needed.

Explanation

The middle school child needs and should receive counseling on many matters. Each teacher should "counsel" the child regarding his learning opportunities and progress in respective areas. Each child should perhaps be a member of a home-base group led by a teacher-counselor, someone who watches out for his welfare. Puberty and its many problems require expert guidance for the youngsters, so a professional counselor should be available to the individual youngster.

Independent Study

What and Why

The program should provide an opportunity for students to spend time studying individual interests or needs that do not appear in the organized curricular offerings.

Explanation

A child's own intellectual curiosity motivates him to carry on independently of the group, with the teacher serving as a resource person. Independent study may be used in connection with organized knowledge, or with some special interest or hobby. The student pursues his work, after it has been defined, and uses his teachers, various materials available in and out of school, and perhaps even other students, as his sources. He grows in self-direction through various activities and use of materials.

Basic Skill Repair and Extension

What and Why

The middle school program should provide opportunities for students to receive clinical help in learning basic skills. The basic education program fostered in the elementary school should be extended in the middle school.

Explanation

Because of individual differences some youngsters have not entirely mastered the basic skills. These students should be provided organized opportunities to improve their skills. Learning must be made attractive and many opportunities to practice reading, listening, asking questions, etc., must be planned in every classroom. Formal specialized instruction in the basic skills may be necessary and should be available.

Creative Experiences

What and Why

The middle school program should include opportunities for students to express themselves in creative ways. Student newspapers, dramatic creations, musical programs, and other student-centered, student-directed, student-developed activities should be encouraged.

Explanation

Students should be free to do some divergent thinking and explore various avenues to possible answers. There should be time allowed for thinking without pressure, and a place for unusual ideas and unusual questions to be considered with respect. Media for expressing the inner feelings should be provided. Art, music, and drama provide opportunities for expression of personal feelings.

Security Factor

What and Why

The program should provide every student with a security group: a teacher who knows him well and whom he relates to in a positive manner; a peer group that meets regularly and represents more than administrative convenience in its use of time.

Explanation

Teachers need time to give the individual student the attention he needs, to help in counseling and curriculum situations. The student needs someone in school that he can be comfortable with.

Evaluation

What and Why

The middle school program should provide an evaluation of a student's work that is personal, positive in nature, nonthreatening, and strictly individualized. The student should be allowed to assess his own progress and plan for future progress.

Explanation

A student needs more information than a letter grade provides and he needs more security than the traditional evaluation system offers. Traditional systems seem to be punitive. The middle school youngster needs a supportive atmosphere that helps to generate confidence and a willingness to explore new areas of learning. Student-teacher planning helps to encourage the students to seek new areas. Student-teacher evaluation sessions can help to create a mutual understanding of problems and also to provide a more meaningful report for parents. Parent-teacher-student conferences on a scheduled and unscheduled basis should be the basic reporting method. Competitive letter grade evaluation should be replaced with open pupil-teacher-parent communications.

Community Relations

What and Why

The middle school should develop and maintain a varied program of community relations. Programs to inform, to entertain, to educate, and to understand the community, as well as other activities, should be a part of the basic operation of the school.

Explanation

The middle school houses students at a time when they are eager to be involved in activities with their parents. The school should encourage this natural attitude. The middle school has facilities that can be used to good advantage by community groups.

Student Services

What and Why

The middle school should provide a broad spectrum of specialized services for students. Community, county, and state agencies should be utilized to expand the range of specialists to its broadest possible extent.

Explanation

Health services, counseling services, testing, opportunities for individual development (curricular and co-curricular) meeting the interests and needs of each child should be provided.

Auxiliary Staffing

What and Why
The middle school should utilize highly diversified personnel such as volunteer parents, teacher aides, clerical aides, student volunteers, and other similar types of support staffing that help to facilitate the teaching staff.

Explanation
Auxiliary staffing is needed to provide the individual help students require. A variety of teacher aides or paraprofessionals may be used to extend the talents of the professional staff.

Notes

1. "Middle School in Theory and Fact," *NEA Research Bulletin*, Washington, D. C., May 1969, p. 49.

2. Morris Mellinger and John A. Rachauskas, *Quest for Identity: National Survey of the Middle School 1969–1970* (Chicago: Chicago State College, 1970), p. 18.

3. Donald Eichhorn, *The Middle School* (New York: The Center for Applied Research in Education, Inc. 1966), p. 3.

4. Paul A. Witty, "What Children Watch on TV." *The Packet*, XIV, Boston: D. C. Heath and Company, 1960.

Bibliography:
Introducing the Middle School

Alexander, William M. "What Educational Plan for the In-Between Ager?" *NEA Journal*, May 1966, pp. 18-19.

——. "The Middle School Movement." *Theory Into Practice.* Columbus: College of Education, The Ohio State University, June 1968, pp. 114-17.

——. *A Survey of Organizational Patterns of Reorganized Middle Schools.* Final Report, Project No. 7-0-076. Gainesville: University of Florida, July 1968.

——. "The New School in the Middle." *Phi Delta Kappan*, February 1969, pp. 355-57.

Baruchin, Fred. "Middle School for Elementary." *New York State Education*, February 1967, pp. 44-47.

Baugham, Dale. "Organization and Administration of the Modern Junior High School." *Teacher's College Journal*, November 1962, pp. 50-54.

Bough, Max. "Theoretical and Practical Aspects of the Middle School." *NAASP Bulletin*, March 1969, pp. 8-13.

Brinkman, Albert R. "We Call It the Middle School . . ." *The PTA Magazine*, June 1968, pp. 12-14.

Compton, Mary F. "When the Middle School Student Enters High School." *Impact*, N.Y.S.A.S.C.D., Winter 1967-68, pp. 20-23.

——. "The Middle School: Alternative to the Status Quo." *Theory Into Practice.* Columbus: College of Education, The Ohio State University, June 1968, pp. 108-10.

Curtis, Thomas E. "Crucial Times for the Junior High School." *New York State Education,* February 1966, pp. 14–15.

———. "Rationale for the Middle School." *Impact,* N.Y.S.A.S.C.D., Winter 1967-68, pp. 6–10.

———. "Middle School: The School of the Future." *Education,* March 1968, pp. 228–31.

———. "The Middle School in Theory and Practice." *NASSP Bulletin,* May 1968, pp. 135–40.

Di Virgilio, James. "Administrative Role in Developing a Middle School." *The Clearing House,* October 1968, pp. 6–10.

Eichhorn, Donald H. "Middle School Organization: A New Dimension." *Theory Into Practice.* Columbus: College of Education, The Ohio State University, June 1968, pp. 111–13.

Gatswirth, Paul. "Questions Facing the Middle School." *The Clearing House,* April 1967, pp. 472–75.

Georgiady, Nicholas P. "The Emergence of the Middle School." *Michigan Journal of Secondary Education,* Summer 1971, pp. 16–20.

Glatthorn, A. A., and Monone, Carl J. "The 9-10 School: A Novelty or a Better Answer?" *Educational Leadership,* January 1966, pp. 285–89.

Heller, Robert W. "Needed: A Rationale for the Middle School." *New York State Education,* January 1969, pp. 35–36.

Howard, Alvin W. "Which Years in Junior High." *The Clearing House,* March 1959, pp. 227–30.

Johnston, Mauritz, Jr. "The Magic Number of 7-8-9. Is This Structure Really the Best for Junior High School." *NEA Journal,* March 1963, pp. 50–51.

Johnston, Robert J., and Casmey, Howard B. "Golden Valley Confirms Middle School Philosophy." *Minnesota Journal of Education,* November 1966, pp. 16–17.

Kittel, J. E. "Changing Patterns of Education: The Middle School Years." *College of Education Record,* XXX (1967), 62–68.

Lounsbury, J. H., and Douglass, Harl J. "A Decade of Changes in Junior High School Practices." *The Clearing House,* April 1966, pp. 456–58.

McHugh, Edward A. "The Middle School That Evolved." *Impact,* N.Y.S.A.S.C.D., Winter 1967-68, pp. 27–30.

Mehit, George. "Middle School: A New Design for Learning Holds Promise for the Education of Early Adolescents." *Ohio Schools,* October 1966, pp. 23-24, 39.

Mellinger, Morris, and Rackauskas, John A. *Quest for Identity: National Survey of the Middle School 1969-1970.* Chicago State College, 1970. 32 p.

"Middle Schools." Educational Research Circular No. 3, 1965. Washington: National Education Association, May 1965, p. 16.

"Middle Schools in Theory and in Fact." *NEA Research Bulletin.* Washington, D.C.: National Education Association, May 1969, pp. 49-52.

Moffett, G. D., and Bingham, L. D. "Casa Grande Plans a Middle School." *Arizona Teacher,* May 1967, pp. 8-9.

Moss, Theodore C. "The Middle School Comes—And Takes Another Grade or Two." *National Elementary Principal,* February 1969, pp. 37-41.

Murphy, Judith. *Middle School.* New York: Educational Facilities Laboratories, 1965, pp. 1-18.

Nickerson, Neal C. "Regroup for Another Try." *Minnesota Journal of Education,* November 1966, pp. 14-15.

Noar, Gertrude. "A Movement Emerges." *Educational Leadership,* May 1957, pp. 468-72.

Popper, Samuel H. "Institutional Integrity and Middle School Organization." *Journal of Secondary Education,* April 1968, pp. 184-191.

Pumerantz, Philip. "Relevance of Change: Imperatives in the Junior High and Middle School Dialogue." *The Clearing House,* December 1968, pp. 209-12.

————. "State Recognition of the Middle School." *NASSP Bulletin,* March 1969, pp. 14-19.

Rankin, Harold J. *Jamesville Dewitt Central School: Position Paper on Middle School.* November 1966.

"Recommended Grades or Years in Junior High or Middle Schools." A Statement by the Committee on Junior High School Education, National Association of Secondary School Principals, *NASSP Bulletin,* February 1967, pp. 68-70.

Regan, Eugene E. "The Junior High School Is Dead." *The Clearing House,* November 1967, pp. 150-51.

Riegle, Jack. "Middle Schools: Ghosts of the Truth." *Michigan Journal of Secondary Education,* Summer 1971, pp. 46-47.

Robinson, Glen. "Principals' Opinions About School Organization." *National Elementary Principal,* November 1961, pp. 39-42.

Rowe, Robert N. "Why We Abandoned Our Traditional Junior High." *The Nation's School,* January 1967, pp. 74-82.

Sanders, Stanley G. "Challenge of the Middle School." *Educational Forum,* January 1968, pp. 191-97.

Schipper, Julius F. "Truly a Middle School." *MASB Journal,* July 1967, pp. 15-18.

Schwartz, Terry. "An Evaluation of the Transitional Middle School in New York City." EDRS No. ED 011 020, Cleveland, Ohio: ERIC Document Reproduction Service, Bell and Howell Company.

Toepfer, Conrad F., Jr. "The Middle School: Implications for Elementary and Secondary Education." *Impact,* Winter 1967-68, pp. 3-10.

Treacy, John P. "What Is the Middle School?" *Catholic School Journal,* April 1968, pp. 56-58.

Turnbaugh, Roy C. "Middle School, A Different Name or a New Concept?" *The Clearing House,* October 1968, pp. 86-88.

Vars, Gordon F. "Change—and the Junior High." *Educational Leadership,* December 1965, pp. 187-89.

Williams, Emmett L. "The Middle School Movement." *Today's Education, NEA Journal,* December 1968, pp. 41-42.

Williams, Emmett L. "What About the Junior High and Middle School?" *NASSP Bulletin,* May 1968, pp. 126-34.

Woodring, Paul. "The New Intermediate School." *Saturday Review,* October 16, 1965.

Part II

This Is the Transescent

Although the objectives of American public schools, both elementary and secondary, have long been concerned with problems of effective teaching-learning processes which meet the individual needs of their students, it seems that today pre-adolescence as a field of inquiry is the object of a double discovery.

From public opinion and various mass media of communication, one is informed about the struggles of the pre-adolescents for self and social identity, their ambivalent behavior, their needs for autonomy and wild experimentation; and all create a desperate feeling in many parents. At the same time pre-adolescents project a delightful tendency toward dependency, affection, and security with respect to their family. Also one has to read professional journals and publications in behavioral sciences in which specialists such as psychologists, sociologists, and educators provide us with insights from the results of their scientific studies on and experiences with the transescent.

This growing interest, the objective analysis of the pre-adolescent, bears important relationship with the present social and intellectual state of affairs. For ours is an age in which socialization and enculturation are as multivaried as is our American society, effectively creating a generation gap. Also the recognition that pre-adolescence as a phase of life is a new phenomenon of civilization in need of analysis and study.

While scholars today are deeply interested in pre-birth formation, adolescence, and adulthood, very little is known scientifically about the transition period of pre-adolescence. Mead, Coleman, Wattenberg, and others have discussed the lack of scientific studies on this topic. Furthermore, they point out that because of the lack of information, educators and parents have not provided the necessary experiences to meet the pre-adolescents' basic needs. This is especially reflected in the junior high school organization where the early adolescent is looked upon merely as a "junior" rather than as a transescent with definite and unique characteristics.

Examination of salient and common features of the early teens reveals that too many of us are taking for granted that these years are a period of transition referred to as the "gang age." This implies that the transescent is sometimes antagonistic while at other times he seems to conform to accepted standards of his parents.

Truly enough, the pre-adolescent is still a child and not yet an adult. He has lost the security of childhood and not yet reached the full status of adolescence. There is an instability between these stages that characterizes the pre-adolescent years.

However, another and more positive view of early adolescence is emerging which does not merely consider this as a period of turmoil but rather looks upon it as a period for formation. Maturing earlier physically and socially than his predecessors, the pre-adolescent still shares with them the need to find his sense of identity and to understand the world that surrounds him. He is faced with the problems of finding out who he is and of integrating his discoveries of himself into a coherent and meaningful pattern of behavior, thereby making the necessary adjustment to 21st Century modes of living and thinking.

Pre-adolescence then is by definition a period of changes, physical, social, emotional, and psychological, and at the same time it is a period of intellectual awareness. The adolescent's thinking, formerly tied to the concrete and immediate, is now freed, and for the first time the transescent is capable of logical and deductive reasoning, of comparing the actual with the ideal, of relating himself to the past and to the present, and of understanding his place in society, in history, and in the universe. Given a relatively benign environment and the freedom necessary for growth to occur, the transescent begins to reassess himself in relation to his own body's new potential, to his social world and his family, and to greater psychological autonomy and self-direction. It is important to recognize that his personality is not yet settled, that he is polymorphous and polyvalent. He is not like soft wax in which any print will leave its trace, but he has a plasticity and a permeability to influences which are an outgrowth of his educational experience. To acknowledge and recognize rationally this point can be of great advantage to persons involved in the educating process of this age group.

This section will deal more specifically with present knowledge about what is encountered in the process of growing up or of being a transescent. There is evidence to show that today's adolescent experiences earlier a great spurt in physical growth. Mentally, he develops to the stage of formal thinking. The emotional stress that takes place within him during this period causes problems unique to his present needs that neither the elementary nor the secondary school is equipped to handle. A large number of options in ways to organize middle schoolers is identified here, and the pros and cons are fairly well explored. New ideas or renovations of old ones continue to appear which should command the attention and creative thinking abilities of the readers in this involving subject.

1

Margaret Mead

Early Adolescence in the United States

When the behavior of young American adolescents is compared with the known behavior of adolescents in other modern industrialized societies and in developing countries, and with their own behavior in past decades, several things stand out.

American adolescents are expected to mimic the ways of adults, long before they are emotionally ready for them. The category *teenager,* inclusive from 13 through 19, has resulted in a public image which expects great precocity from the *young* teenager and irresponsibility from the *old* teenager. This category inappropriately lumps together immature children whose growth spurts have hardly begun and mature young people who are permitted to marry and produce children and expected to support themselves. By making "the teens" a category, within which a nineteen-year-old hoodlum's vicious destructiveness and a thirteen-year-old's mischief are bracketed together, we have endowed the younger teenager with a whole series of real and potential precocities that are not only inappropriate but also burdensome.

One of the striking features of the last two decades has been the steady spread downwards in age level of dating; going steady; pairing-off (rather than one-sex friendship); and in emphasis on vocational choice, criminal behavior, competitive athletics, religious affiliation, and permission to spend money on an increasingly lavish scale. The recent book, *Teen Age Tyranny,* which reifies the teenager into a kind

---

From *NASSP Bulletin* (April, 1965): 5–10.

of mass menace, documents this money-spending phase heavily, perhaps too heavily, relying on quantity—amount spent in the United States—to overwhelm the listener with numbers.[1]

This precocity, which exists in all fields of life, may be partly exaggerated by other trends in the society—the enormous dependence upon the automobile for transport; the dependence of this age group on their parents' driving them wherever they go; the increased importance of the mass media, especially television (which means that individual homes and even individual schools have a hard struggle against a commercially supported and propagated national style); the expectation of many more years of schooling which is complemented by a demand for some real life now. The student, who has entered school in kindergarten or nursery school, and who has traveled laboriously through every grade of elementary school, with high school and post-high school education all to come, feels as if school would last forever. The fact that the schools have been geared to help the more poorly prepared students, have insisted on children staying within their age group, and have discouraged the participation of parents in their young children's education, all adds to the thirteen-year-old's feeling that school is an endless and wearisome process. It might as well be enlivened by as much simulation of adult life—which seems impossibly far off—as can be arranged.

This early reaching for the signs of adulthood, such as clothes, dates, spending money, alcohol—all the things to which age and work were once the tickets of admission—is undoubtedly accentuated by the orientation of older brothers and sisters. They, at sixteen and eighteen, are being forced to reach for adult status parenthood for which they are neither economically nor emotionally ready. The attempt of the older adolescent to become a parent before his time reflects the general uncertainty in American society today about the future of the world. Our apprehension that any change may be a change for the worse leading to economic depression, if not to nuclear catastrophe, makes for a restless drawing upon the possibilities of the present and a decline in the willingness to save, to postpone spending, or to defer marrying, buying a house, having children, or taking a trip. The pervasive fear that the future can only be worse than the present is accompanied by this clinging to and exploitation of the present, which parents in turn express in letting their children do everything earlier rather than later. The American tendency of noting what other people are doing and attempting to do it a little bit better means, now that national mass media are so important, that every time some precocity is reported, other towns, other high schools, other junior high schools, other clubs will try to emulate it. And the direction of emulation since World War II has been toward precocity, marrying younger—and among juvenile delinquents, sensitive to the world stage on which the mass media place them, committing crimes younger.

This emphasis on earlier and earlier participation in adult activities is superficially incongruent with the junior high school movement designed as it was to protect the young adolescent by a separate pace of slower induction into the complexities of high school life. The whole movement began when thinking in chronological age group terms had not been amplified by our knowledge of the great extremes of variation in the ages that boys and girls enter their growth spurt and enter puberty. Junior high schools were designed for children in three "grades" of school: 7th, 8th, and 9th. The grades were postulated on age and not on size, strength, or stage of puberty. They have resulted inadvertently in classifying together boys and girls at the age when they vary most, within each sex, and between the sexes, and are least suited to a segregated social existence. Also, they have divorced them from the reassurances of association with the children like their own recent past selves and older adolescents like whom they will someday become. When a type of school that was designed to cushion the shock of change in scholastic demands has become the focus of the social pressures which were once exerted in senior high school, problems have been multiplied.

Killing the Ability to Experience

Young adolescents today are bored. They have received too many slight and superficial communications about almost everything. They have "had" something about almost everything, and the tendency to give predigested easy previews of what will come later acts as a kind of deadening of the ability to experience. Bright children are bored with this repetition, and other children are not stimulated to more effort. During the early adolescent years children are now developing one strong definite purpose, to get it over with—school, or college, or living at home—and get the real autonomy and independence that is now only spuriously theirs, as mother drives a 14 year old boy and his "date" to the movies.

The appropriate experiences of the early teens are pair friendship with members of their own sex, a just-emerging recognition that the other sex can after all be interesting, admiration and emulation of adult models, heroes, and ideals (who reincarnate the early childhood sense that the parents and teachers were all-knowing and wise), and an enormous curiosity about the outside world, about their own changing bodily responses and shifting sense of identity. At present all of these are inhibited by the present cultural style of aping of a later stage.

Another set of pressures on this age comes from the present styles of education and social life of smaller children. The dull routine of schools, in which children learn a tenth of what they could, results in blunting the curiosity that might carry them through junior high school. More ambitious kindergarten and elementary school programs, entrance to school based on readiness and not on birthday date, might produce a group of early teenagers with more capacity to be interested in what the junior high school could offer them.

The delimitation of the teens has also produced a decrease in the sense of individual growth; where the onset of puberty for a boy or girl once marked a stage in the individual life cycle, emphasis is placed on grade and age alone. Just as we keep children born a day too late out of school for a year, doing an injustice comparable to some of our worst forms of ethnic discrimination, so the fine nuances of individual growth and change are obscured by the magic of the 13th birthday. Assurance that one will be a "teenager" for seven whole years is like being handed life on a silver platter at 13. It is an intolerable tyranny at 19 when—grown, subject to the draft, married, and a parent—the drinking laws and car insurance rules treat one as a child.

The crying out against conformity which has been such a prominent feature of the post World War II years is partly a response to this kind of stylization of a whole decade of life in which the most dramatic changes occur as if it were in fact, one single decade, the sections separated by junior high school, senior high school, and college, with the overall style still that of a teenager. "She's a typical teenager," says the older sister. "She might have come right out of television." And indeed she did.

There are further complications. The children of today mature earlier and grow taller than their parents. These coupled with clothes which thirteen-year-olds share with nineteen-year-olds, make them seem bigger, older, more able to handle adult activities. The parent compares his son with his own image of himself as a boy. His junior high school son looks like a college student to him; often without consciously recognizing his own feeling, he treats him as older than he is.

Furthermore, through the mass media, adolescents who know about adolescence, consider themselves as *teenagers* and include in their self picture the research that is done on their age group. Just as adult educators have tended to take behavior that was found to be average, and transform the average into the norm, and therefore the desirable, so every bit of uproar over teenage characteristics helps form their self-image. By locating most of the behavior which is appropriate to the late teens in the early teens, we have increased this quality of acting out a kind of behavior which has no emotional or intellectual basis.

It is true that the greatest tragedy of our present day adolescents are the millions that are condemned by social circumstances to learn very little at school, and to live a life in which their potentialities are practically unrealized. This great wasting of youth is due to the present inability to manage cities, deploy resources, and deal with economic and ethnic minorities. The specific smaller tragedies of our present cultural style for the junior high school age are dropouts in high school, after high school and college, too early marriage, too early parenthood, under-achievement for a third of our young people.

What About the Future?

Corrective measures are on the horizon: far better early childhood education, including the permission to parents to teach their own children what they know; school admissions as a result of readiness not birthday month; more differentiation by special interests within junior high schools; more association of junior high school students with younger and older students; consciously diversified summer experiences; and not least important but with possibilities for great good and great harm, the increasing strength of the organizations for junior high school teachers, principals, and curriculum specialists. If this increasing organizational strength of a field that has always been treated as somehow transitional and with very little sense of special status and identity is used to increase sensitivity to the problems of the junior high school students, great changes for good may be expected. But it might work the other way. We have imprisoned our adolescents within a category, *teenager,* and our early adolescents with all the striking differences and discrepancies within a category— *junior high school student.* To date the junior high school teacher has been less categorized, more transitional, just out of elementary school or just moving in to senior high school styles of teaching. If the organizing of junior high school administrators, teachers, curricular specialists, is spelled with a capital, and results in their being frozen in a single style, this may intensify the way in which all junior high school students are treated alike, regardless of their levels of physical, emotional, and intellectual maturity. This would be a loss rather than a gain. Junior high school students are more unlike each other than they have ever been before or ever will be again in the course of their lives. If a lively sum of these differences can be maintained and strengthened among those who plan for them and teach them—the whole school system, and the adolescents of the coming generation will be the gainers.

Notes

1. Grace and Fred M. Hechinger, *Teen Age Tyranny,* New York: William Morrow and Company, 1963.

2

Herschel Thornburg

Learning and Maturation in Middle School Age Youth

Of all studied areas of human development, the stage of preadolescence has long been the most neglected. This age range, typically described as 9 to 12 or 10 to 13, is a uniquely awkward range that somehow bridges the gap between childhood and adolescence. It has been expressed as the period of time when the nicest children begin behaving in a most awful way (17).

Children of this age are difficult. Their unconventional mannerisms and their unpredictable behaviors make them a very difficult group to research. Teachers find them uncooperative. Parents find them annoying. In general, it is easier to deal with youth that are either younger or older than with the preadolescent. Yet, this should not fail to make us recognize the need for more knowledge about children within this age range.

Some hope for recognizing and meeting the needs of preadolescents may be found in the emerging middle school. By definition the middle school is a school built to cover the developmental range of late childhood, preadolescence, and early adolescence. It may best be thought of as a "phase and program of schooling bridging but differing from the childhood and adolescent phases and programs (2, p. 5)."

Those who support the middle school feel that the failure of the junior high school to function as a bridging school between childhood and adolescence has forced educators to seek out an alternative. The faults inherent in today's junior high system appear to be twofold: (1)

From *The Clearing House* (November, 1970): 150–55.

The ninth grade has tended to maintain its philosophical and practical ties with the high school. (2) Many seventh and eighth grades have still followed an elementary format such as the older 8-4 organizational plan used (7). One additional problem has resulted throughout the years of the 6-3-3 plan. The junior high school has tended to model after the high school. Extracurricular activities, interscholastic athletics, cheerleaders, bands, banquets, and proms, all activities enjoyed during high school, have become a way of live in many junior high schools. There is increasing support by several proponents of the middle school (5, 7, 15) to have the middle school function as a transitional school and leave the above-described activities to the high school.

Eichhorn has tried to justify the middle school organization by advancing the concept of transescence.

> Transescence is the stage of development which begins prior to the onset of puberty and extends through the early stages of adolescence. Since puberty does not occur precisely at the same chronological age in human development, the transescent designation is based on the many physical, social, emotional, and intellectual changes that appear prior to the puberty cycle to the time when the body gains a practical degree of stabilization over these complex changes (7, p. 111).

Granted, there is no specific line separating childhood and adolescence. Rather there are gradual developmental and learning changes involving the physical, intellectual, and social life of youth. Through such maturation and learning, the well-knit pattern of childhood personality is considerably loosened as youths experience identifying behaviors with other youths, and thus move toward adolescence. Alexander (1) found from a sample of middle school programs now in operation that 44.6 per cent stated "to provide a program specifically designated for students in this age group" as a reason for establishing such a school. It is not the intent of this article to justify the middle school or describe reasons for its existence. However, since the concept of the middle school program is an increasing one, several developmental and learning tasks which youths encounter during pre-adolescence are presented to give proponents of the movement a basis to more realistically realize an educational program based on meeting student needs.

(1) Developing and Organizing Knowledge and Concepts Necessary for Everyday Functioning.

At ten and eleven years children develop interest in highly organizing and structuring their knowledge. The preadolescent develops a "mode of intellectual functioning" (9, p. 43). The child initially operates toward the end of Piaget's stage of concrete operations. During this stage the individual is capable of reasoning about concrete objects experienced within his environment. By the fifth and sixth grade the preadolescent is not as dependent on immediate concrete objects in systematizing and understanding basic ideas about relevant phenomena and objects. Once the meaning of an object is established through experience, the 10- to 11-year-old is capable of comprehending it without any current reference to the concrete object. Therefore, the intellect has developed to the point where it is increasingly independent of concrete objects, which suggests that the individual is ready for more advanced intellectual thought.

Within the structure of the middle school, learning experiences can be guided for youth so that there is easier transition to advanced stages of thought. Thus, by grades seven and eight, most students should be capable of reasoning about hypotheses and deducing conclusions, two characteristics of Piaget's stage of formal operations. Now all information which was ordered, organized, or structured within the mind is characterized by more flexible thinking and sets the basis for the ability to deal with reality.

One of the things that facilitates these increasing intellectual functions is an enlargement of interests within the preadolescent. Through his own intellectual curiosity, the preadolescent now becomes an experimenter. Particular academic subjects interest a youth and he has increasing tendencies to check them out. This promotes moving out of the realm of fantasy and questioning, and into the realm of experimentation and reality. Thus, his social and physical world take on increasing significance.

How may the middle school provide for a greater realization of this task with youth? First, ten- and eleven-year-old's intelligence functions on a junior high school level more so than on an elementary plane. Therefore, if students ages 10 to 13 fall within the same general period of intellectual development, it seems reasonable to develop an educational program in a manner more suitable to their needs and abilities. Thus, a middle school program with a more highly organized curriculum, staffed with teachers who are specialists in their discipline (5), can better realize student needs and abilities.

(2) Accepting Increasing Changes in One's Physique.

Preadolescents begin experiencing several physiological changes during the transitional period of childhood to adolescence. The term "pubescence" is applied to such changes and indicates that the body is rapidly approaching puberty which is characterized by sexual maturation.

Physically the average girl has her growth spurt after 10 with the peak being reached around 12. Girls experience the beginning of breast development about 10.5 years, pubic hair development around 11, and menarche about 12. Approximately 80 per cent of all girls reach menarche between 11.5 and 14.5 years (14). Boys initially experience growth in the testes and penis around 12 and pigmented hair at 13. Involuntary rigidity of the penis and irregular seminal emissions may be experienced at this age. All such activities are part of the male growth spurt which begins about 12.5 and peaks around age 14 (20).

Throughout the age range represented by the middle schools virtually all youths will experience significant physical changes. To reduce anxiety, it is helpful if they have an awareness of what physiological changes will take place. Research has shown that they are concerned about their height, weight, fatness, thinness, and facial features. Of special concern to girls is largeness or smallness of the hips and breasts. Boys are similarly concerned about the largeness or smallness of the genitals (3). If preadolescents are made aware that different rates of growth are not abnormal, they can learn to accept their physique better. The middle school could help them learn this if it can put physical and physiological changes into a normal developmental context for its students.

(3) Learning New Social-Sex Roles.

Our culture sets patterns of accepted social behaviors throughout childhood and adolescence. In early childhood, this has meant aggressiveness in boys and dependency in girls. Boys are expected to be rough, active, adventurous, and rugged. On the other hand, girls are expected to be docile, ladylike, and interested in household or domestic type activities. Through perpetuation the sex roles unfolded into the traditional work role for men and the wife-mother role for women.

In today's society, some varying social-sex roles are being suggested. By preadolescence most youngsters have had exposure to role behaviors that are not as distinctly masculine or feminine as they once were. The hair of little girls is shorter and of little boys is longer. Both have learned to play and accept mannequin dolls, i.e., G.I. Joe and Barbie. In the case of girls, Barbie represents a sexy teen-ager who is involved in all types of social events as her diversified and descriptive wardrobe indicates. While it is hardly fair to give Barbie credit for accelerating female social interest, it is true that one's fantasies may later be transferred more readily to reality if such fantasies have been rewarding.

What today's 10- to 13-year-old is faced with is an increasing unisexuality, and an accelerated flexibility for women in American social structure. The effect has been felt in the emergence of one's sex role. Now less distinct masculine-feminine roles exist in our society. Most positively affected has been less emphasis on the developing girl to accept the traditional wife-mother role.

It is not intended to minimize the importance of identifying with contemporaries of the same sex. But, it is suggested that preadolescence is not the period of quietly accepting one's own sex role as it was once. Earlier socialization has brought about change. The most accelerated has been female aggressiveness (18) and earlier heterosexual involvement. Havighurst (12) suggested that around 13 or 14 most boys and girls become preoccupied with social activities with more intimate companionships, i.e., double-dating, with couple-dating following. Still, there are increasing indications that today group social activities begin around 11 or 12 with more selective dating following (19). Research indicates that many preadolescents are feeling pressures from their parents and peers to be involved heterosexually by grade six (13). Perhaps the task of learning new social-sex roles is more difficult for girls than boys. While it is quite obvious that learning appropriate social-sex roles will not be totally realized during the middle school period, there is no doubt that what is learned during this period will have significant effects on the emerging adolescent and eventually emerging adult.

It is quite possible that the middle school movement may contribute to earlier adolescent socialization. While it is not possible to determine what the social impact might be, it is certainly possible that having 10- to 13-year-olds together will increase earlier socialization (19). This effect will be most likely determined by the philosophy of the school district. If the intent is to build a mini-high school, then it is most certain that earlier socialization will result. On the other hand, if the middle school emerges as a new school geared to the social, educational, and physical needs of its pupils, then early socialization will not be accentuated and emerging social-sex roles may be more realistically realized.

(4) Developing Friendships with Peers.

Most peer relationships that are formed during preadolescence are with those of the same sex. Typically boys express a dislike for girls, and girls show a general lack of concern that boys are in their environment. Most close friends are of the same sex. With this group preadolescents learn to get along. On a general basis "they form teams, committees, and clubs and are very much aware of the personalities of people their own age" (11, p. 121). The importance of preadolescent peer groups should not be underrated. They, too, feel many of their behaviors being shaped by their peers. "Even though children may resist inwardly or feel threatened, they attempt to produce the behavior they think the group expects of them" (10, p. 223).

The initial stage of peer development is formed among isolated unisexual cliques. It is considered isolated in terms of any relationship with corresponding groups of the opposite sex. Dunphy (6) suggests that this represents the persistence of the preadolescent gang into the adolescent period. As preadolescents move into grades seven and eight, their peer associates may begin becoming heterosexual, although on a more limited basis than in later adolescence. Such heterosexual interaction is often done cautiously and is often only undertaken within the security of group settings where members of the same sex are also present.

The middle school could provide a structural framework where its students can develop meaningful and cooperative relationships with peers. This can be facilitated by (1) stressing the importance of socialization with members of the same sex and (2) by allowing heterosexual group activity to evolve out of the students own natural development and personal interests. It seems important that in forming peer relations pre- and early-adolescents feel they are not being forced into such roles. Within the conceptualized middle school it may be possible to create this kind of environment better than in the existing junior high school where many social acitvities approximate high school behaviors.

(5) Becoming an Independent Person

This task has been described by Havighurst (11) as the time when preadolescent youth are expected to become physically independent. He stresses that this should not be equated with emotional independence but that it is strictly physical independence. Havighurst asserts that such independence is obtaining the ability to be away from home at night or go to a summer camp without being terribly homesick or needing mother in his environment.

The preadolescent should begin looking upon himself as a maturing individual and look upon adults as adults. He should see his parents in a new relationship. While maintaining such emotional dependency, the preadolescent should not exercise blind faith in his parents such as he did during childhood. In the process of normal development he gradually begins exercising his right to make choices. While his behavior may become increasingly independent of adults, such behavior should not be misconstrued by adults to think that he is independent and does not need guidance and continued support. Rather adults, i.e., teachers and parents, should recognize the preadolescent's growing concern of making choices and provide for him suitable experiences that allow the gradual acquisition of independence.

How might the middle school help its students with this task? First, by definition, it should provide a more independent and complex structure than the elementary school. Secondly, since its functions are transitional, it should provide a less complex model than the existing junior high school although it may be highly departmentalized. Havighurst (11) makes an important point here. He has observed that not all youngsters 10 to 12 years have enough self-control to get along in this structure. He sees the middle school requiring of its students the ability to adapt one's behavior to a variety of situations. Therefore, quite realistically, Havighurst has pointed up one real test for the middle school—the ability to solve the problems of motivation and method so that this complex structure might aid in the process of becoming an independent person.

(6) Developing Elementary Moral Concepts and Values.

As the preadolescent begins identifying more with his peers, and adult identity declines, there is a shift in the way in which conscience develops. Children between the ages of 10 and 13 can make much progress in reasoning, sympathy, esthetic sense, love, and morality. These youth can now learn a greater regard for truth and fairness, especially within the activities of peer groups. Then as youths move out of preadolescence into adolescence, they can better begin assuming increasing self-responsibility and increasing responsibility to peer, school, and community activities.

In today's society much stress is being placed on individuality. Accompanying individuality should be self-responsibility. The middle school is in a good position to assist students in this task. Through departmentalization, students can learn responsibilities through many different academic and social approaches, since they are exposed to several different teachers and students in one day's time.

Probably the most detrimental factor to the student's learning this task is the effect of adult moralizing. Many teachers attempt to deal with stealing, lying, laziness, cruelty, and bullying by moralizing with the student. "Good" wins rewards and "bad" suffers consequences. If teachers are really interested in helping youths develop moral concepts and values, they might better help children "(1) make free choices whenever possible, (2) search for alternatives in choice-making decisions, (3) weigh the consequences of each available alternative, (4) consider what they prize and cherish, (5) affirm the things they value, (6) do something about their choices, and (7) consider and strengthen patterns in their lives" (16, p. 47). The flexibility of the middle school potentially makes this possible.

Conclusion

Discussion has focused on the physical, intellectual, and social development of 10- to 13-year-old youths during their transitional period from childhood to adolescence. Six maturational and learning tasks have been described as occurring during this age range. The ability for the middle school child to cope with these tasks and realize as many of them as possible should strengthen his ability to acquire increasingly more complex maturation and learning tasks during adolescence. Learning to cope with bodily changes, exercise a new mode of intellectual functioning, and taking steps to be a person in his own right present a tremendous challenge to the youngster from 10 to 13. The challenge is significantly as great to the emerging middle school to develop and implement an educational program which will foster greater maturation and learning on the part of its students.

Bibliography

(1) Alexander, William M., "The Middle School Movement," *Theory into Practice,* 1968, 7, (8), 14–117.

(2) Alexander, William M., Emmett I. Williams, Mary Compton, Vynce A. Hines, and Dan Prescott, *The Emergent Middle School.* New York: Holt, Rinehart and Winston, 1968.

(3) Angelino, Henry and Edmund V. Mech, "Fears and Worries Concerning Physical Changes: A Preliminary Survey of 32 Females," *Journal of Psychology,* 1955, 39, 195–198.

(4) Breckenridge, Marian E. and E. Lee Vincent, *Child Development.* Philadelphia: W. B. Saunders, 1960.

(5) Di Virgilio, James, "Switching from Junior High to Middle School?" *The Clearing House,* 1969, 44, 224–26.

(6) Dunphy, Dexter C., "The Social Structure of Urban Adolescent Peer Groups," *Sociometry,* 1963, 26, 230–46.

(7) Eichhorn, Donald H., "Middle School Organization: A New Dimension," *Theory into Practice,* 1968, 7 (3), 111–13.

(8) Eichhorn, Donald H., *The Middle School.* New York: Center for Applied Research in Education, 1966.

(9) Flavell, John, *The Developmental Psychology of Jean Piaget.* Princeton: Van Nostrand, 1963.

(10) Gordon, Ira, *Human Development: From Birth Through Adolescence.* New York: Harper and Row, 1962.

(11) Havighurst, Robert J., "The Middle School Child in Contemporary Society," *Theory into Practice,* 1968, 7 (3), 120–22.

(12) Havighurst, Robert J., *Developmental Tasks and Education.* New York: Longmans, Green, and Company, 1952.

(13) Martinson, Floyd M., "Sexual Knowledge, Values, and Behavior Patterns of Adolescents," *Child Welfare,* 1968, 47, 405–10.

(14) Meredith, Howard V., "A Synopsis of Puberal Changes in Youth," *Journal of School Health,* 1967, 37, 171–76.

(15) Oestreich, Arthur H., "Middle School in Transition," *The Clearing House,* 1969, 44, 91–95.

(16) Raths, Louis E., Merrill Harmin and Sidney B. Simon, *Values and Teaching.* Columbus, Ohio: Charles E. Merrill, 1966.

(17) Redl, Fritz, "Pre-adolescents—What Makes Them Tick," *Child Study,* 1944, 21, 44–48.

(18) Reiss, Ira L., *Premartial Sexual Standards in America.* Glencoe, Ill.: Free Press, 1960.

(19) Thornburg, Herchel D., "Adolescence: A Re-interpretation," *Adolescence,* 1970.

(20) Winter, Gerald D., "Physical Changes During Adolescence," in *The Young Adult.* G. D. Winter and E. M. Nuss (eds.). Glenview, Ill.: Scott, Foresman, 1969.

3

Sister Mary Amatora, O.S.F.

Developmental Trends in Pre-Adolescence and in Early Adolescence in Self-Evaluation

A. Introduction

Persistent study of personality poses numerous and complex problems. Yet, if development of a person's personality is to proceed in the direction of wholesomeness, analysis must be made, and guidance and direction offered during childhood and adolescence. Many, though not all, cases of warped personalities can be traced to the childhood days of the maladjusted adult.

Friedlander (16), after studying the personality development of children who later became psychotic, is of the opinion that "certain characteristics in the home background and early emotional development . . . may account for the disorders." In fact, in 55 per cent of the cases she found definite evidence of gradually increasing maladjustment of personality throughout childhood and adolescence.

Havighurst, Robinson, and Dorr (17) maintain that the "environment of the child has a great effect upon the ideal self." They express a similar opinion when they state that "individuals in the child's environment influence his ideal self, especially if they are young adults." They conclude: "The inference is clear that schools, churches, and youth-serving agencies influence the ideals of youth as much or more through the presence and behavior of teachers, clergy, and youth-group leaders as through their verbal teachings."

From *The Journal of Genetic Psychology* 91 (1957): 89–97.

"What is needed," writes Anderson (9), "is a much more complete approach to the problem of persistent and fluctuating traits and characteristics with an analysis of all data in terms of span of time. When this is done we will locate the factors that produce modifications and find that change is orderly and consistent. . . . By locating in the stream of stimulation and response the recurring factors which are subject to control, we will be able to guide the process of growth and development more effectively and improve the adjustment of all children. We not only need to know how to create a good environment for children; once created, we need to know how to maintain it."

As he points out, the child's "personality becomes organized around nodal points or experiences which have received particular emphasis and much reiteration." After enumerating some of these factors, he affirms that the child "is not a simple passive creature molded exclusively by external forces; he is very much a creature in his own right, moving through his own experiences and creating his own world. This is not to deny the value of nurture in creating the best possible world for children, but to plead for a study of the child as he is rather than to use him as a convenient locus for images which fit adult conceptions and convenience."

Adler (1) raises a plea for better evaluation of all material collected for the guidance of the child. Cattell (14) has shown that major life events produce simultaneous readjustments in several personality variables and also that "beyond the primary ergic factors there are second-order factors." Tryon's study (20) of personality during adolescence indicates a "marked tendency for self-mention to decrease as age increased." McQuitty (18) makes the definition of personality integration meaningful as he shows its implications in relationship to the concept of self. Bonney (12, 13), studying the relationship of sociometric scores to personality self-ratings and the relative stability of the several variables, found the scores fairly constant. These and numerous other studies including those of Evjen (15), Anderson (8), Argelander (10), Winslow (21), and Precker (19) all point to the significance of the early development of a well-adjusted personality. Self-knowledge is essential to improvement in personality. More research on the adolescent and pre-adolescent's evaluation of self will help to illumine the problem.

B. Purpose of the Study

The present investigation of the adolescent and pre-adolescent self-concept was undertaken for the purpose of facilitating the understanding of today's youth in these age brackets. The study seeks to analyze developmental trends in a number of independent personality variables as evaluated by the self in pre-adolescent and early adolescent boys and girls. Specifically, the experiment seeks to ascertain whether or not there be observable trends in age-level development for boys and girls during pre-adolescence and through the years of early adolescence.

C. Method of the Study

The Child Personality Scale (2, 3, 4, 6, 7) was administered to 500 children in several public and private schools in the Midwest. Participating in the study at each age level, 9 through 13 years, were 50 boys and 50 girls. *The Child Personality Scale* permits of ratings on each of 22 personality variables on a 10-point continuum. The measuring instrument as well as the meaning of the numbers from 1 to 10 were explained to the children. Hereupon each individual was asked to evaluate himself on each of the 22 scales.

D. Analyses of Data

Data were analyzed both by sex and by age level for each of the 22 scales separately. The results in terms of means for individual personality variables are shown in the accompanying figures. To facilitate interpretation, all computed means were multiplied by 100.

Scales for energy and pep, intelligence, sociability, generosity, nervous-calmness, coöperation, popularity, and entertaining are depicted in Figure 1. In this figure it will be noted that developmental trends do occur in self-evaluation on some of the personality variables. An over-all view of the self-evaluation portrayed in this figure reveals a general downward trend from the 9-year-olds to the 13-year-olds. This holds true for both sexes in the graphs on the right half of the figure, namely, for intelligence, generosity, coöperation, and entertaining. In the scale for energy and pep, the trend is in the opposite direction. As the pre-adolescents emerge into adolescence, the self-scores rise.

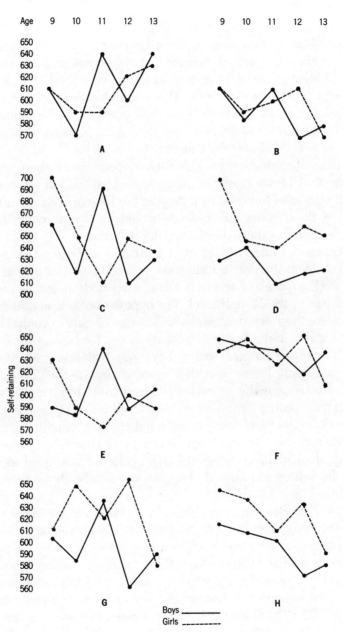

Figure 1
Mean Self-evaluation: **A,** energy and pep; **B,** intelligence; **C,** socialbility; **D,** generosity;
E, nervous-calmness; **F,** cooperation; **G,** popularity; **H,** entertaining.

For the scales measuring sociability, nervous-calmness, and popularity, one notes again a general downward trend in self-appraisal, with the exception of a unique feature in boys' scores of a rise to the 11-year-old level followed by a drop to the 13-year level. This is not the case with the 11-year-old girls. This same phenomenon was noted by Ausubel, Schiff, and Gasser (11) in their graph for "perception of own status" which indicates a rise from the age of 9 years, with a peak at about 11 years, followed by a decline to the 13-year level.

In the self-evaluation by girls there appears in all these eight personality variables a moderate, though decided, rise in self-opinion at the 12-year level followed by a drop at the 13-year level. A further self study of these young adolescence would be warranted to ascertain possible causes of these developmental differences.

A somewhat different picture is portrayed in Figure 2. Though one observes again the rise in ratings for self-evaluation of girls at the 12-year level, in most of the scales one notes a drop in the boys' self-evaluations at the 12-year level. The opposite holds true at the 13-year level. Here there is a drop in the self-ratings of girls, considerably so in several scales, and a rise in four of the scales for boys at the same age level. On the other four scales, boys' self-evaluations are either the same or slightly lower than they were at the 12-year level. Another point of interest is the general downward trend of ratings in many of the scales from the 9- and/or 10-year level to the 11-year level. At all age levels in the four scales, namely, punctuality, disposition, courtesy, and honesty, and at most age levels in the remaining four scales, namely, dependability, sense of humor, patience, and good sportsmanship, the self-evaluations of the girls are clearly above those of the boys.

The mean self-evaluations given in Figure 3 are for scales on neatness, interests, religiousness, persistence, boisterous-quietness, and thoughtfulness of others. Each of the graphs in this figure present a picture somewhat different from those in the preceding figures. In all cases and for both sexes, except for the boys on the last-named scale, the highest ratings are those at the 9-year level. Self-evaluations are lower at the 10-year level and, in most cases, still lower at the 11-year level. Following this one notes developmental trends again indicating in most variables a rise in self-opinion.

Most conspicuous in this group of personality traits is the large drop in self-opinion among boys on the scales for religiousness and for

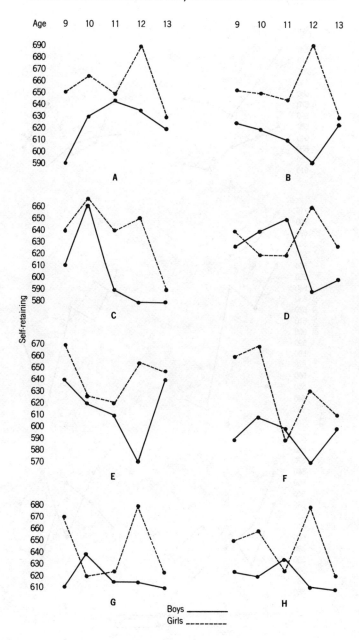

Figure 2
Mean self-evaluation: **A**, punctuality; **B**, disposition; **C**, courtesy, **D**, good sportsmanship; **E**, honesty; **F**, patience; **G**, sense of humor, **H**, dependability.

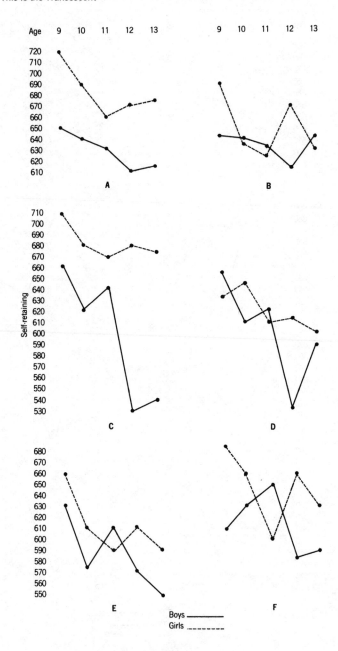

Figure 3
Mean self-evaluation: **A,** neatness; **B,** interests; **C,** religiousness; **D,** persistence; **E,** boisterous-quietness; **F,** thoughtfulness.

persistence. One wonders why there should be so large a drop, 103 points for religiousness and 101 points for persistence, from the 11-year-old to the 12-year-old boys. This is not evident in the girls' self-ratings. On the contrary, girls' ratings show a slight rise between these two age levels. One also wonders why the girls' self-evaluations are so much and so consistently higher than are those of the boys on the scales for neatness and for religiousness at all age levels.

A few over-all observations on all three figures collectively are also important for brief consideration. There is more shift in mean ratings from scale to scale evidenced in the self-evaluations of the 9-, 10-, and 11-year-olds than there is in those of the 12- and 13-year-olds. This seems to hold true for both sexes. Another point of interest is noted in the fact that on all scales, save two, the sexes come closer together in their ratings at the 13-year level. It would be interesting to carry this study on into subsequent year levels to note whether or not this proximity between boys' and girls' ratings maintains.

In an earlier study (5), the present writer analyzed children's self-appraisal at various grade levels. While not directly comparable, in as much as the present study was based on age-level groups, some comparisons of pre-adolescent and early adolescent's evaluations to-day with those of the children of a decade ago may be interesting. In the earlier study there was a distinct tendency for the boys to under-rate themselves. The amount of underrating decreased at each grade level from the fourth through the eighth grades. If the former grade levels and the present age levels are in any way comparable, it would seem that almost the opposite is true today. In nearly all the scales there is more of a downward progression until the twelfth year and then a rise to the 13-year level.

E. Conclusion

After one fashion or another, teachers everywhere are concerned with evaluation in the classroom. While this evaluation is frequently limited to ability to learn and achievement in learning, it is of vital importance for the teacher to evaluate his knowledge of his pupils. This cannot be complete without the knowledge of the child's own self-concept. If the self-concept of the pre-adolescent is such that it does not seem indicative of good mental health, something can be done before the child emerges into early adolescence and adolescence proper.

The present study shows that self-evaluation is possible at the lower age levels. It has revealed developmental trends during the five-year period, namely, from 9- through 13-year age levels on 22 personality variables. It has revealed differences in these developmental trends between the sexes and among the five age levels studied. With more widespread experimentation on the self-concept of adolescents and pre-adolescents, one should come to a better understanding of children and youth at these age levels. As the findings of research become more widely circulated among teachers, its results can and will function in the classroom.

References

1. Adler, A. Influence of early experiences upon the formation of the personality. *Nerv. Child,* 1947, **6,** 318–320.

2. Amatora, S. M. A twenty-two trait personality scale. *J. of Psychol.,* 1944, **18,** 3–8.

3. ——. Child Personality Scale. Cincinnati: Gregory, 1951.

4. ——. Factor analysis of children's personality scale. *J. of Psychol.,* 1944, **18,** 197–201.

5. ——. Self-appraisal of children. *J. Educ. Res.,* 1945, **39,** 25–32.

6. ——. Norms on a child personality scale. *Elem. Sch. J.,* 1950, **51,** 209–213.

7. ——. Reliability of personality scale. *Educ. & Psychol. Meas.,* 1952, **12,** 132–136.

8. Anderson, H. H., & Brandt, H. F. Study of motivation involving self-announced goals of fifth grade children and the concept of level of aspiration. *J. Soc. Psychol.,* 1939, **10,** 209–232.

9. Anderson, J. E. Personality organization in children. *American Psychol.,* 1948, **3,** 409–416.

10. Agelander, A. The personal factor in judging human character. *Charac. & Personal.,* 1937, **5,** 285–295.

11. Ausubel, D. P., Schiff, H. M., and Gasser, E. B. A preliminary study of development trends in sociempathy: Accuracy of perception of own and others' sociometric status. *Child Devel.,* 1952, **23,** 111–128.

12. Bonney, M. E. The constancy of sociometric scores and their

relationship to teacher judgments of social success and to personality self-ratings. *Sociometry*, 1943, **6**, 409–424.

13. ———. The relative stability of social, intellectual, and academic status in Grades II to IV and the interrelationships between the various forms of growth. *J. Educ. Psychol.*, 1943, **34**, 88–102.

14. Cattell, R. B., & Cross, K. J. Comparison of the ergic and self-sentiment structures found in dynamic traits by *r*- and *p*-techniques. *J. Personal.*, 1952, **21**, 250–271.

15. Evjen, V. H. Evaluating the adjustment of school children. *J. Educ. Sociol.*, 1940, **13**, 323.

16. Friedlander, D. Personality development of twenty-seven children who later became psychotic. *J. Abn. & Soc. Psychol.*, 1945, **40**, 330–335.

17. Havighurst, R. J., Robinson, M. Z., & Dorr, M. The development of the ideal self in childhood and adolescence. *J. Educ. Res.*, 1946, **40**, 241–257.

18. McQuitty, L. L. A measure of personality integration in relation to the concept of self. *J. Personal.*, 1950, **18**, 461–482.

19. Precker, J. A. Similarity of valuings as a factor in selection of peers and near-authority figures. *J. Abn. & Soc. Psychol.*, 1952, **47**, 406–414.

20. Tryon, C. McC. Comparisons between self-estimates and classmates' estimates of personality during adolescence. *Psychol. Bull.*, 1939, **36**, 568.

21. Winslow, C. N. A study of the extent of agreement between friends' opinions and their ability to estimate the opinions of each other. *J. Soc. Psychol.*, 1937, **8**, 433–442.

4

Dorothy H. Eichorn

Variations in Growth Rate

Most adults and, indeed, most children are well aware that some persons are large or small, strong or weak, bright or dull, socially mature or immature for their ages. Developmental scientists have confirmed these impressions. For most aspects of physique and for many physiological functions, significant differences in rate of growth are known to exist between boys and girls, among individuals within either sex, from generation to generation, from country to country, and among ethnic or cultural subgroups within a country. There are also wide variations in the rate of mental development among individuals and perhaps some smaller variations across successive generations and cultural subgroups. Further, maturity of social interests and behavior tends to be related to physical and mental development. Before we examine the extent of these variations, their interrelationships, and their implications, we should review briefly ways in which developmental rates are measured.

Measurement of Developmental Rates

Across all major areas of growth—physical, physiological, intellectual, and social—the common organizing concept is developmental age. Physical and behavioral studies have shown that with increasing age,

From *Childhood Education* (January, 1968): 286-91. Reprinted by permission of D. H. Eichorn and the Association for Childhood Education International, 3615 Wisconsin Ave., N. W., Washington, D.C. Copyright © 1968 by the Association.

from conception to adolescence, chronological age becomes a progressively poorer predictor of a child's size, shape and behavior. Increasing differences with age in developmental status imply variations in the rate at which change occurs, hence the concept of rate of maturing. For most types of growth, methods have been devised for expressing variations in developmental status in at least partially quantified form. Among the sorts of measures used to assess *physical and physiological development* are: ratings of secondary sexual characteristics (for example, breast or penis development, amount and pattern of distribution of pubic and axillary hair); age at reaching certain stages in such characteristics; age at menarche or first ejaculation; morphological age (such as height or weight age); age at reaching a certain percentage of mature height; and skeletal age. All measures that have as their basis some aspect of pubertal development cannot, of course, be used until the child reaches the stage in question. Once he has, preceding and succeeding chronological ages can be designated as, say, one year, two years or three years before or after that point. Age at reaching 90 percent of mature height has been shown to be an excellent method for differentiating between maturity groups, but one must have longitudinal measures of height through to the completion of growth in order to use this method. Such measures as height or weight age are less differentiating. For example, eight-year-olds who have height ages of 10 or 6 may not be fast or slow maturers, respectively, but rather average maturers who are genetically large or small. Similarly, a child may be 12 years old and have a height age of 12 yet be a fast maturer who is genetically small. Morphological ages of this type do have the advantage of being determinable at any age without waiting for further growth.

Skeletal Age

The most widely used method of assessing degree and rate of maturing is skeletal age, because it is a highly differentiating measure, is unaffected by absolute size, and can be determined at any age. The various bones of the body pass through a regular series of changes in shape, and the epiphyses of long bones eventually unite with their shafts. The developmental sequence is essentially the same for all individuals, regardless of sex, individual or other variations in the age at which the changes occur. Maturity is assessed on the basis both of the number of ossification centers present and the degree of development of each. In most instances only a hand-wrist X ray is used, for the rate of development of different parts of the skeleton is very similar and a hand-wrist X ray is the easiest and safest to take. From X rays of considerable numbers of healthy children, standards representing the average degree of development for each sex at successive ages have been assembled. An individual child's film is compared in one of several ways to the standards for the appropriate sex and a "skeletal age" assigned. Because the range in absolute skeletal age within a normal group increases from gestation through about the middle of adolescence (for example, from about one year in either direction during late infancy to as many as two years during midadolescence), children are not termed *early-* or *late-maturing* on the basis of an absolute difference in bone age from the average. Instead, the distribution of skeletal ages at each chronological age is determined, and a child is called early- or fast-maturing only if his skeletal age exceeds that of, say 75-85 percent of the children of his age and sex. Conversely, he is called slow- or late-maturing if his skeletal age is below that of 75-85 percent of the group.

Height and other morphological ages show the same sort of increase in variation with age that bone age does. Ratings of secondary sexual characteristics typically are done on a five-point scale, and the usual time intervals between stages may not be equal. Therefore, these scales yield only an ordinal ranking and not an "age."

Mental Age

To measure mental age, tests are devised, pretested and then standardized on sizeable groups of children of each age. Each item in a test is allotted a certain number of months of mental age or a certain number of points. A child's total score is the sum of the items he passes. If the score is in points rather than mental age, the mean and variation of point scores at each age are determined. Again the extent of variation within groups increases with age. Intelligence tests are deliberately designed to yield equal average scores for the two sexes. However, there may be sex differences in mean score on subtests.

Social behavior is sometimes assessed by ratings, although often on a broader scale than that for secondary sexual characteristics, and sometimes by point scores on a test or questionnaire. In either case, if the range of scores is sufficient, standard scores may be derived.

Correlations

In general, the degree of development and rate of change in skeletal maturity, physical size and shape, sexual development and physiological function are very similar. Thus, a child who is advanced in rate of skeletal maturing also grows more rapidly than the average in height, weight and other dimensions; his proportions show typical age changes earlier; and he is precocious in, for example, the usual decrease of heart, respiratory, and metabolic rate with age and in the development of secondary sexual characteristics. The acceleration in physical and physiological development is usually accompanied by greater maturity of social interests, attitudes and behavior, particularly during the junior and senior high school years. Although usually positive, correlations between any of the physical or physiological variables and mental growth are low. A true biologic linkage probably underlies the physical-physiological interrelationships and, at least in part, the correlation of social development with physical and physiological variables. Positive correlations of the latter variables with intellectual development may stem largely from different environmental factors which usually occur together. Children from advantaged homes tend to be accelerated in physical, physiological and mental growth, whereas children from disadvantaged homes are, on the average, retarded in these areas. The physical care—diet, housing, medical attention, and the like—provided in the home affects the rate of physical and physiological advancement. Because the level of intellectual stimulation and encouragement in the home influences mental growth and this level often parallels the adequacy of physical care, some degree of positive correlation between intellectual development and the other two areas may result from what is actually an indirect association through other variables.

Interrelationships between mental and social maturity arise primarily in the more cognitive areas and usually do not extend to, for example, heterosexual interests, unless physical and physiological acceleration or retardation is also involved.

Even the physical and physiological interrelationships are not perfect, however, and some of the regular as well as special exceptions will be noted as we discuss sex, secular and other sources of variation in rate of maturing.

Girls Mature Earlier Than Boys

As a group, girls mature more rapidly than boys and the extent of the difference increases with age. For example, skeletal development in the male lags behind that of the female by about two weeks at a fetal age of twenty weeks, by four weeks at birth and by two to three years during adolescence. Quantitative comparative statements cannot be made about intellectual and social development, because mental tests deliberately equate the sexes and unit scales of social development are rarely available. However, there are many studies and case reports of advancement of social interests and attitudes in girls, particularly during adolescence. Further, the incidence of behavior problems indicative of immaturity, such as incontinence and temper tantrums, as well as of reading and other difficulties in school, is considerably higher in boys. Despite the difference in rate of maturing, males are on the average larger than females at most ages, the only exception occuring during the brief period when girls are entering upon their adolescent growth spurt. Thus, at most ages the basic sex difference in size overrides the relationship of size to rate of maturing.

Individual differences within each sex also exist. And one must remember, for example, that an early maturer may not be large for age if he is genetically small. He is larger than he would be if his maturation rate were slower; but the genetic limit on his potential size may keep his absolute size within the average range during much of the growth period, although he is advanced in the percentage of final height to be achieved. Maturation rates are also positively and moderately correlated among family members. Thus, a fast-maturing parent is more likely to produce fast-maturing offspring than is an average or slow maturer. Both genetic and environmental variables influence this association.

Accelerated Rate of Maturation in Succeeding Generations

At least since the late nineteenth century, children and youth in succeeding generations have been getting larger earlier in most sections of the world. The average length of newborns is probably greater, and average adult heights are not only definitely greater but also reached at a younger age. However, the secular trend is maximal during adolescence and next largest during childhood, indicating that accelerated maturation underlies much of the increase in size. During the last seventy years, for example, the average height of five- to seven-year-olds has increased about .4–.8 inches each decade, while the increment for ten- to fourteen-year-olds was .8–1.2 inches. Over a comparable time span, age at menarche decreased about .4 years per decade. Improved nutrition, housing and medical care are probably largely responsible for the accelerated rate of maturing in succeeding generations. Such factors, plus some genetic differences, would account for ethnic differences.

Whether one is speaking of sexes, generations or individuals, it is generally true that those who reach puberty early are also advanced in development at younger ages. However, discontinuities occur, particularly between childhood and adolescence. Children who have grown at an average rate during infancy and childhood may become either late or early maturers during adolescence. The greatest consistency is found among those who grow very rapidly or very slowly.

Unfortunately, relatively little systematic research has been done on group or individual differences in physical maturation and its behavioral correlates during infancy and childhood. However, there are extensive data for the periods of most extreme variation—preadolescence and adolescence. Representative findings, primarily from studies done at the Institute of Human Development, University of California, Berkeley, are summarized below. From these and less adequate observations on younger children, some inferences about the earlier years may be drawn.

Preadolescence and Adolescence

Among boys physical and physiological variation is greatest at about fourteen years. Early-maturing boys of this age in one of the Berkeley studies exceeded the late maturers by an average of 8 inches and 34 pounds. The former were, on the average, at the 75th percentile in strength for age and well above this level in height and weight; the late maturing stood at about the 15th percentile on these measures. On a 5-point scale of secondary sexual characteristics, the early maturers averaged 4.5 (almost adult); the late, 2.0 (almost childlike). Ratings of physique characterized the accelerated group as masculine or hyper-masculine. The slower group fell in the asexual, bisexual and disharmonious categories. Over most of the junior and senior high school years, adults rated the early maturers as above average and the late as below average in attractiveness of physique and interest in the opposite sex. Slow maturers were rated above average in a large number of traits associated with more immature kinds of expressiveness, sociability and activity. By the end of high school, group differences in size, physique, and adult perceptions were less marked. Peers ranked the groups differently at all ages. They considered the slow maturing bossy, attention-demanding, restless, less good looking, less grownup, and less likely to have older friends. More than half the early maturers were selected for important offices or athletic teams; only two late maturers were so honored. Neither adults nor peers, however, saw these groups as different in such attributes as popularity, leadership and poise when in small, same-sex groups. Nor did the extreme groups differ in mental age or socioeconomic status (more representative samples of the general population do differ in these respects). Judging from the boys' responses to projective tests and from adult ratings, the late maturing had more negative self-concepts, difficulties with parents, unfulfilled needs for succorance and for heterosexual affiliation, and conflicts over the expression of aggression.

In contrast to boys, girls showed maximal physical variation at about age twelve, and differences in size and physique did not disappear by adulthood. During early adolescence, the early maturing were taller than average; but as adults the late maturers were taller, lighter for their height and narrower of hip. By and large, the direction of differences on adult and peer ratings was similar to that for boys, although sometimes more extreme. For example, not only were late-maturing girls above average in expressiveness and activity, the early were below average. Unlike boys, the groups did not differ in attractiveness of physique or in relaxation, and later- rather than early-maturing girls were more prominent in school activities. Paradoxically, projective tests and self-report inventories showed the early maturing to be well-adjusted, indeed more so than the late in some respects. A cross-sectional study by an investigator at Stanford[1] suggests an explanation for the inconsistency between self-perception and peer or adult perceptions. Girls in grades 6-9 were categorized as prepuberal, puberal, post-puberal or late adolescent on the basis of age at menarche. These groups were differentiated by peer ratings of "grown-up" and "having older friends," but the group to which the labels were applied changed with grade. In the sixth grade, where most girls were prepuberal, the least mature group was favored. Throughout junior high school, the traits were more often attributed to the most mature group within the grade. In toto, the relative advantages and disadvantages of early or late maturing are less consistent for girls than for boys. For both sexes, behavioral findings may be expected to vary somewhat with community groups.

Problems of Variations in Maturation Rate

Parents, teachers, recreation leaders and others who work with children are faced with two problems stemming from variations in maturation rate. *First, during the junior and senior high school period a group of youth of the same chronological age will usually have a range of at least six years in maturational age.* Because most classes contain a three-year spread in chronological age, the variation in maturational age may well be considerably greater. Adjusting activities to so wide a span of abilities and interests and the equipment to the range of sizes is a real feat. Settings that provide sufficiently large numbers of children at different stages of maturity and ease of movement among these groups help individuals to seek out their maturational peers and thus ease the strain on both children and adults. Special arrangements may be particularly needed for early-maturing girls and late-maturing boys, the groups who represent the extremes in maturation within an age bracket.

Less-marked variations occur among younger children, yet a considerable spread in size, abilities and interests is evident even in the preschool. Again, flexibility of program and provision for self-selected grouping are desirable. An additional problem, more likely to be met by younger children, results from the false impression given by physical size. While strength and maturity of behavior do tend to parallel growth rate, the association, particularly before adolescence, is sufficiently low as to be a rather invalid criterion for judging individuals. A large four- or six-year-old may be expected, unreasonably, to behave as if he were as old as he looks. Conversely, sufficient challenge may not be given to the child who is small for age.

The second general problem derives from the secular trend—the greater maturity of children for a given age than was typical for the adults who now supervise them. Small wonder that many adults are disturbed by what appears to be the precocious social behavior of today's youth. Perhaps the data reviewed here will reduce the anxiety of those who fear that the younger generation is well started down the primrose path.

Bibliography

Bayley, Nancy. "The Accurate Prediction of Growth and Adult Height," *Mod. Probl. Paediat.,* 7 (1962), 234–55.

Eichorn, Dorothy H. "Biological Correlates of Behavior" in H. W. Stevenson (Ed.), *Child Psychology,* Yearbook. Nat. Soc. Study Educ. (1963), 4–71.

Espenschade, Anna. "Dynamic Balance in Adolescent Boys," *Res. Quart.* 24 (1953), 270–75.

Jones, H. E. "Adolescence in Our Society," in *The Family in a Democratic Society.* New York: Anniversary Papers at the Community Service Society of New York, 1949. Pp. 70–82.

————. *Motor Performance and Growth.* Berkeley: University of California Press, 1949.

————. "Skeletal Maturing as Related to Strength." *Child Development,* 17 (1946), 173–85.

Jones, Mary C. "A Study of Socialization Patterns at the High School Level," *J. Genet. Psychol.,* 93 (1958), 87–111.

————. "A Comparison of the Attitudes and Interests of Ninth-Grade Students over Two Decades," *J. Educ. Psychol.,* 51 (1960), 175–86.

Jones, Mary C. and Bayley, Nancy. "Physical Maturing Among Boys as Related to Behavior," *J. Educ. Psychol.,* 41 (1950), 129–48.

Jones, Mary C. and Mussen, P. H. "Self-Conceptions, Motivations, and Interpersonal Attitudes of Early- and Late-Maturing Girls," *Child Developm.,* 29 (1958), 491–501.

Mussen, P. H. and Jones, Mary C. "Self-Conceptions, Motivations, and Interpersonal Attitudes of Late- and Early-Maturing Boys," *Child Develpm.,* 28 (1957), 243–56.

———— and ————. "The Behavior-Inferred Motivations of Late- and Early-Maturing Boys," *Child Develpm.,* 29 (1958), 61–7.

Nicolson, Arline B. and Hanley, C. "Indices of Physiological Maturity: Derivation and Interrelationships," *Child Develpm.,* 24 (1953), 243-56.

Shock, N. W. "Basal Blood Pressure and Pulse Rate in Adolescents," *American Journal of Diseases of Children.* 63 (1944), 16-22.

————. "The Effect of Menarche on Basal Physiological Functions in Girls," *Amer. J. Physiol.,* 139 (1943), 288-92.

Tanner, J. M. *Growth at Adolescence,* 2d Ed. Oxford: Blackwell, 1962.

————. "The Secular Trend Toward Earlier Physical Maturation," *Tijd Schrift Voor Sociale Geneeskunde,* 44 (Delst, 1966), 524-39.

5

William W. Wattenberg

The Junior High School—
A Psychologist's View

The junior high school, as a psychologist might look at it, has two paradoxical distinctions: First, its clientele is composed of so bewildering an assortment of young people at crucial turning points in their lives as to defy orderly description. Second, at colleges of education there is a tendency to make believe that there is no such institution: schools are considered either elementary or secondary; young people, either are children or adolescents.

Three major strands of fact give texture to the junior high school: First, due to the fact that young people do not develop in accordance with time tables, junior high school populations are heterogeneous not only as to ability and all the usual variables, but also as to developmental stage. Second, during the years over which this institution presides, youngsters may make sharp changes in the course of intellectual growth, emotional adjustment, and social goals. Third, our knowledge of what forces cause the changes is fragmentary at best.

Perhaps it would be best to pick up these strands one at a time. In doing so, we can bring an illusion of order to what probably will always be a scene of confusingly shifting patterns.

Let us begin by picturing more concretely what was implied by the observation that the junior high school student body is composed of young people in assorted phases.

Writers and research workers have found it convenient to divide human existence into a series of stages. Although everyone knows that

From *NASSP Bulletin* (April, 1965): 34-44.

some poetic and prosaic license is involved, that no living human being is ever entirely childish or adolescent or adult, yet it helps us to organize our thinking if we highlight commonalties.

Recognizing that with actual individuals there will always be variations and shadings and contradictions, there are three stages that concern us at the junior high school level. Of these, the least demanding is what we might call later childhood. At this point in the development of young people, especially those from middle class homes, the individual remains fundamentally dependent upon adults. The general orientation is one of pleasing or getting along with the grown-ups. And, in the last years of this phase, most children are skillful enough as young psychologists and strong enough in their self-control so that they are usually quite delightful.

By gradual steps, young people drift into a contrasting stage which earlier writers called early adolescent but for which Redl's designation "pre-adolescence" has come to be the standard term. Here, three major shifts take place. The young people react very strongly to their agemates: Some become utterly dependent upon their peers; an equally normal but puzzling minority court relative solitude. There is considerable vacilation in attitudes toward adults; strong revolt against childishness and sporadic displays of enmity toward parents and teachers may punctuate displays of childishness or its opposite, adult-like responsibility. While all this is happening, the young people are quite conscious of sex—their own sex roles. The boys may show the importance to them of masculinity by shunning or teasing girls; the girls, by unending, giggling conversations, or by needling the boys demonstrate their concern about femininity. Physically, rapid growth and puberty are on the agenda.

The surest sign that pre-adolescence is coming to an end is that boy-girl interests become open. Yet, there are other shifts, also. Where the pre-adolescent was concerned negatively about childishness, the true adolescent is reaching for adulthood. Now, comes the series of steps marking progress toward grown-up status: the driving of cars, the concern with grooming, the cultivating of social skills, the interest in earning money and in vocations, and the organization of values.

What has all this to do with the junior high school? In which stage are its students? The answer is that they are in all three, but at different times! To provide a clue, let us oversimplify the facts by stating that among thirteen-year-olds, half the girls but only ten per cent of the boys will have reached pubescence. At fifteen, the comparable figures are ninety per cent of the girls and fifty per cent of the boys. Only when they are seventeen and safely ensconced in senior high school classrooms will ninety-nine per cent of both sexes be fully adolescent.

If, for the sake of having numbers easy to remember, we were to assume a "typical" class of forty, then, in the sixth grade it would be composed of two fully adolescent girls, eight pre-adolescent girls, ten childish girls, four pre-adolescent boys and sixteen childish boys. A ninth grade class of the same size would consist of sixteen young ladies (adolescents) and four pre-adolescent girls, plus two childish boys, eight pre-adolescent boys, and ten fully adolescent boys.

This, then, is the first and most important fact about the junior high school. Its classes are unstable and constantly changing admixtures. There is no uniformity in needs, motivational patterns, favorite modes of relating to adults, or even social predilections.

Among experienced teachers one finds two exactly opposite but equally "successful" techniques for dealing with what can truly be termed a juvenile hodgepodge. One, often found in many math classes, is to have the work divided into short units whose duration and content permits no leeway for significant spread in time or interest. The other, used frequently in social studies or core programs, is to have the class work in small committees chosen to give some useful organizational form to the diversity.

Usually, junior high school teachers are left to find their own techniques for coping with the extreme heterogeneity of their classes. True, there is quite a bit of useful folk wisdom on such matters transmitted from teacher to teacher. Yet, from the viewpoint of a psychologist one can ask why there has been so little direct study of this aspect of the junior high school, why there has been almost a complete neglect of grouping problems as a subject for scientific study.

This, then, gives us an initial reason for introducing a theme to which we may want to return later: The existence of the junior high school provides an opportunity to cope with a set of problems for which we otherwise would not have suitable administrative structures. But, and this is a most important "but," much too little has been done to make use of the opportunity.

The second major aspect of the junior high school's student body derives from the evidence that, during and immediately after the stage here termed "pre-adolescence," rather abrupt changes may take place in the course of an individual's development. The older writers tended to speak of the changes produced by puberty. The more objective research workers who have engaged in longitudinal studies are likely to write of changes which are associated with the year of maximum growth. For, just as the curves of individual physical growth tend to reach a plateau in late childhood, then abruptly swing into the so-called "growth spurt," and then level off, so too do the curves for various psychological functions change their slope or shape.

Let us recall a few obvious indices. There is comparatively little delinquency charged against eleven and twelve-year-olds; juveniles offenses reach their peak among the fourteens and fifteens. The number who have to be hospitalized for mental illness rises tenfold after the fifteenth birthday. For quite a while psychiatrists have been bemused by the fact that pre-adolescents may display conduct amazingly similar to that shown in the most serious mental illnesses, and spontaneously recover.

At the present point in American educational history we are also struck by the fact that the phenomenon of dropouts is concentrated in the junior high school age range.

The question to which we must address ourselves is whether the personality qualities which are symptomized by delinquency, mental illness, and social maladjustment result from changes taking place at the time of their appearance or are merely the final result of events which occurred earlier in life.

From two apparently contrasting sources of ideas there has come a tendency to regard adolescent changes as the inevitable result of what had happened to the young person during his babyhood or early childhood. Behaviorists, from the boastful Watson to the Walden-thinking Skinner, have emphasized the primacy of early conditioning. Although positing more subtle but even more potent processes, the Freudians agree.

From the latter viewpoint especially, the appearance of any form of pathology later in life is likely to be considered as the precipitating out of the effects of early trauma or early relationships. The search for causes traditionally implicates malformation of personality at the oral, anal, or phallic stages.

One notes, for instance, that use of the Glueck Social Prediction scales apparently permits a fairly accurate selection in the elementary schools of the boys who will be delinquent in junior high school. Good second grade teachers are almost as accurate. Moreover, we find that the bulk of school dropouts were children who had trouble in reading and arithmetic from the start; indeed, many appear to have betrayed their future pattern of failure even as they entered kindergarten.

The facts which support the viewpoints placing prepotency on early childhood would make us hope for relatively little from the junior high school period. True, the results of childhood events finally show themselves, but can they be changed? If the cause is indeed deep-seated, the traditional recourse is to the deep therapies, which take extended periods of time. Moreover, the turbulence of emotions accompanying puberty have been long regarded as psychoanalysts as tremendously complicating the work of the therapist.

Not only is this true, but it is equally true that the kinds of trouble with which we would be concerned blossom rapidly. The causes may have been operating for years and have acquired great momentum: The results appear suddenly. Delinquency becomes full-blown in a matter of months, the decision to drop out of school becomes firm in weeks, and who would want to decide how long it takes a disturbed girl to get herself pregnant? As one thoughtful psychiatrist summed up the dilemma, "It's too late too soon."

Since hopelessness is not a congenial frame of mind for educators, we have equipped junior high schools with counselors, installed various programs of group counseling, and opened the door to courses ranging in title from home and family living to life adjustment. Is there any evidence to justify all this?

The answer is a somewhat puzzled, "Yes." A rather striking set of facts have been brought to light by the group of research workers who have made longitudinal studies of young people and applied one or another technique of curve-fitting to those sequences of data which can be placed in numerical series. Cecil Millard noted, for instance, that there was enough of an orderly character to the growth patterns of most children so that one could predict with some confidence from the early years to the later years up to the year of puberty or the year of maximum growth. Then, so to speak, the bets were off. A new growth curve with a new set of parameters appeared on the charts.

Using difference techniques and working with the data which had earlier been gathered in the Harvard Growth Study, Cornell and

Armstrong, while the Research Division of the New York State Education Department, found four rather distinct patterns of shift in course of intellectual growth which occurred at the year of maximum growth. The first is the one which we have regarded as traditional and universal. That is, the relationship between chronological age and tested mental age is a straight line. Then, there were found a large group of curves where after the year of maximum growth, there was a slowing up of apparent intelligence. In a third group, the year of maximum growth marked an upslanting change—these are the so-called "late bloomers." The fourth group followed a pattern of growth by "fits and starts;" throughout life their curves showed a step-like pattern. For us, the thing to hold our attention is that there were many cases where changes were sharply defined and where the turning point occurred during the junior high school years.

There is a smattering of evidence that similar turning points may occur in the emotional, characterological, and social spheres. At the University of California, another center for longitudinal study of juvenile development, it was noted that boys tended to have a firm masculine identification and all the goods that went with that if they had had a non-stressful relationship with their fathers either when they were four or five on the one hand or during pre-adolescence on the other. Apparently, damage done by a poor relationship early could be significantly corrected later.

In a similar vein, a pair of studies of Warbois and Cantoni on counseling processes with the same population in Flint, Michigan, found that it was almost as though good counseling on his or her personal problems could put a youngster on another track from the one he had been following.

If these data come as a surprise, if they are not among the most important intellectual equipment of junior high school teachers and administrators, isn't that fact revealing in its own right? Here, then, to return to our theme we have the interesting facts that the junior high school is the scene of events significant enough to justify its existence but that much too little has been done to seize and exploit the opportunities it offers.

Now, let us look for a moment at the fact that so little is known about the reasons behind the changes which we have been emphasizing. The extent of our ignorance is symbolized by the fact that during the past four decades, years during which 50,000 books a year on the most detailed and even inconsequential subjects of all kinds have appeared in these United States, there have been exactly three books devoted to pre-adolescence, the pivotal psychological stage of the junior high school population. Back in the late 1920's Father Furfey published a book called, *The Gang Age*. More than twenty years went by before Blair and Burton published their book on pre-adolescent development. After another decade passed a book on the same subject was authored by Loomis.

The junior high school is an established institution; it is an element in most school systems. Why has its student body apparently been comparatively ignored as a field of study? Why the paucity of publication? Part of the answer lies in the fact that relatively little is known, and that with marginal reliability. The group has puzzling qualities; the changes which take place are difficult to relate to factors over which we have control.

Let me give a sampling of the information we do have. We have data gathered at the Fels Research Institute, for instance, which seem to show that the achievement motivation of elementary school children reflects the value placed on achievement by the parent of the opposite sex. Studies of high school students indicate that they are more likely to identify with the values of the parent of their own sex. Somewhere in between, presumably during the junior high school years, the shift takes place. We lack details as to how this occurs and what can be done by school people. The phenomenon of the "academic tailspin," as evidenced by adolescent boys who were pushed scholastically by their mothers, is the main topic in the chapter on adolescent pathology in English and Pearson's classic work on "Emotional Problems of Living." They are able to give some fascinating explanations using orthodox Freudian concepts. Yet, today, twenty years after this material has appeared, there is nothing approaching a reliable application of the ideas whether by counseling techniques or deep-probing psychotherapy.

Let us take another illustration brought to light by the careful comparison of data gathered by the Adolescent Growth Study in Berkeley, California. They noted that at about the time boys and girls first displayed interest in each other and became preoccupied apparently with their lack of boy-girl social skill or rather with the success or failures of their attempts to gain such skill, at that very time the youngsters were attacking and making life miserable for even the best trained group workers at a clubhouse established for observational purposes, and at that very time their teachers were reporting a falling off in scholastic interest and quality. A short while later, when the boy-girl activities had reached the point of taken-for-granted skills, the clubhouse leaders reported that the very same young people were now behaving helpfully, as apprentice adults, and teachers reported that their scholastic work had picked up again.

Quite interesting, we'll all agree. But, now let's ask some questions. Do we know which of these three relationships stands in the causal position? Have we any tried-and-true rationale for dealing with this matter, or even for deciding whether we should do anything at all? Yes, and when Bestor and Rickover were enjoying a field day with their sneers at "life adjustment education," why weren't these relationships mentioned? If there is reason to brood over such questions, let's compound the puzzlement with an intriguing fact: the study to which I have been referring was published more than 25 years ago; it was one of the first studies making good use of the existence of a junior high school, in this case the Claremont Junior High School.

It would be interesting to regale ourselves with the many other illustrations which could be given, but the two cited above are adequate to help define the dimensions of the situation. What we appear to have is not a total absence of information, but rather a broad and relatively shallow stream of largely descriptive information whose application is not firmly determined. This exhibits a marked contrast with the tremendous volume of material on early childhood and the not-quite so voluminous but still massive accumulation of data on adolescence.

The situation as to studies on development is paralleled to some degree by the accumulation of material on pedagogical issues. We have for no junior high school subject anything coming even close to the study of psychological factors and teaching methods involved in beginning reading or arithmetic. However, research relevant to teaching fields in the junior high school does not suffer by comparison with that for the senior high school or even the colleges. In the upper reaches of all our educational institutions there has been some fascinating experimentation by a goodly company of hardy souls, but the research problems are quite intricate and the prevailing atmosphere often permeated with suspicion of educationists.

Let us return once again to our theme. Both what we know and we don't know about the young people themselves support the wisdom of establishing an institution, the junior high school, which can minister helpfully to their special needs. In this institution the very demands of the situation require faculty, administrators, and other professional personnel with the knowledge, patience, durability, and other attributes to cope wisely with rather unique opportunities for serving young people. The institutions exist. The personnel is on the job. Yet, there has been a notable lag in the appearance of professional training for this situation; there is an equally serious lag in painstaking research on the part of either junior high school people or child development experts.

Let us attempt to come to grips with the twin questions of why this should be so, and what can be done about it. Now, with cold malice aforethought, I am going to use what is a typical psychologist's trick— I am going to call attention to the very name, its implications, link to it associations, which some will regard as far-fetched, which will make others righteously indignant. So be it! The name with which we have endowed this unique educational institution, this challenging opportunity for education, is junior high school. *Junior* high school.

Let us free-associate for a moment to both halves of the title. What are our usual feelings and our usual associations, our hunches, about juniors? Sons, overshadowed by fathers, even having to bear a name not quite rightfully theirs, having to be chips off the old blocks, always having to live up to a model not of their making, not quite people in their own right. Think of the junior in Junior Achievement—not quite real, playing at being grown-up, in apprenticeship to being serious.

And high school. High. The first step to college. Emphasis upon intensive effort. Where there are departments composed of experts in subject matter, with graduate degrees in the academic disciplines, just like college professors!

Viewed wryly from the proper (or perhaps, improper) angle, there is a comic note to the juxtaposition of terms. And, as is so often true of veritable comedy, there is beneath it a deep layer of pathos, bordering on the tragic. Yes, seriously I am suggesting that a portion of our problems in fulfilling the potential of the junior high school arises from the fact that the professional staff has let themselves be caught in a situation where powerful and usually unverbalized status considerations turn their eyes away from the very difficulties which should be a source of pride.

Now, this is neither a demand nor a hint that merely changing the name will in and of itself be of any value. The situation is too deeply rooted for that; the possibilities for gain are too vital.

Well, then, where do we find the answers? For the purpose of inaugurating discussion, of triggering that comparison of ideas and matching of dissents from which knowledgeable and experienced professionals may bring into the open their own solutions, let me have the temerity to suggest a few items in a strategy for basic reorientation.

First, it may be necessary to focus sharply on what makes the junior high school distinctive from the senior high school. (We do not need to worry about proclaiming a function different from the elementary school; that is easy to do emotionally, and has been done well.) The uniqueness consists in the fact that this school's population is in transition. During an older period we might have compared it to the marshalling yards of a railroad. In an era of motor travel we might find an analogy in the elaborate interchanges which link major routes with interstate freeways. This uniqueness poses problems which are included in the construction of any other road, and then call for an additional set of skills for the engineers, for the construction workers, and for the drivers.

Second, the teachers and administrators responsible for such schools may have to be painfully insistent on bringing their special needs forcefully to the attention of our teacher-educating institutions. Possibly to avoid complicating the curricular structures, partly to guard jurisdictional rights, our education faculties have assumed that the similarities between junior high schools and senior high schools so greatly outweighed the contrasts that both could be embraced as "secondary education" and, accordingly, there was positive disadvantage in looking at the differences which might require distinctive preparation and differently aimed research.

It must be admitted that to emphasize distinctivenesses which would logically lead to "fragmentation" in teacher-preparation at the present time would be to swim against the tide. But, then, there is no point in learning to swim if one is only going to go with the tide. Today one hears much talk of K through 12 programs. The implication is that there is a universality to educational principles and problems which call for so little specialized expertise as to militate against preparation or research based on meeting the peculiar needs of different age groups.

Yes, if we are to base our educational programs upon simpleminded acceptance of Skinnerian conditioning, and consider that the major mode of learning, then there is such universality. But, if that is our fundamental belief, let's turn our schools over to electronic gadgetry and clear out. However, if we are concerned with differences in cognitive styles, if we are concerned with motivation, if we are to recognize the significance of social adjustment and utilize the full power of group processes, then, we must force acknowledgement of the fact that the junior high school population is, in fact, very special. Its specialness calls for understandings in genuine depth concerning the phenomena of pre-adolescence and the ways of utilizing heterogeneities so massive as to constitute differences in kind rather than differences in degree.

The wisdom and experience of many educators gave rise to the movement which brought the junior high school into being as an institution. Now we have the grueling task of realizing the hopes and expectations with which they launched the enterprise. There can be no doubt but that the task is proving much more complicated, much more obstinate than the founders could have believed. Their expectation was that creating a new institution, engaging as it were in a neat bit of administrative legerdemain, would almost in and of itself solve the problems. It has turned out that the creation of the institution has provided a setting that has opened opportunities. Yet, progress has been slower than earlier leaders might have expected.

If we and our thousands upon thousands of colleagues could now get to work to take full advantage of the opportunities, perhaps within a generation one could boast of great achievements, could say with pride that we had learned how to help our youth negotiate the pre-adolescent transitions with confidence, had found answers to dropout problems, had brought self-destructive delinquency under control.

The jobs to be done are worth doing. Let's intensify the zest with which we tackle them.

6

William W. Wattenberg

Preadolescents in the Junior High

The change from childishness to adolescence takes place for most youngsters some time between the dates they enter the seventh grade and leave the ninth grade. The period of transition, often marked physically by rapid growth, is one which has received until recently little careful scientific study. In the terminology now current, this is the period of preadolescence.

To place preadolescence in its sequential setting, and at the risk of some oversimplification, it is necessary to give a brief summary of the psychological characteristics most likely to be associated with childhood, adolescence, and preadolescence:

A child can be considered, for this purpose, as a young person who is in almost all respects dependent upon adults, whose chief sources of need gratification are grownups, and who tends to assume without struggle the status and roles accorded children in his culture.

An adolescent is a young person whose reproductive system has matured, who is economically dependent upon adults, whose chief source of need gratification is his peers, who has open interest in the opposite sex, and for whom status and roles as defined for children and adults in his culture are confused. He tends to be moving toward adulthood.

The term "preadolescent" has taken a special meaning within recent years. It refers to a fairly well-defined transition stage between childhood and adolescence, as described above. Some writers would call it "early adolescence." Others, singling out salient characteristics found in limited groups, have referred to "the negative stage" and "the gang age." A more accurate but cumbersome designation would be "the circum-pubescent years." Preadolescents are young people who, physically, are in a period of growth spurt which transforms their builds from that of children to that of young adults and which includes maturation of the reproductive system. Their attitude towards adults is often one of open ambivalence. These young people are shifting emotional dependence from parents to peer groups. Their budding interest in the opposite sex may show itself more by hostility than by open attraction. Play groups are almost entirely self-segregated by sex. The personality structure often goes through a temporary disorganization. There is likely to be movement, without positive goal, away from childishness as characterized by docile submission to adult domination.

A Flexible Setting

Although the majority of students will go through preadolescence at some time during their junior high school careers, the most striking thing about the junior high school student group as a whole is that it consists of a mixture of psychological stages. For no youngster is the change from child to preadolescent to adolescent so sharp that he moves from one to another in the course of a single month. Rather, each change is gradual and for many months a given student may combine qualities belonging in different areas to two, and sometimes all three, of these phases. Each boy and girl follows his own timetable. Hence, chronological age is a poor index of psychological qualities. The girls, as a group, tend to move through preadolescence into adolescence about eighteen months to two years before the boys. Within each sex group there is likely to be a four-year cycle extending from the time the first significant fraction enter preadolescence until the last enter adolescence.

The resultant situation is that, if we use physical status as a rough index and engage in willful oversimplification, we can think of a typical sixth grade class of forty as composed of two fully adolescent girls, eight preadolescent girls, ten childish girls, four preadolescent boys and sixteen childish boys. A ninth grade class of the same size would be composed of sixteen fully adolescent girls, four preadolescent girls, two childish boys, eight preadolescent boys, and ten fully adolescent boys.

Although junior high school classes will usually show this type of mixture, always in each class there will be a significant fraction of preadolescents. Because of the personality qualities associated with that phase of development, this fraction will usually call for more attention by the teacher and be the source of more strain on group organization.

The genius of the junior high school is that it can provide a setting where a psychologically mixed group can develop in a framework not dominated by any one subgroup. An eight-year elementary school is likely to be geared to the needs of little children. Those seventh and eighth graders who reach adolescence are apt to present difficult problems; rules and regulations needed to protect little folk are to them childish restrictions. Yet, to make exceptions for the large, prestige-bearing, early maturers may produce unfortnuate group repercussions. Socially, the first girls and boys to mature may feel unduly conspicuous and isolated; there is no large group to accept them and into which they can blend.

A four-year high school creates the opposite problem. The late-maturing boys may appear in its halls as bewildered children moving aimlessly among giants. Social life and physical activities are geared to adolescents; class procedures are fitted to the type of teacher-student relationship suited to their maturity. The immature minority may be allowed to stay lost.

It is clear that the span of chronological ages encompassed by the junior high school is one which presents unique situations that can most easily be handled in a separate administrative unit. Unfortunately, in too many instances the possibilities of special helpfulness to young people remain relatively unexplored. Although there are many promising exceptions, junior high schools too often tend to suppress the differences among young people which might better be cherished.

For example, there is good evidence that changes in interests and needs accompany the changes in physique and physiology at sexual maturity. Thus, in a class containing a mixture of children, preadole-scnets, and adolescents, one would expect to find striking individual differences not only in mental ability and personality but also in the appeal of any topic. To meet this situation, there is need for classroom procedures which will permit of subgrouping in accordance with differences in felt need. If there is any one place in the educational system which requires use of committee work it is at the junior high school level.

An illustration of a typical dispersion of interest was observed in a seventh grade class visited recently by the author. The general topic on which the group was at work was Indian life. One committee, composed largely of mature girls, was delving intensively into family life in various tribes. At the opposite extreme, another group, composed entirely of young-looking boys was discussing and acting out how Indians made war.

There is need for a study to discover general topics which will permit subgroups to follow such a range of interest and yet contribute to the progress of larger group projects. Much too often when one enters a junior high school class he finds a procedure and choice of topics almost identical, except for level, with what would be found in a senior high school or college. Psychologically, this represents as bad a loss of educational opportunity as though kindergartens were to imitate second grade class procedure.

Another important set of problems with which the junior high school can deal, and does so very effectively in many cases, arises from the fact that sex identification and development of self-concepts relative to sex roles are taking place for many young people. To a large extent, departmentalization by ensuring that every child will have substantial contact with adults of his own sex helps to meet the resultant need. Certainly, a boy should have masculine guidance in the important areas of learning game skills and industrial art skills; a girl in exploring home making skills. The present author would question the wisdom of the recent trend to ignore or suppress real sex differences by converting the traditionally sex-segregated shop and home economics classes into mixed home mechanics and family living classes at the junior high school level. Of course, both sexes at some point in their schooling should gain the benefits of recognizing the responsibilites for joint planning and shared skill in the home. Such classes from a psychological viewpoint might better be placed in the early elementary or the later high school grades.

A related complex of problems, more often ignored, is symptomized by the changes in relationship of boys to girls which frequently occur. Quite often in the seventh grade, girls emerge as class leaders. If elections are held, girls tend to vote for other girls; boys, inclined to regard class officers as being straw bosses allied to the traditional enemy tribe of Adults, may be willing to see girls assume that role. By the end of the ninth grade, the boys are yielding to standards of decorum and grooming more typical of young adults. Now, when elections are held, they tend to vote for other boys. Meanwhile, the girls' admiration of girls in general has been dropping and many girls feel that boys make better leaders.

Behind what appears to be an unimportant and amusing minor shift in voting habits, a crucial drama has been unfolding. At issue basically is the girls' evaluation of their femininity. In later years, for many women the striving for masculinity as a desirable condition is a key element in mental health problems. The change in attitude of which such difficulties is born takes shape during the junior high school years, although its basis is in earlier experiences. Little is done in junior high schools in relation to this fundamental attitudinal change; usually it is allowed to go ignored.

Counseling Services

This and other personal developmental problems point to the need for provision of counseling services. In many communities, the legal limit for compulsory attendance comes within a year or two following junior high school. In fact, many young folks arrive at their decision to "serve out their time" and then quit school when they are in the eighth or ninth grade. Here, again, although the basic attitudes become visible at the junior high school level, the experiences from which they arose are often of earlier origin. The availability of personal counseling might be of significance to many individuals. This would require rather special arrangements and changes in policy.

In the problems of elementary shool children, the present activities of parents are so significant that the procedure of choice in dealing with personality problems is to contact the parents. Accordingly, there is a justifiable tendency to use available funds to increase the number of visiting teachers or school social workers. By the junior high school years children are mature enough and their relations with parents are such that direct counseling with the young person may be a more efficient remedial procedure than contact with the parents, although parents should never be ignored. At any rate, for most boys and some girls social distance between child and parent is rapidly widening by the time of puberty.

Unfortunately in too many junior high schools, the flare-ups of disciplinary difficulties result in a drift toward using counselors as high-powered punitive agents. This prevents all but the most exceptional from being able to establish with most youngsters who have personal problems the relationships needed for genuine counseling. Also, the type of problem already mentioned requires a program of several counseling sessions; if, as is generally the case, junior high school counselors have heavy case loads and other duties, they may be forced toward ineffective one-shot attempts to deal with basic attitudes and reserve multiple-contacts for only those boys or girls sent repeatedly to the office for dressings-down. To date, attempts to reduce early school-leaving by counseling have proved usually to be ineffective. One probable reason is that it has come too late and been too diluted.

Interestingly, the junior high school years have been found good ones for attempts to introduce programs for direct study of human relations and other psychological problems. Students are vividly aware of social relationships; many are experiencing conflicts of values between home and peer group. When opportunity is provided they are ready and eager to discuss issues related to popularity, family relations, emotional reactions, and values. Experimental programs for stimulating concentrated discussion of these topics have been successful, and seem to produce durable results. The curricular context for such discussions may vary much from school to school. In some cases, the intensive study of human relations and personal adjustment is given a course name and is assigned separate time, more often it develops within the setting of a core program, an English class, a social studies sequence, a family living, a science, or a group guidance program.

The purpose of the present article has been to point out some characteristics of student groups at the junior high school level and, in doing so to indicate possible gains to be won by having an administrative educational unit devoted to meeting the needs of these young people. While an administrative arrangement would undoubtedly make it easier to serve the group well, it is by no means a guarantee that this will happen. There are altogether too many schools where the staffs try to suppress the striking individual differencs which are so typical of the young people. Above all other qualities, the psychological needs of the students require that the junior high school have a flexible curriculum and utilize educational procedures which nurture individual differences. How many junior high schools have those qualities?

In many communities, an eight-year elementary school or a four-year high school has developed a program for meeting individual differences which provides a more hospitable atmosphere for preadolescents and for mixed groups than have some junior high schools. The administrative inconveniences involved have been quickly swept aside.

Regardless of the structure of institutions, whether it be an 8-4 plan, a 6-3-3 plan, or a 6-4-4 plan, the significant educational objective should be to create a setting where groups mixed as to developmental phase may work together on problems which are vital to the individual young people. The argument should begin at that point rather than assume that the structure will determine the program.

7

Douglas R. Jones

Pressures and Adolescents

The junior high youngster today faces many pressures. Probably the greatest pressure comes from his parents who wish the best for him. Even while they are anxious about what the future will bring to their children, parents understand that junior high school students also are often silly, moody and loud with many different reactions and behavior patterns. One can safely predict that they are unpredictable. Parents may fail to realize, however, that their children are growing up, facing special problems, and having individual needs. They may fail to understand that junior high students are experimenting with new situations in life rather than simply trying to rebel against their parents.

Another great pressure placed on the young adolescent is from the teachers. Many of the teachers may understand child growth and development but fail to use this knowledge to the best interest of the youngster. Frequently, teachers do not have a thorough understanding of the characteristics of the 12-, 13- or 14-year-old student, and, therefore, encounter difficulties with him. Teachers who understand what to expect from the early adolescent in all probability will be more effective in the classroom.[1]

Social pressures are too varied to list. The greatest pressure may be

From *Educational Leadership* (December, 1965): 209–11. Reprinted with permission of the Association for Supervision and Curriculum Development and Douglas R. Jones. Copyright © 1965 by the Association for Supervision and Curriculum Development.

that which is exerted by the idea of conformity thus causing the youngsters to conform to the demands of the right crowd. In every junior high school, there is at least one leading group which exerts a powerful force in controlling the energies of the students. This group dictates the activities and interests of the young adolescent.

These social pressures may be in the form of wearing the right brand of shirt, or shoes, or it may be an extreme hair style similar to that of the Beatles. In many of the junior high groups, there are peer pressures to conform by drinking or smoking. The present-day youngster is exposed to many ideas and concepts which he cannot control because he may lack information and security.

The youngsters are searching for status and recognition in society. The social classes of the students and the cultural background of the family group play a very significant part in the child's life. The child from a lower socioeconomic status may realize that children from the families of a higher income bracket seem to have a definite advantage. Research shows that middle and upper class families seek to instill in their children a greater motivation to achieve, which is an important factor in their growth. Often children from a lower socioeconomic group are sensitive because of their dress, speech or habits which may differ from some of their peers.

As a child grows, he has many conflicts in the family role and finds that he is expected to behave in contradictory ways. The role that he might play may be dictated by the demands of his parents. How the youngster resolves these problems depends on the background of the family, individual personalities, and a particular situation in which a young person may find himself.

Homework and grades add additional pressures. In the modern schools, increasing importance is placed on grades for the college-bound student. With the population explosion, colleges hold that they must be more selective. Therefore, teachers and parents preach continuously about grades and accumulating knowledge so that students can make high scores on the college entrance examinations. This pressure has moved from the senior high school down to the junior high school. With the concept of high grades, some teachers often emphasize quantity in assigning homework and, therefore, do not take into account the individual differences. In other situations, the accelerated classes are given so much homework the students do not have time to play and act their age. Since most junior high students are conscientious about completing their homework, they may actually endanger their health or start family squabbles by trying to complete all the assigned tasks.

Many people believe that murder, horror and gangster shows have devastating effects on the morale of children and young people. Programs with themes of crime, violence, brutality and sex can definitely influence the young mind.

What Should Be Done?

1. Teachers and Teaching Must Be Improved.

In too many schools a junior high school teacher is not qualified for this area of specialization. Actually he may have been prepared to teach in a self-contained classroom in the elementary school or he may have had a specialty in subject matter which prepared him to teach at the senior high school level. A curriculum for the teachers in the junior high school must be developed which will place the teacher in situations where he can understand adolescent problems and the characteristics of the growth and development of the 12-, 13- or 14-year-old.

This teacher should be an educated person who has love and understanding for adolescent children and realizes that he can help these youngsters to solve their problems. It is also imperative that teachers and parents be sympathetic with this age group and help them find solutions for their many problems. Even though the problems may seem insignificant to adults they are monumental to these youngsters at this particular time.

Curriculum authorities have offered many suggestions for improving the junior high school course of study. Regardless of the educational jargon, the child must be taught at his basic level of ability. In the junior high school the youngsters should be kept with their peers and given an opportunity to succeed in whatever endeavor they pursue. In many of the modern junior high schools, the students are expected to perform impossible tasks. By scheduling blocks of time, the child could be successful at his basic level of ability.

2. Problems of Adolescents Must Be Detected Early and Given Attention by the Guidance Counselor.

By the time a youngster arrives at the junior high school level, his potential and ability should be known. If he does not have the ability or desire for a program in college preparation, then another program must be offered to meet his individual needs. The guidance counselor may need to inform the parents that he believes their child does not have the ability to go to college.

In a good public relations program, information must be provided for the parents so that they may understand that college is not for all students and that individuals can be happy in other professions which do not require a college degree. In order to accomplish this objective, more guidance must be available at the intermediate level. Consistently educators have used the words, articulation, transition and exploration, but the curriculum may not offer the opportunities to meet these goals. The future programs must allow the youngster opportunities, under guidance, to explore all possibilities as he seeks excellence in his own way.

3. Pressure of College Preparation in Accelerated Programs Should Be Balanced.

Grouping and homework practices ought to be reexamined in schools so the youngster may be afforded an opportunity to live in a normal environment rather than in abnormally tense situations. If administrators decide that acceleration is a necessity, then it should be horizontal rather than vertical.

The teacher must assign homework in terms of individual differences. It is imperative that parents be given some idea as to the amount of time students should spend on their homework so that they can offer help if this is needed.

4. It is Mandatory that Leadership and Membership Roles Be Studied, Understood and Practiced in the Junior High School.

Students must be able to recognize the effective and wholesome kinds of leaders. Leadership abilities should be sought and opportunities should be provided for students to perform as leaders. By giving an early teenager information about effective leadership, he will be able to determine the kind of leader he should follow in a democratic society.

As the curriculum is revised to meet the crisis at the junior high school level, it is not a matter of utilizing new ideas but rather of applying *immediately* basic principles of learning and teaching which will help to improve the program. With love and understanding, the adolescents *can* survive this period of "transition in chaos."

Notes

1. Klapper, Joseph T. *The Effects of Mass Communication.* Glencoe, Illinois: The Free Press, 1960.

8

James S. Coleman

Social Change: Impact on the Adolescent

Adults have a special reason today to shake their heads and mutter, "the younger generation . . . ," as adults are wont to do. For today's adults and today's teenagers have special problems of communication that make it more and more difficult for each to understand what the other is up to. These communication problems arise not because teenagers are in some strange new way different than ever before, but because of changes in the structure of our society. These changes have produced a number of special problems in education and in the whole process of growing up, of which the communication gap is only one. I would like to indicate what some of these structural changes are, and some of their consequences for adolescents.

Societal Changes and Family Cohesion

A number of changes have combined to make the family a less cohesive, less effective agent within which to raise children than ever before. One of these changes is the entry of large numbers of women into the labor force. Prior to World War II, in March 1940, 16.7 per cent of married women held jobs outside the home. By March 1961, this had doubled to 34.0 per cent. (In 1890, it was 4.5 per cent.) This change need not, of course, make a given family less tightly knit, nor give adolescent children a less rich "psychological home," but it tends to do so, and the overall social impact must be in this direction.

From *NASSP Bulletin* (April, 1965):11–14.

Another change is the smaller and smaller number of families that have relatives—aunts, uncles, grandparents—living in the household. This means that the typical family of today in America is parents and children, with nothing more. Thus the family's strength depends far more on the parents than ever before. The relatives are not there to provide adults for the children to model themselves after, or adults in whom they can confide.

A third change, which reinforces the preceding one, is the greater geographic mobility of families, particularly since World War II. An urban or suburban family today does not have a homestead that passes from one generation to another; nor does it even have a stable place of residence for a single generation. More and more, the typical "life cycle" of a family begins with a newly-married couple living in an apartment in the city; then with the first child comes a move to a suburb of families with young children; then later, as income and family grow, to a suburb of larger houses and older children; then finally, after the children are gone, back to an apartment in the city.

Such moves mean that the adult neighborhood, which was once an extension of the household itself, is hardly so now. Children make neighborhood friends quickly, but their parents do not; and perhaps most important, the children have few contacts and even fewer stable relationships with other adults in the neighborhood.

Finally, a change that has been going on for a long time is the shift of the father's work from the home or the neighborhood (e.g., the farmer or merchant) to a distant office or factory. Thus, the son knows only abstractly what his father does; and he can never enter into the father's work.

Consequences of Change

The effects of these changes on the adolescent are many. One of the most interesting indicators is the recent large increase in "going steady" among adolescents. This phenomenon, virtually unknown in Europe, can be explained only in terms of overall changes that have taken place in the teenager's life. Looking closely at the practice of going steady indicates that it is not (as some adults fear) principally a license for sexual freedom. Instead, its basis is more nearly in the kind of psychological security it provides, a psychological closeness that today's adolescents seem to need. When we ask why they need it, the answer is clear: the family no longer provides the closeness and security it once did. Because of the structural changes indicated above, the family fails to provide the kind of close, secure relationships that the adolescent had as a child and will once again have when he himself forms a family. His response comes by finding that close security in an attachment to another.

Going steady is only one of the consequences of these structural changes in society. Another is the greater and greater burden that falls on the school. The school was once a supplement to the activities of the family in making adults of its children. But the roles have reversed for today's adolescents: the home is more and more merely a supplement to the adolescent's life, which focuses more and more on the school. It may be, as some school administrators feel, that this places too great a responsibility on the school. Yet the condition exists, and many families, with their working parents, high mobility, and lack of other relatives in the household, are in no position to change the condition. The adolescents turn to one another, to the school, and to the entertainments of the larger society, for these are their only resources.

Another consequence of the family's weakness, one that stems from the same needs as does going steady, is the earlier age of dating and of interest in the opposite sex. The consequences of this for interest in schoolwork is particularly marked for girls. There is a sharp shift in early adolescence from a high evaluation of the bright girl to a much lower evaluation—for the girl who appears especially bright does not fare well in dates with boys. Among schools I studied a few years ago, this shift started slightly later in the rural schools than in the urban and suburban ones. In the former, the shift occurred during the ninth grade; in the latter, the shift had largely taken place before the ninth grade. In both sets of schools, the devaluation of brightness and the emphasis on good looks and popularity with boys was at its peak in middle adolescence. In the rural schools, it had sharply declined by the senior year in high school, while in the urban and suburban ones, the decline had already begun in the junior year. It appears that the most intense focus of adolescent girls on problems of popularity and dating, and the greatest devaluation of schoolwork occurs when the rating and dating system is still unsettled, and the uncertainty of who will ask whom for a date is at its height. These years, among modern adolescents, are earlier than ever before—in junior high school and early high school. The consequence for schools may be a peculiar one: to make the junior high school years more difficult ones than in the past, for adolescents and for teachers and school administrators, and to make the senior high school years (in three-year high schools) less difficult.

The earlier age of interest in the opposite sex, and the consequent earlier shift of adolescent values in this direction derives only in part from weakened family ties. It derives in part from all the changes in society that bring about early social sophistication among adolescents. Partly urban and suburban living, partly television and other mass media (for example, both popular music and movies have come to be more and more oriented to teenagers), partly the money they now have to spend, partly their better-educated parents, and partly the school itself, have made adolescents more wise in the ways of the world.

The Desire for Sophistication

In the schools I studied recently, the sharpest difference I found in the adolescents of the most rural schools and those of the most middle-class urban and suburban ones, was in the sophistication of the latter. The rural 9th graders were still children, obedient to teachers, and the middle-class suburban pupils were already disdainful of the ways of childhood. Such sophistication, and desire for sophistication, is a double-edged sword. It means that adolescents are more ready for new ideas, new experiences, quicker to grasp things. But it also makes them far less easy to teach, less willing to remain in the role of a learner, impatient with teachers, less likely to look at the teacher as a model or an authority. It need not make them more interested in school, but perhaps even less so. For the world whose sophistication they are taking on is one outside the school. Schoolwork, with its daily assignments and homework, they associate with childhood. Many of these children learn only years later, in college or after, that hard work and carrying out of assignments, attention to the demands of the teacher, become more important, rather than less, the farther they go in school.

Of all the recent changes in adolescents, this early desire for sophistication poses perhaps the greatest problem and the greatest challenge for secondary schools. Teenagers are less willing to respond to the teacher just because he is a teacher; less willing to "be taught." But they are more responsive *if* their imagination is captured, more able and willing to respond to a real challenge. It makes the school's task more difficult, for it cannot take the adolescent's interest for granted; it must find new ways of capturing this interest and energy. It has no other alternative but to accept these more sophisticated adolescents, and turn their sophistication to the advantage of education.

Altogether, recent changes in society have had a sharp impact on our adolescents. They present now, and they will present even more in the future, both difficulty and opportunity to the schools.

9

Francis C. Bauer, M.D.

Causes of Conflict

A comparison of today's adolescent with his counterpart of the 20's and 30's would certainly suggest that he has undergone considerable change. Whether this change is essential, however, or whether we are dealing primarily with a surface phenomenon seems a valid subject to debate.

To enumerate some of the apparent changes, today's adolescent is on the average slightly taller and enjoys better nutrition. He is physically healthier, perhaps more intelligent and certainly more sophisticated. He enjoys greater mobility, has more freedom and spends more money than any adolescent in history. But he is fundamentally the same adolescent struggling with the same basic problems that are characteristic of this somewhat disturbing phase of emotional development. Indeed his conflicts are greater today since not only is the adolescent expected to find himself, but he must do so in a world which refuses to remain the same for two consecutive weeks.

The basic conflict of adolescence is the struggle between his need to become independent on the one hand and his equally strong but opposite tendency to remain dependent on the other. Although present at birth and for some not resolved until death, this conflict is most disturbing during the adolescent period. Intellectual development enables the twelve to fifteen-year-old to see the future more clearly, and accordingly he yearns for independence and adult privilege. At the same time, however, he is reluctant to accept the responsibility of

From *NASSP Bulletin* (April, 1965): 15–18.

that state and desires for yet a little while the protective dependence of childhood. Since physical growth and development make it less appropriate to turn back than ever before in his experience, the conflict becomes intensified.

Today's adolescent is fundamentally no different from the adolescent of previous generations. He is a child in the body of an adult, engaged in role playing, trying out emotions and assuming attitudes. He is confused, indecisive, insecure, self-conscious, and acutely in need of direction. He is fearful of his own inner impulses and more especially fearful of the consequences resulting from their satisfaction. Why then are his problems more numerous and more acute today? This question is more logically answered by examining today's radically different social structure than by postulating a change in the nature of the adolescent.

We have, in recent decades, made something of a fetish of progress. The need to change, often for its own sake, has embraced every aspect of our living including, unfortunately, our methods of infant and child care. As a result we have literally pushed our children out of infancy by weaning, toilet training, and sending them off to school before they are really ready for any of these events. We have robbed them of their childhood by organizing their games and structuring their play activity according to adult rules and standards. We have placed great significance on performance and achievement thereby encouraging the attempt of status conscious parents to accelerate the process of childhood development. We have indeed propelled our children toward maturity and independence and insisted that they assume responsibility sometime before they are ready for it. Excessive permissiveness and self-determination are two examples of these social trends. But in so doing, we have failed to indulge the dependency needs of children allowing them to persist into adolescence.

Having attempted to accelerate the natural development of childhood, it appears that society then reverses the process during adolescence and the weight of adult pressure becomes redirected toward retarding growth. Instead of strengthening the adolescent's striving for independence, we now deny him experience with practical problems, we indulge and overprotect him and in effect keep him in a dependent state of existence for ever-lengthening periods of time. The adolescent then is pressured from both directions and is told to, "Hurry up and wait!"

Money, mobility, and the use of goods have also had an effect on today's adolescent, making him appear quite different from his counterpart of a generation or more ago. It seems more reasonable, however, to assume that he is the same adolescent but that he is reacting to many more and radically different situations than were formerly found in his realm of activity. And it should be especially noted that today's adolescent is asked to react to some situations involving rapid change with which today's adults are themselves not familiar. It is probably for this reason that so many youngsters seem to have lost faith in adults and retreated to the more secure and highly structured society they have built themselves. It is always interesting to note, in this connection, that while adults seem fearful of setting limits on youngsters, the gang, the group, the club or whatever a particular segment of adolescent society may be called, set far more stringent limitations on its members and in place of rebellion receive cheerful compliance. The obvious conclusion is that children demand external controls.

Certainly money and the use of goods have increased the material advantages of our twelve to fifteen-year-old set. These can never realistically compensate, however, for the less tangible but more important advantages that have been replaced—consistent values, family unity, and the authority of the parent.

The contamination of a value system by unrealistic notions of democracy has had a significant influence on the inability of the adolescent to resolve his conflicts. Idealism predominates the emotional life of the adolescent and his need to believe in something is never stronger. If during his formative years, however, his parents were consistently indecisive regarding values, the twelve to fifteen-year-old has few resources to sustain him during the adolescent search for an ideal of his own. His parents may have disagreed on religion, for example, and rationalized their own inability to resolve the difficulty by allowing the child to develop without any religious influence and to choose for himself at sixteen. While this may be considered a mark of great sophistication and is certainly democratic, all that it means to the growing child is that neither parent cared enough to teach that child what he thought was right. How notions of democracy ever became involved in family living could well be the subject of a separate paper. Suffice it to say that if the family unit, the foundation of our social structure, becomes further eroded by commercialism and materialism, the adolescent of tomorrow will appear to have changed to even a greater degree than the early teenagers of today.

Adolescence has always been a time of conflict inasmuch as it hurts more than a little to grow up and to become involved with the reciprocal relationship between privilege and responsibility. The normally occurring conflicts are necessarily intensified when the youngster's childhood experiences provide a weak foundation upon which to build. And this is becoming rather more usual than extraordinary. When we reflect on the tired old statistic that in our society one of every four marriages terminates in divorce, thereby removing the most important source of stability in childhood, it becomes easier to appreciate why so many youngsters are overwhelmed by the challenge of adolescence. And if we recognize that in at least two of the three remaining marriages, the parents have abdicated their position of authority and have joined the adolescent they should be leading, we are still closer to an understanding of the problem.

Human nature is the one constant in an ever-changing universe. It has the unique capacity to effect change and to adapt to change without itself changing in the process. For this reason, if we are concerned with the adolescent today we must consider him not as essentially different from his predecessors. We must consider rather those changes which make him appear different from other adolescents at other times in other settings.

10

Margaret Mead

Are We Squeezing out Adolescence?

We complain today that our young adults are narrow, selfish, interested only in the security of their own families, without horizons and without dedication, although they are good, hard-working husbands and wives, fathers and mothers. One explanation is that we turn them into potential husbands and fathers, wives and mothers far too soon. We stunt their moral and intellectual growth as it was once stunted by the narrowness of a primitive culture or a stringent poverty. But for us there is no such excuse.

Man is born with the capacity to acquire any knowledge that his forefathers have gained. To absorb this knowledge, man needs the long learning period of childhood and youth, and this long childhood is one main reason why he has been able to advance so rapidly.

What a society does with this learning period is a decisive element in determining not only the level of its culture but its survival in a socially competitive world. How fast are its children to be made to grow up?

The more primitive the society, the shorter the learning period has been. But one of the first signs of an advancing civilization is the lengthened learning period of adolescence, which postpones adult responsibility.

In the United States today, the common man lives as kings once lived. The house of the common man has luxuries no ancient palace could afford—heating and lighting, foods from all over the world, new

From *PTA Magazine* (September, 1960): 4–6.

and wonderful materials. In this house, news of the world is brought to him, and from it messages are sent, both with astounding rapidity. Without leaving his easy chair, he has gained an extensive knowledge of what is going on in the world.

As we have produced these and other marvels of well-being for family life, we have thought also that we were giving our children something no other children had before. We offer them, combined, the onetime advantages of the highly privileged with the new possibilities of an industrialized country. Not only do we educate the children of the rich or the future elite, but everyone. First came elementary education for all, then high-school education for all—a goal undreamed of two short centuries ago.

Something Is Wrong

But we are in serious danger of falling short of our ideal, no matter how near it may appear when we see the hordes of bright-faced youngsters pouring out of our impressively beautiful school buildings. For something is wrong. The symptoms have been enumerated often: the increase in juvenile delinquency and crime, the number of young people whom we permanently stigmatize as failures, the waste of talent, low academic standards, the high drop-out rate. These are the obvious deficits of an educational system that has become too impersonal and too standardized to take account of the individual child whose first failure, if caught in time, need not lead to retardation, truancy, and delinquency.

Just as severe a price is being paid by the children who make high grades, have an admirable record in extracurricular affairs, and have good chances at higher education. Along with their conformity to the school's demands goes conformity to another kind of demand, one begun in the junior-high school—that they be adult beyond their years.

The very phrase *age mate* becomes a kind of absurdity in junior-high school, where tiny youngsters several years away from puberty are classified with well-developed girls who look almost ready to be the mothers of another generation. Some of these youngsters have scintillating intelligence and the bodies of children. Others are still childish in mind though mature in body. Yet all are pushed into a common mold, pushed ahead to match not the highest intellectual development but the most precocious physical development.

This means that in our junior-high schools the pace is set by the girls, as it has been ever since the children entered first grade. Little girls are more docile and more verbal than boys, more anxious to please; and because these are qualities that our schools reward, the girls appear to excell the boys. If the schools would place as high a value on other qualities—originality, creativity, stubborn individuality of style, refusal merely to conform to please—the boys, recent investigations show, would come out better. Docility, verbal compliance, and the wish to please don't go very well with originality.

So, from the start, our grade schools expect girls to set standards in schoolwork, standards of orderliness, accuracy, legibility in handwriting, and proper outlining. The boys, for the most part, simply remove themselves from this world. They play games, think about cars, follow the major leagues. Meanwhile, the girls forge ahead.

In Junior-High School

Then comes junior-high school, which accentuates the differences in each sex and between the sexes because it is limited to the years of greatest disparity in growth. By this time the girls are, on the average, two years ahead of the boys in physical development. The boys, on the other hand, are not only farther behind the girls than before but incredibly diverse in size and shape, from Tom Thumbs to tall, thin creatures. Or they may be inordinately fat.

Hardly any of the boys have a sufficient internal stirring of approaching manhood to turn them spontaneously in the direction of the girls. Girls appear to them as alien creatures—too big, too demanding, too sure. Left to themselves, the boys would pull the girls' pony tails, pelt them with snowballs, or ignore them altogether. Once in a while a boy might defend a smaller girl and thus begin to think about protecting his own and other boys' sisters, a habit which has almost disappeared in the United States. But most junior-high boys would have nothing to do with girls their own age.

Neither would the more mature junior-high school girl be attracted by the reluctant, fumbling dance steps of her boy classmates. She would much prefer older boys, much older, even college "men."

Real Adolescence Denied

From first grade on we have trapped our boys in a female-modeled environment, in which the kind of lessons girls do well are the kind of lessons everybody does. Later we insist on keeping children of the same age together, which means that the more mature girls dominate the scene. Both boys and girls, therefore, are denied a real adolescence and forced instead into premature adult activity. Rich and privileged as no nation has ever been, do we have any reason to push our children into such premature adulthood, as if they lived in a country where the majority of the people still do not know where tomorrow's meal will come from?

This sorry situation has come on us gradually. As high schools broadened after World War I to include all sorts of children, the separation of children by age became more and more rigorous. The junior-high school seemed a good idea—a way of introducing young people by degrees to the different structure of high school. But it was invented without due regard to what we already knew about the tremendous discrepancy between boys and girls of that age. Nor have we reckoned with the evergrowing pressure toward precocity, toward becoming adult before one really becomes adolescent. Long pants, lipstick, nail polish, and dating have crept down into the grades, and social, not intellectual, preparation is emphasized in the junior-high school.

For the stimulating and exciting challenge of friendship with members of one's own sex, we have substituted "going steady." Mothers report that this makes the boy "much more serious about his work," not recognizing that such seriousness, though it leads to good grades, early career choice, and early adulthood, cuts the boy off from the searching, exploring, and experimenting that will some day result in real maturity.

The fruits of all this are bitter: lowered educational standards, a world that is much harder for boys than girls (although it is from our boys that most of our scientists and leaders will come), shortcircuited careers, low levels of aspiration, the tremendous hostility of men toward women, and the uneasy contempt of women for men.

None of this can be changed overnight. But there are things that every responsible community can do. First, it should urge a different kind of emphasis in elementary school, so that the special abilities of boys will be recognized more and their greater waywardness and variability penalized less. Second, there should be a determined effort to reduce social activities at the junior-high level, to encourage solitary pastimes, and to promote separate activities for boys and girls (all of which are discouraged today by parents and teachers alike). Third, adolescent social affairs should cut across high-school and college lines. Then maturing girls can meet older boys who are ready, physically and emotionally, for the pressures of dating. Fourth, there should be a serious exploration of the advantages of growing up slowly. The long days of adolescence will never return—those days in which both boys and girls have their last leisure to search their souls and to try, without commitment, the many possible roles they may take in the world.

11

Edward Bantel

Pre-Adolescent: Misunderstood

Sandwiched between two more perceptually impressive developmental stages is the terminal cycle of late childhood. This stage of development by its nature is probably the least likely to attract the penetrating interest of adults except those who must either live with or teach him. For the average child in the nine-to-twelve group there comes the maturational closure of important antecedent years of growth and anticipation of what lies ahead. Normally, as there is consolidation in behavior that assumes neo-adult qualities, there is being produced in him a stability and integration that will become the foundation for the ensuing period of youth.

In the framework of psycholanalytic theory this stage is within the "latency" period. The urgency of sexual strivings toward the parent of the opposite sex is greatly diminished. Thus, the average child is now free to invest a vast fund of energy in his own growth and learning, meeting major cultural expectations and adult demands. The disposition to come to grips with reality is salient and thus there is an increase of the adult tendency to overstructure learning events.

In this phase mutual, reciprocated attachments provide strength that heightens autonomy. Through successful social and affective transactions with agemates the child can diminish extravagant roman-

---

tic claims to the parent. Relinquishing excessive demands and bridging the gap with others establish the firm basis for surmounting the turbulence of ensuing years.

For the child who is not successful, needing to cling to parental support imperils his immediate adjustments and makes him a greater risk in the pubertal cycle of change. His self-made assurance is needed to move successfully into the adolescent world. To become certain of self, to become certain of "what is me" and "not me but others" is a salient feature in the terminal phase of childhood.

The Need for Time

For example, the child's capacity to understand (grasp temporal relations) and function in relation to a time schedule often leads to excessively demanding regulation and ordering of his behavior. Thus, linear time is an American cultural reality, thought of as a vessel to be filled with quality events of adult discretion. However, the child needs more rather than less time to himself (so evident in harried adult life yet overlooked as a child's need). He needs time to "play out" or "dream out" solutions to the problems with which he is grappling. Privacy, undisturbed by intrusions and thrusting of others, is essential to work at unifying perceptions of the physical and social world. Time, too, to be in the company of other children to explore, share, participate in innumerable life crises. This play relationship with real people of *his own age* serves to rework unresolved problems, to make and sustain affective ties that are tested in the reality of everyday life experiences.

The Struggle for Self

Some forms of parent- or teacher-pleasing, academic excellence, mask the basic developmental struggle for self. To exclude others, to avoid hard work or to engage in spectacular diversions, thus drawing greater parental and adult attention and support is behavioral or learning deviancy. Many a child, referred on this account, easily establishes a relationship with a guidance counselor, social worker, psychologist or other adult ancillary school personnel yet finds intimacy and comfortable association terrifying, as he either avoids others his own age or intimidates them to maintain social distance.

To take a chance—to venture and seek to make a friend, to be a friend—means giving up a part of self for a share in the other. Only a child secure in himself can take the risk.

In this period the modality of behavior is incessant involvement in gaining knowledge of a world which is increasingly important to him. His energy is invested in sharpening perceptive skills, building knowledge, mastering the essential tools and symbols of his culture, and it is this learning which provides new opportunities for him to become more of himself.

All his abundant energies are directed toward mastering the world of things, people and meanings, and upon this mastery is founded healthy self-esteem.

Thus it is essential that needless barriers (time schedule, space, classroom regulation) not be erected between child and child; peers provide essential yardsticks to measure success or failure, an extrafamilial dimension to criteria for measuring the accomplishments of self-effort and the degree of self-improvement. The uniqueness of the individual is enhanced by the tight interdependencies of the group. Paradoxical as this may seem at first glance, autonomy proceeds out of mutual dependency at this stage.

Growth in Cognitive Capacity

Piaget describes this level of intellectual maturity as the stage of "operational thought." At the later period, nine to twelve, come mental experimentation and the ability to order the world along criteria lines independent of his intuition, personal reference and proximity in experience.

In contrast with the younger child who will put into his "tool kit" cookies, personal treasures near at hand as well as the necessary hammer, saw, etc., in the nine-to-twelve's kit are relevant task-oriented tools only. That is, as he studies parts and understands their relation to each other he is led to understanding the whole.

There is an emergence of complex hierarchal systems of classification in this stage based on conceptualizations of the internal relations of parts to create the inclusive whole (nesting); and the expansion of subclasses of objects linked by logical connective parts (lattices) to form an orderly world. Presumably schooling gives him a major assist in these mental operations.

Thus, in most matters directly concerning him, the child can order life experiences and be aware of their realistic relationship to each other and to himself. This does not mean to imply that anxiety is necessarily less.

Children tend to be only moderately afraid of possible immediate realistic dangers but are strongly afraid of remote, very unlikely or impossible events, e.g., ghosts, wild animal attacks. Often these can be interpreted as symbolic substitutes for feared, more approximate dangers (parental wrath, defeat and humiliation in school and social encounters).

In effect and through his own efforts, his increasing comprehension of multifaceted experiences provides great stability and feelings of assurance. His more accurate and consistent perceptions of the environment strengthen his certainty. His many stable points of reference permit a firm anchor for his interpretations and experiences in numerous learning and social settings.

Moral Code and Values

Appearing too are the value geometries basic to conscience. Conscience reflects cognitive capacity to internalize a sense of morality—a wrongness-goodness continuum applied, however, without regard to behavioral intent or ameliorated by concern for underlying motivation.

In general, the content of conscience reflects the incorporation and organization of adult standards and expectations and at times reverse application of the standard to the parents' behavior. It is largely a practical system consisting of maxims and homilies systematically pieced together without theoretical foundation.

Rules that will regulate the mutal activities of children nine to twelve are explored and developed in great detail. Children's clubs at this age often may have more designated officers with specified and elaborated functions than they have members! And while these club groups last a comparatively short period, the cohesive force is the refinement and expansion of the regulatory rules governing behavior. Social transactions lead to notions of *fairness* and equality. Describing actions and reactions in light of "fairness" is a preoccupation of this age. Equality judgments once hammered out provide the moral outlook when regarding teacher, parent or peer behavior. For a punishment to be fair it must be objectively applied and in only exact proportion to the misbehavior. Blanket punishments of the whole class, for example, for the deviancy of one or a few is indignantly and angrily reacted to. To be "fair" the teacher must know what is going on, move in on time with appropriate enforcement of rules. Disciplinary actions wide of the mark lead away from productive learning involvement to higher deviancy and management problems.

A View of Self

Tranquil self-certainty comes clearer to the child that has his own world as well as an objective one which is common to all. The child operates in both turning away from the common world toward his own quickly and spontaneously and, vice versa, turning toward it. The common shared world is rational and logical, culturally blueprinted; the private world of fantasy contains numerous possibilities of being and is thus free to design itself. The private person comes into being with the genuine possibility of being oneself and the possibility of being "we" in a group. There is the ability to see that others have "private worlds," for indeed the self and the world are reciprocal concepts at this stage.

In this stage the average child comes to view himself and others as autonomous actors reciprocating respect and adherence. Violation of the code, such as that found in a "white lie" intended to deceive is a denial of respect and consequently is the worst crime of this age. Pledging and swearing to tell the truth are important rituals of obedience, for the necessity for collective obedience is at the center of the system of morality.

There is an Irish folk tale of the rural young man who during a dispute clouts his father with a shovel and flees to town claiming to have killed the old man, thereby becoming something of an audacious hero. When the furious father appears, quite alive, the indignant villagers run the son out of town as a *liar,* ignoring the fact that he perhaps was a murderer first.

Up to this age the child might be regarded as having been confined to a "situational circle" with himself occupying the center. But the nine-to-twelve has a world, the foundation of which family and school provided, the blueprints of which his culture prescribed, but which *he can transcend.*

The years from nine to twelve are most difficult for adults to grasp and there are many features of this age likely to cause adults to err. There is a tendency to overschedule, fill up time, without regard to value and necessity for children. There is the likelihood of using techniques that reflect moral precepts adults use in reciprocal relations with adults. All violations to personal integrity are serious at this age.

Now the outlook of the child is near to our own, but it is also often too easy to confuse our needs with the child's. He is more capable of vastly greater learnings (sock it to him!), highly imitative of adult behavior (social dance schools) because he is interested in judgments we pronounce too much. Preadolescence culminates with a sense of mastery, of healthy esteem for self-feelings of certainty and mutuality. It is the important structure necessary for the child to embark upon the difficult road to adulthood.

Difficulties in This Age Group

In part, difficulties in this period stem from adult organization, regulation, direction of time, situations and conditions for behavior. Because the child reacts rather well to our expectations for him—he is curious to learn, to "objectify" his world—we are strongly disposed to add on in such ways, in such amounts of conformity and regulation that there is an excessive burden of restraint.

The demands made by others are excessive when external arbitrary dictates of home and school do not permit internal impulse to reign and prescribe the suitable activity.

We have not given sufficient credit for the great amount of responsibility children of this age have assumed and yet how often his own parents and teachers lament the "lack of responsibility" at this age! We take him for granted until external coercive demands exceed his ability to adapt and the frustration spreads in all areas of life, disrupting other abilities and accommodations in normal situations, and when he finally reacts emotionally and behaviorally to excessive demands he is regarded as a problem child or a child with problems.

We fail to realize that when a child of this age "plays" with his friends for two hours that he has been hard at work adapting to very new and unfamiliar demands of others, learning the basis of mutuality and reciprocity in human terms that are the basis of later human adjustments. He works hard for peer acceptance; this striving can create major tensions. It is difficult for a child to get away from the constant demands and expectations of others. If one looks at life honestly one sees that the child's consumption of energy is vast and that his waking hours are completely filled by learning and social experimentation. Our perception of what it means to play distorts our interpretation of the child's behavior. He is not able to sidestep reality.

A tremendous respect is owed the child, for in fact he meets, on the whole better than many of the adults around him, the great social cultural demands placed on him.

A member of society grasps reality only as it is presented to him in its cultural code. The assumption is that the objective world is codified in the language and behavior patterns of the culture and as mastered and accepted is experienced as reality.

Terminal Cycle

The child achieves in this terminal cycle of childhood the symmetry of foundation on which he will build his adolescent life and then his adult life. But this all takes time. Hastening maturation may prolong childhood personality. Inevitably the child must come to terms with himself, establish himself with certainty, preferably in these years rather than be allowed to postpone the confrontation with himself as a human being growing toward adulthood.

12

*Prepared under the direction of
Mary Jane Loomis*

Early Adolescence
(Ages 11-14)

I. Maintaining Personal Health and Promoting Healthful Living

A. Meeting Needs of Rest, Diet, and Freedom from Infection

1. Rest needs are approaching the rest needs of adults—8 to 8½ hours of sleep each day.

2. These children are likely to feel that they have unlimited resistance and unlimited sources of energy. In many instances, they are unwilling to get as much sleep as they need and tend to go beyond the normal fatigue point, especially in strenuous play.

3. Boys usually have more physical energy and endurance than girls. Girls tend to tire easily and do not have the physical endurance to play as strenuously as boys, even though they are interested in many of the same activities.

4. Childhood diseases have usually run their course prior to this period. But since resistance to infection may be low in many of these children, frequent health examinations are extremely important. This is a period of many minor illnesses (with many but short absences from school) but a period of few deaths.

5. Rapid growth is likely to cause either a tremendous increase in appetite or sometimes, particularly in girls, a finickiness with loss of appetite. Both diet and eating habits are involved.

From *How Children Develop,* Chapter IV, The Ohio State University, Faculty of the University School (1964): 41–53.

6. Boys usually have a more adequate supply of nutrients than do girls of the same age because they consume more food. Teenage girls do least well of all children in the adequacy of their food intake. Both boys and girls must be urged to keep in mind that an adequate diet is one that provides all the known essential nutrients in sufficient quantities to meet the needs of the body.

7. Knowledge of food values helps to eliminate the unwise choices of food that children tend to make at this age. They need to know that eating the necessary foods to supply the nutrients in an adequate diet satisfies the appetite to some extent and helps to curtail the consumption of nonessential foods.

8. Most of these children can be taught to take complete responsibility for treating minor cuts, wounds, and sprains, and to realize why it is important to care for them.

B. Achieving Optimal Physical and Organic Development

1. This is a period of rapid growth, especially of the long bones of the body, with great differences apparent among individuals.[2]

2. Most girls of these ages are taller and proportionately heavier than the boys. Differences tend to decrease by the age of 14.

3. Most boys are growing broad-shouldered, deep-chested, and heavier. Voice changes occur more noticeably among boys.

4. Children with rapidly growing bodies may have difficulty in learning how to carry themselves, or they may feel tired and inclined to slump. Self-consciousness accompanying rapid growth causes some adolescents, especially girls, to assume unhealthy postures in an attempt to look small or less ungainly. Special attention to posture is advisable at this time.

5. Skin disorders, especially acne, are a major concern. Acne is caused by the discrepancy in growth between the small ducts which carry oil to the skin and increased activity of the glands secreting the oil.

6. During this age period, vision and hearing are often altered by the child's rapid physical development. To help ensure the child's maximum response and comfort in the classroom, he should be given the prescribed number of medically recommended vision and hearing tests.

7. Some girls at this age level are physically mature; menstruation begins, and the development of breasts and hips is becoming noticea-

ble. Many young girls are bewildered and frightened by the first menses. The girl who is ill-informed often mistakes the menarche for a mysterious illness or injury. Even girls who have been well prepared may pass through a period of considerable emotional disturbance and of exaggerated concern over health.

8. Most investigators agree that masturbation is practically universal in the male adolescent for varying periods of time, and also that quite a few girls masturbate.[3] It is usually at puberty that the child first becomes aware of the genital organs as sources of pleasure. From now on the sex activities of the child, which have been infantile in their expressions, tend to become adult. Sexual tension will find release in playing games, romping, walking, dancing, skating, and engaging in baseball or other sports. Straightforward discussions of sex also are helpful.

C. Engaging in Suitable Recreational Activities and Promoting Healthful Living

1. Games popular with these children are team games that involve increasing organization—baseball, volleyball, football, and softball. However, children are still unable to choose recreational activities wisely in terms of strength and need for development. Also, they still need adult supervision in this area.

2. Sometimes there is self-consciousness about undertaking new physical activities in which an individual is unskilled. Children who are skilled are usually more inclined to try new physical activities than those who are awkward.

3. This age group prefers active types of social recreation and exhibits a willingness to practice in order to become adept in physical skills and games.

4. The child of this age begins to broaden his understanding of group health problems, such as contagious diseases, and of the importance of preventive measures.

5. These children are becoming aware of the theoretical need for proper eating habits and the need for rest, but they do not always apply this awareness to their own behavior.

6. This is a period of relatively poor physical coordination. Growth is often rapid; and since some parts of his body grow more rapidly than others, the child may have difficulty becoming accustomed to his increased size and coordinating his movement.

7. Children of this age show a decided preference for group games and individual activities of a self-testing nature.

8. Some of these children may feel frustrated as a result of physical inadequacies; others may be stimulated to improve. Physical superiority may lead to "showing off" and exhibitionism. Withdrawal from group activities or exhibitionism may imply the existence of a more basic problem.

9. Differences in interests often cause difficulties in social adjustment. Girls dance earlier than boys. Dancing with girls is rejected by some boys.

II. Achieving and Maintaining a Sense of Security

A. Gaining and Holding Affection, Confidence, Esteem, and Status

1. These children often achieve status in the family and feel happy in it if the responsibilities they are given are within their capacities to perform; however, the main concern of children of these ages is their standing with their peers. They feel it necessary to conform in their appearance, possessions, and activities.[4]

2. An attempt to gain adult status may be made by trying to imitate adult behavior in language, dress, and use of cosmetics.

3. However, a 13- or 14-year-old wants to retain child status in some areas where the family wants him to grow up—for example, in assuming some home responsibilities and in acquiring more adult manners.

4. These children experiment with various roles in an attempt to find status. One day a boy will be the suave diplomat; the next, the "tough guy." On one occasion, the girl is the demure and petite maiden; on another, the sophisticated young lady.

5. There is a tendency for children to refer to the privileges of their age mates to exert pressure to gain similar privileges for themselves. This is especially significant to parents and teachers.

6. The amount of freedom allowed children of this age differs greatly between lower- and middle-class families as well as among families in each class.

7. The desire for group approval increases the child's participation in clubs and groups. He also expects his family to recognize the importance of his friends, clubs, and group interests.

8. This desire for attention and association is frequently expressed through close friendships with age mates, "crushes" on adults, and such forms of behavior as poking, teasing, and kidding.

9. Preadolescent children are capricious in their friendships and their enmities in that they do not understand other children and do not know why they associate with them or dislike them. In contrast, hero worship is a usual accompaniment of the "emotional" friendships of 13-to-14-year-olds. The hero or heroes are usually playground supervisors, camp counselors, and older friends.

10. "Dates" are beginning to be a factor in a girl's achieving group status, but boys at this level often lose status with other boys if they show an interest in girls or dating.

11. Children who are slow to grow, especially boys, worry about losing status because of their small size.

B. Becoming a Social Personality

1. Most of these children are congenial in their relations with others. They are rapidly learning the "niceties" of social relations where personality comes into play, but are most likely to display these traits when dealing with adults (other than parents.)

2. These boys and girls are well aware of and respond to the pressure of the group concerning acceptable behavior; however, rivalries and conflicts do arise between individuals and groups who are maturing at different rates.

3. Children with similar intellectual abilities, social skills, or physical skills quite frequently group together at this level. Isolation results from the inability of children to solve their personality problems or from their having little to contribute to group activities rather than from any desire to display social independence.

4. Adolescents who are not accepted by an already established group tend to drift into a group of their own. The group may either conform to social codes or become antisocial.[5]

III. Developing and Maintaining a Sense of Achievement

A. Gaining a Sense of Personal Adequacy and Control over the Environment

1. Insecurities and feelings of inferiority may develop in both rap-

idly and slowly maturing individuals. The person who is either too far behind or too far ahead of his age group is likely to have problems in connection with such things as participation in sports, dancing, and activities requiring physical strength and endurance.

2. These children generally enjoy doing things that yield the satisfaction of achievement and of self-improvement, especially in some activity valued by their group.

3. The child's feeling of adequacy in family relations may be somewhat strained during this period by his attempt to gain adult status and privileges without being ready for full responsibility.

4. These children frequently ask for help in learning effective means of group participation—for example, parliamentary procedure, committee organization, and discussion techniques.

5. Adolescents begin to grope for means of community participation, but it remains on an elementary level—for example, carrying papers, caring for children, doing odd jobs, joining dancing clubs, and taking part in interschool sports.

6. In his desire to achieve and to "shine," a child may choose an activity that is neither constructive nor wholesome. Likewise, he may put his energy into achieving, with his group, a code of behavior in direct conflict with adult codes.

7. Children of these ages should be able to handle money and budget allowances to the extent of buying some of their own clothes and paying for some of their own recreation.

8. Most boys and girls at this age are able to care for their personal grooming in terms of their own standards. These standards may be far from acceptable to adults. Lack of grooming is a characteristic of most boys; good grooming usually coincides with an interest in girls. The desire to be attractive on the part of both boys and girls may not include cleanliness, however, unless adults have managed to establish it as part of the group pattern.

9. The child has already acquired many of the mechanics for meeting simple needs and understanding his environment better.

10. Thirteen- and 14-year-olds are interested in learning to do almost anything useful that they see adults doing, but they frequently conceal this interest because of the adult tendency to pass routine responsibilities over to them.

11. These boys and girls also do not want to "carry through" if adult activities are too difficult or devoid of sensory experience.

12. Young people of these ages frequently are able to plan on a higher level than they can execute.

13. They have a short attention span in group discussion; it is still difficult for them to concentrate for a long period of time. Girls tend to have a greater capacity for concentration than boys.

14. The 12-to-14-year-old youths tend to be concerned with the activities of the moment and rarely plan for the future.[6]

15. These children are beginning to understand the relationship between their material wants and the size of the family income.

16. They become increasingly able to distinguish between necessities and luxuries in terms of their allowances or the family income, and they begin to judge values.

17. There is a great interest in moneymaking activities. Some of these children are learning to supplement an allowance with other earnings; however, a child's "need" for money to satisfy his new desires frequently outruns his earning ability.

18. Most early adolescents are still dependent upon the family for their major financial needs, and many of their opportunities to make money still come from doing chores at home and in the neighborhood—for example, carrying papers, cutting grass, washing cars, and minding small children.

19. The child's growing but limited understanding of his environment leads to overgeneralizing.

B. Developing Sensitivity to the Opposite Sex

1. In the early part of this age range, there is a tendency to prefer one's own sex. This more marked in boys than girls.

2. Boys and girls at this age frequently have "crushes" on age mates and adults.

3. The girl of this level who tends to be a tomboy retains status with both sexes. The boy who tends to be feminine is labeled "sissy" and hence loses status in his group.

4. Interest in the opposite sex sometimes shows itself in action that is contrary to the expected, such as teasing, pulling hair, and poking. Affectionate boy-girl relationships may be expressed in such forms as

"swiping" or hiding notebooks and other possessions and untying shoes.

5. Boys go through a short period of roughness and rudeness to all females, even older ones. This is followed by a period of overt interest in the other sex.

6. Girls show social awareness earlier than boys and take the initiative in their relations with boys. They prefer parties attended by both boys and girls.

7. Children of these ages develop a keen interest in their own bodies and in sex and sex processes, including human reproduction. There is a continued interest in other living organisms.

8. Most children of these ages desire associations with the opposite sex. Some of the least mature children still respond without reference to sex. This tendency is more marked in boys than in girls.

9. Less mature youngsters tend to shy away from the opposite sex, and most youngsters are somewhat insecure in their relationships with the opposite sex.

10. Puberty is accompanied by increasing sexual impulses. Nearly all normally growing personalities feel a desire to express sincere, idealistic affection by some physical means. Holding hands, walking with arms around one's companion, even fairly intense kissing remain for most young people expressions of friendship rather than erotic excitations. Overly suspicious adults may by the wrong attitude create a sexual consciousness in the young person that does not naturally exist.

11. At this age level, there is an increased desire for information about sex. The amount of information possessed differs greatly among individuals and between children of different social groups.

12. Some adolescents experiment with sexual intimacies in order to allay unconscious self-doubt of their sexual adequacy. Sometimes, in a desire to assure himself and others of his adequacy, the adolescent may boast of sexual intimacies that he never experienced. Sometimes, an adolescent's mixed feelings about the ethical implications of his sexual impulses may lead him to find gratification in an eroticism that is devoid of companionship.[7]

13. Masturbation may become a source of future personality difficulties if the matter is not properly handled.

IV. Developing and Deepening Interests and Appreciations

A. Achieving Intellectual and Aesthetic Interests and Appreciations

1. Imaginative play virtually disappears at this age level.

2. Children of this level enjoy the manipulation of concrete things. Their understanding of abstract concepts continues to grow but is still very weak.

3. Children of this age level choose art experiences that broaden and deepen past experiences.

4. They have an interest in experimenting with color and media and derive a sense of satisfaction from developing new skills.

5. If children of this age level are given enough freedom of expression, they find enjoyment both in a process for its own sake and in the resulting product.

6. During this age period, children begin to take more responsibility in planning and evaluating their work. They also derive enjoyment from individual problem-solving experiences rather than from teacher-directed experiences.

7. At this age, they are ready to study art on a comparative basis and to develop generalizations concerning specific works of art or types of art. Like the 6-to-11-year-olds, this age group maintains a spontaneous enthusiasm for recognized works of art, but 11-to-14-year-olds are much more responsive to new experiences.

8. A child of this age may be able to read and grasp as many words per minute as a mature person, but this does not mean that he will enjoy adult reading material.

9. At this age, children will try almost anything for experience, but they tend to lack confidence if their results are to be made public.

10. The child's ability to memorize tempts teachers and other adults to teach him a multitude of facts rather than to challenge him to think.

11. Toward the end of this age range, children are able to read and think for long periods without becoming restless. It is a great age for reading and exploring. Girls prefer to explore vicariously through books; boys prefer first hand experiences.

12. At these ages, sensory impressions are sharpened and emotional responses become more diversified by the onset of adolescence.

13. It is also a time for learning the skills of problem-solving and for

practicing the skill of finding "third alternatives," which are new and more creative solutions.

14. Children of this age range are more capable of intellectualizing their experiences than at earlier levels, and for some individuals intellectual activity is a satisfying end in itself. However, other individuals will attempt these activities because they are trying to imitate the intellectual group.

B. Developing Social Values and Respect for the Cultural Heritage

1. After passing through a negative phase in which adult opinions are considered a hindrance, these children may seek adult companionship and guidance.

2. At this time, there is growing recognition of the possibilities of cooperative endeavor. Under proper guidance, these children can become increasingly conscious of the value of group service. They also learn to do things for others when no immediate and tangible rewards are involved.[8]

3. Most children of these ages show an awareness of the codes of moral conduct and are usually willing to exhibit behaviors that are implied by these codes. Some children adopt the codes of such organizations as the Scouts and Camp Fire Girls and try to live by them.

4. Small groups of adolescents often develop codes of acceptable group behavior that are in direct conflict with adult codes. Such codes are frequently a challenge to, or actually a defiance of, adult codes.

5. Undemocratic organizations are very common at this age. However, most individuals have begun to recognize the need for cooperative endeavors, and the drive towards group activity makes it possible for teachers and group leaders to develop principles of democratic living.

6. Children of this level show a continued interest in factual information concerning the building of culture. They are particularly curious and interested in specific dramatic aspects of the present culture—for example, space travel and automation.

7. There is also an intense interest in the scientific aspects of the culture and its imaginative derivation, science fiction.

8. In beginning to understand the contributions of past achievements to present living, these children show a continued interest in the dramatic episodes of the past, especially the colorful opening of the West, historic battles, and the World Wars.

9. Some hobbies are carried over from earlier age levels. Other interests develop during this period and often continue into adult life.

10. Solitary hobbies practiced in moderation are normal for these children. Absorption in a hobby to the exclusion of all other interests may, however, sometimes be symptomatic of a poor personal adjustment, and it may in turn make the child's withdrawal and isolation more pronounced.

Notes

1. This period tends to overlap with late childhood, especially for girls. The first pubertal changes start as early as 10 or 11 in some girls, at 11 in others, and at all ages between these and the end of early adolescence. In boys the changes usually begin between 12 and 16.

2. McCandless, "Physical Factors and Personality," pp. 295-309, in *Children and Adolescents.*

3. *Ibid.,* pp. 292-94.

4. Friendenberg, *The Vanishing Adolescent,* pp. 17 ff.

5. Rogers, Chapter 9, "The Adolescent in the Peer Group," pp. 337-75, in *The Psychology of Adolescence.*

6. Torrance, *Guiding Creative Talent,* p. 98.

7. Zachry and Lighty, *Emotion and Conduct in Adolescence,* pp. 390-91.

8. Powell, *The Psychology of Adolescence,* pp. 181-215.

13

*Louis G. Romano,
James D. Hedberg & Mark Lulich*

Developmental Characteristics
of Pre-Adolescents
and Their Implications

A close examination of the transescent of the 70's with his counterpart of the 20's and 30's would show that there have been a number of changes. Much discussion has recently centered on whether or not these changes are insignificant.

Studies tend to agree that 5th, 6th graders and 9th graders of today are more mature and more closely related to 6th and 10th graders of previous generations respectively in terms of physical development,[1] attitudes and interests,[2] and levels of maturity.[3] Because of the transescent's earlier maturation physically, socially, and intellectually, the middle school has emerged as a bridge between the elementary school and the senior high school. The bridge function serves as a transitional period for the transescent, but concern has been expressed by Mead[4] and others who see that this new organizational structure may result in a dangerous evaluation of the middle school student precocity rate by its accent on social development and all of its concomitant pressures.

It becomes imperative that the administrator and teachers have a thorough understanding of the growth characteristics of the 11-14 year old students and to provide those activities which are challenging, but within the capabilities and interst of the transescent.

The growth characteristics outlined fall within what we call the "normal range" for the transescent as a group. But it should be emphasized that each boy or girl at a given age grows at his own rate which may differ from the rest of the group.

The following chart of physical development, emotional and social characteristics, and mental growth characteristics; and their implications for the pre-adolescent and for the curriculum was developed to guide the middle school educator in the planning of learning activities consistent with the growth needs of these children.

	Implication for the Pre-Adolescent (11–14 years)	Curriculum Implications for the School	Questions for the Teacher
I. Physical Growth Characteristics *A. Body Growth* The growth pattern is the same for all boys and girls, but there are wide variations in the timing and degree of changes. The sequential order in which they occur is relatively consistent in both sexes.	Develop an awareness that individuals grow at varying rates of speed and begin this rapid growth at different ages.	Emphasize self-understanding throughout the curriculum. This can be done by: a. Providing health and science experiences that will develop an understanding of growth such as: (1) weighing and measuring at regular intervals and charting gains or losses; (2) observing growth of plants and animals; (3) learning about individual differences in growth.	Do I expect that there will be a tremendous range of maturity levels in any one class, e.g. some 14 year old boys may be biologically and physiologically 10 years old, whereas some 14 year old girls may be 19 years old biologically and physiologically?
Each person rapidly accelerates before pubescence and decelerates after pubescense.[5]			
During the transition between childhood and adolescence,[6] the greatest	Learn to accept one's own body; realize, too, that classmates may de-	b. Providing guidance at the classroom level and by utilizing school coun-	Do I provide guidance within the classroom knowing that it's more

Physical Growth Characteristics	Implication for the Pre-Adolescent (11–14 years)	Curriculum Implications for the School	Questions for the Teacher
amount of physical (as well as psychological and social) change in an individual will occur.	velop differently; each individual is unique.	selor(s) as a resource person.	important than help provided by the school counselor(s)?
a. growth hormone (anterior lobe of pituitary gland) stimulates overall growth of bones and tissue. This hormone is largely responsible for the growth rate.		c. During physical education classes, providing for individual differences by having several groups of differing abilities.	Do I use pre-tests to group according to skills during team sports? Do I provide appropriate activities and objectives for each group?
b. gonad - stimulating hormone causes gonads (testes and ovaries) to grow, which produce hormones of their own. When gonads reach maturity they seem to dry up the growth hormone.			
c. changes in thymus, thyroid, and possibly adrenal glands result in			

changes in rate of energy production (metabolism), blood pressure, and pulse rate.		
d. bones grow fast, muscles slower; legs and arms grow proportionately faster than trunk. Hands and feet mature before arms and legs. This split growth is called *asynchrony.*	Understand that others will be changing as well as oneself and that all pre-adolescents have similar difficulties in coping with these changes.	Provide opportunities for interaction among students of multi-ages.
		Do I provide activities which include the sixth, seventh and eighth graders?
Girls are usually taller and proportionately heavier than boys (ages 11–14). Some girls at this age are mature; menstruation begins (12–13), and development of breasts and hips becomes noticeable.	Understand that reproductive organs are developing. Girls should know that menstruation will soon occur and should know how to deal with it.	Provide instruction related to growth of the body so that one can better understand changes in himself and in others and be prepared for future changes and problems.
		Am I aware that the pre-adolescents may be extremely self-conscious during these physical changes, and minimize potentially embarrassing situations?
Boys are growing broad-shouldered, deep chested and heavier with a voice	Boys should know that they may have nocturnal emissions.	Do I provide rules for entering or leaving the classroom that are flexible?

Physical Growth Characteristics	Implication for the Pre-Adolescent (11-14 years)	Curriculum Implications for the School	Questions for the Teacher
change being more noticeable than with girls. Most rapid growth has occurred by 13½-14 and most have experienced ejaculation.	Develop the habit of periodic visits to the doctor and dentist.	Provide school examinations of eyes, ears, and teeth. Keep complete health records including height, weight, medications, and emotional problems.	Am I aware of special health problems in the classroom—diabetes, poor vision, students on medication, epileptics, etc.?
Facial proportions change as nose and chin become more prominent.		A nurse should be available on a full-time basis for first aid and as a resource for the teachers.	Do I know what to do in an emergency?
Secondary sex characteristics develop—hair appears on face and in genital area.		Health classes should especially emphasize exercises for good posture.	Do I encourage good posture habits and ignore awkwardness?

B. Health

Continues to enjoy comparative freedom from diseases; however, eyes, ears, and especially teeth may require medical at-

tention. Minor illnesses of short duration are fairly common during early pre-adolescence.			
Poor posture and awkwardness become increasingly evident.	Learn to accept the fact that some awkwardness and accidents caused by it are likely to occur. Make an effort to improve posture.		Do I require periodic rest especially during highly competitive sports? Do I provide adequate time for showers?

C. Body Management

Endurance is usually not high, perhaps because of the rapid growth spurt. Pre-adolescents can overtire themselves in exciting competition.	Develop good habits for diet, exercise and rest. Nine hours of sleep is usually needed.	Physical education classes should provide health instruction as well as exercise. Periods should be long enough to allow adequate time for showers—which should be required.	
For many, this is a period of listlessness, possibly of an emotional or physical cause.	Develop a balance between mental and physical activities.	Formulate school policy regarding homework assignments to insure adequate play time.	In making homework assignments, do I consider the student's need for free play time?

Physical Growth Characteristics	Implication for the Pre-Adolescent (11–14 years)	Curriculum Implications for the School	Questions for the Teacher
Pimples and excessive perspiration become problems as glands produce only secretion.	Learn good health habits such as to bathe regularly.		
	Be aware of sales propaganda for beauty aids which may be harmful.		

II. Emotional and Social Characteristics A. Emotional Status (Stability)	Developmental Tasks for the Child	Curriculum Implications for the School	Questions for the Teacher
The comparative serenity of later childhood is left behind and emotions begin to play a more obvious part in their lives. They frequently appear unable to control them and lose themselves in anger, fear, love. Often no relationship between the	Understand that he is in a period of extreme violent moods with emphasis on exerting some control.	Discuss values, morality, and what's important. Get children's feelings on these. If consideration emerges, stress this for children to remember in relationships.	Am I understanding of the needs and feelings of this group and not over sensitive to retorts to me?
	Understand that peer friends who "blow up" at	Help child find activities at which he excels. Pro-	Do I provide means by which students can role

importance of situation and violence of reaction. Extreme variance in moods.

him are not necessarily bad guys. They are only doing what is natural to all peers.

vide for an ample variety of outlets to emotions and for educational learning.

play and discover the violence of their moods and how it affects them and others?

Uncertainty may begin and a strict self-criticism. Also strict criticism of others. Tend to suppress feelings later in age and to keep things to themselves in contrast to early part of age when they immediately express all feelings.

Learn to judge self and others with less criticism.

Provide dramatic experiences which allow the child to release tension, to take different roles, and to achieve satisfactions in the eyes of peers.

Do I provide a variety of activities and allow for emotional outlet yet provide good learning situations?

Do I provide games, plays, self-expression situations?

Strong positive feelings toward ideals that are effectively presented. Frustrations grow out of conflicts with parents or peers, an awareness of lack of social skills, or in failure to mature as rapidly as others. Anger is

Become aware of the new feelings and realize they are part of the growing process.

Encourage youngsters to be critical of their work but in a way that will help them not to feel inferior.

Realize the turmoil of the period they are in, the

Do we demonstrate the value of analysis and show children how some learn things slower or faster than others—such as some babies crawl sooner or some boys make better athletes sooner, or girls learn to dance

Developmental Characteristics and Behavior	Developmental Tasks for the Child	Curriculum Implications for the School	Questions for the Teacher
common and may grow out of feelings of inadequacy, fatigue, rejections, uncertainty.	gap that exists between older and younger, and that younger sibling has feelings, too.		sooner, but eventually all learn?
B. Feelings for Self and Others			
Feelings about parents and peers change. View them more realistically. May be quick and vociferous. May cause younger sibling to younger sibling which may cause younger sibling to tease to get a rise out of older child. Later in period, he gets along quite well and may in fact be nice to have around.	Learn to realize that no one is perfect but that there is a great deal of good in each.	Learn to accept others for what they are.	Does each youngster get a chance to assume a leader role in group?
		Learn behavior necessary to add to the group.	
		Develop appreciation for individual company as well as group.	Do I allow youngsters to plan their own activities?
Group is all important. Compulsion to dress con-	Learn that group behavior means giving as well	Be aware that criticism can be constructive and	Do I make certain no one or two dominate con-

formity, language, possessions, and behavior. Tend to look down on less mature. Failure to achieve status or belonging may lead to self pity. Often fights in group but may make up quickly. By end of stage the gang changes to the crowd.	as taking, that there are "rules" in any society.	see the merits of accepting some of it.	stantly? Do I stress cooperation and success vs individualism and failure?
		Punish the act when necessary. Be firm and fair.	Am I cheerful and warm when reprimanding and let the child know I reprimand his act and not him?
Begins by boys loathing girls but girls liking boys. Each stay with own sex. Boys later tend to tease girls and to "steal" loose articles of clothing. Late in period both prefer mixed parties.	Learn how one functions with the opposite sex.	Develop an understanding of the opposite sex through readings, discussions, role playing, etc.	Do I provide opportunities for the transescent to discuss personal-social problems?
C. Tendency to Have Fears Tends to pooh-pooh fears but is apprehensive in dark. Likes flashlight near	Realize that there are scientific causes for the things that are happen-	Discuss worries and fears in class. Encourage freedom of expression of feel-	

Developmental Characteristics and Behavior	Developmental Tasks for the Child	Curriculum Implications for the School	Questions for the Teacher
by or light shining into room from without. Not comfortable on dark streets. Will reject baby sitter but is afraid at home alone. Unexplainable noises or objects stir a wild imagination.	ing. Understand that everyone worries and that fear is natural. Learn to discover those sources where he can seek personal assistance such as counselor, pastor, teacher, parent, other.	ings and in communicating problems. Show examples of people who have had problems and have learned to overcome them. Show by illustration peers and adults who have learned to overcome them.	Am I aware that fears play a large part in the child's behavior? Do I attempt to understand him and empathize with him?
Fears are more in form of worries. Worry over non-acceptance primary. Can imagine that report grades and peer criticism are cues of non-acceptance. Worry over school work, exams, promotion. Boys may worry over money, physical ability,	See how worry tends to beget worry and that emotional outlet in some form is necessary for everyone—physical activity, involvement with others, reading, other. Realize that self-examina-	Explain that many adults strive to help this group. Attempt to build faith in home, church, school, with emphasis on parent, clergy, and teachers and counselors and who to consult when necessary. Find ways to release ten-	Do I study the needs of each and attempt to provide means for satisfaction of needs? Do I assure each of success roles as well as failure roles? Do I show the need for failure as a means to learn? Do I provide for leadership roles as well as follower

facial blemishes. Girls worry about development (too fast or too slow), belonging, and later to acceptance by opposite sex.

At end of age is apt to feel caged or penned in—confined by crowd. Doesn't fear death but wonders about it. Perfers to die in sleep.

Worries because of increasing demands of self as well as of school and home.

D. Personal Ideals and Values
Conscience becomes more apparent at this stage. Exhibits strong

sions.

Show how to accept disappointment because there is always another way to seek rewards.

Realize that nearly everything is not absolutely right or wrong, black and

Let the children help develop a method for establishment of some class-

roles?

Do I listen? Really listen? to words and to non-verbal cues?

Do I plan, plan, plan, for every individual in the room and to cover every type of concern the students bring up?

Do I provide a positive example of good citizenship as a teacher, as a

Developmental Characteristics and Behavior	Developmental Tasks for the Child	Curriculum Implications for the School	Questions for the Teacher
feelings about fairness, honesty and values in adults but may "relax" their own. Example: boys cheating in school; girls shoplifting.	white, but that there are many gray areas. Also to learn that there are two sides to every interaction.	room rules. Show the need for rules in a simple society and for a complex society.	friend, as an authority figure, as a person?
		Attempt to instill a respect for rules, for law, for school, for all authority.	Do I attempt to show how experience makes each of us see life differently from each other?
This may grow out of greater need for wide variety of articles, greater chance of success in not getting caught, pressure of gang, general emotional instability of age.	Understand that there are pressures on every person of every age and understand what forces these pressures are—parent, gang, friend, etc. Learn that each person is accountable for his own actions and behavior and pays his own price.	Discuss those problems of concern: Marriage, divorce, dating, sex, wars, whatever. Attempt to discuss these problems objectively.	Do I constantly seek to help child strengthen those bonds which he considers important and do I help him to establish and reestablish values and goals?
	Learn to develop a re-		

spect for others' feelings, others' rights, others' property.

Sense of simple justice strong. Want fair teacher and are quick to challenge anyone unfair. May become martyr to include peer left out of crowd. Expect high levels from teachers and parents. Accept drinking and swearing in moderation. Want independence but may feel anxiety when parents' expectations are not met. Want to do what's right. Pressure of crowd strong.

E. Independence
Begins to cut loose from parents. May look for an adult other than parent for help in understanding

Develop sense of responsibility, that each of us is responsible to someone or something every minute of our lives.

Expect that they respect each other in everyday courtesies and politeness. Discuss the role of authority in a society.

Develop a respect for self, for self-inspection, and plans for improvement.

Give opportunity for each child to be independent at times and yet attempt to help each develop se-

Am I patient? Do I emphasize the success in students rather than the negative qualities?

Do I keep track of individual student needs and background and use them to plan?

Understand that it is normal at this age to want to be independent. Provide learning activities which

Developmental Characteristics and Behavior	Developmental Tasks for the Child	Curriculum Implications for the School	Questions for the Teacher
complexities of life. Wants to cut loose from authority and to figure things out for self. Protests he is no longer baby. Gripes when restricted.	curity within the group.	include independent study.	Do I give chances for independent planning for self-improvement?
Much behavior is role playing and cannot be taken at face value. He must respond as the group would expect. May say "the rest of the kids are doing it." Could show lack of concern for family but look out if one is in bad health or needs help. He shows much concern.	Recognize those conformists who are tied to the group, help them realize this is natural, help each to become confident within himself somewhat as well. Help him learn polite meaningful ways of persuasion, to talk and express self to parents, peers, and others with a minimum of antagonistic characteristics.	Analyze the behavior of the group and attempt to sort out desirable and undesirable characteristics. Provide role playing activities to understand personal and family problems.	Do I show the benefits of group action in certain situations and also show that independent work is better in other situations? Can I give living examples in the known adult world?

Parents often misunderstand and can cause problems by demanding level of performance far beyond child's ability.		Provide opportunity for group to plan such as use of time, group activity, independent activity, projects, other.	Do I respect each student?
During early stage may need help and rules at parties. Later is able to work along quite independently. True in school as well. Often when class is left alone teachers may find them creatively employed when returning.	Understand how responsibility and privileges often go hand and hand.	Provide opportunity for students to work independently when they desire to.	Do I help the child realize that the more responsibility he assumes and handles the more faith others will have in him to do the job right?
Wishes to preserve a self-identity. Often wishes to be alone. Often goes to room to read alone or to be alone. Spends time in reflective thinking toward end of age.	Understand that at times he wants to be alone rather than with the group.	Provide a quiet corner for independent study both in the classroom and in the Learning Center.	Do I make provisions for independent study?

Developmental Characteristics and Behavior	Developmental Tasks for the Child	Curriculum Implications for the School	Questions for the Teacher
F. Responsibility and Sensitiveness			
Home hostilities are expanded but if channeled right by giving choice, they are more apt to select an activity to do. Generally hate to work early in period. Especially at home.	Show youngster the need for responsibility in group situations and in own. Let him know that his feelings in situations may be another's feelings in another situation. Try to get students to understand, to empathize, be fair and considerate.	Provide opportunities to discuss feelings displayed at home and how to cope with them.	Do I plan release of hostility when things build up so that he learns how to improve his social interaction?
Beginning to accept views of others and to live in harmony with those with whom they disagree.	Learn how to live with others in many different life situations.	Provide many situations where he grows in his ability to work with the group or other individuals.	Do I emphasize cooperative living in a positive manner? Do I do the same for independent living?
Able to wash car, dishes, babysit and other home responsibilities. The ac-	Acceptance of work responsibility is part of growing up.	Provide activities which help him to work well, complete jobs, and to be	Do I help him to realize that there are many tasks to be completed because

ceptance of work responsibility seems natural at first. Enthusiasm is great then may slack off toward end of period.

increasingly responsible.

of need, and not merely to be paid or praised?

G. Play

At early stages the competitive spirit and the will to excel are primary. One boy in desire to win may ridicule another who makes an error.

Encourage all to participate in some game.

Provide opportunities for a variety of activities so that a student may excel in one.

Do I set a good, firm example of desirable behavior involving team games?

Encourage all to be considerate of each other in the game with understanding that some are naturally better at game than others.

Provide opportunity for all girl, all boy games; for mixed activity; and for activity where the best in it compete against one another to exclusion of poorer ability students.

Do I follow vigorous play periods with quiet games?

Team play is understood and practiced. They can work reasonably well together but ground rules should have first been es-

Attempt to provide at least one group activity in which each person can excel and one where each will experience some

Provide activity for increasingly difficult coordination in both boys' and girls' interests.

Do I seek the knowledge of what's best for each child and continue to work on that interest?

Developmental Characteristics and Behavior	Developmental Tasks for the Child	Curriculum Implications for the School	Questions for the Teacher
tablished and a supervisor should be in attendance, especially at the earliest stage.	sense of inferiority.		
Girls lose interest in dolls and become increasingly more aware of their appearance and of boys. Boys detest girls at earliest age, later tease them, push them in water, steal little articles of clothing and run expecting to be chased. Much chasing of one another in halls of school, on street, or wherever with "wait 'til I get you." Toward end of period boys and girls prefer mixed parties.	Participate in vigorous exercise but also in the quiet and spectator games. Learn that on a team, all must contribute. Learn that criticizing each other on a team can cause internal decay. Building each member is a way to win.		

Some may collect, others write in diaries. Most prefer to play with others. Those alone may need much individual consideration. An especially good time is summer camp as all enjoy swimming, group activity, and running.

Roller skating, baseball, swimming, jumping rope are favorite activities. Also just chasing one another.

Near end of period, group play is still appreciated, but not for winning. Participants are more concerned about how well each did. Rules not needed as much. Group more able to make up rules as needed.

Learn to develop leadership qualities and also follower qualities.

Know that there are many kinds of activities to enjoy throughout life, some active and others more passive. That a truly rounded person will participate and appreciate to some extent all of them or at least to appreciate and understand another's participation.

Participation, encourage family types of games so child can introduce them to family. Games such as archery, bowling, tennis, swimming, etc. are family type games.

Provide active and quiet team activities in curricular and noncurricular learnings.

Do I discuss valuable ways of spending our leisure time?

III. Mental Growth Characteristics

General Statement

As the child matures physically, increasing in body size and developing more and more motor skills, there is a concurrent growth in mental skills. His world widens with each succeeding experience, and he can cope more readily with abstract ideas. He develops his ability to generalize and to discover relationships. Because of the great differences in mental and physical characteristics, a single, preconceived standard for all may cause extreme pressure on many.

Implication for the Pre-Adolescent (11–14 years)	*Curriculum Implications for the School*	*Questions for the Teacher*
To participate in activities which will challenge his growing intellectual capacity.	Provide opportunities for critical reasoning and problem solving.	Do I provide a variety of learning activities which are challenging to the transescent?
To participate in mental activities consistent with his abilities yet challenging.	Use hypothetical situations occasionally in language arts and social studies situations.	Do I provide opportunities to exercise and develop this new reasoning power?

A. Intellectual Development

Characteristics	Needs	Experiences	Questions
Have already learned to make comparisons and to recognize likenesses and differences. Can meet failure and disappointment and accept criticism. Can face reality as well as admit strength and weaknesses.	Learn to make decisions based on the evidence at hand and to take responsibility for the decision.	Provide experiences such as in science and social studies where the student must look at the data and arrive at suitable conclusions.	Do I provide for teacher-student planning? Do I provide problem solving situations in the various instructional areas?
Is capable of making judgements. Can make generalizations and do reflective thinking.	To engage in activities which enable him to grow in his ability to carry out concrete operations.	Provide for the full range of intellectual development through the provision of activities to meet the needs of the student.	Do I have a multitude of activities to meet the varying learning personalities within my group?
Can carry out concrete operations (7–11 years) dealing with the properties of the present world.[7]			

Mental Growth Characteristics	Implication for the Pre-Adolescent (11–14 years)	Curriculum Implications for the School	Questions for the Teacher
Develops ability to use hypothetical reasoning, formal operations, using objects (12–15 years). This is the final childhood stage preparatory to adult thinking.	To grow in his ability to solve problems.	Provide activities in both the formal and informal situations to improve his reasoning powers.	Do I give all youngsters opportunities to grow in reasoning powers?
Develops concepts of volume (11 or 12 years).			
Some will be satisfied in learning the characteristics of electric bell circuits, as one example; others will go on to discover the basic laws of work and apply them to new situations.	Understand that others will differ in intellectual interest and abilities. Learn to be tolerant of these differences.	To provide experiences to challenge each youngster's thinking abilities in the instructional program.	Do I provide challenging activities in the science program and other instructional areas?
While brain and other neural developments are	Realize that one's experience is limited, and that	Provide opportunities for a variety of experiences in	Do I understand that experiences are limited? Do

almost complete, experience is lacking to solve adult problems.	others who have more experience may have something to offer.	curricular and co-curricular activities.	I build on these experiences? Do I provide opportunities to share in the decision making?
Charts, maps, and diagrams are now useful means of communication.	Broaden means of communication by learning the skills necessary to use maps, charts, and diagrams.	Provide experiences which will help the student learn how to read charts, maps, and diagrams effectively.	Do I provide instruction in using maps, charts, and related skills?
Attention span continues to increase with all activities, with the most striking gains being in problem solving.	Participate in many activities so that he will increase his attention span in those activities which he enjoys.	Recognize that students have varying attention spans and make provisions for this variation in the instructional program, homework, etc.	Do I vary classroom activities to provide opportunities for involvement of the pre-adolescent in relation to his attention span?
Reading rates may become adult.	Continue expanding interests while selecting books which continue to challenge.	Keep an adequate number of books at all levels of reading ability.	Do I allow for choices in selecting reading materials while continuing to build the necessary skills?

B. Interests
Interests are related to

		Provide reading materials	Do I realize that emo-

Mental Growth Characteristics	Implication for the Pre-Adolescent (11-14 years)	Curriculum Implications for the School	Questions for the Teacher
accelerating physical growth, increasingly strong emotional reactions, and the awareness of new roles awaiting them in society. Problems of human relations become increasingly important.		which contain examples of emotional problem-solving, various occupations, and problems of human relations.	tional problems, although seemingly minor, may be very important for the pre-adolescents? Do I help them sympathetically over these hurdles?
There is a wide variety of interests and individual differences become greater.	Recognize that everyone does not have the same interests.	Provide reading instruction which is individualized. This is more effective than level grouping.	Do I develop an individualized reading program within the classroom?
Reading and collecting equal or exceed the high rates of later childhood.	To recognize that reading can be an avenue to open up many new experi-	Provide opportunities for reading individually and in organizing clubs in various interest areas.	Do I encourage hobbies and clubs?
This is the period of excessive day-dreaming.	Excessive day-dreaming can be avoided through	Provide a program of learnings which is excit-	Do I accept day-dreaming as a normal function

involvement in many activities.

ing and meaningful.

of the transescent?

Girls become more preoccupied with themselves and their appearance.

Provide experiences in clothing and textiles, food and nutrition.

Do I develop units in makeup, hair styling, dress and nutrition?

Do the best you can when expressing yourself. Recognize that mistakes will happen. Be tolerant of the mistakes of others.

C. Creative Ability and Appreciations

Individual differences in creative ability are pronounced. Exceptional talent, if given opportunity and training, develops rapidly. Some students are self-conscious and highly critical of themselves.

Provide experiences for individuals to express themselves by writing and participating in dramatic productions.

Do I vary assignments to capitalize on individual interest and abilities? Do I provide opportunities so that each student can be successful?

Writing, dramatizing, and painting are particularly appealing for self-expression and creative expression.

Provide experiences in the various arts for all transescents.

Mental Growth Characteristics	Implication for the Pre-Adolescent (11–14 years)	Curriculum Implications for the School	Questions for the Teacher
Diaries, poetry, and letters are used for expressing thoughts.	Recognize that these forms of expression are useful in organizing thoughts.		Do I encourage diaries, poetry, etc.? Do I expect that letters and notes will distract at times, but regardless of reaction, they are normal and inevitable?

Notes

1. Forbes, Gilbert, "Physiological Implication for the Middle School." (Unpublished Speech) August 10, 1965.
2. Jones, Douglas R. "Pressures and Adolescents," *Educational Leadership,* December 1965, pp. 209-211.
3. Dacus. W. Pence, "A Grade Structure for the Early Adolescent Years," *Bureau of Education Research and Service,* University of Houston, 1963, p. 62.
4. Mead, Margaret, "Early Adolescence in the United States," *NASSP Bulletin,* April 1965.
5. This is called the transition period. Duration for each individual is 3½-5 years. Some boys enter this period at 10 years of age and reach adolescence at 13½; others enter at 13½ and reach adolescence at 15½. Girls enter this period at 8½-11½ years.
6. Adolescence is defined here as six months after puberty.
7. Piaget divides intellectual development into three periods or stages: (1) period of sensory-motor intelligence, birth to 2 years, (2) period of preparation for and organization of concrete operations, 2 to 11 years, and (3) the period of formal operations, 11 to 15 years.

Bibliography

Alexander, William M. *et al. The Emergent Middle School.* New York: Holt Rinehart and Winston, 1969.

Bossing, Nelson L. and Roscoe V. Cramer. *The Junior High School.* Boston: Houghton Mifflin Company, 1965.

Breckenridge, Marian E. and E. Lee Vincent. *Child Development: Physical and Psychological Growth Through Adolescence.* Philadelphia: W. B. Saunders Company, 1965.

Britton, Edward C. and J. Merritt Winans. *Growing From Infancy to Adolescence.* New York: Appleton-Century-Crofts, Inc., 1958.

Gesell, Arnold, Frances L. Ilg, and Louis B. Ames. *Youth: The Years from Ten to Sixteen.* New York: Harper & Row Publishers, 1965.

Loomis, Mary Jane. *The Preadolescent.* New York: Appleton-Century-Crofts Inc., 1959.

Stone, L. Joseph and Joseph Church. *Childhood and Adolescence: A Psychology of the Growing Person.* New York: Random House, 1968.

Wisconsin Cooperative Educational Planning Committee, *Guides to Curriculum Building: Intermediate Level,* Problems Approach Bulletin No. 4, Curriculum Bulletin No. 12, State Superintendent, Madison, Wisconsin, June 1962.

Bibliography:
This Is the Transescent

Havighurst, Robert J. "The Middle School Child in Contemporary Society." *Theory Into Practice.* Columbus: College of Education, The Ohio State University, June 1968, pp. 120-122.

Hull, J. H. "The Junior High School Is a Poor Investment." *The Nation's School,* April 1960, pp. 70-81.

Johnson, Mauritz, Sr. "The Adolescent Intellect." *Educational Leadership,* December 1965, pp. 200-04.

Jones, Mary C. "A Comparison of the Attitudes and Interests of Ninth-Grade Students Over Two Decades." *Journal of Educational Psychology,* August 1960, pp. 178-79.

Riessman, Frank. "Low Income Culture, The Adolescent, and the School." *NASSP Bulletin,* April 1965, pp. 45-49.

Wass, P. B. "The Economics of Teenagers." *NASSP Bulletin,* April 1965, pp. 29-33.

Wattenberg, William M. "Today's Junior High Students." *Educational Leadership,* December 1965, pp. 190-93.

Part III

Curriculum Strategies
for
the Middle School

The rationale for many changes and innovations that occur in education today focuses on the individual. Team teaching, programmed materials, continuous progress, non-gradedness, independent study, and other approaches all present ways to respect the individuality of each pupil in carrying on his learning experiences. Presented in this chapter are several viewpoints discussing how individualization is made possible in a middle school organization.

For the proponents of the middle school, individualization and flexibility are key concepts. They attempt to provide educational programs that fit the needs and characteristics of eleven- to fourteen-year-old students. Such programs help the transescent to achieve the emotional, social, intellectual, and physical development that is required to bridge the gap between childhood and adolescence. In terms of curriculum construction and planning, the student is helped to make the often difficult transition from the child-centered program of self-contained elementary classroom instruction to the subject-centered and highly departmentalized program of the high school.

Once these basic approaches have been decided upon and provided for, the next question is how to create and foster the settings and the atmosphere, and how to decide on the content and procedures that encourage transescents to exercise all the dimensions of their humanity. As we have seen in Section II, most people involved in educational programs recognize that there is growing range of differences among transescents and that the use of an individualized approach is imperative in curriculum planning in order to accommodate this wide range of abilities and interests. By the same token, educators acknowledge that the great variations in maturity and readiness, growth and development at this stage require that the instructional methods be relatively flexible and informal so as to provide for continuous pupil progress.

Not only do these support the change and demands of a new societal generation of students but, in terms of what a program should be or do, they are important criteria to be taken into consideration if the school experience is to be meaningful and challenging. In this group of readings are included some informal and formal thoughts concerning this approach to middle school instruction content and methods.

219

The content and methods of instruction must also seek to cope with continuous education in developing the intellectual capacity of the transescent maximally. As pointed out by Havighurst, Johnson, and Partin, it is an appropriate goal for the transescents whose need for discovery and exploration are acute at this age. Transescents have a strong need to cultivate the mind, to learn how to play with ideas, to find means of inquiry which will help them to attain objectives that are of importance to them. At no other moment in their lives will children be so ready and so open to intellectual discoveries.

Although the preceding paragraph limits itself to a discussion of the intellectual approach, one must keep in mind that one of the objectives of the middle school is concerned with the transescent's role in adult life.

It is a difficult task for teachers to use the on-going needs of the students as an approach to teaching as suggested by the middle school philosophy. It requires of them that they be highly qualified in and sensitive to subject matter as well as to the child's need to explore. But trained in this respect, they will eventually learn that the main difficulty is to select and decide among the many interests of the children, the most important to be dealt with during the school hours. The greatest obstacles to implementing this approach of participation and active involvement in curriculum planning and instruction are the skepticism and passivity of educators which in turn perpetuate passivity and maintain the rule of authoritarianism in the classroom. For students, the result is a stultifying experience rather than one which motivates their necessary curiosity for learning experiences. A variety of instructional strategies are presented here which demonstrate clearly how a specially developed middle school curriculum and methods of instruction help the students to make personal and social development a thrilling experience for both the student and the teacher.

1

Mauritz Johnson, Jr.

The Adolescent Intellect

American adolescents have been exceedingly well studied. They are known to be bothered by acne, to reject adult authority, and to have an awakening interest in the opposite sex. They conform slavishly to peer group standards, and, except for a few abnormal ones, they are either overly aggressive, submissive, withdrawn, or characterized by psychosomatic symptoms. All but about 95 percent are juvenile delinquents. The female type reaches puberty approximately two years before her male age-mates and between ages 11 and 13 exceeds them in height as well as in school marks.

According to James Coleman, adolescents value popularity and athletic prowess; according to Robert Havighurst, they have nine developmental tasks to carry out; according to Erik Erikson, they have four such tasks, the first being to achieve industry while working toward identity, fidelity, and intimacy. It is widely recognized that they have changing bodies, ambivalent feelings, and numerous problems, worries and needs, but until recently few have suspected that they also have intellects.

Indeed, the very term "intellect" is rare in the literature of education. The crucial concept has been "intelligence," a global capacity for solving problems, according to David Wechsler; existing in three

From *Educational Leadership* (December, 1965): 200-204. Reprinted with the permission of the Association for Supervision and Curriculum Development and Mauritz Johnson, Jr. Copyright © 1972 by the Association for Supervision and Curriculum Development.

forms—theoretical, social and mechanical—according to E. L. Thorndike; composed of general and specific factors, according to Charles Spearman; and increasingly differentiated at puberty into some seven or more primary mental abilities, according to L. L. Thurstone. But intelligence has been viewed as an attribute that is largely determined genetically, subject to cumulatively substantial, but nevertheless comparatively limited, modification by environmental influences. Educators have seen intelligence essentially as the raw material for their work, providing possibilities and imposing limits. Their preeminent goal has been "intelligent behavior," overt and observable, rather than the development of any such inferred abstract quality as intelligence, much less one as abstruse as an intellect.

Finally, however, a time was reached when the world had been so drastically changed by intellectual efforts that attention was drawn to the intellect's increasing importance. Belatedly, scholars began to participate in curriculum reform.

Curriculum Reform

Jerome Bruner called attention to the value of students' discovering fundamental relationships among key concepts within a disciplinary structure and suggested that intellectually honest discovery in some form is possible with children at any age. Joseph Schwab stressed the importance of both the conceptual and the syntactic structures of disciplines. Philip Phenix defined learning not as a change in behavior but as the discovery of meaning, and he classified meanings as symbolic, empiric, aesthetic, ethical, synoetic, and synoptic. B. O. Smith took a new look at the teaching act and saw logical operations on subject matter as an important element. We were reminded of Jean Piaget's earlier contention that in acquiring meanings children pass through a stage of concrete operations before entering, sometime before reaching puberty, the stage of formal operations.

Piaget's studies show that, while the sequence in which stages are reached is invariant, the specific age is affected genetically, experientially, and culturally. Even in Martinique, where development is slower, the stage of formal operations is reached before the period known in America as the junior-high-school years. Moreover, it has been demonstrated that when children are given appropriate intellectual experiences, prevalent notions about readiness prove to be untenable. Robert Davis has found that fifth graders can not only readily discover truth sets for open mathematical statements, an achievement traditionally considered difficult for ninth graders, but can also invent mathematical laws of their own, something that students are seldom encouraged to do at any level. Patrick Suppes has successfully taught young children to engage in mathematical reasoning.

Professional reaction to these demonstrations and to the shift in goals and changes in curriculum that they imply has been interesting and, to a degree, disturbing. In many schools, to be sure, enlightened teachers and administrators have eagerly seized the opportunity to experiment with radically revised curriculum arrangements and new instructional approaches that challenge students and inject an unwonted intellectual vigor into their schooling. But from those who have resisted have come expressions of concern regarding undesirable "pressures" on children and youth and protestations that social-emotional development is fully as important as intellectual growth, that education should provide practical preparation for living and earning, that learning experiences should be "lifelike," and that recent reforms represent a return to "subject-matter centeredness."

These are sincere reactions and understandable ones, given the clearly demonstrated and freely admitted lack of intellectual interest in the society as a whole and among a large segment of the teaching corps. Of all the reactions, however, the most disturbing is that based on the erroneous belief that the current ferment is a retrogression to the uninspiring peddling of vast quantities of unrelated, out-dated, inert factual minutiae for rote memorization by apathetic students. Many lackluster traditional teachers who characteristically practice such vapid peddling share this belief and mistakenly applaud recent developments on the assumption that their practices are vindicated thereby.

Given this misconstrual of intellectual activity on the part of some and the antipathy toward it on the part of others, it is extremely difficult to assess the true characteristics of the adolescent intellect. Certainly it is no compliment to junior high school students to assert that most of them are quite as capable of engaging in intellectual activity as is the average adult.

Those who come from homes in which intellectual interest exists, located in communities in which intellectual achievement is valued, and attending schools in which intellectual activity is stressed at all levels—those adolescents can be expected to conceptualize, reason, and engage in inquiry of a far different order from that which can be expected where one or more of these three factors is missing. Significantly, the only place where the vicious cycle can be broken is in the school, though perhaps this is impossible without a substantial infusion of new teachers who themselves have a strong intellectual orientation and commitment.

A Sound Base

Unfortunately, beginning teachers of such persuasion will not long remain in a school where the principal's primary concern is the athletic program and where only a few teachers read, have a scholarly interest in their subjects, and prefer serious discussion to faculty lounge gossip. Where enough kindred spirits are to be found, however, a substantial transformation of the junior high school, giving greater play to the adolescent intellect, can be effected.

Underlying any such transformation is a basic change in the "climate" of the school. Some junior high schools today are characterized by a repressive rigidity and stultifying stagnation; others by a sentimental indulgence of the frivolous and the trivial. Neither type exalts either ideas or inquiry. The desired atmosphere is one in which the examples set by teachers and the policies set by the school give clear indication that intellectual pursuits are valued above all others. In view of the long-standing entrenchment of countervalues, the mere honoring of intellectual accomplishment will probably be insufficient. Temporarily, at least, it may well be necessary not only to ignore and de-emphasize, but actually to discourage, occasions for extolling popularity and athletic performance.

Equally as important for adolescent intellectual development as a hospitable atmosphere in the junior high school is an appropriate grounding in the elementary school. A sound conceptual base must be established through long experience with concrete operations in the empirical realm. Even more vital, however, is close attention to linguistic and mathematical symbolic structures. The outlook in mathematics is hopeful, with the increasing emphasis on correct terminology, properties of the real number system, and unifying mathematical principles. In the area of reading, however, nothing short of a complete overhaul of the system that prevails today seems likely to bring about the necessary reform.

Regardless of how unsatisfactory for currently accepted purposes the insipid stories in conventional readers and the excessive reliance on a look-say approach may be, these defects are minor compared to the general overemphasis on entertainment and neglect of language structure. Children must at an early age come to view reading primarily as a source of ideas and information and secondarily as a means of recreation. At the same time, whether pupils are encouraged to recognize words at sight or decode them analytically, they must attend not merely to the meanings of words but to their functions and positions in sentences.

Intellectual Emphasis

By the time they reach the junior high school the majority of students should be ready for formal operations. They should then regularly engage in framing definitions, identifying assumptions, dealing with cause-and-effect relations, classifying individual phenomena, generalizing from recurring particulars, and determining necessary and sufficient conditions for a conclusion. In short, they should, in the terms of Robert Ennis's definition of critical thinking, become able to assess statements correctly. Concurrently, they should be gaining fundamental insights into matter, energy, and biological phenomena and acquiring a conceptual basis for explaining man's interaction with his geographical environment and with his fellow men, through economic, political and social institutions. Students should continue to advance in mathematical sophistication instead of endlessly applying elementary concepts to every conceivable practical situation.

These intellectual activities assume their rationale under a conception of general education which, in the terminology of Harry Broudy, B. O. Smith and Joe Burnett, emphasizes the "interpretive" use of knowledge. A junior high school guided by this conception will abandon the notion of prevocational exploration and premature vocational decisions. It will consider its intellectual emphasis the most practical kind of preparation for both the vocational and the leisure-time realities of the future, and its teachers will refuse to acknowledge students' demands to know the specific practical value of their studies. It will protect students from having to attempt to devise solutions to complex social problems until they have mastered the fundamental concepts of the relevant disciplines and are aware of both the assumptions and the methods of inquiry underlying the disciplined search for truth.

Particularly bothersome is the problem of providing a coherent program in the humanities. Efforts must be made to maintain the highest possible artistic standards in selecting works for study in literature and the fine arts. The cultivation of critical tastes demands a radical departure from current desultory efforts in the arts and requires continuation throughout the senior-high-school years, which is impossible until the diverse elective program at that level is abandoned.

It is an affront to adolescents to assume that they cannot or will not respond to a program with a serious intellectual emphasis. Provided with a suitable background and placed in a setting in which intellectual activity is not deprecated, most of them are quite capable of dealing formally with abstract notions that serve to explain the world around them and invest their experiences with meaning. Dealing with ideas diverts adolescents from their preoccupation with themselves. Even the slower learners can more readily grasp significant ideas than retain masses of inconsequential facts. By definition they cannot progress as rapidly as the average adolescent can toward the consideration of more complex concepts, and the program must account for such differences. A curriculum that is arranged on the basis of the level of intellectual comprehension required cannot, of course, be bound to conventional grade designations. Until a more coherent curriculum has been arrived at, however, teachers will have to rely on the use of a discovery approach to gauge the intellectual level at which a particular group of students is ready to function.

Charles Armstrong and the late Ethel Cornell found that most individuals pass through two cycles of mental growth, the second beginning around puberty, often after a plateau period of relatively little progress. Possibly this plateau is the result of the school's failure to confront the young adolescent with a timely challenge to his changing intellect. It seems unlikely that the physiological and emotional aspects of maturing at that stage usurp so great a proportion of some fixed reserve of psychic energy that little is left for intellectual activity. Indeed, when an individual is putting away childish things, he is anxious to think about serious matters.

The adolescent intellect deserves more respect and greater expectations.

2

Robert J. Havighurst

Lost Innocence: Modern Junior High School Youth

It is uncomfortable and disquieting to watch one's children growing up in a way which differs from one's own experience. This is happening to parents and teachers now. It has been happening to every generation of parents and teachers for a long time; but perhaps the change between generations is greater now than it was a hundred years or even fifty years ago.

There are some constants that make adolescence the same at all times and places and for all youth. At the same time there are differences in adolescence among various societies and between adolescence in two consecutive generations within a given society.

First, let us look at the constants. Biologically, adolescence is the same in all races and in all the centuries where we have any knowledge of human development. Nature's built-in time clock controls the changes of puberty, their order, and their timing. There is some evidence that sexual maturity comes now perhaps a year earlier than it did a hundred years ago in Western Europe, but this change came slowly and is hardly perceptible between parents and their children.

Socially, adolescence is a moratorium between childhood and adult roles. During this time, a youth slowly acquires adult roles by a process of trial and error, with the help of educational institutions and of his own peers. Each generation must find a way of life that grows out of its own childhood and fits into what it perceives to be the historical process leading to the future.

From *NASSP Bulletin* (April, 1965): 1–4.

Psychologically, adolescence is a period of time during which a youth acquires an identity. He narrows and focuses his personal, occupational, sexual, and ideological commitments to the point where he is perceived by others to be an autonomous adult.

When we look at adolescence from the sociological or psychological points of view, we find great differences, both in the *social situation* and in the *self-concept* of the present day adolescent compared with his parents in their adolescence. From the base-line of the earlier generation, the adolescent of today is more *precocious* and more *complex.*

When we say that the modern adolescent is more precocious we mean that he has many experiences *earlier* than his parents had these experiences. He starts going to parties and having dates at an earlier age. Through the greater frankness and brutality of the mass media, he gets acquainted with death and with human depravity earlier. As a high school student, he is apt to read such a book as *Lord of the Flies* and thus comes face to face with the naked evil of human nature ten years earlier than his parents did.

The danger and the complexity of a world armed with the power of self-destruction are not kept from him. He reads or hears the speeches of presumably responsible politician urging nuclear war and at the same time he reads and hears discussions of the danger of fallout from nuclear bomb-testing.

The serious nature of life comes home to the junior high school youth more frequently and earlier than it did to his parents. At the same time he sees a complex and difficult world, in which the distance from childhood to adulthood seems so great as to be almost unbridgeable. He hears that it is difficult to get into a good college. He hears that there are few jobs for youth, and if he tries to get a part-time job he finds it almost impossible. He is likely to live in a metropolitan area, with complex arrangements for moving around and communicating with people.

It is no wonder that the average junior high school boy or girl has some doubt about his ability to grow up and to cope with the life he sees ahead of him. If we had a good way of measuring self-doubt, or its opposite, self-esteem, it is likely that we would find a substantial increase of self-doubt among 15-year-olds since 1920 or 1930.

Self-esteem is pretty largely *bestowed* on a boy or girl by his family and teachers and friends up to adolescence. He feels good about himself because other people show him in many ways that they feel good about him. He feels self-doubt when important people (to him) show that they doubt his value or competence. But during adolescence a boy or girl must begin to *earn* his own self-esteem, and to feel that he deserves it because of his own efforts and abilities. The earning or achieving of self-esteem is more difficult for a 15-year-old today than it was in 1920 or 1930.

On the positive side, a junior high school youth is more complex today than his age-group was in an earlier day.

For one thing, he knows more about the reality of society and of human nature. Living in an age of greater exposure of human behavior and greater frankness about human motives, he becomes *acquainted with* these things much earlier than his parents did, though he probably does not *understand* much of what he sees. He is exposed through the TV screen, the contemporary novel and short story. He learns about the complexities of sex and of the power drive and he learns of the dangers of mass suicide and the perilous game of brinksmanship.

He is a much more sophisticated person than ever before. He has been over-protected in some ways, and under-protected in other ways.

He knows more about art and music and literature than his predecessors, and often more than his parents now know. Modern parents are often baffled by the extent of the knowledge their teenage children possess in areas which they hardly know about. Also, on the positive side, the junior high youth has ahead of him a long period of time for learning to understand and deal with the complexity of modern life. He will spend an average of two or three more years of time in school preparing for adult life than did his preceding generation. If he can organize himself for reflective study during this extra period, he will be better started on a competent and productive career.

The problem for practical school people as well as for researchers is to find out under what conditions the *self-esteem* and the *social faith* of teenagers can be increased. What part can schools have in this process, as compared with churches and youth organizations? To what extent is this something that only the family can accomplish?

The writer's view is that the junior high school can contribute in an important and indeed essential way to this process. There appear to be three ways in which the school might work.

■ One way is to give boys and girls opportunities to be of *service* to the society. Contributing to the welfare of society cements the bonds of loyalty and interest. At the same time it increases one's self-esteem to do something which is valued by others. This is the Peace Corps idea. How can the school make use of the service motive with boys and girls in local community and school service projects?

■ A second way is to teach about the heroes of a modern self-renewing society. In their courses in literature and social studies, boys and girls may study such people as Dag Hammarskjold, Dr. Schweitzer, and some of the contemporary scientists, business men, and statesmen who have committed themselves to making the world more productive and more peaceful. Some films and biographies of such people are now being produced for use in the schools. Hero-worship can be put to good use by teaching about heroes of the present and the immediate future.

■ A third way is to study and analyze contemporary social problems with an emphasis on positive solution. No doubt the teaching of social studies will undergo major changes in content in the next few years, with greater emphasis on the study of such problem areas as economic growth, urbanization, population expansion, international interdependence, and the effects of automation on the labor force. It would be possible to study these subjects purely as problems of scientific analysis, and certainly they should by analyzed scientifically. But the teaching should carry with it a conviction that positive constructive solutions are possible and that the decisions made by ordinary people as citizens and workers will influence the outcome. Otherwise such teaching might only result in greater self-doubt and resultant apathy on the part of boys and girls.

For this objective, it is essential that teachers possess and exhibit a faith in the future, a belief that they are working together with a benevolent cosmic force to make history, and to make history turn out better than it would if they did not exert themselves. If there is one essential requirement of the teacher of junior high school youth, it is that he or she should have this faith and should be able to transmit it to boys and girls.

3

George W. Batezel

The Middle School: Philosophy, Programs, Organization

Philosophy

A carefully thought out philosophy is essential as a guide in developing the program and organization of a good middle school. The following points should be considered:

(1) A good middle school ought to provide for a gradual transition from the typical self-contained classroom to the highly departmentalized high school.

(2) Provision should be made by program and organization for each student to become well known by at least one teacher.

(3) The middle school ought to exist as a distinct, very flexible, and unique organization tailored to the special needs of pre-adolescent and early adolescent youths. It ought not to be an extension of the elementary nor seek to copy the high school.

(4) The middle school ought to provide an environment where the child, not the program, is most important and where the opportunity to succeed exists.

Program

While the child is the important factor, the program provides the vehicle to move him along intellectually in such a way that his self-image is enhanced. Transcending any program, then, is the way in

From *The Clearing House* (April, 1968): 487-90.

6th Grade	Periods Per Week
Language arts, social studies, reading	12
Mathematics, science	12
Physical education	3
Foreign language	5*
Music	5**
Art	5**
Industrial arts—home economics	5**
Health	5**
Special interests or homeroom	3
* shortened periods	
** for one evaluation period	

which it is implemented. A middle school program, properly conceived, is not just a series of hurdles which a child must jump, but a means to a far broader and nobler end—developing and/or increasing the self concept of each child as a valuable human being.

It is in this frame of reference that the following curriculum, program, and activities of a 6-7-8 middle school are proposed.

General Observations. In laying out specific programs for 6th, 7th, and 8th grades, a 40 period week of 40 minutes each, plus a 40 minute lunch period has been assumed. While this does not necessarily represent an ideal, it is being used to indicate the proportionate share of available time to the various subject areas.

Sixth Grade. In planning a sixth grade program it is desirable that the benefits of the close teacher-pupil relationship inherent in the self-contained classroom be maintained as far as this is possible, while still taking advantage of the enrichment which the utilization of special teachers and/or special facilities offer.

The sixth grade ought to contain a large enough block of time with one teacher so that each child is well known by that teacher.

(1) In the above program the student in sixth grade would have only five teachers at any one time.

(2) Teachers in the major subject areas would be paired into teams in which each team would consist of a Language Arts-Social Studies-Reading and Math-Science teacher.

Two classes of 25 each would be assigned to this team. Each

member of the team would be the homeroom teacher for 25 youngsters and, as such, be responsible for the guidance, general supervision, and welfare of the homeroom student in all phases of his school career. The team would work together in developing a total coordinated program. While the two classes would be scheduled on a turnabout basis for normal operations (e.g., "A" group would be having L.A.—S.S. while "B" group was having Math-Science in the morning, and vice versa in the afternoon), nothing would preclude the team from rescheduling for days or weeks at a time into large and small groups in order to carry out a well planned unit or units within the team or in conjunction with other two-member teams.

(3) Students would have foreign language instruction in Spanish, French, or German five times per week for 25 minutes per day.

(4) Students would have a 15 minute recess or free time.

(5) There would be four evaluation periods per year. At least one—possibly two—of these would involve a parent conference with each student's homeroom teacher.

(6) The special interests program would be designed to provide:

a. Enrichment for those who have an unusual interest in a specific subject.

b. Opportunity to try out some skills not offered in the regular program (e.g., Typing).

c. Opportunity within the school day for students being transported to partake in some intramural, music, and club programs.

Some suggested special interest programs might be:

Art	Mathematics
Band	Mechanical drawing
Foreign languages	Newspaper
Future Homemakers of America	Nursing
Choral groups	Orchestra
Clothing	Photography
Debating	Science
Dramatics	Shop
Food	Sports
Typing	

(1) The seventh grader would be assigned to a homeroom teacher who *would be responsible for knowing the child well* and for provid-

7th Grade	Periods Per Week
Language arts, reading	7*
Mathematics	5
Science	5
Social studies	5
Foreign language	5**
Physical education	4
Music	5***
Art	5***
Industrial arts—home economics	5***
Health	5***
Special interest and homeroom	4

* plus 5 shortened periods
** shortened periods
*** for one evaluation period

ing help, guidance, and general supervision of his welfare in all aspects of school life. This teacher would remain his homeroom teacher through 8th grade. Ideally, a homeroom teacher would teach the child in at least one class while he has the child in homeroom.

(2) Interdisciplinary teams would be encouraged so that teams of four teachers would have the same (approximately 100) youngsters in the major subject areas.

(3) Foreign language instruction would continue daily for 25 minutes per day. Students would be encouraged to continue the foreign language begun in 6th grade.

(4) The special interest groups would be the same as for sixth grade.

(5) There would be four marking periods with the homeroom teacher responsible for providing his students with needed assistance.

(1) The eighth grader would continue with the same homeroom teacher, who, with two years' experience, will be better able to guide the student throughout the year and in the initial selection of his high school program.

(2) Foreign Language instruction would be for five full periods per week. The language would be elective, the student selecting either Spanish, French, or German.

(3) Each student not selecting a foreign language will receive reading instruction (developmental and/or remedial) designed to meet his

8th Grade	Periods Per Week
Language arts, reading	7
Mathematics	5
Social studies	5
Science	5
Foreign language or reading	5
Physical education	4
Music	5*
Art	5*
Industrial arts—Home Economics	5*
Health	5*
Special interest groups and homeroom	4
* for one evaluation period	

individual needs. (The student's needs, coupled with his experience in 6th and 7th grade foreign language will provide a basis for guidance in this area.)

(4) Science will have one double period per week to introduce laboratory techniques. (Assuming 9th grade program becomes a laboratory science.)

(5) Special interest groups would be for the same purpose as 6th and 7th grades.

All grades would have the benefit of a reading specialist to work with youngsters in a flexible program of small-group instruction. This specialist would also be responsible for in-service training of all our language arts teachers in reading instruction.

The physical education program would be expanded. Remedial instruction would be provided. Hopefully, swimming instruction will be possible.

The interscholastic athletic program for 7th and 8th grades will be carefully evaluated to determine its place in a middle school. An intramural program will be developed for the 6th grade and the present program expanded for the 7th and 8th grades.

Organization and Staffing

A middle school organization should not be overwhelming. Every possible device should be built into it so that each child will become a well known individual. Size is an important factor here. Large and small schools each have their distinctive advantages. Only a large enough school can provide the services and facilities a good middle school should have. On the other hand, only a small school can enhance the close personal communication and atmosphere for teacher and pupil alike. The house plan organization comes closest to making possible the advantages of a large school while maintaining the warm, human, very personal environment of a smaller school. Therefore, it is proposed that the new middle school be organized and staffed for a 900 pupil middle school as follows:

(1) The school would be divided into three distinct houses of approximately 300 students each.

(2) Each house would have a 6th, 7th, and 8th grade of about 100 students.

(3) Each house would have
   a. A full-time "Dean" or "Housemaster" in charge of and responsible for the program in his house
   b. A full-time guidance counselor
   c. A full-time secretary

(4) The "large" or overall school would have
   a. A principal
   b. An assistant principal
   c. Two secretaries
   d. One guidance director
   e. A library staff consisting of
      1) Two librarians
      2) An audio-visual specialist
      3) One secretary
      4) Lay personnel
   f. A nurse
   g. A psychologist
   h. A reading specialist

(5) Common facilities and personnel would be available to all houses equally in minor subject and special interest areas.

The above organization and staffing represents what a really good middle school ought to have in order to provide the services necessary to carry out its basic philosophy and function well.

Facilities. In order to implement the program, philosophy, and organization, the new middle school should provide for

(1) Three separate and distinct areas for each house and its own facilities as described above.

(2) A central area convenient to all "houses" for administration, guidance, and health services.

(3) Provisions in each house for at least one large group instruction area.

(4) One small theatre large enough to seat 300 to 400 students. (This theatre could double as the large group instruction area for *one* house.)

(5) The industrial arts, home economics, music, gymnasium, art, and health facilities located for convenient use by all houses.

(6) An instructional materials center (library, A-V, reading laboratory, etc.) located in the most advantageous and central position possible.

(7) Two smaller dining areas, kitchen between, which might also be used for large group instruction.

(8) A special education classroom located in one of the house units.

The facilities ought to be designed so that no one system is irrevocably locked in. They should be flexible to accommodate changes and modifications.

General Observations. The implementation of the program should be consistent with the aims expressed in the philosophy of the middle school and should strive for the following attributes:

(1) Close coordination and cooperation between teachers in developing programs tailored to the needs of the youngsters involved.

(2) Close, warm, and wholesome relationship between teacher and student.

(3) Flexibility to provide for thoughtful innovation.

(4) A new concept of evaluation designed to lessen anxiety about grades and increase self-esteem of the pupils.

(5) Individual programming for each youngster according to the level of his ability.

4

Gordon F. Vars, editor

Guidelines for Junior High and Middle School Education

Curriculum and Instruction

The curriculum is the sum total of the learning experiences provided by a school for the achievement of its purposes. The program of studies is that portion of the curriculum offered through courses, seminars, or supervised study. Learning experiences provided through less formal activities are discussed in later sections on student activities and guidance services.

Program of Studies

Individual subjects in the junior high school program were not examined in detail by participants in the NASSP discussion. Rather, the *guidelines* stress ways in which instruction in all subjects contributes to the broad purposes already indicated.

The times require that students examine the impact on their own lives of such factors as the evolution of nations and cultures, the interdependence of peoples caused by improvements in transportation and communication, the increasing complexity of the social, economic, and political worlds, and the changing role of the United States in relation to the individual and the world. Vital curriculum

Excerpts from *Guidelines for Junior High and Middle School Education, A Summary of Positions*, National Association of Secondary School Principals, 1966: 4-6 and 11-12.

content and methodology develop in students an interest in keeping informed and provide them with the skills needed to do so.

3. The curriculum emphasizes the tremendous changes taking place in the world and how the young adolescent, himself in transition, copes with the changes.

4. Every subject is taught to reveal opportunities for further study, to help students learn how to study, and to help them appraise their own interests and talents. In addition, the junior high school continues the developmental program of basic skills instruction started in the elementary school, with emphasis on both developmental and remedial reading.

5. The curriculum highlights the worthwhile contributions and character traits of individuals in order to help adolescent youth develop desirable goals. Social mores are examined to help students develop sets of values that will guide them into socially acceptable and personally satisfying standards of conduct. Democratic ideals and principles are stressed.

Curriculum Organization

A block-time or core program, in which one teacher provides instruction drawn from two or more subject areas, may be an effective means of bridging the gap between the elementary and junior high school. The extended period of time permits a greater variety of learning experiences than typically occur in a conventional class period. Also, the block-time teacher is in a good position to serve as teacher-counselor for his pupils. Desirable social development may be fostered in the stable social group represented by the block-time class.

Since few teachers are equally competent in several subject areas, an interdisciplinary team teaching approach provides a promising alternative to the single-teacher block-time class. For example, a teacher of English, a teacher of social studies, and a teacher of science may teach jointly ninety or more pupils meeting in a three-period block of time. Such an arrangement enables each teacher to remain a specialist while fostering subject correlation whenever appropriate. The size of pupil groups may vary from time to time and independent study is emphasized. Students find that working with a team of teachers for an extended period each day provides a satisfactory transition from the single-teacher, self-contained classrooms typically found in elementary schools. Judicious use of small groups as part of the team operation can provide students with a continuity of relationship with one teacher.

6. The junior high school curriculum is organized to provide a gradual transition form the typical self-contained elementary school instructional pattern to the highly departmentalized senior high school program. Positive steps are taken to show students the inter-relationships among the conventional school subjects.

Instruction

Teacher-student planning involves students in many decisions concerning what will be studied and especially how it will be approached. Flexible assignments are designed to encourage creativity in pupils. Independent study opportunities provided in many team teaching programs also are valuable. Here students exercise considerable initiative in selecting and carrying out individual studies in contrast to conventional class assignments, in which the teacher makes all the decisions and identical tasks are set for all students.

7. As young people seeking more and more independence from adult control, junior high students are helped to assume increasingly greater responsibility for their own learning.

Study Skills

Although the foundations for effective study are laid in the elementary school and refinements are made as late as graduate school, the junior high school assumes a major role in helping young people to acquire effective study skills and desirable attitudes toward learning. Leading pupils to want to learn and teaching them how to study are part and parcel of all instruction, not a bag of tricks or something "extra."

Pupils need such skills as map reading, use of reference materials, adjusted reading rates, listening, observing, and preparing for and taking examination. Instruction in the use of the typewriter may be provided as an aid to effective learning. Parents should by advised how to help their children improve study skills.

8. Study skills are developed through a planned program of continuous and coordinated instruction.

Homework

As a general rule, textbook assignments and practice exercises should be carried out at school. More appropriate as homework are such activities as writing reports and compositions, conducting experiments, or reading for pleasure and information. When instruction is individualized and student independence stressed, the distinction between homework and classwork disappears.

Differences in students' abilities and interests make uniform policies on homework difficult to implement. So do variations in both the facilities and the support for home study provided by the family. Teachers need to plan cooperatively the long-term or special out-of-class assignments given to students so that they will not be overloaded at some times with very little to do at others.

9. Homework is a logical extension of classroom learning designed to develop students' responsibility for their own learning. Students are allowed considerable initiative and reasonable choices in what they do and how they do it.

Individual Differences Among Pupils

A unique feature of the junior high school unit in the educational continuum is the great diversity of its students in physical, emotional, and social maturity. The diversity typical of any human group is aggravated at this age level by differences in rate of maturation, both within and between youngsters. Therefore, the junior high school needs to be even more flexible than other schools units and to devote more attention to the individual differences among its students. The goal is to see that each student is sufficiently challenged but not to pressure him too much for success or to grow up "too fast."

Some educators favor providing for individual differences through acceleration; that is, permitting the able student to complete the junior high school program in less than the usual time. Others prefer some kind of selective enrichment, keeping the student with his age mates but adjusting the scope and depth of his studies to fit his abilities and interests. The junior high administrators in the NASSP disscussions opposed one type of acceleration—grade skipping. On the other hand, they did call for thoughtful experimentation with nongraded programs, which provide for acceleration without some of the drawbacks of grade skipping.

10. Insofar as possible, each pupil has a program especially de-

signed for him. Not only do students follow different course schedules, but within each course there are opportunities for each student to make some choices of content to be studied, to use a variety of learning aids, and to carry out individual or small group projects.

11. Recent developments such as programed instruction, language laboratories, individual recording and listening devices, and other multisensory aids to learning are used to provide a variety of instructional aids geared to individual differences among students.

12. The junior high school provides special programs for students talented in such fields such as music, art, and dramatics. Wide participation at less advanced levels in all these activities also is encouraged. Depth study in all areas is provided through electives and independent study. Remedial help is made available for those who need it.

13. Selected enrichment in content is preferable to grade skipping for most students.

Diversity of home backgrounds also results in individual differences among students. Both curriculum and teaching methods need to be modified for some groups of pupils. Extraclass activities and an effective guidance program also may help to provide for the uniqueness of individuals. Teachers realize that the school can do little directly to change the home and cultural conditions of youth, but they can help pupils adjust to the differences among home, school, and community standards.

14. Schools develop specific programs to help teachers understand and deal effectively with cultural differences that affect pupil behavior in school. Special cultural enrichment programs are provided for students who deviate markedly from the norm.

Exploration

The junior high or middle school designs exploratory experiences to help the student broaden his horizons, develop his interests, and identify his aptitudes, strengths, and weaknesses with respect to educational, vocational, and avocational pursuits. These experiences are provided in courses, in student activities, and through the guidance program. Exploration is especially important during early adolescence when young people are beginning to think of themselves as men and women and to make some of the choices that will determine many aspects of their future lives.

Each teacher contributes to this function by utilizing a wide variety of learning experiences and by encouraging students to consider educational, vocational, and avocational opportunities relevant to a particular subject or activity. All classrooms and activities may serve as places to try out talents and interests. The student needs enough time at an endeavor to determine whether or not he can achieve the success that is fundamental to the development of continued interest. The goal is to help each student to capitalize on his strengths, to overcome any correctable weaknesses, and to learn to live with any permanent disabilities he may have.

Since exploration permeates the entire program, it is important especially that the junior high school principal exercises effective leadership—keeping this specific goal constantly before the staff, coordinating, stimulating, and reviewing their various efforts, and encouraging positive improvement.

15. The goal of exploration characterizes the philosophy and operation of the entire school program, not in just one department or in one subject.

Pupil Personnel

A sound school program takes into account the health, social, and economic needs of youth in addition to their educational needs. All who work with junior high school students need to foster their growing maturity, while recognizing that many are still extremely immature and general instability characterizes behavior at this age.

Guidance

The term guidance refers to the school's efforts to assist each boy and girl to make plans and decisions regarding a career, education, employment, and personal problems, so that each may gain as much as possible from school. The guidance program focuses on each pupil in relation to his total experience, helping him to develop realistic goals based on the best possible understanding of himself, the world, and the tremendous changes taking place in both.

The school's guidance team consists of the principal, assistant principal, deans, psychologist, nurse, social worker, guidance specialists, and designated teachers. Each student needs a personal advisor who may be a block-time teacher, homeroom teacher, or any member of the staff who has the time, inclination, and preparation for the role of teacher-counselor. These teachers who carry special guidance responsibilities are especially trained to counsel with students and their parents.

Cumulative pupil records include such data as careful reports of conferences, course selections, scholastic records, test results, health information, referral records, and staff recommendations. It is essential that elementary school officials pass on to the junior high school adequate information including that needed to identify potential early-school-leavers and others who require special guidance. Likewise, pertinent data are forwarded immediately when a student transfers out of the junior high school.

16. Every student is well-known in all respects by at least one teacher. This "first echelon" guidance provided by teachers is coordinated and supplemented by guidance specialists who work with classroom teachers as they carry out their guidance responsibilities.

17. The guidance team, or a representative committee of such personnel, meets regularly to establish policies, deal with special problems, consider available resources, make referrals to specified persons or programs, and evaluate the school's services to each pupil.

18. Adequate cumulative records are essential. Interschool communication is improved when uniform record forms and procedures are used.

Rules and Standards for Student Conduct

Pupil behavior is greatly influenced by the nature of the total school environment as developed by students, counselors, teachers, and administrators. What school staff members *do* is more influential than what they *say* or *write.*

Cooperative planning stimulates student participation in activities designed to promote good school citizenship and enhances their respect for and acceptance of necessary rules and standards. Establishment of codes and standards should be accompanied by appropriate, constructive instruction.

19. Pupils, teachers, and parents share in the development of codes of dress, grooming, and classroom and audience behavior, along with policies for dealing with extreme deviations. Codes are reviewed periodically so that current students have a hand in their formulation.

Student Activities

Extracurricular activities appeal to students because they allow more responsibility and freedom than typically is permitted in the classroom. The goals of the activities program are similar to those of other aspects of the curriculum. One particular emphasis is the development of wholesome leisure-time interests that can be continued into adult life. Activities programs also aid in developing school spirit and in maintaining student interest in school.

Although student participation in the activity program is voluntary, all students should be encouraged to take part. Leadership needs to be spread as widely as possible, not clustered in the hands of a few students.

20. Student activities are carefully planned and evaluated to make certain that they have definite educational values and that the goals actually are realized.

21. Activities are given financial support and facilities that compare favorably with other aspects of the school program. Time for activity programs is provided within the daily class schedule. Teacher competence, interest, and work load are considered in assigning staff advisors to student activities.

22. A personal guidance approach, rather than uniformly-applied standards, is utilized to help students avoid either under- or over-participation in activities.

Student Participation in Government

The junior high school student council provides a laboratory for students to learn how to make wise, moral, and informed choices, and to carry them into action. Every school needs a program for developing and training both leaders and participants in student activities, so that democratic citizenship is learned through practice. Homeroom programs, class work, and club activities make important contributions in this regard.

It is important for the principal to promote effective student participation and appoint as student council advisor a staff member dedicated to its full development. The goal is for *all* students to participate through representation or direct action in student council programs.

23. The student council establishes, promotes, regulates, evaluates, and also discontinues student activities, subject to school policies and

the principal's approval. The council also contributes to the formulation of policies and regulations governing student conduct.

Clubs and Service Groups

Ideally, student activities emphasize both service to others and personal enjoyment and benefit. A well-rounded program includes: service clubs, interest clubs, subject-extension clubs, and honor societies. Examples of service groups are: office assistants, library assistants, audio-visual equipment operators, school store assistants, and safety patrols.

An honor program, such as that of the National Junior Honor Society, recognizes outstanding students of high scholastic achievement and also fosters high standards of character, citizenship, leadership, and service. However, the junior high school principals who participated in the NASSP study were divided on the desirability of honor societies at this level. Other means of recognizing meritorious service and achievement also are desirable, whether or not the junior high school has a chapter of the National Junior Honor Society.

24. Clubs and other acitvities are formed, maintained, and evaluated in terms of services to potential and existing student interests and contributions to desirable educational goals.

Athletics

The junior high or middle school athletic program needs to be "pupil-centered" rather than "high-school centered." In other words, its purpose is to serve students *now* rather than to prepare them for senior high school athletic teams. Such a program includes activities that are likely to be pursued by boys and girls for their personal enjoyment both now and in the future. In a carefully controlled interscholastic program, the number of games is limited and most of them are held in the afternoon, after school hours. Admission is free. Travel distances are short. Dads' or Boosters' Clubs are discouraged, publicity minimized, and awards de-emphasized. League championships and tournaments are not permitted. These and other policies, plus constant supervision, are provided to protect the welfare of students and to keep interscholastic athletics in balance with other aspects of the total program.

25. Emphasis is on intramural sports in which all interested students may be included. Interscholastic athletics, if conducted at all, are carefully controlled and supervised.

Evaluation

Evaluation is the process of judging progress toward agreed-upon goals. School innovations and experiments as well as existing programs need continuous evaluation. When such appraisal is an integral part of curriculum and methodology, the findings are translated directly into improved teaching and learning.

Evaluation of pupil progress includes situational performance, attitudinal development, and behavioral changes, in addition to and separate from subject matter and skills achievement. All tests given should be interpreted, reported, and used to improve instruction.

26. Teachers, parents, and pupils understand the school's purposes and how progress toward them is defined. Adequate time for evaluation is included in the teacher's professional assignment.

Marking and Reporting Pupil Progress

Each student's progress may be: (1) evaluated in terms of his own past achievement, (2) compared with the performance of other students, and (3) measured against a set of accepted standards. Most of the junior high school administrators who participated in the NASSP discussions gave primary emphasis to the first criterion.

A grading system based solely on comparisons among pupils was opposed by the principals because it results in eliminating some pupils from school and hence represents a significant barrier to education for many youth. Similarly, calculation of a junior high student's rank in class was judged indefensible, and considerable question was raised about the value of honor rolls at this level. The junior high principals also rejected arbitrary standards, urging that grade-level standards that result in pupil retention (non-promotion) be replaced by curriculum organizations that permit continuous progress. In short, they called for emphasis on the individual and how well he is using his abilities, not on how his performance compares with either an arbitrary standard or with that of other students.

Conventional grading symbols and report card systems hardly can be expected to communicate results of the kind of multi-dimensional evaluation program recommended by the NASSP study groups.

27. The progress of each pupil is measured in relation to his or her own past achievement. The single-letter, multi-purpose mark is supplemented or replaced by parent-teacher conferences and a variety of written reports.

5

Samuel R. Porter

The School in the Middle

With increasing frequency, the school districts of this nation are making the decision to abandon the junior high school as presently organized in favor of some type of "middle school". This change in grade pattern is not a small isolated incident in educational practice; with the announcement that the vast New York City system will drop the present 6-3-3 plan and adopt a 4-4-4 plan (four grades each in elementary, middle and high school), a trend is definitely established.

The exact grade composition of the new middle school is still not firmly fixed in actual practice, although grades 6, 7 and 8 are often included, with grade 5 sometimes being added, as in the case of New York City.

The demise of the junior high school will not only be a great disappointment to many educators who have invested their careers in this type of school, but all of the disciplines which have developed curricula purported to be uniquely suited to the needs of pre-adolescents in grades 7, 8 and 9 will have to be rethought, readjusted and refocussed; industrial arts is clearly one of the disciplines most affected by the change.

Marshall Schmitt has compiled figures (1) which indicate that the greatest concentration of enrollment in industrial arts is found in the present junior high school grade 9, with enrollments falling off sharply thereafter. With a shift in grade level for this school, many questions arise: How will new school organizations (5-3-4, 4-4-4, 6-2-4) affect

From *Journal of Industrial Arts Education* (Nov.-Dec., 1967): 26–31.

the enrollments, programs and practices of industrial arts at all grade levels? Will the middle school offer new opportunities that have been unavailable or unpracticed in the junior high school? Will industrial arts face the future in this confusing situation by clinging to the practices of the past, only offering these practices one year earlier?

It is the purpose of this article to examine the history of the junior high school and its industrial arts offerings, to summarize the arguments for a change to the middle school, to project the opportunities and problems attendant to this change, and to make some suggestions regarding possible solutions to the perplexing problems which will ensue.

Junior high schools have often been called the "black sheep" of the educational world. Created some fifty years ago in order to provide a bridge between childhood and adolescence, the junior high school has never been totally successful in developing a program suited to the physiological and psychological needs of its enrollees.

The other schools of the educational sequence have been more fortunate than the junior high school in achieving stature. On one hand, the elementary school has seldom been the center of controversy regarding its general educational purpose; parents have traditionally shown an active concern for an enriched environment in the elementary school and have demonstrated fervent participation in its affairs. On the other end of the continuum, it can be observed that the high school enjoys widespread importance. With the possible exception of those located in the inner-city, it is almost the rule that the high school is an important adjunct to community life and is blessed with the best faculty and newest facility that can be afforded. With the frantic anguish over the standards of college preparation, the public scrutiny of the local athletic program, and the current obsession with the teen-age culture which centers in the high school, there is little question that the high school is accepted as an important institution worthy of all the money and attention it receives.

The junior high school, on the other hand, has had a long history of problems which have plagued it in its attempt to establish program and prestige distinctive to itself. The April, 1965, issue of the *Bulletin of the National Association of Secondary School Principals* is devoted to an examination of the problems of junior high schools and its students. There is clear evidence of the second-class citizenship of the junior high schools.

In spite of a few examples to the contrary, there is no doubt that the junior high school has inherited all of the accoutrements of high school programs. Most surveys indicate that the junior high school program is highly departmentalized, given to the "academic cycle" (lectures, homework, mid-term and final examinations), and fraught with high school traditions which were, incidentally, borrowed in turn from the colleges. Examine, for instance, the number of junior high schools that feature formal dances, interscholastic athletics, graduation exercises, and Kodachrome-studded yearbooks—all under the guise of being important, in some unproven way, to the regular program.

In industrial arts, very few junior high schools have designed programs and facilities which are very distinguishable from their high school counterparts. Most new teachers know that "exploration" is the primary purpose their professors have expounded for the junior high school industrial arts program, yet they have not been shown exactly how this exploration differs from doing "whatever you want" in the chaotic context of the general lab. Naturally it is easier and safer for the new teacher to establish high-school-like programs which are specialized in materials, processes and projects and carefully structured so that the "academic cycle" will operate smoothly. Indeed, there is evidence that "exploration" in the junior high school is limited to experiences in courses and labs identical to those of the high school, except that the work is often confined to smaller sizes, hand tools and perhaps lower standards. With our present elective system, many students elect to "explore" woodworking for six years in the junior and senior high school.

The teachers' colleges have done little or nothing to prepare teachers for dealing with the unique characteristics of youth during preadolescence. Wattenberg (2) has summarized it this way:

> The junior high school, as a psychologist might look at it, has two paradoxical distinctions: First, its clientele is composed of so bewildering an assortment of young people at critical turning points in their lives as to defy orderly description. Second, at colleges of education, there is a tendency to make believe that there is no such institution: schools are considered either elementary or secondary; young people either are children or adolescents.

One might ask the question: How many industrial arts methods courses exist which are addressed solely to the difficult task of teaching 12-year-olds in the lab situation?

The junior high school has long been the proving ground for secondary teachers and administrators. A coach is often "promoted" to the high school level if his teams are outstanding. An administrator who is successful in developing a noteworthy junior high school (according to local criteria) will be offered the first high school opening. At the same time, the mediocre teacher who attracts little attention, either for an outstandingly good or bad record, runs the risk of being shanghaied at the junior high school level for the rest of his career. Dr. Conant has substantiated these tendencies and has recommended that the best teachers available be placed and retained in junior high schools where teaching difficulties culminate; in industrial arts, as in other subjects, these recommendations do not seem to have been heeded.

If there is any validity to the accusations leveled at the junior high school, one cannot help looking toward the movement to a new form—in this case, the middle school—with great anticipation and hope. However, since the junior high school has been somewhat less than successful, it is useless to propose a substitute organization which is not clearly superior—at least in potential.

It should be stated at this juncture that there is no proof that the middle school will guarantee anything. To quote one author:

> On the basic question about the efficacy of one pattern or the other (6-3-3 or 5-3-4), we have very little evidence and much conjecture.(3)

Although the trend toward the middle school is based on little evidence, approximately 10 percent of the nation's school districts have seen fit to join the trend, and in most cases their experience with it has led to expressions ranging from cautious optimism to open enthusiasm.

The rationale for making the shift seems to center about several middle school "advantages" which deserve close examination.

The middle school seems to cater to a student body more homogeneous in psychological and physiological character. Margaret Mead (4) has commented on the inappropriateness of the traditional junior high school grouping in terms of maturation. Studies of the social, emotional and physical differences between children find close similarities between students in grades 6 and 7 and also grades 9 and 10; the middle school does not separate these grades as does the junior high school.

The middle school allows for an expanded curriculum one year earlier. For reasons yet unknown, children are reaching adolescence somewhat younger than in the past. Many courses traditionally reserved for the high school grades are now being taught earlier, and 6th graders are ready for the excitement and challenge of an expanded school curriculum, according to the proponents of the middle school. It should be pointed out, however, that the general "pushing down" of subject matter is not necessarily a good thing and could well be the most forceful argument against the middle school unless the movement of subject matter down into the grades is accompanied by changes to methods appropriate to youth at an earlier age. In short, the content and methods of the junior high school should not be transplanted *per se.*

The middle school is free of the Carnegie Unit (the unit of measure that indicates high school preparation for college), since the 9th grade is shifted into the high school. With this relief, the middle school has no pressure to prepare an impressive transcript for college entrance. In the opinion of this author, this change is the strongest case for the middle school because it removes many of the influences of the secondary school; the middle school is not a junior anything and is free to experiment with non-graded schools, flexible scheduling, ungraded coursework, individual teaching, resource centers and all of the other theories which have too often been abandoned in favor of traditional methods which result in transcripts for college. (As a side effect, the four-year high school is able to prepare a more meaningful college entrance sequence and report it on a well-coordinated transcript.)

Because no 9th grade is included, the middle school has the opportunity to avoid many of the social activities and school affairs which are associated with high school life. Close scrutiny can be given to marching bands, inter-scholastic sports, dances and similar activities before they are sanctioned.

The middle school results in a smoother transition from the practices of the elementary grades to those of the high school. It is usually proposed that students start their middle school careers in self-contained classrooms which are under the direction of one teacher, although this teacher's work is augmented by assistance from the specialists in science, mathematics, foreign language and the practical arts. The more departmentalized offerings of separate subjects in separate facilities are reserved for the upper middle school grades and are introduced in increasing amounts. Thus, students enter in the elementary school atmosphere and leave in one similar to that of the high school.

Proponents of the middle school hope that teacher education and certification laws will recognize the middle school as something unique and will not prepare and certify teachers in the usual secondary patterns.

There are several administrative opportunities which arise whenever there is a shift of grades within school organizations. In many local situations the middle school might be installed in order to deal with such problems as crowded buildings, *de facto* segregation or over-loaded bus schedules. However, if the shift to the middle school is made for these administrative reasons, it should be viewed as a temporary solution, and the real reasons must be honestly declared instead of claiming educational advantages for ulterior motives.

Again, there is little quantitative proof for the rationale stated above; indeed, many of the arguments for the middle school are the same ones advanced for the junior high school upon its inception. Furthermore, the arguments, though often compelling, do not guarantee good results—that is, they contain the seeds of a worse situation as well as those of opportunity. The middle school will only represent improvement if teachers and administrators recognize the opportunities involved and work with imagination and creativity toward a distinctive new school which is suited to students who have unique intellectual, social, physical and emotional needs.

Regardless of the controversy surrounding the trend to the middle school, the trend itself cannot be ignored or denied. Throughout the nation, groups of teachers are being asked to make proposals regarding the place of their disciplines in the middle school. Those in subject areas which are sometimes considered "non-central" or "peripheral" to the primary purposes of education, even more than others, will have to postulate a well-grounded and defensible series of offerings. There is some evidence that industrial arts has often found a diminished role in many new middle schools because the articulate academicians cut the pie to their liking while the industrial artists bogged down in indecision.

Two steps must be taken when industrial arts faces a move to the middle school.

First, a set of working principles must be compiled. Too often this idealistic and philosophical step is hurried over. The final place and prestige of industrial arts in the school must come out of the beliefs that teachers hold, state and defend about their subject.

Secondly, the realities of the local situation (enrollments, scheduling possibilities, facilities, faculty and financial support) must be adjudicated with the working principles so that the emerging middle school program will be idealistically conceived yet realistically structured.

Taking these two aforementioned steps can be done only by the industrial arts staff that is willing to invest thoughtful effort as they grapple with their content in the middle school context. While Step 2 must be based entirely on local data, it is possible to discuss Step 1 here and to present a sample list of working principles which are related to the place of industrial arts in the middle school and which portray the type of generalizations upon which actual practice can be based.

The study of industry and its impact upon the lives of individuals should be an important part of the work in each grade of the middle school. It is not implied here that all content about industry should be confined to industrial art courses, nor that separate units of study courses in industry must be offered at all grade levels. It does mean, however, that the role of modern industry in contemporary society cannot be ignored at any point in the middle school. For example, the study of history should not be confined to military and political history. Science and mathematics should not remain so pure that they fail to apply their concepts and principles which are so amply illustrated in the industrial products and processes in everyday life.

The organization of the middle school should exploit the use of the specialized industrial arts staff and facility in developing a curriculum that is characterized by unity and articulation. Disjointed fragments of knowledge are probably not suitable to any age, but especially not to the middle school youth who is attempting to organize the structure of knowledge into rational thinking. The industrial arts teacher has, therefore, curricular obligations which are twofold: in addition to the careful delineation of his own coursework, it is not too much to expect that he become familiar with the content of other subjects so that he can contribute insights and experiences related to industry wherever and whenever possible.

Like all other subjects in the middle school, industrial arts should adapt itself to the transition from the self-contained classroom in the early grades to the more segregated offerings in the upper grades. Teachers in middle school self-contained classrooms, like those of the elementary school, will probably hesitate to include industrial content and activity in their classes because they feel inadequately prepared in this area or think that including industrial arts (as they know it) requires facts, facilities and skills beyond their grasp. The industrial arts teacher should stand ready to assist the regular classroom teacher in his attempt to deal with these facets of learning.

Separate specialized industrial arts experiences should be offered (or even required) in increasing amounts as students move through the grade levels of the middle school. Local conditions must surely dictate when and how these experiences change from integrated classwork to full-fledged courses.

Industrial arts in the middle school must be characterized by exploratory experiences in a wide variety of media. There are several reasons why courses and experiences should be broadly conceived; the ability and interest of middle school youth vary widely, the content of industrial arts should be related to the diverse activities of other subjects, and experiences in industrial arts will terminate, for many students, in the middle school. Therefore, exposure should be broad.

Courses in drafting should include all phases of graphics, including graphic arts, photography, sketching, technical illustration, etc.

The traditional troika of woodworking, drafting and metalworking should be expanded to include graphic arts, photography, electricity, power mechanics, industrial crafts and any other industrial activity arising out of the interests of the students and the curriculum of the total school.

Laboratories should be flexible in organization to accommodate any worthwhile activity that seems appropriate to the occasion, and formal coursework should be unstructured enough that it can give way quickly to more compelling tasks which might achieve the same ends. This is not to say that coursework has no direction whatever; however, there are often many means to an end and too often the means are so formalized that they stand squarely in the way of spontaneous educational experiences, and individual students are squeezed into administrative structure and convenience rather than the other way around.

It is interesting to note that the comprehensive general lab is the form of organization most frequently advocated and chosen for early industrial arts, although it must be admitted that very often this promising lab organization is used in a restricted manner, with students working at pre-set requirements in a rotational scheme in such a way that exploration and experimentation are squelched.

The middle school and all of the disciplines within it should feature emphasis upon individualized instruction. The authors of the original junior high school aspired for an institution that fostered individual teaching; surveys indicate that this goal has not been attained. The proponents of the middle school once again pose this goal. Industrial arts can and must make this possible for two reasons: (a) the very nature of industrial arts as an activity offering allows for methods of very individualized instruction, and (b) industrial arts at this level will enroll the complete gamut of abilities (unlike the high school) and cannot presume to require identical content and method of all. Individualized instruction is the only alternative under these circumstances.

The middle school, and industrial arts within it, should place primary emphasis on factors that lead to the continued quest for knowledge. If there is any one factor that stands out in Marshall Schmitt's report, it is that the holding power of industrial arts is poor. In order to increase enrollments in high school courses, steps should be taken to bring the work of the earlier levels into line with the recommendations of those who study motivation. Educational psychologists seem to agree that early success in challenging and interesting experiences which are related to the goals of the learner are most likely to whet the appetite for continued experiences which are even more challenging. It is the opinion of this author, then, that the middle school industrial arts laboratory should be a place where youth can experiment, investigate and explore in a relatively low-pressure atmosphere without too much concern about competing for predetermined goals of proficiency in certain basic skills deemed "necessary for all" by the teacher. The elective courses of the high school, rich in industrial content and structured in approach, will do little good if no one elects to take them after sampling conformity and perhaps failure in the middle school.

If it is impossible (and it is not) for industrial arts to be both interesting and educational, one should settle for the first, so students will continue their quest for the second.

A continuing in-service program should assist teachers in understanding the middle school student and the methods which are most appropriate to the unique characteristics of this age. As stated previously, the preparation and certification of teachers generally ignores the problems of teaching pre-adolescents. One common text in industrial arts devotes more space to the problems of students who are either left-handed, mentally retarded, defective in speech or otherwise deviate than to the great majority of normal or above-normal students who enroll in industrial arts with all of the problems associated with being 12 or 13 years old.

Because the curricula of the teachers' colleges are already bulging with requirements of many kinds, it seems unlikely that the pre-adolescent will receive any attention from that quarter. Therefore, this study should be taken up with vigor by those in middle schools through in-service courses and activities.

The authors of the middle school concept hope it will become what the junior high school failed to become. Industrial arts can contribute to this hope if it can chart a future that is truly adapted to the mission of the middle school. Ideally, the industrial arts laboratory should become a resource center not unlike the library where students and teachers can investigate, experiment, explore and learn, either individually or in groups, as they attempt to understand themselves and their industrial society.

(1) Schmitt, Marshall L., Industrial Arts Education, A Survey of Programs, Teachers, Students, and Curriculums, OE-33038, *Circular No. 971, US Office of Education, 1966.*

(2) Wattenberg, William W., "The Junior High School—A Psychologist's View", Bulletin of the National Association of Secondary School Principals *(April 1965), p. 34.*

(3) Vars, Gordon F., "Junior High or Middle School? Which is Best for the Education of Young Adolescents?," The High School Journal, *Vol. 50 (December 1966), p. 109.*

(4) Mead, Margaret, "Early Adolescence in the United States,"

Bulletin of the National Association of Secondary School Principals, Vol. 49 (April 1965), pp. 5-10.

(5) Alexander, William, and Williams, Emmett L., "Schools for the Middle School Years," Educational Leadership, Vol. 23 (December 1965), p. 217.

(6) Brod, Pearl, "The Middle School: Trends Toward its Adoption," Clearing House, Vol. 40 (February 1966), p. 331.

(7) Editorial, "The Junior High School—Where is it Heading?" Ohio Schools, Vol. XLIV (October 1966), p. 18.

(8) Hull, J. H., "Are Junior High Schools the Answer?" Educational Leadership, Vol. 23 (December 1965), p. 213.

(9) Madon, Constant A., "The Middle School: Its Philosophy and Purpose," Clearing House, Vol. 40 (February 1966), p. 329.

(10) Shuster, Byran, "An Ungraded Multi-Activity Program," School and Community, Vol. LIII (January 1967).

6

Edward A. McHugh

The Middle School
That Evolved

Central School District #4, East Patchogue, like most school districts on Long Island, has experienced rapid pupil growth in the last ten years. The district was centralized in 1956. At that time all of the elementary schools in existence were K-8. With centralization, a junior-senior high school (7-12) was created and the elementary school grade organization became K-6.

Many changes in the elementary grades followed between 1956 and 1967. The schools remained K-6 until 1962; from 1962-64 the elementary schools became K-7; in 1964-65 they once again became K-6 only to change again during the year 1966-67 when they became K-5 schools.

What has taken place in our district is not unusual. In order to avoid split sessions, or because of lack of space, children and grades are moved constantly. Many times local Boards of Education are not able to house children according to any philosophical educational plan because of the realities of pupil enrollment and space needs.

Since September of 1965 a middle school in our district has "come to be" without any special premeditated commitment to the middle school concept. We hesitated to adopt a philosophy based primarily on available classroom seats.

As the junior high school principal of the district, I felt I should do two things. First, I should make the maximum use of all our educational facilities to make the present grade organization in my building

From *Impact* (Winter, 1967-68): 27-30.

(6-7-8) as fruitful as possible for the children of the district. Secondly, I should review the old junior high school grade structure in order to serve as an advisor to the district on the future grade organization within the district. I felt the day would arrive when the Board of Education would be asking, "Should we return to the K-6-3-3 school organization or should we separate grades 9 through 12 and then decide what combinations of elementary grades seem to work best for the children of our district?"

The Junior High Pattern

The ninth grade has brought unusual administrative and curricular problems. The learning process of the junior high school has been, in many instances, subverted to the Carnegie unit. Strickland[1] attempts to give some insight into this "ninth grade" question. Extensive study clearly shows that differences in academic success in the ninth grade do not rest so much with its placement in either junior or senior high school as they do with the program of instruction and instructional staff involved.

During the fifty years of its existence, the junior high school seems to have changed very little. The following practices seem typical of most junior high schools throughout the country:
1. There is a trend to increase the number of classes.
2. Periods continue to average about 50 minutes. (Module scheduling offers flexibility in many schools.)
3. Departmentalization is characteristic.
4. Three fourths of all separate junior high schools are made up of grades 7-8-9. Two year junior high schools of grades 7-8 are common and make up nearly a fifth of the schools.
5. Many classes have 25–29 pupils but a typical class might be 30–34.
6. Most junior high schools have their own library, gymnasium, science and home economics facilities.
7. Usually electives are found only in the eighth and ninth grades.

Lounsbury and Douglass[2] say that the junior high school continues to develop and show changes. They feel it has reached a level of maturity that brings some standardization. They also feel that the junior high school will not change suddenly and that practices that will become common in the future are already in the making.

The Middle School Pattern

In the 5-3-4 plan, grade 6 is moved from the elementary to junior high school and grade 9 is returned to the high school. When the sixth grade is removed from the elementary grades, not all educators feel it is the best move for the children. Elementary principals quickly point out that the "heart" is taken out of their buildings. At first, the teachers are fearful of the change. After all, some teachers have been doing an excellent job in self-contained grades for a good many years. They have surrounded themselves with teaching aides to their curriculum and feel perfectly satisfied to remain in the elementary building. Parents are apprehensive about the change. Do sixth grade children belong with seventh and eighth graders? Will they be pushed socially and pressured academically?

Alexander[3] feels that the 5-3-4 plan spans the years between childhood and adolescence better than the common 6-3-3 setup. Brod[4] says research has fairly well confirmed that children in grades 6 to 8 are developmentally more alike than those in grades 7-9. The middle school concept gives the intermediate unit a status of its own rather than a junior classification. It is NOT a high school in miniature. Such a grade organization helps to slow down the "growing up" process from K-8 because the oldest group is removed from each level.

Eventually local objectives must be set for the middle school and immediate resources utilized to give the students the best possible educational opportunities. The following are the objectives we have developed for our local programs at Central District #4 in a sixth through eighth grade program:

I. Overall Plan for the Middle School.

Naturally such a plan should serve the needs of all the children in the school. This school should be free from the rigidity of total departmentalization and from the pressures of interschool competition and older adolescent social functions. Madon[5] says, "It is important to maintain the balance between specialized instruction and the need for security that comes through a self-contained classroom."

II. Basic Program of General Studies.

Science, Social Studies. Language Arts, and Mathematics make up the so called standard subjects. French and Spanish are offered as electives in the eighth grade. The content of the basic subjects relates to the elementary and senior high programs for continuity within the district. Efforts should be constantly made to create a climate in which learning is respected and yet remains exciting.

III. Program for Student Exploration.

The earlier opportunity for the students to explore many interests is one of the reasons for a middle school. Someday the sixth grade curriculum might include the Industrial Arts and Home Economics that are now offered to the seventh and eighth grades. However, activities that offer the student many leadership opportunities are photography; creative writing; ceramics; assisting in library, the office, the dining room plus taking part in assembly programs, school publications, band, orchestra and chorus.

Within the last few years four 10-week electives that have been created locally in the areas of Industrial Arts, Home Economics and Art have been added. The clubs that are in existence also serve as an individual interest outlet. We have eliminated interscholastic competition. A very active intramural program is encouraged with students assembled to watch honor team playoffs or final individual intramural matches.

School dances do not take place in the evening. The last period of the day plus the activity period are utilized with the student council assuming responsibilities such as providing for refreshments and music. Sixth grade students do not participate in this activity. The boys' and girls' gymnasium, the shop, the art room, and so forth are kept open so that dancing is not the only outlet for the seventh and eighth grader.

IV. Independent Study and Emphasis on Learning Skills.

The combination of direct instruction and the student discovery method lead children to seek additional information and learning. Children are encouraged to ask questions. There is ample opportunity to use the library and other learning resources placed throughout the building. Eight of our rooms are electronically looped for individual and small group work. Some students are issued an honor pass which enables them to be responsible for their own learning and time distribution. Individual elective study programs are catalogued in the library.

V. Teacher Aides.

We have employed approximately fifteen teacher aides for the last two years. All of these women are graduates of liberal arts colleges. We are fortunate to be located near the Brookhaven National Laboratory and the wives of scientists offer us a fabulous community resource. The teacher aide programs are always requested by the teacher. We have been very successful with a lay reader program. Students work on a one-to-one basis with an adult. A remedial mathematics program for the average student who needs concentrated help for a short period has worked well. Two seminars that really proved exciting were conducted by one of these ladies, one on the "short story," the other in "mythology."

VI. Scheduling.

We have scheduled horizontally as much as possible. With four English classes or four mathematics classes meeting at the same time, the student is able to be moved without any great strain on himself or the office at any time of the year. Of course, one can easily see the possibilities for team teaching and large group instruction.

VII. Evaluation.

Statements of sixth grade teachers indicate strong support for the 6-7-8 grade organization. Without exception, teachers, administrators, and guidance personnel who were questioned at levels 6 through 12 favored the 6-7-8 grade organization.

Teachers were asked to list their reasons for favoring the 6-7-8 grade organization. The following statements would constitute the thinking of the group:
1. I was able to confer with my colleagues at any time.
2. A wealth of supplementary materials is available.
3. The 6th grade teachers may follow academic achievement of former students through grades 7 and 8.
4. Large group instruction is possible if the situation warrants it.
5. The sixth graders mature faster and become more independent when they associate with junior high students.

6. The sixth graders, in my opinion, are eager for specialization in subject matter instruction.
7. The sixth graders are ready for many teacher personalities rather than the one in elementary school.
8. The organization of conferences is easily arranged for coordination of curriculum and student problems.
9. A.V. material is centralized and used for large group instruction.
10. Grouping of students at different levels in math and reading may be achieved more efficiently.
11. Team teaching can be coordinated with grades 7 and 8.
12. The maturity level of sixth graders is more compatible with 7th graders than to 5th graders.
13. There is a more effective pooling of resources and materials at this level.
14. The curriculum coordination enhances the sequence of matter provided.
15. Team teaching and team guidance efforts are included.
16. Partial departmentalization in sixth grade promotes, in my opinion, better teacher preparation and a higher quality of teaching.
17. There seem to be fewer discipline problems in both sixth and ninth grades when the middle school exists.
18. These children are on the threshold of adolescence and are socially, physically, and emotionally closer to junior high than to the elementary grades.
19. The partly self-contained, and partly departmentalized arrangement seems to fit the moods and needs of children of this age. At times they need the security of seeing the same teacher for long periods of time and at other times the excitement and stimulation of a different teacher pleases them.

Summary

Perhaps the most important thing is not what the school is called or what organization it uses, but what goes on in a school between teachers and students that counts. Good schools are made by good teachers. I feel that the middle school offers a second opportunity for those interested in the education of youngsters of this age.

Finally, I would hope that someday administrative organization will be determined on educational grounds rather than for such reasons as building efficiency, economy, or racial balance.

Bibliography

1. Strickland, Virgil, "Where Does the Ninth Grade Belong?" *Bulletin NAASP #316,* February, 1967.

2. Lounsbury, John H., and Douglass, Harl R. "A Decade of Changes in Junior High Practices," *Clearing House,* April, 1966.

3. Alexander, William M., and Williams, Emmett L. "Schools for the Middle School Years," *Educational Leadership,* December, 1965.

4. Brod, Pearl, "The Middle School: Trends Toward Its Adoption," *Clearing House,* February, 1966.

5. Madon, Constant A. "The Middle School: Its Philosophy and Purpose," *Clearing House,* February, 1966.

7

Ernest O. Melby

It's Time for Schools to Abolish the Marking System

The marking system is damaging in its impact on the education of our children. It should go the way of the hickory stick and dunce cages. It should be abandoned at all levels of education.

Our marking system is no longer relevant to the needs and educational programs of our society. It says nothing meaningful about a pupil. It glosses over exceptional effort on the part of some pupils and lack of effort on the part of others. It says nothing about the most important outcomes of education. It leads us to measure the outcomes of our educational programs in terms of what people know, when we ought to be measuring them in terms of what people are and are in the process of becoming. It tells us a little about what the pupil has done to the subject he studies but nothing about what his study of the subject has done to him. We think we must use this worn-out system to motivate pupils, but all the studies I have seen show that marks have no motivating effect.

But the marking system is not only irrelevant and mischievous. It is destructive. It destroys the self-concepts of millions of children every year. Note the plight of the deprived child. He often enters school at six with few of the pre-school experiences that the middle-class children bring to school. We ask him to learn to read. He is not ready to read. We give him a low mark—we repeat the low mark for each marking period—often for as long as the child remains in school. At

From *Nation's Schools* (May, 1966):104.

the end of perhaps the ninth grade, the child drops out of school. What has he learned? He has learned he cannot learn. We have told him so several dozen times. Why should he think otherwise?

We have lied to him. He can learn. If we were worth our salt as teachers and as a school, we should have taught him he can learn. We should have asked him to do things he can do, not what we know he can't do. Every day we should have sent him home with more confidence in himself, liking himself better than when he came in.

But don't tell me it's only the deprived who suffer from our marking system. All children are injured. They are injured because they are induced to seek the wrong goals—to be satisfied when their performance reaches a given level, rather than when they have done their best. They are injured because they develop a dislike for subjects in which they get a low grade, literature for example. Often these dislikes are lifelong. Think of all the college graduates and high school graduates who dislike mathematics, for example. The low grade they received told them they were deficient in mathematical ability when most often they were merely the victims of bad teaching.

When I say these things about our obsolete marking system, someone always asks "What shall we tell the parents about the child?" "What shall we report to the university?" My answer is let us be both informative and conducive to the growth of the pupil's self-concept. Let us describe his growth in meaningful terms that are really descriptive of the pupil's effort, unique qualities, interests, attitudes, and behaviors. As for standards, we should evaluate each pupil in terms of his own capacity and growth, not in comparison with others, who are very different. A slow learner may become a better self-actualizing person than a fast learner.

We should be engaged with parents in the joint undertaking of helping the pupil to grow as a self-actualizing person. Our marking system injures the self-concepts of many children and is an obstacle to self-actualization. As for university entrance, from four years of high school experience, we should be able to decide what kind of post high school education the student should undertake. We either recommend him to a state university or junior college. On what basis?

When you go to a doctor for a history and physical check-up, the doctor writes constantly as you talk, describing your condition. He accumulates your medical history. He does not give you an "A" or a "C." He does not use meaningless terms which blot out your individuality. He uses descriptive language which when he reads it causes you to come alive as a unique person—in health terms.

Why can't we in education do the same? Why do we bury the observations of a pupil's teachers over a dozen years in meaningless symbols? Why do we ignore the specific judgments of all the teachers who worked hard with the pupil and had much to pass on both to parents and the next teacher?

In American schools today perhaps a third of the children get very little in effective education. What is worse, their experience in school destroys their self-confidence. On a nationwide basis we are belatedly coming to grips with the problem. We are trying many plans. But, unless we abandon our crude and destructive marking system, nothing else we do will have much value.

8

Victor B. Lawhead

A Block of Time—
for General Education

The best grounding in all formal schooling at all levels, both
for special tasks and for general responsibilities, is a broad
education in which the social, biological and physical sciences, mathematics, the humanities and the arts are learned
in concert and in their relationships.[1]

The significance of reorganizing instruction into more meaningful
units and the necessity for blocking instructional time for effective use
of direct, firsthand experience have been the concerns of thoughtful
educators for many years. Early in this century, the introduction of
half-day programs for vocational education, double periods for laboratory courses, and unlimited time after classes for extracurricular activities reflected the necessity for flexible scheduling to make learning
more meaningful. On the contemporary scene fresh approaches in the
form of educational television, the Trump proposals, independent
study, and others have challenged time-honored concepts of the orderly 50-minute schedule and the neatly packaged bodies of subject
matter apportioned to the school day.

An additional development of the past three decades to challenge
further the efficacy of the fragmented daily program has been the

From *Educational Leadership* (December, 1960): 148-52. Reprinted with permis-
sion of the Association for Supervision and Curriculum Development and V. B.
Lawhead. Copyright © 1960 by the Association of Supervision and Curriculum
Development.

steady growth of core programs in general education. Such programs have been characterized by an integration of learning within a longer block of time than the usual class period. A 1958 report from the United States Office of Education[2] indicated that approximately one-third of the separately organized junior high schools in this country now provide an extended block of time for general education.

Despite these encouraging developments toward unifying learning in general education, one may discern a number of current efforts to direct the curriculum of the junior high school toward more atomistic and fragmented patterns of organization. Although Dr. Conant recommends a block-of-time in Grades Seven and Eight in which a student's classes in English and social studies would be staffed by the same teacher, his curricular recommendations imply rigid departmentalization. Educational television, which has a potential for programming viewing experiences of an interdisciplinary scope, has not capitalized on this possibility to any great extent. If the tentative schedule of courses proposed by the Midwest Program on Airborne Television Instruction[3] is indicative of patterns in this field, further departmentalization of instruction may be fostered by this medium not only in the junior high school but in the elementary school as well. Curriculum innovations in the areas of mathematics and science during the post-sputnik era have reflected an emphasis on early specialization, a condition that complicates further the task of offering a broad general education. In the light of these developments, it seems useful to look again at the nature and scope of core programs organized around the values, skills and knowledge required for common citizenship and to restate the case for such a program in the junior high school.

What is the core program and what advantages does it offer for the improvement of general education for early adolescents? The term "core" refers to that part of the curriculum which utilizes two periods or more for education that meets common or universal needs of students in modern society. Thus, two distinguishing characteristics are noted. *First,* the core is concerned with general or liberal education in contrast to special or technical education, which is also necessary but organized for the variety and differences in talents and interests. *Second,* instead of short, separate periods for isolated subjects, the core embraces a larger block of time for a unified organization of experiences which cuts across the major disciplines. These comprehensive and integrating characteristics foster conditions which lead in practice to other discernible values of a core program. Of these, the following three have special significance for improving secondary education on the junior high school level.

Case for an Integrating Program

The core program encourages students to establish relationships between and among fields of knowledge.

Effective core programs have a planned content of problem areas. From these areas instructional units are developed that help students pull together knowledge from several disciplines in solving the problems of common citizenship. That modern systems of communication make possible the application of knowledge from many disparate fields to the common problems of living has been demonstrated by the scientists. In building a basic education for adolescents, we can recognize with them that, ". . . the very survival of our society itself may depend upon our ability to reaffirm in the most concrete and specific ways the unity of all human knowledge, both theoretical and practical."[4]

In dealing recently with the sequential and lateral relationships discernible in an effectively organized curriculum, Tyler wrote:

> From the standpoint of the achievement of continuity and sequence, the discrete subjects, the discrete courses for each semester or year, and the discrete lessons, all impose difficulties that make vertical organization less likely to occur. There are too many boundary lines from one structure to another to assure of easy transition. Vertical organization is facilitated when the courses are organized over a period of years in larger units and in larger general framework.[5]

In making a case for establishing lateral relationships he continues:

> . . . to achieve integration is difficult if the organizing structure is composed of many specific pieces, since the tendency is to arrange the elements of each piece into some more unified form but to work out the relationship of each of these pieces to each other becomes more difficult as more pieces are involved. Thus, fifteen or sixteen specific subjects

in the elementary school present more hazards to the achievement of integration than an organization which has four or five broad fields like the language arts, the social studies, health and physical education, and the like. A core curriculum involves even less difficulty in achieving integration so far as the interposition of boundaries between subjects is concerned.[6]

The core program facilitates guidance and counseling of students.

Since the core program takes its name from the fact that it represents the heart of general education, we should not overlook its secondary responsibility for nurturing specialized interests and abilities up to a point short of technical competence. This additional responsibility of general education defines further the guidance role of the core teacher. In placing primary emphasis on common learnings we sometimes overlook the additional task of general education of fostering unique interests and talents of pupils. The problem here is not one of meeting fully such needs but of bringing them into clearer perspective so that the student can choose wisely his experiences in the elective or special interest offerings. To assist him in this process is to provide him one of the most significant of guidance services— whether such service is called "counseling" or just good teaching.

The longer block of time that characterizes the core program has several implications for effective guidance of students. In contrast to other teachers on a staff the core teacher is likely to spend more time with a given group of pupils and hence should be in a better position to know them as individuals. Furthermore, sound testing procedures support the practice of having tests administered by persons who are close to the students and who probably will be in a better position to interpret results.

The content of the core is problem centered and hence more conducive to personal and social guidance. The core program with a planned structure of problem areas increases the possibility that the real life concerns of the students will be given attention in the classroom. An examination of proposed problem areas similar to those listed by Lurry and Alberty[7] reveals that all such areas offer opportunities for students to relate individual problems to those being studied in a wider context. Some areas, however, are more provocative than others. Consider for example, the learning units that might fall under the broad areas of Self Understanding or of Employment and Vocation.

The core program connects the curriculum content more directly to the needs of students and demands of society.

A flexible content of problem areas enables the school staff to relate curriculum content more directly to student needs and to societal demands than is possible in the subject-centered program. Courses for students in separate disciplines often promote ground-covering attempts at teaching. Such attempts may have little direct bearing on the real problems of personal development or on the needs of the society that supports education.

In recent years curriculum design for the schools has drawn from two general sources its concept of the learner's needs—studies of individual development and of the social milieu in which children mature. The former source, having as one of its antecedents the emphasis on the "unfolding process" of Rousseau's naturalism, has encouraged a curriculum devoid of any discernible structure. The second source, orienting the curriculum primarily to societal demands, has been largely responsible for incorporating the logically organized bodies of subject matter into basic curriculum structure. Lyman Bryson, formerly with the Columbia Broadcasting Company's "Invitation to Learning" series, reflected this social emphasis when he wrote:

> The first task of every teacher is to arrange, out of superior knowledge and training and years, those experiences for the students which will bring out in them the qualities society has need of. The young learn by their own experiences—as the old do also. The difference is that the experiences out of which the adult finds and creates and criticizes the principles of his living may be accidental; those of the child are arranged by the teacher, who is deputy of the culture.[8]

The core program of general education reconciles these divergent tendencies by organizing for instruction signficant problem areas around which student needs seem to cluster. Emphasis is placed on the personal-social nature of adolescent needs and the qualities of interaction in human experience. Viewed in this light, a concept of youth needs implies study of the adolescent behavior at various maturity levels and also an examination of the whole environmental pattern in which people operate. Study of the adolescent in his culture reveals needs that reflect the regularities and uniformities of the cultural pattern, but also deviations and variations of the individual. A core program with a flexibly planned block of time enables a staff to develop a general curriculum based on common needs in such areas as communication, value clarification, family life, intercultural relations, consumer problems and others of educational significance.

The core offers additional opportunities for improving instruction.

In addition to the foregoing values other obvious advantages of such a program, which call for less analysis, should be cited. For example, the core makes classroom practice consistent with sound learning principles by encouraging genuine problem solving. With curriculum content rooted in the persistent problems of living such as communication, family life, vocational planning, value clarification, community understanding, and others, the learning experience can reflect the important roles of interest, involvement and meaning in the educative process.

The core, with its extended bloc of time, provides the teacher with a curriculum organization which fosters the use of community resources in teaching. Direct firsthand experiences in the community with industrial, social and cultural agencies can be planned and developed without encroaching on time scheduled for other studies.

Furthermore, such a program in the junior high school provides a better transition for the pupil in the shift from the self-contained classroom of the elementary school to the departmentalized program of the senior high school. A junior high school having a core program offers students an experience which contains elements of both the elementary and secondary program. Such an arrangement assures a continuing of emphasis from one level to the next and helps the student make the shift with a minimum of distracting adjustments.

An additional advantage is gained by reducing the amount of pupil-accounting by the teacher. In a time of bulging class enrollments, the core offers the possibility of reducing materially the "student load" of the teacher. In contrast to having six separate classes with an aggregate of 150-180 pupils, the teacher with two core sections has about one-third the number of pupils with whom he may become closely acquainted for effective teaching and guidance.

Finally, the flexibility of organization offers increased possibilities for curriculum revision and improvement. Curriculum modification and improvement are more readily achieved in the flexible structure of the core since here it is not necessary to eliminate, add or rearrange specific courses each time a change seems desirable. Representing a reorganization of general education along a design that would eliminate the necessity for adding new courses constantly, the core offers the possibility for continuous appraisal with changes in emphasis being made as needed.

With education at all levels decrying the rigidity of curriculum structure based on narrow specialization, it seems most crucial in the junior high school to consider a program which asserts the unity of human knowledge but recognizes the need to extend individual talents toward diverse competencies.

Notes

1. The Fund for Adult Education. *Education for Public Responsibility.*

2. Grace Wright. *Block-Time Classes and Core Program in the Junior High School.* Bulletin No. 6, 1958. Washington, D.C.: U.S. Department of Health, Education, and Welfare, p. 1.

3. *Midwest Program on Airborne Television Instruction.* Lafayette, Indiana: Purdue University, 1960, p. 12–13.

4. J.H. Shera. "Knowledge Goes Berserk." *The Saturday Review* 39:69, December 1, 1956.

5. Ralph Tyler. "Curriculum Organization." *The Integration of Educational Experiences.* 57th Yearbook, National Society for the Study of Education. Chicago: The Society, University of Chicago Press, 1958, p. 123.

6. *Ibid.*

7. Elsie Alberty and Lucille Lurry. *Developing a High School Core Program.* New York: The Macmillan Co., 1957, p. 69–89.

8. Lyman Bryson. *The Drive Toward Reason.* New York: Harper and Brothers, 1954, p. 38.

9

Mildred L. Krohn

Learning and the Learning Center

Is it pertinent to the topic to ask how we learn? By questioning, examining, exploring, experimenting, even sometimes when browsing without purpose. To help pupils learn more effectively, it is necessary to make available as many of the tools of learning as possible. To learn independently and at maximum potential for each pupil, instruction in work-study skills is basic. Such instruction can be enhanced and accelerated by the use of a wide range of materials and resources, in addition to books.

For the past two years work-study skills have been taught to elementary school children in Shaker Heights, Ohio, using large group instruction, and with the aid of an overhead projector. This approach grew out of an experimental plan that was tried for a year and then was presented to the Ford Foundation's Fund for the Advancement of Education for a possible grant. Purpose of the project was to help develop ideas for further experimental study. In May 1962, a matching grant was given in the amount of $45,000 to be used over a three year period to teach work-study skills and develop independent study habits. This involved pupils in grades 4, 5 and 6 in two schools: Lomond, with an enrollment of 625, and Ludlow, with 300 pupils.

Self-directed, independent study skills generally have been considered as suitable to the college and graduate study level. This experiment is attempting to prove that these skills can be acquired and used by pupils at an earlier age.

We must recognize that as the volume of knowledge becomes greater the teacher can no longer have all the answers. Consequently, there must be a shift in emphasis from the teaching to the learning aspect. We now see the self-motivated child bringing information to the classroom as a result of independent study which becomes a sharing, with teachers learning from as well as teaching pupils.

This requires a revolutionary shift in the teachers' thinking. Can Johnny actually learn without the teacher being present? We believe he can and does, as he has access to a wide range of materials, direction from teachers and librarians, and as he has motivation to interest him in finding answers, reports, truths, and in how to use these materials to his own best advantage.

Many school libraries today are known as materials centers where all types of materials are provided to enrich and support the curriculum. However, "materials center" does not truly describe the activity taking place there, but rather suggests a place to store or house materials. For the schools in this project a more unique term was wanted that would indicate activity and the role of the library in the learning process. "Learning Center" was selected as the best descriptive term.

The Learning Center

To implement this project, program changes in physical facilities were necessary. In the larger school a wall had to be removed to enlarge the room to about three and a half classrooms in size. Free-standing double-faced shelving is arranged in U-shaped areas down the middle of this large rectangular room to hold the 10,000 volumes. We find that books arranged this way absorb sound and allow several alcoves to accommodate children simultaneously doing different things without noise interference.

At one end of the room are five built-in study carrels, each with an electrical outlet and a filmstrip viewer, well lighted with cork board space on the walls which allows notes and papers to be tacked up for easy viewing. These carrels are extremely popular with the children and help to make their research and viewing a satisfactory and individual experience.

The listening area was developed by building a shelf in a small offset of the former main room and installing jacks so that earphones can be plugged in for student use. Tapes and records are also used here.

Another alcove has filmstrips and viewers on a built-in shelf. Here are also programed materials in the following areas: Organizing and Reporting; Reading Graphs, Charts and Tables; and Basic Library Skills. These are used independently by children, or assigned by the classroom teacher or librarian.

At the smaller school the center moved into the kindergarten room, the largest and one of the most attractive rooms in the school. Here perimeter shelving is used and is adequate for the 7,000 volumes. In this center six free-standing commercially built carrels are used instead of built-in carrels. These have a shelf where encyclopedia sets can be shelved and, with books in proximity, can create a reference area. The viewing area was formerly a closet, but by building a shelf on three sides, boys and girls can sit on stools and use the viewers which are placed on the shelf. The listening area is a table with earphones in one part of the Learning Center.

With this available space and a wide range of materials—books, filmstrips, pictures, recordings, tapes, transparencies—the tools of learning are readily available to the advantage of the learner. Learning becomes attractive in this kind of situation and achievement brings its own satisfactions.

A guide, outlining large group lessons, was used last year in grades four through six. This was rewritten this summer and expanded to two booklets, one a guide, "Suggested Activities To Motivate and Follow Up Large Group Lessons" for the teacher and the other, a "Curriculum Guide for Large Group Instruction in Work-Study Skills," for the librarian.

Teaching Needed Skills

Last year large group lessons were held every other week. This year the group lessons are being held every week, leaving the second semester for reviewing and reteaching skills where needed and for enrichment lessons. From the first year's experience it was learned that all the skills need to be taught as early as possible rather than spacing them throughout a school year. What was taught last May would have helped children use the skills more knowingly if they had been taught as needed.

The basic lessons outlined in the guide are as follows: Orientation to Learning Center; Listening; Card Catalogue; What Study Is; Outlining; Note Taking; Dewey Decimal Classification; Reference Books and Tools; Using the Audio-visual Section of the Learning Center; Techniques of Reporting; Oral Book Reports; Graphs, Charts, Tables and Diagrams; Using Many Sources in Preparing Reports; Map and Globe Studies; Bibliography; Parts of a Book.

These lessons are not listed in the order in which they are being taught, some are repeated in all three grades, but the scope and development varies for each lesson according to the grade level. These lessons are taught in the auditorium weekly by grade level. By teaching all classes of a grade at one time, the center is free from rigid scheduling and blocks of time are thus made available for practicing skills taught and for individual research.

For these lessons pupils are seated on folding chairs to which an arm has been attached to permit them to write. Each child is given a participation sheet which has blanks to be filled in as the librarian teaches the lesson. When completed, these sheets provide a good summary of what has been taught and are also helpful for absentees who miss the lesson.

Transparencies, shown on the overhead projector, have proven to be a most effective teaching aid, and the participation sheets have been the best method of getting total class participation which is not possible orally with a large group.

Last year lessons were taught by the three librarians, one being a former teacher who had recently completed her master's degree in library science. She taught the units that would ordinarily be considered classroom areas, e.g., maps and globes, outlining, graphs, charts, tables and diagrams. This year some lessons will be conducted by teachers and children as well as by the library personnel.

The total staff for this project includes, besides the three librarians, a library aide in each school, an audio-visual clerk and a half-time technician in the larger school. Having a technician to produce transparencies for use with the overhead projector is helpful to staff and students. They are used, not only for large group instruction, but also for class purposes, or for students giving special reports.

Overnight books and reserved book shelves have usually been associated with secondary and college levels. However, the project program has made it necessary to initiate these practices in our two program schools.

Teachers are asked to observe each lesson for their own information and for help in classroom follow-up. They are asked to write constructive criticism for whoever conducts the lesson to strengthen and improve wherever possible any future presentations.

Also this year the classroom teacher is to emphasize follow-up of lessons and utilize specific skills taught in large group lessons by applying them to use in current units in their daily teaching and thus make them more meaningful.

Help for Individuals

Last year's emphasis was on the facilities and their use in the Learning Centers. This year the teacher is to play a more important role by utilizing skills in classroom follow-up and by checking and helping individual children improve their techniques.

In grades 4-6 there are no regularly scheduled library classes except for large group instruction. Instead, teachers are urged to permit pupils to come to the Learning Center as the needs arise logically in the classroom. In talking with teachers, they agree that this is the most difficult change to make in their teaching day. Their teaching methods have not changed, but their concepts of learning are being shifted. Children are not sent to the Center after work in the classroom has been completed, but rather as class discussion requires or provokes the need for immediate information.

One of the problems is what to do with the children in the classroom while six or ten of their classmates are sent to the Learning Center. With emphasis on independent study and individual learning according to ability, the individualized reading time is best to free children to do research without loss by being separated from the group, according to many teachers. Also available are times when children are working individually on projects in science, mathematics or social studies and no class presentation by the teacher is in progress.

Because good teachers are concerned about what and how much the children in their care learn they are naturally reluctant to allow them to leave the classroom and go off "on-their-own." However, after a year of trial, persuasion and observation, teachers are altering their thinking, revising their classroom schedules and witnessing children studying independently, using many kinds of materials on problems of real interest and value to them.

Eagerness for Growth

In summary, the "Activities" guide describes the goals of this experimental program in these words: "If we subscribe to the theory that children *want* to learn, that they are *eager* to grow in knowledge and their ability to apply this acquired knowledge to purposes which are meaningful to them, then we are ready to accept the basic goals of the experimental program in teaching work-study skills and in independent study. If the assignments we make to children in the intermediate grades have real meaning for them in that they help them to find answers to their immediate questions or to fill some present need (rather than as preparation for some nebulous career in the future), the children will not need to be *driven* to finding answers, nor will they need us, as teachers, to stand over them forcing them to study. These children will be ready for *independent study,* the ultimate goal of the experimental program."

After one year, the guide has been rewritten to become two, one for the teacher and one for the librarian; shifting teacher emphasis from factual to conceptual, emphasis has been shifted from the Learning Center to follow-up in the classroom; teaching large group lessons will now include teacher and student personnel. Additional changes will be made as experience warrants these.

Interest in this experiment has brought many visitors and inquiries for information and materials. To free the librarians and principals from conducting tours and answering correspondence, additional funds were granted this year by the Fund for the Advancement of Education. This money provided for an Information Officer to coordinate these duties; also to arrange visitors' schedules, and to publicize and promote the project. In the past month more than 150 sets of the "Curriculum Guide" and "Suggested Activities" books,[1] which were requested have been sent out.

How does one evaluate this project? The Iowa Work-Study Skills Test and the Educational Stimuli Library Skills Examination are being used but are inconclusive in their results to date. However, there is no test, to our knowledge, that truly measures how children have grown in independence in using the varied resources in the Learning Center. The use of the card catalogue and the location of materials improved considerably during the year, as did pupils' ability to work independently. Perhaps with more experience a test can be developed that can objectively evaluate this type of program.

While only two schools are involved in this experiment, all of our elementary schools have either moved libraries into larger existing quarters (kindergarten rooms or auditoriums), or have plans to enlarge by moving or enlarging existing libraries. It has also necessarily affected our secondary schools. If children are being taught work-study skills and have the opportunity to work independently in the Learning Center, this must continue in junior and senior high school.

The most important consequence of this experiment, hopefully, will come through the experiences children have in this program. If they can be developed into secondary and college students who pursue their academic interests in an independent, meaningful and increasingly successful manner, the true purpose of learning will have been served.

Note

1. Available for $5.00 from Information Officer, F. A. E. Project, Shaker Heights City School District, 15600 Parkland Drive, Shaker Heights 20, Ohio.

10

Charles S. Partin

To Sample—
or to Explore

Since its inception the junior high school has justified its existence through the stated objective that it meets the educational needs of adolescent age students. Educators often state that in this period a special program is needed for and special help is required by the student. They hold that students at this age level, the transition from childhood to young adulthood, should, in addition to the general educational experiences, be provided an opportunity to identify their specific talents and abilities.

The junior high school student needs to explore his world. He is becoming more aware of himself as a person and is concerned with questions that have to do with himself as a person and his identity as such. He is concerned about the use that he makes of himself in attaining objectives that are important to him.

The adolescent knows that achieving adulthood is important. He is searching for ways to achieve this goal. He is interested in knowing what the adult world is like and how a feeling of being adult differs from that of being a child. He can remember what it is like to be a child and in imagination he has played at being an adult and at doing adult things. He needs to "check out" these imaginings against reality and to find out what he is—what he is in this transition zone between

From *Educational Leadership* (December, 1965): 194-99. Reprinted with the permission of the Association for Supervision and Curriculum Development and Charles S. Partin. Copyright © 1965 by the Association for Supervision and Curriculum Development.

childhood and adulthood. The exploratory program may provide each student an opportunity to retrace through memory the road that he has traveled, to look around himself at his present world, and to project himself into the future through imagination.

A Search for Meaning

To make its position clear on the purpose and function of the exploratory program the National Association of Secondary-School Principals recently presented this definition:

Exploration is that function of the junior high school which provides each student a breadth of experiences that will broaden his horizons, develop his interests, and identify his attitudes, strengths, and weaknesses in vocational, educational, and avocational pursuits (1).

The meaning of exploration as defined here hinges on the word *experience.* If experience is looked upon as both an active and a passive affair, as Dewey (4) defined the term, exploration becomes a comprehensive activity. The activity becomes a well-planned, coordinated unit within which the student does something to things and ideas and they in turn (the passive phase) do something to him. The activity becomes an experience as the student takes meaning from what is done to him. He is passively taking from the activity a meaning, a way of seeing, that affects his future behavior and becomes a guide for future action. Meaning is dependent upon both the active and passive phase of the activity.

A child puts his hand into a flame and withdraws it suddenly. The child actively does something to the flame when he puts his hand into it. He receives the action of the flame and takes from it the meaning "hot" or pain. The flame now takes on new meaning for the child. It is seen in a different way; it is something to avoid, something that can cause pain. There has been no experience, according to Dewey, unless both phases of the activity have been completed.

In the classroom or shop the active phase of the exploratory experience occurs when the student does something with or to a thing, idea, etc.; when he is pursuing an active course. The activity may be of short of long duration. The passive phase of the activity occurs when the student sees or gets the meaning of the activity—when the meaning of the thing or idea is established for the student. The passive phase occurs when the student answers for himself the question, "What does it mean for or to me?"

More Than Sampling

In many school situations students are scheduled for short periods in various kinds of activities that are called exploratory, but which are really only sampling operations. In such activities the student is given a chance to do something to things but the meaning of what the things do for him is left to chance. Anything that is learned in this type of activity is fortuitous. In such situations the activity becomes activity for activity's sake. In a sampling operation, working with the refrigeration unit may become a routine mechanical operation for the student. He would probably see only the parts of the machine and learn how to fit part with part so that the machine would function. Any learning other than what one does to the machine is left to chance.

A much more profitable operation for the student would be the opportunity to round out the process. Through the exploratory activity the student may have an opportunity to look at the machine in relation to man. Such questions as "What does refrigeration contribute to the health, welfare, comfort and happiness of people?" "What is it like becoming a refrigeration mechanic?", may be answered by the student for himself.

He needs to explore the questions: "Does this vocation offer me the opportunity to actualize my potential?" "What opportunity does this vocation offer me to gain the community status or esteem that I need?" These and other questions that the student will ask need to be explored. The student needs to find the answers both from within himself and from the responses he hears his peers make to the questions. He needs to have a significant (to him) adult help him in his search for valid answers to his questions.

Although getting into "right" courses and a "right" vocation or profession is important, an individual's success or failure in school and in life is dependent upon other factors about which the school may do something. How one feels about himself, his way of seeing himself, is such an area. It may be that as important as native ability to the success of an individual in any vocation or profession is his feeling about himself.

The Self Is Important

Each student is constantly trying himself out and taking in meanings through which he views himself. He is constantly searching for answers to such questions as "Who am I?" "What am I like?" "What things can I do well?" "How do people feel about me?" These and other questions that relate to the idea of self are pressing concerns of adolescents. Each, in his own way, and in unsupervised and often destructive ways, is constantly finding answers to these questions. The answers one finds, on his own, are quite often invalid and unsound. The answers that young people get to these questions, when they search on their own, may actually thwart self-fulfillment.

Self-exploration that leads to a knowledge of what self is like may be very productive in terms of personal satisfaction and growth. Not only may the student get insight into his own inner being but he may gain, through experience, a knowledge of the conditions conducive to self-exploration and self-discovery. This knowledge and understanding may help students find some solid footing in what Norman Cousins calls "Life Inside the Centrifuge" (3). He has the opportunity to bring his emotional knowing and his intellectual or conceptual knowledge into congruency.

The atmosphere that is made safe for self-exploration will also be one in which what is discovered in exploration can be accepted. The accepting teacher can create an atmosphere in which the truth one finds about himself can be accepted without efforts at distortion, refutation or repudiation (2). It is in the accepting atmosphere that the student is given a chance to find that he is more than a thing with which something is done. It is in this type of atmosphere that he comes to see himself as a thinker of thoughts, a doer of deeds, a maker of decisions, a fully human person.

Acceptance of self by any individual may conserve great amounts of individual emotional and intellectual energy. If the individual is unable to accept himself he will be forced to expend undetermined amounts of time, energy and effort in defending the unacceptable facets of himself. He may, on the other hand, join a group where normally undesirable behavior is acceptable. A student is unable to devote adequate time and attention to scholarship when so much is consumed in proving to himself and his peers that he is an acceptable person.

Need To Explore Feelings

Students bring to school their feelings about themselves, about others, about school and home, about adults and the adult world, about adult expectations of them and about teachers and their expectations (5). There may be feelings of hostility and resentment that are expressed in outbursts of anger or other overt, destructive behavior. They bring to school with them their feelings of fear; fear of failure, fear of non-acceptance, and other fears. They bring their feelings of frustration and futility—the gamut of feelings with which people live. The physical expression of these emotions may take many forms from open hostility to extreme withdrawal. Although these emotions are present, students are taught, through external pressure, that only positive feelings are permitted in the classroom. "You mustn't feel that way," students are told.

The feelings that students have are there and should be looked at by them. Students need to explore these feelings, label them and discover the reason for their existence. They need to be permitted to search for acceptable ways of expressing all of the feelings they experience. In the safe atmosphere of an exploratory situation one may say, "I feel angry when . . ." and find the feeling of anger not demanding expression in destructive outbursts. They may look at their fear of failure, their fear of being disliked and find them less awesome when brought into the light of open discussion.

Feelings of fear are threatening and people who operate under a cloud of threat are unable to function in an optimum way. If students are able to deal with their fears and frustrations through verbal identification of cause and effect the energy formerly used to defend could be used to gain and maintain growth momentum.

Patterns of feeling are the stuff in which patterns of thought are rooted. Erich Fromm, in his book *May Man Prevail?*, says, "Patterns of thought are rooted in patterns of feeling . . ." (6). Since patterns of thought and patterns of feeling seem to be so inextricably interwoven, a change in thought patterns requires a change in patterns of feeling. This change cannot occur in a vacuum nor can ignoring feelings bring about a change in them. Like any other subject matter they must be "looked at" and the meaning out of which feelings arise must be discussed and become a part of the knowledge an individual has.

As one learns to take realistic meanings from his environment, his feelings come to match reality. As this occurs the individual can afford to *be* his feelings. His anger at injustice becomes indignation, and his behavior a rational program designed to alleviate a situation that to him seems unjust. As one becomes able to accept his feelings, to experience them, he is able to function more fully, effectively and creatively (7).

Need to Know What One Values

The values one holds are important. It is important that each person has opportunity, through exploration, to identify those values which he really holds and those to which lip service is given. The student needs opportunity to find out what he really values as well as what he values because others think he should. In an exploratory program, a student has opportunity to hear others express their values and their reasons for holding these values. He is placed in a position of being able to express his values and have them looked at and in the looking be able to sift out the pseudo-values from the real ones. The student will probably find that there are values to which all of the other students give allegiance. He may find that he holds values which are common to all people with whom he relates while others are unique to small groups or just to him.

It seems important, in this age of mobility, that students become aware of the value systems of others and come to respect the different systems while maintaining their own. They may understand that certain values, such as the Golden Rule, the value of human life, honesty, truthfulness, integrity, chastity, have universal application and that becoming a fully-functioning member of society requires allegiance to these.

In a society such as ours which professes a belief in freedom, this concept needs to be explored and clarified by students. Too often in our history freedom has been seen by individuals and groups in a very selfish way. Such persons or groups have seen freedom as applying only to them. They have seen freedom as the right to deny it to others, to exercise and apply one's own prejudices, to deny privilege and rights, to demand conformity to one's own values or system. Through exploration of the meaning of freedom, students may come to see that the freedom of each is dependent upon the freedom that each other one is given.

The need to be free seems to be a part of being human. People, to be fully human, need to be free and the meaning of being human needs to be explored. The road from savagery toward full humanness has been long in terms of time and effort. People need to explore the meaning of humanness, of becoming, and of being human. The understanding of the meaning of human growth and maturity is important. This kind of exploration may be a part of the humanities program.

For the economy, the technology, and the culture to remain healthy and vigorous, the uniqueness of the individual must be valued and respected. Through exploring the meaning of uniqueness, students may come to see that valuable contributions to the world of science, mathematics, technology, literature, art, etc., have been made by people because of their uniqueness; because they think differently. Yet the success of the exploratory program depends upon the complete respect for uniqueness and the right of the individual to express this uniqueness, the right to express divergent opinions and ideas. The entire exploratory program may contribute to this value which is so important to a free and open society.

A Time, A Place, A Group

The gratification of the need to feel esteemed, to experience success, to feel safe in one's world will not be put off into some distant future. If the student is unable to find satisfaction of these needs in socially approved ways, he may turn to unacceptable activities in search of satisfaction. The adolescent "gang-world," for example, may become the medium through which he satisfies his needs. Power as a gang leader may be seen as a means of satisfying the esteem need. Membership in the gang may be seen as a way of satisfying the safety need, and becoming effective in the performance of gang activities may be seen as satisfying the self-fulfillment need. In the larger social scene, however, any or all of the substitute activities become need frustrating and growth inhibiting. The struggle to satisfy these needs may become so great that all energy and every inner resource is devoted to gratifying them.

If, through exploration, students, with understanding help, can identify their strengths and competencies, they can use these as means to satisfy needs. They will be able to elect courses and select activities in which they can experience the satisfaction of accomplishment and success. They will be able to identify themselves with a group holding similar interests and abilities and gain a feeling of safety through belonging. They can gain esteem from peers and teachers and utilize their abilities and talents which need to be used.

We must not confuse sampling with exploring. In sampling we get the sensation but we may not get the meaning. We may savor the bits of food laid out on a table without understanding the meaning of the specific food for the human body. In exploring there is the search for the deeper meaning—not only for how things seem but how things are.

This type of exploration can provide faculties and administrators with the information they need as they strive to build programs to hold the dropouts in school and meet the needs of all students. In a free-flowing, exploratory program, students will give the school information about their needs, their talents, abilities and goals. As this information comes to the faculty, it can be used as elective courses are developed, and as activity programs are evaluated and planned. Course content may be selected and materials and methodology can be adapted to the identified need and ability level of the student served. The exploratory program may offer the student the opportunity to explore, vicariously and in safety, the culture and ways that he would like to fit into it.

A comprehensive exploratory program, operating under optimum conditions, can give students an opportunity to find their way. It can provide them opportunity to develop a realistic view of self and a positive regard for others. It can give them an opportunity to scan the world of work and the world of values. It can provide them a time, a place and a group where they can feel emotionally safe and personally esteemed. It may be the only time in their daily lives that some students can experience this feeling.

An exploratory program may become the medium through which both student and teacher discover the means at the student's disposal for the achievement of their joint enterprise.

References

1. Delmar H. Battrick. "What Do We Believe About the Exploratory Function of the Junior High School?" *Bulletin of the National Association of Secondary-School Principals*, October 1962.

2. A. W. Combs, editor. *Perceiving, Behaving, Becoming.* Washington, D.C.: Association for Supervision and Curriculum Development, 1962.

3. Norman Cousins. "Life Inside the Centrifuge." *Saturday Review,* August 29, 1964.

4. John Dewey. *Democracy and Education.* New York: The Macmillan Co., 1916.

5. L. K. Frank. *Feelings and Emotions.* New York: Random House, 1954.

6. Erich Fromm. *May Man Prevail?* Garden City, New York: Anchor Books, 1961.

7. Carl Rogers. *On Becoming a Person.* Boston: Houghton Mifflin Co., 1961.

11

Robert W. Heller
& James C. Hansen

The Middle School and Implications for the Guidance Program

The present day interpretation of the middle school concept still presents problems to some educators, school board members, and other lay citizens. This can partially be explained as a result of the unusual organizational patterns of the middle school and, perhaps more importantly, by the lack of sound educational rationale in support of the concept during the early stages of the present movement.

In a publication of the Educational Facilities Laboratory the position for not attempting to solidify a rationale for the middle school is suggested: "In a way, it is no misfortune that the middle-school concept is as fluid as it is. There is a case to be made for keeping it so, and for not endowing this new kind of school with a full-fledged rationale."[1] This raises the question of how educators can endorse the middle school movement if they do not develop supportive rationale. Therefore, the authors will attempt to provide rationale in support of the middle school and discuss in some details the emerging role of the guidance program within this new organizational pattern.

Rationale

Basic to the concept of the middle school is that it should provide an environment that will foster meeting the needs of students who are

From *Peabody Journal of Education* (March, 1969): 291–97.

entering adolescence. The middle school should help students gain a sense of self-identity and an inner stability that will allow them to make the transition from pre-adolescence to adolescence.[2] Popper identified the paramount goal of the middle school in the modern era as:

> The differentiated function—hence, the paramount goal—
> of the American middle school is to intervene protectively
> in the process of education which was begun in the elemen-
> tary school, mediate between the human condition at the
> onset of adolescence and the pressures of culture and con-
> tinue the general education of early adolescents with a
> curriculum applied in a psychosocial environment which is
> functional for learning at this stage of socialization.[3]

Cuff perceives the rationale for the middle school as emerging for four basic reasons. He feels that increased enrollment, integration, pressure to restore the four year high school and the vocal critics of the junior high school precipitated the movement towards today's middle schools.[4] One could not examine the growth of the middle school without awareness of the junior high school movement. The attitude of many educators today is that the junior high school has failed to adequately meet the needs of a particularly unique group of students, the young teenagers. The image "Junior" has been contribu-tory, for instead of providing an identity of its own it has mimicked the senior high school. Conant is only one of many who was ". . . shocked by the Junior High School overemphasis on athletics, preten-tious graduation ceremonies, and other frills in imitation of the high school."[5] Rice further supports this position when he says, "The pat-tern of the junior high school closely parallels the senior high but with little evidence to justify it. . . . Its curriculum is pushed down from the grades above it, so that in all too many instances it really is a prep school for the senior high."[6]

It is not that educators could not have provided for the achieve-ment of the goals established for the junior high school but the fact is they did not. There should be no doubt that the supporters of the present middle school movement are concerned that the junior high school has done little in the past to meet the educational, emotional, and psychological needs of children. A basic precept for the develop-ment of the middle school is that it is designed and planned to meet the needs of children from ages ten to 14. The middle school is defined by Murphy as a school between two other schools. This weaning away period from the self-contained classroom to the subject centered discipline of the high school would take into account special needs and capabilities of children in the years between childhood and adolescence. The middle school, as perceived by Murphy, would best encompass the social, psychological, physical, and intellectual range of children ages ten to 14.[7]

Nickerson states that we must have a middle school "... because the needs of these fifth through eighth graders can be met better in this arrangement than in the three year junior high school of grades seven, eight, and nine."[8] He feels that there is enough evidence to support the fact that children are physically and emotionally maturing earlier than during the period when junior high schools were first conceived.

Madon supports the middle school because it is able to offer a curriculum particularly at the sixth grade level, which best serves children who have intellectual, social, physical, and emotional needs that are similar. Further, he feels that the middle school serves the child best because it takes into account the child's need for peer recognition and at the same time allows the student to become more aware of himself as an individual. This is done best when there is a balance, "... between specialized instruction on a departmental basis and the need for security and recognition which comes through self-contained classrooms."[9]

According to Madon, the real advantages of the middle school are fewer discipline problems, less academic pressure on the middle school youngsters, and the opportunity for the high school counselors to follow a student through four years of high school rather than have a new counselor for a high school student once he leaves the ninth grade. He does provide a word of caution. The middle school is "... not a miniature high school—it is a transition experience that is accompanied by marked physical and intellectual changes which affect the social and emotional responses of the child."[10]

The Middle School Concept

The focus thus far has been on presenting supportive rationale for the presently emerging concept of the middle school. This included a brief discussion of the role the junior high school has played in this movement due to its alleged failure to meet the objectives for which it was organized. However, one might ask, "Just what is the middle school?" The authors perceive it as a separate physical structure (possibly within an educational park) for grades 5, 6, 7 and 8 with an appropriate program for students in these grades. Appropriate program is interpreted as meaning it will provide a curriculum containing advanced placement, remedial placement, and overall more responsible placement of pupils than is now being done in either the self-centered, child-centered upper elementary school classroom or the rather impersonal departmentalized high school oriented junior high school. It is an intermediate school, a school between two other schools, standing on its own merits, and does not represent a watered down high school setting.

The middle school is organized to take better account of the needs and abilities of the children it is serving and provides an opportunity to use a variety of instructional innovations. Grouping patterns may or may not be used depending upon the philosophy of the school plus the needs and interests of the students. The objectives of the middle school may not vary much from those of the junior high school. However, it is being perceived by many as a vehicle through which many of our present economic and social problems may better be solved, particularly for racially integrating schools. Examples of this are New York City and Buffalo who are adopting the 4-4-4 organizational pattern which includes the middle school as an entity different from the traditional junior high school. Buffalo plans to use the first 4-year sequence to preserve the neighborhood school concept and begin integrating students beginning with the second 4-year sequence, or in the middle school.[11] New York City, on the other hand, wishes to promote high quality education and at the same time promote racial integration using the middle school as the vehicle to accomplish these goals. The plan in New York City is to replace all of the 138 junior high schools with a network of middle schools by 1972.[12]

Curricular Program

Because adolescence is a period in which there is a great diversity in rates of growth, differences in ability to do school work and learning rates, the individualization of instruction is of paramount importance.

Consideration of these factors has resulted in flexible curricular construction and the examination of a great number of guidance functions by the classroom teacher. Contemporary views of the curriculum no longer refer solely to the content of special subject areas and required courses. There is a realization that the curriculum must relate to the needs of students for optimal learning to take place. Curriculum includes the sum total of the planned learning experiences and activities that the school provides for the education of students. The curriculum may be regarded as the basic tool through which the school's philosophy, and the philosophy and values of the society are learned. It includes all the experiences under the direction of the school. This point is echoed by Lefever when he says, "The curriculum is nothing less than the sum total of all student experiences, formal or informal, which takes place both within and without the classroom walls."[13]

There may be no period more critical in the span of education than the period which covers the years of early adolescence. At this time the needs of the individual are heavily influenced by social realities and values which impinge upon his life. Learning appropriate set roles and learning to behave independently with social assurance and social effectiveness are also significant.

Guidance Services and the Curriculum

The passage of the National Defense Education Act in 1958 was instrumental in providing guidance services at the elementary level. The establishment of these services has resulted in an increasing acceptance of them as important contributors to the overall objectives of the American educational system. The contemporary view of guidance has expanded a great deal since 1958. It now includes the primary objective of providing guidance assistance to all children in their normal development, both socially and educationally. This objective when applied to the level of the middle school is influenced by the needs of early adolescence which have the greatest importance as determinants of the student's success in setting goals, meeting objectives, and alleviating concerns.

The guidance services most frequently found in the school are organized around four service areas: appraisal, information, counseling, and the service area which includes the service of placement and followup.[14] The appraisal service handles the coordination and analysis of data obtained from any of the appropriate sources available to the counselor which enables him to better understand the needs of the child. Through proper utilization of these data the child is able to achieve a better understanding of himself. The data may be obtained from objective and subjective test results, information from counseling, or other sources which yield a variety of personal, psychological or social information about the student. The guidance activities of the information service are concerned with information about the world around students, i.e., vocational, educational, and personal-social opportunities and the use of such information should afford the student a sound basis upon which to make decisions. The service of planning, placement, and follow-up in the middle school involves helping the children plan their study habits and plan their movement into the senior high school. It also involves the counselors working with teachers and administrators in placing students in the proper groupings, as well as a follow-up to evaluate how effectively the student is coping with his environment. The counseling service is designed to facilitate self understanding. It is through this service that the counselor applies his skills directly with the student. Therefore, the counselor uses individual and group counseling to try to improve the child's interaction with himself and significant others. It is also necessary to provide assistance for all children rather than just those with problems. Counseling may be only partially effective unless teacher and parent attitudes of the child are also modified. Therefore, the counselor will work with parents and teachers to improve their understanding of the child and his situation. It is through communication with the teacher that environmental change can be introduced as it is controlled by the teacher. This is based on the concept that the child's behavior is determined by social reinforcement and, therefore, the changes introduced by his parents or teachers will lead to a change in the child's behavior.

The middle unit in the educational system may have a curriculum which lacks the necessary flexibility to allow for individual differences in the adolescent pupil. The subject centered organization passed down from the high school is, unfortunately, not an exception. In such a system the curriculum may still meet both the common and the special needs of young people to some extent. Certain courses for study may be selected by some students and special needs may in some cases be handled by the teacher. The common needs are allowed for in the curriculum prior to the teacher acquaintance with the individual children. The curriculum, however, must be continually replanned in the light of the individual patterns of strengths and weaknesses. With a subject oriented curriculum this may be difficult. The lack of flexibility does not allow for consideration of various social, emotional, physical, and intellectual factors. It has become increasingly obvious that if the needs of individual pupils are to be met in the curriculum, such needs must be first ascertained. The counselor is in the best position to do this. Guidance in a school with a traditional, somewhat inflexible curriculum generally applies to a service which is offered in addition to the regular curriculum. In such a situation it becomes clear that although the process which takes place in guidance is clearly within our definition of curriculum, it is not recognized as such by many teachers and administrators. The counselor is forced to act in a remedial capacity adjusting students and their programs to lessen the problems that each individual encounters in the school. With a heavy counselor-client load, however, it becomes virtually impossible for the service to meet the individual needs of all students. Therefore, the counselor's main function in this organization must be to facilitate each teacher's knowledge of the needs, abilities, and interests of each child.

However, in the middle school when working individually with the teacher, the counselor assists through giving of information, participating in classroom observations of children's behavior, discussing information obtained from tests and counseling sessions, discussing guidance techniques that the teacher can utilize, referring to other special services that may be available, and explaining to the teacher what assistance can be expected from these services.

In the middle school the counselor must take an active part on the curriculum committee and provide pupil personnel information. With the increase in the number of counselors, teacher aides, psychologists and other specialists, the educational team has been forced to become more open and communicative about what is really going on in the classroom. Working with parents and teachers, the counselor must stress the concept of individual differences as one which has given us productive direction in education.

Guidance functions in the middle school are perceived as a more integrated part of the curriculum through block time, core curriculum, and team teaching. As such, our attempts to help children through the curriculum provide adequate opportunity for teachers to carry on the guidance function. The counselor's competencies in child development, learning theory, human relations, and curriculum design are challenged by this program. He assumes a leadership role in areas of diagnosing student's levels of development, planning learning experiences to complement developmental stages, and re-orienting curricular patterns for alignment of flexible curricular structures. One danger of this curricular plan is teacher susceptibility to "teach for tests." The counselor sensitizes teachers to the whole child evaluation process. The guidance services of appraisal, placement, and consultation become an integral part of the educational program. In addition, much of the counselor's time is spent in individual and group counseling. He provides each student an opportunity to learn about himself and his environment. The counselor helps plan for and maintain an educational atmosphere where each student can engage in meaningful learning.

Summary

Not all educators share the enthusiasm for the middle school as portrayed here. Frequently one hears the danger cry that the middle school will follow the same path as the junior high school which only imitated the senior high and did not develop a specific curricular program based upon the needs of children at that age level. However, the authors have attempted to present sound educational rationale which supports the middle school movement. Of crucial importance is Alexander's suggestion that any plan for the middle school should include instruments for rigorous careful evaluation of results.[15]

It is impossible to conceive of the middle school without a strong guidance program which should be strengthened by the recognition of individual abilities and talents. Student problems will be recognized earlier and there should be benefit to the student from having a more direct contact with teachers and guidance personnel on an individualized basis. The counselor can aid the teacher in better understanding pupils and placement for meeting individual needs.

It is vital to the middle school program that efficient and well-prepared guidance counselors be available, in sufficient quantity, to understand and assist in the development of each pupil's program. To really help this age group of children, the total pupil personnel services staff must know each child, his assets and disabilities. The pupil personnel services staff must work with the classroom teachers in developing the student's total educational program. Not only should they assist in developing academic programs but also offer guidance with the social activities and psychological problems encountered by students. Social competition can often be destructive as we sometimes experience with athletic and academic competition.

The master classroom teacher and the efficient pupil guidance program are the keys to the success of the middle school program. Working together with the administration, the pitfalls which doomed the junior high school may be avoided.

References

1. Judith Murphy, *Middle School* (New York: Educational Facilities Laboratory, 1965).

2. Paul Gastwirth, "Questions Facing the Middle School," *The Clearing House*, Volume 41, No. 8, April 1967, pp. 472–476.

3. Samuel H. Popper, *The American Middle School* (Massachusetts: Blaisdell Publishing Company, 1967), pp. 48–49.

4. William A. Cuff, "Middle Schools on the March," *The Bulletin* of the National Association of Secondary School Principals, February 1967, pp. 82–86.

5. James B. Conant quoted by Fred Hechinger, *Educational Supplement New York Times*, May 24, 1964.

6. Arthur Rice, "What's Wrong With Junior Highs? Nearly Everything," *The Nation's Schools*, 74:30–32, November 1964.

7. Murphy, *op. cit.*

8. Neal C. Nickerson, "Regroup for Another Try," *Minnesota Journal of Education*, November 1966, p. 14.

9. Constant A. Madon, "The Middle School: Its Philosophy and Purpose," *The Clearing House*, Volume 40, No. 6, February 1966, p. 330.

10. *Ibid.*

11. "A Plan for Accelerating Quality Integrated Education in the Buffalo Public School System," The State Education Department, Albany, New York, August 19, 1966.

12. Cuff, *op. cit.* p. 83.

13. D. W. Lefever, A. M. Turrell, and H. D. Weitzel, *Principles and Techniques of Guidance*, New York: Ronald Press, Inc., 1950.

14. Bruce Shertzer and Shelly Stone, *Foundations of Guidance*, New York: Houghton Mifflin Company, 1966.

15. William M. Alexander, "What Educational Plan for the In-Between-Ager?", *NEA Journal, Volume 55, No. 3, March 1966, pp. 30-32.*

12

Louis Romano

A Revolution in Middle School Education— Individually Guided Education

> It is not possible to spend any prolonged period visiting public school classrooms without being appalled by the multilation visible everywhere—mutilation of spontaneity, of joy in learning, of pleasure in creating, of sense of self.
> —CHARLES E. SILBERMAN
> *Crisis in the Classroom*

Dare our schools continue public education where the formal classroom environment is often detrimental to education and casts a "grim" and "joyless" light on learning?[1] Should our teachers and administrators be preoccupied with order and control in our schools? Should we be satisfied with the rigid teacher—the one with neat rows of quiet kids—who sees the school as a collection of assembly-line receptacles to be properly positioned for maximum filling? Should we continue to pay tax dollars for schools where, as Marshall McLuhan states, children go to school to have their education interrupted? The time has come for our public to prepare a quick funeral for the lock-step or strait-jacket school!

The seeds of a revolution in our public schools are scattered, but through the efforts of organizations such as the University of Wisconsin's Research and Development Center for Cognitive Learning, these

From *Michigan Journal of Secondary Education* (Summer, 1971): 7–15.

seeds have been planted, cultivated and harvested, resulting in programs including Individually Guided Education. Several years of research supported by Federal money under the Elementary and Secondary Education Act have provided a means of seeking more effective teaching-learning strategies. Recently, a study of the research results was made by I.D.E.A. (Institute for the Development of Educational Activities), an organization sponsored by the Kettering Foundation, whose sole purpose is the dissemination and implementation of educational innovations. They supported the concept of Individually Guided Education enthusiastically and developed the necessary training materials (films, soundfilm strips, and publications) to implement the I.G.E. program in public schools within the country and American Schools overseas.

The I.G.E. Concept

What is I.G.E.? As defined by the I.D.E.A. staff, *Individual Guided Education is a learning program designed to meet the learning needs of the individual on the basis of an assessment of his achievement, aptitudes, and overall learning personality as these are related to his learning objectives.* To achieve this goal, an I.G.E. school is a "multiunit school," or has a "school-within-a-school" organizational pattern. An I.G.E. school is more than an administrative strategy. It combines differentiated staffing, nongradedness, and team teaching to produce a teaching-learning environment dedicated to individualizing education according to the learning needs of each child—a tailor-made program for each student. Stated another way, *it is a school designed for children rather than forcing the children to fit the school.* The goals of I.G.E. can only be realized through a commitment from the administrators and teachers within a school. With the well-prepared training materials and a trained consultant, the I.G.E. program can be implemented successfully in a relatively short time.

The Administrative Organization

The multiunit school is made up of teams or units of teachers, paraprofessionals and inter-age groups of boys and girls. In the diagram shown below, the teachers have the opportunity to decide in which unit they want to be a working member, and to choose a leader for

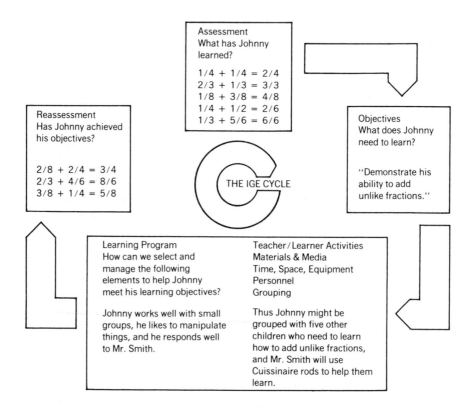

the team. Included is an instructional aide who might be a cadet teacher or a paid paraprofessional. It is imperative that the unit interview the paraprofessional to insure that there will be a good working relationship among the members. Each team includes a clerical aide, who prepares all of the mimeographed materials needed by the unit or team. If a team is fortunate, a talented clerical aide could also be used to develop any graphic materials needed for the teaching-learning situation.

Instructional Improvement Council

Each team leader automatically becomes a member of the Instructional Improvement Committee, which is made up of team leaders, auxiliary staff (Learning Center Director, Music Teacher, etc.) and the building principal. The I.I.C. meets regularly with the principal to help determine policies and guidelines for improving instruction, to help coordinate the use of schoolwide facilities and resources, and to help evaluate the progress of the school in achieving its objectives. Each team leader is the formal liaison between the team and the principal and provides input to the I.I.C. for problems beyond the scope of the team, and provides feedback to members of each team on proposed schoolwide plans and policies. Under this arrangement, the role of the principal changes drastically. He no longer "runs" a school, but rather centers his major concerns and his energy on the problems of the instructional program of each of the teaching teams. As Mary Muehring, principal of Sukiran Elementary School states, "With the I.I.C. the principal is relieved of the entire responsibility for making decisions on the instructional program; I now feel that I have eleven assistants." Furthermore, the role of the teacher changes in an I.G.E. school. She now becomes a decision-maker, not only in the team situations, but also in all school policies and procedures through the Instructional Improvement Committee.

Planned Change Through In-Service

Setting up the administrative organization for an innovative program is easy, but the most important and most difficult task is to bring about behavioral changes on the part of the principal and his staff. These essential changes can only be made through carefully planned and *regularly-scheduled* in-service meetings. Some of the more pertinent changed behaviors essential in the staff to fully realize an I.G.E. school are as follows.

1. *To learn how to plan in a team situation.* Team planning is the key to success in a multiunit school. In the in-service session, the teams discuss the four component parts of planning: goal setting meeting, design meeting, school and group meetings, and situational meeting. Only when the staff learns the ingredients of each of the four components and has an opportunity to be involved in simulated planning, will the team function effectively. As a staff member of one of the units stated: "The excitement of planning together as each team member thought of a new and different activity to challenge all students was truly stimulating. The training and new ideas have added much enthusiasm to my efforts in team teaching. The critiquing after

we finished teaching certainly helped us to see if our activities were helping to achieve our goals, or if they were unnecessary busy work."

But teams will only be successful if time is allotted for them to plan. On Wednesdays the boys and girls of the Sukiran School (Okinawa) are bussed to school at 10 o'clock, which enables the team to have almost two hours for planning sessions. To make up the time, the students remain in school a short time at the end of each school day. Other planning sessions can be arranged by the team through manipulation of their schedules and by using the auxiliary teachers. As Helen Goddard, Coordinator Elementary Education, Okinawa, stated, "It's beautiful to see how the team members pool together all of their ideas and to pick each others' brains. Much better decisions are forthcoming and result in some exciting teaching situations for the youngsters."

2. *To define objectives behaviorally.* During the in-service sessions, the staff learns how to define the objectives for the instructional program in behavioral terms. These objectives are clearly written so that the learner can observe his own behavior, and knows when he has achieved the desired objectives.

3. *To learn the use of pre-assessment and post-assessment tools.* Teachers at all levels assume that the youngsters know little or nothing about a particular topic to be studied. In an I.G.E. school this is not true. Prior to teaching a unit of study in social studies or science, a member of the team prepares a pre-assessment tool on the particular unit to be taught. The team membership then critiques the appropriateness of the assessment tool. Once approved by the team, the pre-assessment tool is administered to all of the youngsters in the team. On the basis of these tests, the youngsters are grouped, i.e., those who cannot demonstrate successful performance on the behavioral objectives defined are grouped in one section, while those who have demonstrated that they understand some of the behavioral objectives are grouped in another section, etc.

A post-assessment tool is designed to be used with the children after they have been exposed to the materials and activities for the various behavioral objectives in the unit of study. If the child shows that he has achieved the objectives, he can move on to the next unit. However, if the child has not attained the objectives, he is re-cycled in the

Principal			
INSTRUCTIONAL IMPROVEMENT COMMITTEE			
Unit A	Unit B	Unit C	Unit D
1 Unit Leader	1 Unit Leader	1 Unit Leader	1 Unit Leader
4 Teachers	4 Teachers	4 Teachers	4 Teachers
1 Instructional Aide	1 Instructional Aide	1 Instructional Aide	1 Instructional Aide
1 Clerical Aide	1 Clerical Aide	1 Clerical Aide	1 Clerical Aide
150 Pupils Ages 9,10,11	150 Pupils Ages 8,9,10	150 Pupils Ages 7,8,9	150 Pupils Ages 5,6,7

teaching-learning situation until his performance shows that he understands and has mastered the defined objectives.

4. *To learn the techniques employed in critiquing the work of the teaching team.* The evaluation of teacher performance is imperative if teachers are to improve their teaching, but in an I.G.E. school the methodology is vastly different. Rather than the principal supervising in a teacher's class two or three times a year, the critiquing of teaching may be done by the principal and/or teachers in the form of an observation team. The techniques to be used by the teaching team prior to teaching and in preparation for meeting with the observation team, and the techniques to be used by the observation team are discussed. Every effort is made to assist the teaching team to improve its performance, but at the same time the observation team improves themselves by critiquing the teaching situation observed. Approximately once a month, each teaching team participates in a critiquing session with an observation team.

5. *To learn how to ungrade the skills taught in reading, mathematics and spelling.* Teachers in an I.G.E. school become involved in developing a sequential list of the skills to be developed in the fore-

going instructional area. After these lists are developed, they are divided arbitrarily by the staff into levels. These materials are then used to determine where a child is at a particular time; to determine groupings within the team; to know what skills are to be developed on a particular level, to determine how much a child has accomplished in the skills included in the level, and to help parents know the progress being made by their children in these skill areas.

6. *To develop a unit of study based upon ideas presented.* As was pointed out, planning is essential to the success of an I.G.E. school. In the first component of planning, the goal setting meeting, the team teachers define the topic to be covered in the next science or social studies unit. This decision is made on the basis of past units covered, and interests and needs of the boys and girls in the team. Each member of the team must develop a unit of study by defining the behavioral objectives, the activities and materials needed to realize the defined behavioral objectives, and the most appropriate activities, to meet the various learning personalities of the boys and girls in the team.

Self-Direction Goal of I.G.E.

All types of grouping practices or modes are used in an Individually Guided School, including large group, small group, independent study and one-to-one relationship. Although common in team teaching, large group instruction is used less frequently in an I.G.E. school. Small group, independent study and one-to-one relationship are modes continuously used to give children opportunities to grow in self-direction. Through these modes youngsters can realize the instructional objectives through activities and the use of materials of their choice. In cases where a student progresses rapidly, a contract of work is developed with one of the team members. Once the independent study is carefully defined and agreed upon, the student pursues his work. The team member, learning center staff, and even other students in the team play an important part in helping students with their contract of work.

Concluding Statement

In an I.G.E. school many of the traditional modes of operation are gone. Flexibility in grouping, in schedules, in planning, and in any other activity related to teaching and learning is the keyword. The teacher no longer stands before the group to lecture, but becomes more a diagnostician, one who studies the needs of each student and then provides a stimulating learning environment. No longer do students march to the library or from room to room. Children earn the freedom to move from one station to another, as necessary, to gather materials to learn about an instructional objective. As one student stated, "School's different now. I'm having a ball learning about so many different things." A mother stated, "We may have had a good program, but now with I.G.E. we have a superior program. I know, Billy loves school."

Is your school ready to meet the challenge? Are you willing to make some significant changes in the educational program? I.G.E. schools can improve growth in the academic areas, but more importantly boys and girls will grow in self-direction, improve their self-concept, and as an added bonus—they will love school!

Note

1. Silberman, Charles E. *Crisis in the Classroom*. New York: Random House, 1970.

Bibliography: Curriculum Strategies for the Middle School

Anderson, Robert H. "Team Teaching in Action." *The Nation's Schools,* May 1960, pp. 62-65.

Association for Supervision and Curriculum Development. *Developing Programs for Young Adolescents.* Washington, D. C.: The Association, 1954.

―――. *The New Elementary School.* Washington, D. C.: The Association, 1968.

Atkins, Neil P. "Rethinking Education in the Middle." *Theory Into Practice.* Columbus: College of Education, The Ohio State University, June 1968, pp. 118-19.

Baillie, John H. "Laboratory Experiences for Disadvantaged Youth in the Middle School. *School Science and Mathematics,* November 1970, pp. 704-06.

Curtis, Thomas E., and Bidwell, Wilma W. "Rationale for Instruction in the Middle School." *Educational Leadership,* March 1970, pp. 578-81.

Devita, Joseph C. "No Homework . . . No Report Card Grades . . . Ungraded." *National Assocation of Secondary School Principals Bulletin,* October 1961, pp. 180-84.

Dravitz, Bernard, and Soroka, Diane Jural. "Inquiry in the Middle Grades." *Social Education,* May 1969, pp. 540-42.

"Enter the Era of the System." *Reading News Report,* III, 1 (October 1968), 32–35.

Hines, Vynce A., and Alexander, William M. "Evaluating the Middle School." *National Elementary Principal,* February 1969, pp. 158–66.

Kopp, O. W. "The School Organization Syndrome vis-a-vis Improved Learning." *National Elementary Principal,* February 1969, pp. 42–45.

McCarthy, Robert J. "Nongraded Middle School." *National Elementary Principal,* January 1968, pp. 15–21.

Powell, William. "Training Teachers for the Junior High and the Middle School." *Michigan Journal of Secondary Education,* Fall 1967, pp. 22–26.

Redl, Fritz. "The Technique of Sex Information." *Child Study,* Fall 1944, pp. 9–11, 17.

Rice, Arthur H. "What's Wrong With Junior High? Nearly Everything." *The Nation's Schools,* November 1964, pp. 30–32.

Rizzo, Michael E. "An Active Activities Program." *The Clearing House,* November 1969, pp. 182–84.

Strickland, Joann H., and Alexander, William. "Seeking Continuity in Early and Middle School Education." *Phi Delta Kappan,* March 1969, pp. 397–400.

Taormina, Francis R. "Team-Teaching in the Middle School." *New York State Education,* April 1969, pp. 22, 46.

The Transitional Years—Middle School Portfolio. Association for Childhood Education International, 1968. McSwain, E. T. "Bases for Grouping Within the Class." Yamamoto, Kaoru. "Creativity in Learning." Beery, Althea, and Wirthlin, Lenore. "Acquiring Power in Reading." Chase, Naomi C. "Creative Writing." Arey, Charles K. "Science: Middle School Years." Carlson, Reynold E. "Outdoor Education." Strickland, Ruth G. "Language in the Middle Grades." Olson, Waldemar. "Discovery in Teaching Mathematics." Ambrose, Edna. "Social Studies: Process of Inquiry." Hines, Vynce A. "Perspectives on Evaluation." Synder, Marjorie. "New Concepts of Learning: Multimedia."

Wolfson, Bernice J. "Individualizing Instruction." *NEA Journal,* November 1966, pp. 31–33.

Part IV

The Middle School Multipurpose Plant

The evidence is obvious when school architecture is called a "dismal art." Too often school buildings are built consisting of four walls of mortar and brick with a number of cubicles called classrooms. These buildings have been called "double-loaded corridors with egg crate classrooms." It is very evident that these buildings did not emerge from a philosophy of education. What we find in existence are many school buildings which unfortunately do not provide for the needs of the teachers or pupils who use them.

Often the construction of a school facility becomes a disappointing experience. Superintendents, board members, and architects design and observe a school building taking shape and usually note its imperfections. Such buildings are built without consideration of the educational program which the principals and teachers feel will best meet the needs of the particular group of boys and girls to be served. One can only conclude that the only perfect buildings are castles in the sky.

For the transescent and his educational requirements, a school is needed which ideally will provide the facilities for innovative teaching-learning practices. The school should be constructed to implement an effective program of team teaching, independent study, laboratory exploration, dramatic expression, multi-media use, and other innovative practices. Such a diverse environment, with an emphasis on the individual responsibility with which the transescent will be confronted in the middle school program, can and must be included in the physical plant in the middle school. Teachers in this environment act more as catalysts, as guides to sources of learning, rather than as dispensers of knowledge. The physical plant should both reflect and facilitate this role.

As pointed out in preceding chapters, the clue to middle school organization is determined by the nature of the child it intends to serve. This child is a unique individual who has left the self-contained classroom of the typical elementary school, but who has not yet reached the level of ability needed to cope with the highly departmentalized organization of the high school. In a developmental period best characterized by change and a new awareness of self and others, the middle schooler must adjust to the transitional period, test his new roles, and explore his expanding world. Since the school and schooling period occupy a large amount of time in the transescent's life, the facility which houses him must reflect and promote his special needs and provide an adequate environment for psychological, social, physical, and intellectual growth to occur.

The school plant for the transescent should be radically different from both the elementary self-contained classroom arrangements and the highly departmentalized arrangements of the high school. Too often in the past and probably in the future, the middle school is or will be used as a substitute name for a conventional junior high. The middle school is not a "junior" high school. It is a school with a learning environment built for specific groups of boys and girls at a specific learning stage. It should therefore reflect the learning needs of the youngsters between the ages of 11 and 14. In the past the junior high school plant usually reflected the facilities found in the high school plant. If a school is truly built to meet the needs of the transescent, it will be very much different from the traditional junior high or senior high school. Hopefully, this transitional school will bring about or force changes in the high school as a result of what's happening in the schools that feed it, as happened in Barrington, Illinois.

What building design can promote and facilitate the transition period of the early adolescent? In this section are presented some of the most adventurous and creative new middle school designs which were planned with a philosophy consistent with the needs of the transescent. Plans and proposals included discussing how the school was designed and built. Of greater importance, educators working with architects explored the quality of educational programming needed for the transescent. These are middle schools for middle school boys and girls. They represent middle schools built for individual communities to house individual programs. These schools will not necessarily serve ideally in other communities, but many of the ideas incorporated in them can with adaptation be used in other situations. To use these ideas in planning a new middle school facility without determining the type of educational program to be included in an individual community would only result in chaos. Each school facility must be planned for each individual community and its educational program.

The scope and details of technological inventiveness shown in these reports suggest the complexity of making educational decisions about the purpose of the middle schools and translating them into functional buildings. In this task the school personnel must persist until the school plant is consistent with the educational needs of the transescent. Bold attempts are tried out and considerable attention is given to various building requirements, such as use of clusters, moveable wall arrangements, multi-space utilization, open areas with a minimum of dividing walls, innovative sonic environments, variable climate environment, etc. These bold, broad strokes in building innovation are designed to encourage teachers to be flexible and to meet the diverse needs and capabilities of the middle schooler.

More than just a building and its surrounding grounds, the educational environment of the student should enhance curricular attainment. In the middle school, the teaching-learning situation emphasizes flexibility, independent study, and individualized and large group instruction. The learning area therefore should be adaptable to varying class sizes and group activities.

Experimentation and exploration are important factors in promoting mental growth. The physical facilities should accordingly provide for maximal experiences of an experimental or exploratory nature. Laboratories should be included for group activities, and provisions made for independent studies. There should be a full range of supplies and equipment for this facility including cages for animals, facilities for "plug in" lab work, etc. The library or learning resources center should provide enough space to house a quality and quantity supply of all types of printed and nonprinted materials. Provisions should be made for technology of the future by providing service systems for closed-circuit television, computer-assisted instruction, and a variety of listening and viewing facilities which will be used in tomorrow's schools. Optimum learning requires the best possible acquisition and utilization of teaching-learning tools of instruction and an appropriate environment. A school for "growing up" is multivaried and calls for building facilities that enhance learning activities.

The innovative plans presented in this chapter are results of attempts by administrators and architects to design middle school plants which will be functional for the years to come. Flexibility of plant use is the key word of these schools and schools of the future. But besides having flexibility, the middle school should be a thing of beauty and a source of pride to the middle schooler and the members of the community. Daniel H. Burnham best expressed this thought in the following words:

> "Make no little plans; they have no magic to stir men's blood and probably themselves will not be realized."
>
> "Make big plans; aim high in hope and work, remembering that a noble logical diagram once recorded will never die, but long after we are gone, will be a living thing, asserting itself with ever-increasing insistency. Remember that our [children] and grand[children] are going to do things that would stagger us."
>
> "Let your watchword be order and your beacon beauty."

1

Harold Gores

What Principals Should Know About New Developments in School Design

Chairman

Calloway Taulbee, Director of Secondary Education, State Department of Education, Santa Fe, New Mexico; First Vice President, NASSP

Interrogators

Louis C. Darst, Principal, Central High School, Lawrence, Indiana. Jay W. Formsma, Principal, Holland High School, Holland, Michigan. Louis J. Harbor, Principal, William C. Overfelt High School, San Jose, California

Among the matters principals worry about, the schoolhouse itself does not have highest priority. And this is as it should be. After all, people are the principal's first concern because it is people—the pupils, teachers, parents, and public—who ignite the issues and bring on the condition known as inflammation of the institution.

Granted that people—and the body of ideas, the curriculum, around which they are caused to assemble—are first, it is an unwise principal who concludes that the place and the things of education, the arrangement of space and environment are somehow beneath him and can safely be left to the discretion of well-meaning, non-reading janitorial-types whose reputations derive from a long line of Procrustean Beds. The environment of education should not be dismissed as only nuts and bolts.

First, let's look at the schoolhouse, the most public of public build-

From *NASSP Bulletin* (April, 1963): 190–200.

ings, the public building more people care about, get angry over, and take up sides about. Look at them, if you can, as though you hadn't spent half of your life in one.

With few exceptions, a schoolhouse is a big box filled with equalized little boxes called classrooms. The classrooms are like our kitchens—hard, reflective, reverberative, utilitarian, indestructible, and antiseptic. Their motif is dictated by a municipal desire to frustrate any errant scholar who, unsheathing his jackknife, might try to carve his initials in this ceramic vault the taxpayers have provided for this childhood.

The very architecture sorts the children. It helps the administration to establish groups of uniform size—25 pupils if the community is rich, 35 if it is poor, and 50 if it doesn't care. In each box is placed a teacher who will be all things to all children all day all year. If it be a secondary school, bells will ring to signal the musical chair game that is played a half-dozen times a day as groups exchange boxes. This is known as secondary education.

The interior layout of schools has been this way ever since the Quincy School was built in Boston in 1847, and keyed for 100 years their ice-cube tray arrangement. Incidentally, the Quincy School, now in its 115th year, is scheduled next year for abandonment because Boston, which was once described as becoming a cemetery with lights, now finds the Quincy School a detriment to the existing rebirth of that city.

The new schools being built this year in your town and others may be only a half-life in the year 2,000, when this year's first-grade pupils will be only middle-aged; when one half of all the people alive on this "one inhabited star" will be Chinese and Russian; when Americans, if the author of the recent book, *The Race to the Year 2,000* is correct, will be only five per cent of the world's population; and when the good old U.S.A. may bear the same relation to the world's economy that Switzerland does today—a relatively small nation of inventive people who prosper through their inventiveness and industry.

The difficulty is that many boards of education regard the new school as the solution to a present problem; *i.e.*, we have more children than we have seats, therefore a new school, or addition to the old, is needed to provide more seats. Yet a new school, if it is to make any real difference to America, is more than just more seats. The new school, or even the addition to the old, should help succeeding principals to solve the problems of the predictable future. Whatever you build it not for the purpose of getting yourself out of trouble; it is as much to help succeeding principals to keep out of trouble. Therefore, the principal who today consents to buildings that are unchangeable, immutable, unresponsive to what the future will confront, is not only wasting present funds and setting a trap for future administrators, but is also exhibiting a cultural arrogance that no swift-moving society can afford. The school that sees itself as the end of the line rather than in the stream of change endangers us all.

Let me illustrate what your problem is by citing a personal experience. In 1958 *Time* magazine called a small city school system in New England to inquire how it happened that among the 25,000 contestants in the Westinghouse Science Talent Search, this one high school won that year both first and second places. The answer given to *Time* was a simple one: they were two bright students and *the schools got out of their way*. One of the great responsibilities you have is to see that schools, whether it be the course of study, the subjects offered, or the building itself, get out of the way.

Though the prevailing pattern of arranging pupils and teachers is still by equal groups in standard spaces for periods of equal length, it is clear that substantial reorganization is taking place in many communities. The self-contained classroom in the elementary school is giving way to more sensitive and manageable ways of clustering children from time to time during the day. In the secondary schools, more students are being allowed to escape the tyranny of the standard, block-book divisions to pursue certain portions of their education at their own academic pace. The amount of freedom accorded students varies from school to school—some high schools have begun by creating honors courses available to seniors; one 800-student secondary school, to my knowledge, has 160 students on individual schedules; Florida's Melbourne High School has nearly every student on individual schedule so that students receive instruction by appointment; at Ridgewood High School, in a Chicago suburb, the schedule provides for only independent study, seminars of 150 students, and large-group instruction. These schools are straws in the wind.

The swing away from standard groupism and toward the individual, as learning gradually takes precedence over teaching, as the individual differences among teachers come to be recognized and capitalized upon, the chambered nautilus schoolhouse whose interior is as unchangeable as though its partitions were made of calcium, gets in the way. It is not surprising, therefore, that the rearrangement of pupils and teachers is bringing about the rearrangement of school interiors. Literally, the schools are busting out of their boxes. Within a decade, it is quite possible that the capacity of a school will not be measured by units called classrooms but by zones of space.

Now you may say that concern about space is unwarranted unless you are planning a new building. Actually, from my observation, experimental rearrangement of groups is taking place as much in old buildings as in new. Indeed, if you preside over an old building—say 1920—you may have unusual freedom to reshape and refurbish its interior simply because everyone recognizes that something ought to be done about the old hulk. From the standpoint of accommodation to change, the most unfortunately situated are those in obsolete but relatively new buildings, those built in the early 1950's and whose cost is still green in the taxpayers' memory. In these structures, more than ordinary persuasion is required to cause municipal authorities to knock out partitions not yet paid for and which clearly have a half century of life remaining in them.

But whether your task is to rehabilitate an old school or plan a new one, there are several issues you will have to confront. As I listen to secondary-school principals as they try to reshape their schools' physical environment here are the questions they raise with greatest frequency and puzzlement:

1. What About Flexibility?

Flexibility is a fighting word in educational planning. Architects quail before it when clients demand it without explaining it. Educators as a group have a vague feeling that flexibility is something they should be for, and should demand, if only somebody would describe it. It's an all-purpose word that shrouds the uncertainty of making decisions in uncertain times—a way of asking the question, "How do we act now and not regret it later?" This is a general yearning not confined to educational facilities. Because buildings have a way of being around for a century and their shape cannot be rescinded by taking a vote, decisions about buildings are especially haunting.

In simplest terms, flexibility is the means by which higher utilization of space can be achieved. In ascending order of sophistication and of initial cost, here are some of the ways that schools are creating spaces that yield to the program—indeed, get out of its way:

a. By installing non-bearing interior partitions, free of plumbing and mechanical apparatus. This is the lowest order of response and there is a great hazard to it. You can be sure that the partitions will remain in the way long after their obstruction to the program is apparent. People don't like to take a sledge hammer to public property and somebody is bound to ask when the money is spent to knock down the wall, even if the act occurs twenty-five years from now, who made the mistake of putting it up in the first place.

b. By clustering spaces of varying sizes selected according to one's best guess as to how groups and individuals will be organized in the immediate years ahead. This involves a certain amount of risk-taking because it pitches the design ahead of the *status quo*. A common pattern of clustering spaces is four (sometimes six) classrooms clustered around a central space that is library-like in character.

c. By using salvable and re-useable panels for partitions between classrooms, whether in row-on-row classrooms strung along straight corridors or in clusters.

d. By installing operable walls—partitions that can be withdrawn, either manually or mechanically, at will and at once. A spectacular development in operable walls has occurred in the last two years. Prior to then, operable partitions that would effectively stop sound were hand-crafted and cost about $25 per square foot in place. There were cheaper partitions, a kind of accordion-folding screen often found in faculty clubs and guaranteeing that the jokes and applause on one side of the wall could be heard and appreciated by persons attending a different meeting on the other side. These were nothing really but visual dividers and brought disrepute to the principle of operability. But today there are a dozen manufacturers of operable partitions that stop sound. For $25 a foot, operable at the turn of a switch, they will stop all the sound. For $10 a foot, mechanically operated, they will stop the sounds of conventional instruction. And for $5 a foot, manually operated, they will stop ordinary speech. This means you now have the opportunity to create smaller spaces out of larger spaces when desired, yet recover the large spaces when you want them back. It means you can divide an auditorium or large lecture hall into sub-spaces that can be used independently and simultaneously without acoustic interference, each to the other. One college has currently on its boards a thousand-seat auditorium-theater which, according to the way it is divided at any one moment in time, will serve six different functions. It is in effect a poor man's Loeb Theater. Its economy is not to be gauged by the comparative cost of operable *versus* immovable walls; but rather by the higher utilization of space it offers with consequent reduction in space that otherwise would have to be provided. At last count there were thirty divisible auditoriums in use or under construction in American schools.

e. A fifth step is just beginning to emerge in school and college design. New York University has planned a demonstration school that provides zones of space out of which sub-spaces can be "snapped" according to the dictates of the program, hour-by-hour.

New York City has on the boards a small primary school, actually a separate addition to an existing school, which is not a series of self-contained standard classrooms, but is instead a self-contained unit large enough to accommodate 200 pupils. Ways are being devised to provide visual and acoustic privacy when and where desired for the various groupings within the universal space, which groupings can be selected by the faculty according to the needs of the children rather than the requirements of existing spaces.

An aspect of flexibility often overlooked is its usefulness in reducing overcrowding in existing schools. Professor David Austin's study reveals that the typical high school can gain the equivalent of several additional rooms by using operable walls to divide the larger classrooms in half for those small classes that would otherwise be occupying a standard classroom.

2. What About Science Facilities?

If you are integrating two or more of the disciplines, especially in science, plan also to integrate the space. We are working currently with a number of colleges which are attempting to design multi-use space and equipment that can be used effectively in more than one subject field. One university has invented, at least to its own satisfaction, a single laboratory station that satisfies the departments of physics, chemistry, and biology. And if you are planning a lecture-demonstration hall, consider well the *rotating* stage which allows out-of-sight make-up and knock-down of apparatus while the hall is in use. The rotating stage also helps the facility to bridge a number of subject fields thought heretofore to be incompatible. The Ridgewood, New Jersey, High School is now just completing the installation of a rotating stage in a lecture-demonstration hall.

There is substantial movement toward freeing the student from the tyranny of the standard group by providing time and facilities for independent study. Accordingly we see these trends in science buildings:

a. The melding of the isolated one-discipline laboratory, precisely designed for a single function, into groupings of labs, offices, and lounges so as to increase communication.

b. The rise of the multi-discipline lab bridging two or more sciences, thus encouraging higher utilization.

c. Greater use of the portable snap-in equipment for small group and independent study.

d. The central location of heavy, costly, or complex apparatus, as in a common tool-bin, serving the surrounding cluster of labs.

e. The creating of large, open lab spaces with all service functions, stairs, utilities, toilets, *etc.*, placed on the periphery. At Colorado College, for example, the solution has been described as "grasshopper skeleton" because all the bones—the utilities, exhaust, plumbing—have been placed in the exterior skin of the building, leaving the interior free for maximum flexibility. At Rice University, for example, the utility skeleton is placed as, a spine through the center of the building. In Boston, the Retina Foundation's new lab building is best described as an aircraft carrier flight deck with utilities placed in the superstructure.

f. Several colleges are tackling the inflexibility of the laboratory bench. One inventive solution is the suitcase system, which stores laboratory apparatus in a case apart from the bench.

g. And last, the trend toward increasing demonstration and decreasing time at the bench for students electing, but not majoring in science. This has heightened the interest in lecture-demonstration halls and has placed a premium on closed-circuit television and the use of films and tapes. One of the most thoughtful uses of television in science is at Rensselaer Polytechnic Institute in the East and at St. Mary's on the West Coast, each using television as a means of magnifying and multiplying an image so that many can see simultaneously what only one can see less well.

In sum, whether space for science is an exo-skeleton, a sandwich, or a flat-top, the object is to achieve *generalized* space made *specialized* by the kinds of equipment introduced from time to time through the years.

3. What About the Library?

Of all facilities in secondary education, the library is most in agony, setting as it does at the confluence of two forces: (1) its historic archival function as a place for books; and (2) the new demand that it be the locus of all the carriers of information. In many schools—and unfortunately to my way of thinking—the newer media, the audio-visual, have already set up their separate establishment, usually in the basement, leaving the librarian dusting her books.

I realize there are natural reasons why this dichotomy has occurred: the typical school librarian is female; the typical audio-visual special-ist, who must be neither afraid of, nor unable to lift the hardware, is male. In many schools, the integrator of these two carriers of informa-tion—paper and machines—defies the efforts of both the principal and Cupid.

This dichotomy has been further reinforced by the small amount of space customarily allotted to the library. Many schools have allotted library space equal to five or ten per cent of the enrollment. In some cases, the formula has been "a library is as large as two classrooms." Small wonder that when new carriers of information came to the school and when more and more students were encouraged as individuals rather than as groups to use the library, the audio-visual wound up in the basement or the attic—a respectable place for a man to be seen, but not a woman.

Whatever the reasons for their separation in the past, the book and the machine are being brought together in the same place in the design of new schools and the rehabilitation of old schools. In a forthcoming publication by the Educational Facilities Laboratories (EFL) on school and college libraries, the author, Ralph Ellsworth, is recommending that high schools plan library space for at least thirty per cent of the school enrollment, and to provide space for the audio-visual as equal partner in the library function.

The colleges are already breaking new ground in library design. When Keyes Metcalf designed the Lamont library at Harvard just after World War II, he provided individual study spaces for fifty per cent of the occupants. Recently he was quoted as saying he now would raise the figure to eighty per cent.

Last week I visited a high school which was constructing study carrels in one of its vocational shops for the school library. The carrels were of simple table-top design, costing about $1.50 for materials per student in units of six, and providing visual privacy when the student is seated. EFL has a publication on the design of carrels, several of the do-it-yourself variety, which may be helpful as you confront this problem.

I see these general trends emerging:

> a. Location of the library—though the library is "the heart of the school," don't bury it in the geographic center of a big structure. Put it on the periphery where access, day and night, will be easiest for students, and someday the public. One principal told me that, if he had his way, he would put the library on the front lawn where students and teachers would have to walk by it or through it to get anywhere. At Parma, Ohio, for example, the library is separately zoned near the front of the building and does a land-office business during school vacations.

b. Amenity—the library is no longer a cold, clammy cement-block vault for shelving books under maximum security. Carpeting the floor raises the tone, reduces the noise, and, in the long run, will reduce the cost of maintenance and heating. More surfaces will yield to the touch and absorb sound, and delight the eye.

c. Absolute and total standardization of furniture will give way to a variety of sizes, materials, and shapes. The atmosphere will be more like the living room than the kitchen.

d. Eventually the conventional row-on-row classrooms will be broken up into large zones of library-like space. Someday somebody will design a high school that is mostly library.

4. What About Carpeting?

The notion of carpeting in a schoolhouse is likely to leave the taxpayer in a state of shock. After he hears the case for carpeting, he still has a sense of cultural guilt about the matter. After all, the root of the word curriculum is race track. Consciously or unconsciously, we expect schools not only to teach the young, but also somehow to toughen them for a competitive society and now a competitive world. The image of carpeting is just the opposite—lush, costly (wall-to-wall carpeting and back-to-wall mortgage), and smacking of the good life.

I shall not attempt to argue the case. I only report that in Andrews, Texas, where the high school is carpeted door-to-door, their studies indicate that the higher initial cost of carpeting will have been cancelled out in four-and-one-half years by reduced maintenance; that in ten years, savings will have accrued sufficient to replace the carpeting; and the school district has a 20-year bond on the carpeting. One of their elementary schools has had seven years' experience with carpeting. If you have the opportunity, talk with the people at Shaker High School, Newtonville, New York, where one half of the building is carpeted. Or see what the carpeting of an old school in Amsterdam, New York, has done to improve the environment.

I realize that this is a touchy subject; though what carpeting does to the acoustic surround, the ease of maintenance, the tone and spirit of a school are there to be seen for one's self. I only suggest that, if you are planning to dejuvenilize the schools to increase their performance as places in which to learn as distinguished from institutions of maximum security, carpeting of at least the library seems to be an acceptable and reasonable act even to the richest taxpayer, who is the last to be convinced.

5. What About Air Conditioning?

The question of air conditioning is now so tender that in some quarters it is being called "climate control." But by whatever name it's called, the fact remains that no student has been known to learn faster because he is scratching his heat rash.

If you are running, or planning to run, your school in the summertime—and this is clearly a national trend—you will want to consider reasonable comfort as a necessary condition for efficient learning. The evidence is pretty clear that the school designed in the beginning for climate control will construct at about the same cost as a school designed around the capturing of the natural breeze. A few weeks ago the state of Mississippi changed its regulations to permit state aid to include the cost of air conditioning. (I introduce this relatively unimportant fact only for the purpose of reporting something decent from Mississippi.)

In the meantime, a spirited battle rages between those who would knock out all the glass from exterior walls in order to reduce solar heat gain, and those who believe that glass should not go out the window. Considerable support is gaining for the position that windows bear the same relation to light that fireplaces do to heat. They are essentially esthetic. Some of the earlier compact, windowless schools look like warehouses where administration is by refrigeration. More recently, I observe that where exterior glass has been diminished, the roof is once again returned to visibility and makes architectural statement for the building. The newer schools with diminished use of exterior glass are looking less and less like mausoleums.

In any event, the glass companies should exploit the use of glass in the interior of schools to open up visibility within. The maze has only begun to be explored and its implications for reduced cost of supervision of areas showing high visibility is substantial. For extensive use of glass partitions, see the Bridgeport, Michigan, High School, and Andrews, Texas.

Currently, we at EFL are conducting tests of metallized mylar which, applied to the interior surface of window glass, shows promise of dramatic reduction of solar heat gain without objectionable loss of transparency. Tests conducted last August in Princeton, New Jersey, produced an average temperature drop in unair-conditioned class-rooms of thirteen degrees. For those of you who will be sweating it out in your glass boxes next July and August, I can only say that your comforter cometh.

6. What About the Gymnasium?

The gymnasium, a large box whose dimensions are determined by the rules of basketball, consumes as high as thirty per cent of the cost of some schools. The gym is often planned with more tender, loving care than the rest of the building, partly because of its cost, partly because teachers of physical education have studied the effect of environment more intensively than their academic colleagues, and most because the public visits the gymnasium to watch contests that, as Robert Hutchins, said, "bear the same relation to education that bull-fighting does to agriculture." Tell me the enrollment of a high school in Springfield, Massachusetts, or Springfield, Illinois, or Colorado, or Oregon, or Florida, and I'll tell you the dimensions of its gymnasium. Such is the stranglehold that basketball has on facilities for physical education.

Yet there are stirrings in the hustlings. See the field houses at Holland, Michigan; Bethesda, Maryland; Wayland, Massachusetts, and a host of thin-shelled structures, scoops of the sky with no interior supports that has forever to be walked around, that are on the boards. See our report from Texas A. & M. on semi-enclosed structures—shelters that imply that physical education can sometimes take place without all participants being reduced to their underwear.

Watch what the Forman School, Litchfield, Connecticut, is doing with air-supported structures—a thin plastic or glass fiber membrane that covers an area—a tennis court, a swimming pool, eventually, it is hoped, an acre of play space—and is supported by only two pounds of air pressure. Someday this may be the way that schools in benign climates can acquire adequate and sheltered space for physical educa-tion—with artificial turf, virtually an acre of June. The air-supported membrane may also bring the cost of a swimming pool within the grasp of many a small high school.

It is clear that the trend is toward the round, toward roof shells that provide interiors uninterrupted by supports and barriers that get in the way of change. Incidentally, the University of West Virginia is studying the feasibility of superimposing an airplane hangar on the closed end of its 42,000-seat stadium, thereby achieving an inexpensive field house without diminishing the usefulness of the stadium for football.

In sum, look carefully and sympathetically at these matters:

a. Environments that are comfortable and ????????, both summer and winter; watch out for the over-use of unshaded glass.

b. Flexibility that will allow quick and economical multiplication and division of space.

c. Libraries that give maximum access to all the carriers of information.

d. Gymnasiums that are more than basketball courts.

e. Science facilities that bring utilities to general space—made special only by the specialized equipment installed at the time.

f. Remember, the building you plan today will be at only half-life by the year 2,000. Don't trap your successors.

g. Don't feel guilty if you ask for rooms and buildings that are not rectangular. There are other shapes of space which may serve you better.

h. And last, insist that there be beauty in whatever is done.

John Kenneth Galbraith has said it best: "Government buildings serve their purpose, but no one ever points to them with pride or indeed with any other recognizable emotion. The same box-like, glass and stainless steel austerity characterizes our hospitals, public garages, police stations, and quite a lot of our public housing. Only in our airports and occasionally in our schools do we show signs of letting ourselves go—of doing something that flatters the public eye and nourishes the community pride.

"We act efficiently," he goes on to say, "when we maximize the product of a given expenditure or when we adopt the expenditure which maximizes the product. Beauty and elegance and the pleasure that they provide must be counted as part of the product. We are being inefficient if, by false economy, we deny the community pleasure and pride in its achievement. . . . Those who are unwilling to pay for beauty and some elegance and those who profit from community squalor will say that these standards are too precious. But those who say we cannot concern ourselves with esthetic goals are wrong and I believe dead wrong. These are the natural next concern as people master their economic problems."

2

Judith Murphy

A Middle School
Keyed to "A New Number:
The Number One"

A good three years before construction began, imaginative plans for this middle school were afloat. Some were aired at an unusual two-day meeting convened in September, 1961.

This meeting, co-sponsored by the Bedford Public Schools and EFL, brought together an array of people deeply concerned with society and people and education. In a free-wheeling exchange of ideas, they concentrated on the kind of school that would truly meet the needs of pre-adolescent youngsters in the Bedford school district, and that would be adaptable to the unknown needs of the district's children decades hence.

The Committee of Seventeen numbered 15 different disciplines among its members. It included administrators and a school-board member from Bedford; nationally known educators like Robert Anderson of Harvard and Lawrence Cremin of Teachers College, Columbia; architects and designers; and such notables as Harvard psychologist Jerome Bruner (whose influential *Process of Education* had just been published) and Jane Jacobs, maverick critic of cities and city-planners.

The conferees took off from the premise, presented in a report by a Bedford staff committee, that the district stood in need of a school program and building "suited to the peculiar requirements of children in the 'middle' of their public school life" and that flexibility was of

From *Middle Schools* (New York: Educational Facilities Laboratories, 1965): 28–30 and 45–48.

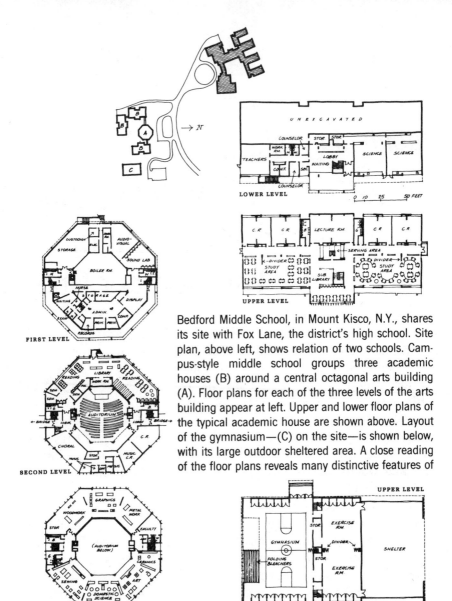

Bedford Middle School, in Mount Kisco, N.Y., shares its site with Fox Lane, the district's high school. Site plan, above left, shows relation of two schools. Campus-style middle school groups three academic houses (B) around a central octagonal arts building (A). Floor plans for each of the three levels of the arts building appear at left. Upper and lower floor plans of the typical academic house are shown above. Layout of the gymnasium—(C) on the site—is shown below, with its large outdoor sheltered area. A close reading of the floor plans reveals many distinctive features of

the Bedford school. The auditorium, for instance, at the center of the arts building on the second level, is essentially a little theater seating 350. It can be divided in half by a double, soundproof folding partition. The raised platform is demountable and can be centered to create a theater-in-the-round. The school's unusual provision for individual study is indicated in the large, open library area adjoining the theater, and in the space each house gives to individual study areas. The audio-visual center in the lower floor of the arts building can eventually provide closed-circuit television for the middle school and for Fox Lane and connect selected individual carrels in the arts building and the houses to programmed material in the sound laboratory.

paramount importance, calling for well-thought-out combinations of teaching and learning groups.

The September meeting was followed a month later by a meeting in which four of the original committee joined Bedford staff members to draw up more precise physical and programmatic specifications for the new school. From that point until construction began in the spring of 1964, men and money revised some of the original ideas. Only two of the 1961 board members are still in office. Some features which proved to be costly were dropped to assure passage of the bond issue. Difficulties with contractors have been slightly above par for the school-building course, though unrelated to the building's architectural or educational innovations. And the district now has a new superintendent. (Charles Richter, who sparked the middle school idea and the 1961 conferences, is now superintendent of schools in West Hartford, Conn.)

Change—a concept important in the planning—has thus overtaken the Bedford Middle School even before its completion. But the basic concept evolved by the Bedford people and their advisors prevails. The new school will be uniquely keyed to "each and every individual child—to the new number in education, the number one." Certain engaging features, along with the swimming pool, will be missing— notably the "acre of June," the year-round verdant area that might have replaced the standard gymnasium. But Bedford still promises to be a school distinctively designed for the intermediate child and unusually sensitive, in fittings and organization, to his manifest needs (e.g., for privacy and sociability) and his unknown potential. Among other unusual assets, the gymnasium will be extended by an outdoor area as big as the gym itself, roofed over, and usable very nearly all year. (The micro-climate study that proved the feasibility of this outdoor innovation was done by Texas A and M, with EFL support.)

The site plan shows the relationship of the middle school to the Fox Lane School, the district's high school, now overcrowded with grades 7 and 8. There will be some interchange between the two schools, and they will share certain facilities (including auditorium, playground, and kitchen). As the plan indicates, the new school is laid out campus-style, with three academic "houses" clustered around an octagonal arts building. The houses are long rectangles, as is the gymnasium.

The three houses are identical except that one of them contains a two-story lecture room accessible from the lower floor, planned to accommodate a planetarium some day. There are 18 standard class-rooms (including 6 science rooms) and 3 large-lecture rooms for an enrollment of over 1,100. Open areas on either side of each house library accommodate individual study-and-storage carrels, outward signs of the school's philosophy of placing confidence in these very young people "to carry out assignments over lengthening periods of time, to pursue new ideas and interests independently, and to main-tain and utilize various resources and materials which relate to their classroom experiences." The new school, in reflecting this consensus of the Committee of Seventeen, will honor its confidence in the individual student by assigning him "a headquarters of his own . . . a headquarters for scholarship."

Actually, when the school opens, there will not be a carrel for every student, partly because of other demands on space, partly because of the feeling that all the children will not be ready for so much indepen-dence. Two-thirds of the students will have their own individual carrels. And to honor sociability (and also to conserve space), the study area is to be used for dining. The table surface of each group of four carrels will provide round-the-table dining. The children not yet assigned carrels of their own will be based in traditional home rooms, and join their fellows for lunch. In general, it is planned that most children will spend an increasing proportion of their time without teachers—working on assignments in the library and elsewhere, study-ing, working on projects.

The arts building, rising to three stories at the center of the school, was conceived as a busy studio. Of particular note is the little theater on the second level, the unencumbered library, and the open third floor devoted to the manual, graphic, visual, and home arts. Insofar as building codes permitted, this floor was designed as one continuous space.

The Bedford people hope that the house (or school-within-a-school) plan will scale the 1,050 student facility down to more manageable size—more important, to a size suited to the 10-to-14-year-olds who will spend their days there. As one of the participants at the 1961 conference said: "At least someone under this system would know whether the kid in the green sweater was one of ours or one of theirs." Each house will be the school in miniature, with all age groups represented, including possibly a few advanced fifth-graders and slow ninth-graders.

One of the architects taking part in the September, 1961, meeting said: "Instead of creating boxes for students and teachers, let's create a community." And Mrs. Jacobs added: "The school for now should

Pleasant Hills Middle School

be a commitment for now. But the structure has to be nurturing—a structure which permits change."

BEDFORD MIDDLE SCHOOL
Mt. Kisco, New York
Size: 137,690 sq. ft.
Cost: $3,070,775
Cost per sq. ft.: $22.30
Cost per pupil: $2,925
Grades: 6-8
To Open: Fall, 1966
Capacity: 1,050
Present Superintendent: Duane Ahlf
(Superintendent 1961-1964: Charles O. Richter)
Principal: Neil P. Atkins, Bedford Middle School and Fox Lane High School
Architects: The Architects Collaborative
Partners in Charge: John C. Harkness, Herbert K. Gallagher, Sarah Harkness
Figures are best available in July 1966, but not final because of pending litigation.

From the Top Down

This middle school, even when half finished in February of 1965, promised to be a bright landmark in this suburb seven miles from the heart of Pittsburgh. Rising three stories in the dish-shaped hollow of its appointed site, the school has a roof rather like that of an enlarged, flattened pagoda. Enhancing the distinctive shape is its treatment: white mastic compound paved with marble chips.

The roof design takes on importance because of the way in which

The architects of Pleasant Hills Middle School translated site problems into design attributes by relating the school to the conformations of its hilly site. Construction photograph shows school from the northeast with main entrance at grade into the buildings upper level. Elevation, below, shows Pleasant Hills from the west, with the two upper levels revealed. Canopied bridge to lobby and administration offices is at left.

the architects handled a difficult grading problem. Only the top of the three-floor school is generally visible from the surrounding area and from the main, or northern, approach to the school. Viewed from the west, the first floor—the principle classroom floor—is also visible. Only from the east and the south are all three floors revealed.

In marked contrast to the middle school in Barrington, Ill., whose architects used grade to minimize the gymnasium, Celli-Flynn made the Pleasant Hills gym-auditorium (which will be in heavy community use) the center of a core of spaces common to the whole school. The roof expresses the gymnasium beneath it; the surrounding parapet houses mechanical equipment. Classrooms flank the gym, with administrative offices to the fore on either side of the main entrance and homemaking, music, and art rooms to the rear.

The stage in the gym-auditorium includes a music area with movable tiers that can be closed off by Coil-Wal partitions. The gym-auditorium itself is divisible by another Coil-Wal partition into two large-group instruction or play areas (like the arrangement at Kennedy Junior High School in Natick, Mass.). On both this floor and the one below, classrooms are grouped by fours on either side of the central core, with a buffer zone of storage space, toilets, conference rooms, and locker rooms between. All classrooms are unit-ventilated and all interior spaces exhausted, but there is air conditioning only in the music rooms.

Both classroom floors include two large-group instruction rooms with operable partitions; they can be converted by hand into standard-sized classrooms. In addition, the lower floor has an extra large area with tiered seats, its high ceiling accommodated by the auditorium stage above. It is planned as a science-lecture hall, and for use by groups of all sizes. Of approximately the same generous size is the library across the front of the same floor, with an extension that looks out on a landscaped vista.

The ground floor, curving around the hillside and less than half the size of the floors above, is devoted to nonacademic functions, such as shop and cafeteria. The architects are particularly pleased with such innovations as the prefabricated, double-barreled teacher's closet and with the arrangements for sound control. The music-practice rooms are isolated from the homemaking and art rooms by double walls, noncontinuous floor slabs, and a separate air-handling system which prevents the transmission of sound via duct work. The gym-auditorium and music-room stage are similarly isolated, vertically and horizontally. For controlling sound within the classrooms, ceilings are fitted with acoustical tile at the back of the room to absorb sound, but are untreated in the front to permit the teacher's voice to carry.

All this design and engineering ingenuity will express an educational program that credits considerable influence to the middle schools of Saginaw, Mich. Supervising Principal William J. Blakley has lived through a good deal of educational history, and he takes a benign wait-and-see attitude toward team teaching and non-gradedness. "Maybe a subsequent administrator will go to team teaching," he says, and he believes the new middle school is flexible enough to accommodate this and other innovations.

But although the West Jefferson Hills administration plans no sweeping instructional changes to match Barrington's, for instance, or Plainview's, the new school will reflect a very definite middle-school philosophy. The West Jefferson Hills Union School District was ready to shift from the prevailing 6-6 pattern, in part—perhaps primarily, because school board and administration were convinced of the superiority of a four-year senior high school. They were also conscious of the draw-backs of the conventional 7-8-9 junior high, with many educators believing, as Mr. Blakley has written, "that while the theory of the junior high school is excellent, in practice it has resulted in junior high schools becoming miniature senior high schools. . . ." The West Jefferson Hills people saw reason to agree "that this movement downward of the patterns of the senior high school . . . has multiplied

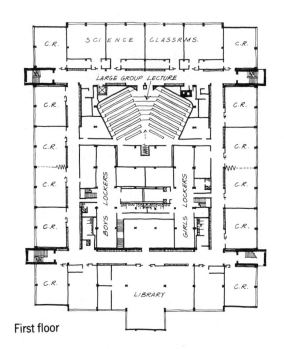

First floor

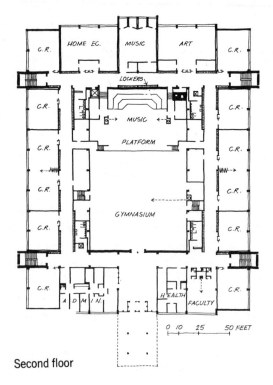

Second floor

and intensified the problems of [the] normal growth and development" of the younger children.

As in school districts everywhere, educational concerns like these were backstopped by sheer necessity and by educational imperatives in other areas. West Jefferson Hills was faced, for one thing, with buildings up to capacity at all levels; and, for another, with the need to improve elementary education by making space in the lower schools for kindergartens and central libraries. The more they looked into the matter, the more school board and administration became convinced that a 5-8 school would not only best meet immediate practical needs but could provide a greatly improved program and environment for youngsters aged 10 to 14—a system that was "forthcoming, rather than continuing a pattern which many feel is no longer considered adequate," in Mr. Blakley's measured words.

Mr. Blakley and his associates feel that even though they propose no radical shift in instructional program ("programs in these grades are pretty largely set by the State"), the new middle school will offer an improved "school society and environment" for the children, with more chance at self-directing activities and intellectual stimulation than an elementary school usually provides. Specifically, it will be possible to group children more homogeneously (with 200 plus per grade, instead of the present 25 to 90 in seven different buildings). The school can afford superior facilities in art, physical education, music, and other special areas—and these will now be available to fifth and sixth graders for the first time. One aspect of this "school for growing up" will be a carefully staged transition from the substantial self-containment of grades 5 and 6 to the departmentalization of 7 and 8.

As a result of their studies and of looking at middle schools in Saginaw and elsewhere, the West Jefferson Hills people see many other advantages to the new arrangement, from cafeteria efficiency to provision for individual differences. In all, Mr. Blakley has presented the district with a good dozen and a half reasons in favor of the middle school (on the negative side, he could report only two minor disadvantages, one being that "girls in the middle school might object because boys are not mature enough"). He has high hopes that the new school, in its striking new building, will prove its worth, and will accommodate the future as it unfolds.

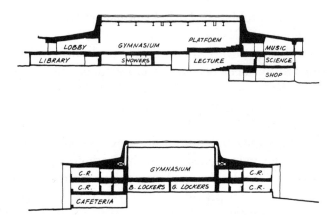

Floor plans, plus sectional drawings, of Pleasant Hills' three levels appear on this page and page 340. The plans on page 340 show first floor and second floor plans. These floors contain all the classrooms, the gymnasium-auditorium, rooms for art, music, and homemaking, the library, and other special facilities. Placing the auditorium, which is expected to serve many community purposes, high in the building made it readily accessible to grade at the main entrance. Sections, above, indicate its central position. Note also tiered lecture room on first floor.

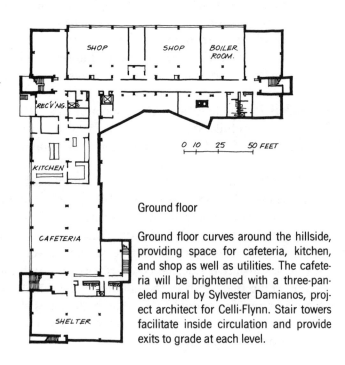

Ground floor

Ground floor curves around the hillside, providing space for cafeteria, kitchen, and shop as well as utilities. The cafeteria will be brightened with a three-paneled mural by Sylvester Damianos, project architect for Celli-Flynn. Stair towers facilitate inside circulation and provide exits to grade at each level.

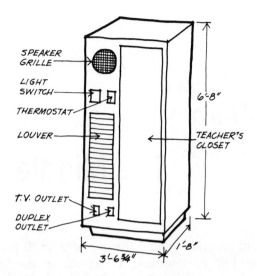

The architects used several original designs in Pleasant Hills, including this unusual prefabricated unit combining a teacher's closet with various functional necessities such as public-address speaker, television outlet, and thermostat. It will extend less than nine inches into corridor. Surface, brightly painted, can be used to display art.

PLEASANT HILLS MIDDLE SCHOOL

West Jefferson Hills School District, Pleasant Hills, Pennsylvania
Size: 110,600 sq. ft.
Cost: $2,090,000
Cost per sq. ft.: $18.90
Cost per pupil: $2,055
Grades: 5-8
To Open: September, 1965
Capacity: 1,017 (960 to start)
Supervising Principal: W. J. Blakley
Architects: Celli-Flynn
Sylvester Damianos, *Project Architect*

3

*Ronald Gross &
Judith Murphy*

The Middle School

Children will progress around the age of 9 or 10 from the primary school to a middle or intermediate school. In the late 1960's this alternative to the conventional junior high was beginning to spring up all over the country, for a variety of reasons—social, educational, and sometimes just plain expedient. A middle school, like the one pictured on pages 346–351, might cover three or four grades in the upper-elementary years, probably grades 5 or 6 through 8. Today's youngsters, it is generally agreed, mature earlier than their parents did. Long before they reach the teens, they seem to be ready for much richer and more concentrated school experiences than the traditional system provides. Ideally, the pre-teen-ager, after four or five years in school, should have a fair mastery of the basic skills and be expected to apply them to progressively challenging and substantial problems.

The drawing suggests in broad strokes an environment designed to meet the diverse needs and capacities of the intermediate-aged children. It offers a marked change of pace and sophistication from the primary school; yet it is radically different from the rigid departmentalization of the conventional junior high, which all too often has simply exposed the young teen-ager to a watered-down version of high school. In the scheme shown here . . . the school introduces the child to departmentalization by grouping together the facilities for related disciplines, in large, open, barnlike areas. Central to the whole design, in fact and in spirit, is the library (or learning-resource center)

From *Educational Change and Architectural Consequences* (New York: Educational Facilities Laboratories, 1969): 56-67.

where each child may be assigned a carrel and storage space. The middle-schooler, as his powers and confidence increase, makes greater and greater independent use of the library and its varied resources.

The drawing shows, in the upper lefthand corner, an arts barn that provides for creative art, industrial art, and the domestic arts. One area flows into the next, with a minimum of dividing walls. The central workspace is for the teachers. Only the noisy power tools are set off by themselves; the little rooms around the barn's perimeter are primarily for storage, with space enough for small groups of students to work on plans or actual projects. The large drawings . . . show the arts barn in greater detail. The central concept is the unity of the creative and practical arts. The design minimizes conventional divisions, including the fusty split between the vocational and creative. In the same spirit it seeks to eradicate the old opposition between artsy-craftsy girl work and rugged manual boy work. A middle school that opened three years ago in Amory, Mississippi, has just such an open art, shop, and home-arts area.

. . . From the arts barn, there is another barn labeled "Science and Math." Here again the intent is to bring together physically disciplines that are intellectually related. The plan shows three laboratory spaces clustered around a storage and preparation room; adjacent to it is a planning center for a team of eight teachers—the combined staff of the science and mathematics departments. Flanking the center are small seminar rooms. Each of these three laboratories can be used for science or mathematics. The design presumes there are no arbitrary divisions between these subjects or spaces; groups can flow from one lab to another depending on the numbers of students and the kinds of interdisciplinary projects on hand. The key to these laboratories is mobility and flexibility. All furniture and equipment, except for the fixed plumbing counters, is movable.

The small spaces abutting from the laboratories are for students working on advanced, long-range projects. The one adjoining the laboratory to the left contains cages for animals and all requisite facilities for "plug in" lab work. The space next to the laboratory on the right contains computation devices and other data-processing equipment. The space off the combined central lab at the bottom of the drawing can be reserved for students working on geometric/chemical models.

Counterclockwise to the next cluster, the scheme shows a communications barn; English, foreign languages, reading, and speech. Cen-

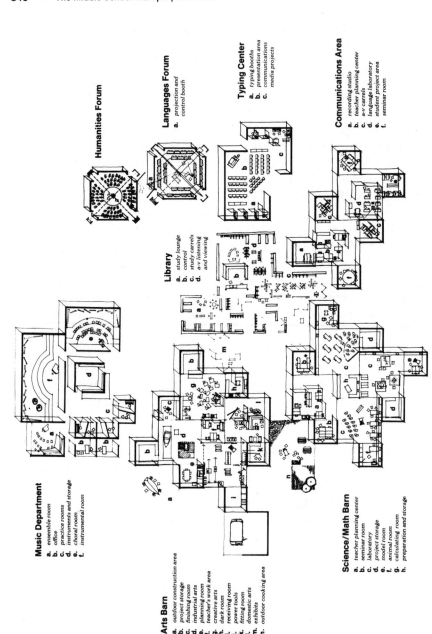

Humanities Forum

Languages Forum
a. projection and
   control booth

Typing Center
a. typing booths
b. presentation area
c. communications
   media projects

Communications Area
a. recording studio
b. teacher planning center
c. a-v carrels
d. language laboratory
e. student project area
f. seminar room

Library
a. study lounge
b. control
c. study carrels
d. a-v listening
   and viewing

Music Department
a. ensemble room
b. office
c. practice rooms
d. instruments and storage
e. choral room
f. instrumental room

Arts Barn
a. outdoor construction area
b. project storage
c. finishing room
d. industrial arts
e. planning room
f. teacher's work area
g. creative arts
h. dark room
i. receiving room
j. power tools
k. fitting room
l. domestic arts
m. exhibits
n. outdoor cooking area

Science/Math Barn
a. teacher planning center
b. seminar room
c. laboratory
d. project storage
e. model room
f. animal room
g. calculating room
h. preparation and storage

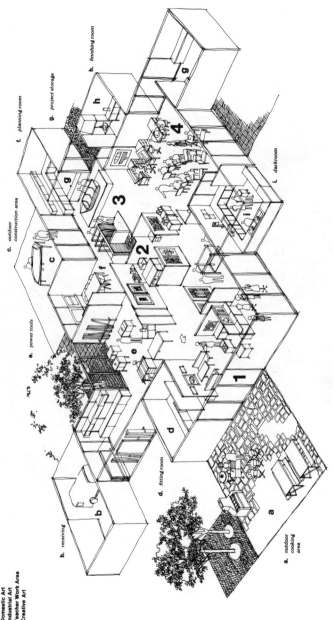

Arts Barn

1 Domestic Art
2 Industrial Art
3 Teacher Work Area
4 Creative Art

a. outdoor cooking area
b. receiving
c. outdoor construction area
d. fitting room
e. power tools
f. planning room
g. project storage
h. finishing room
i. darkroom

Science/Math Barn

1 Laboratory
2 Teacher Planning Center

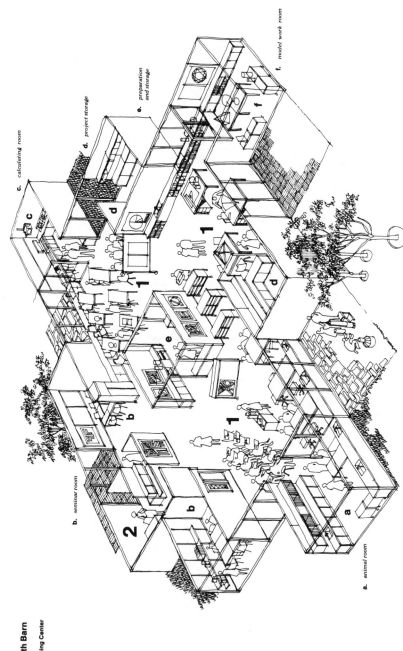

a. animal room
b. seminar room
c. calculating room
d. project storage
e. preparation and storage
f. model work room

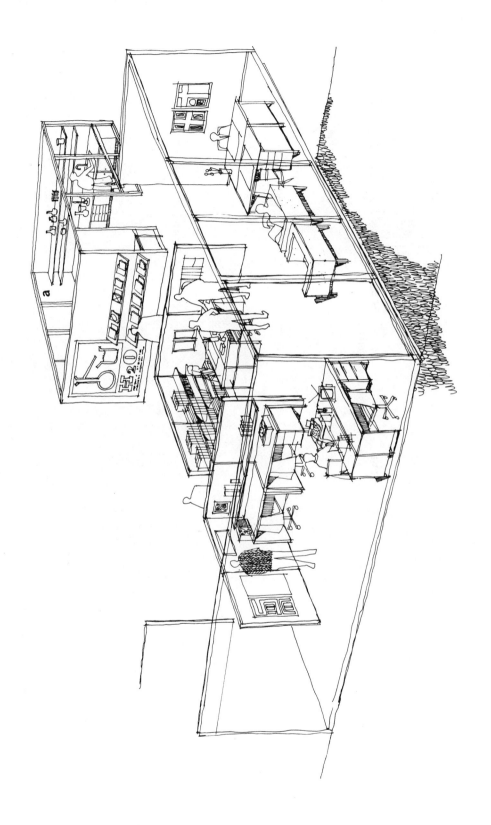

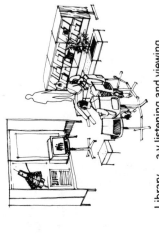

Library. a-v listening and viewing

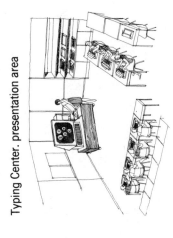

Typing Center. presentation area

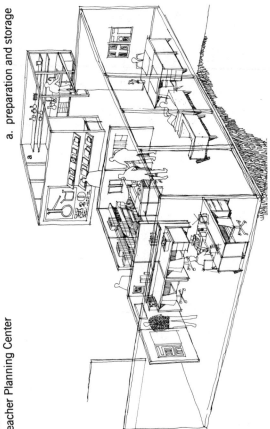

a. preparation and storage

Science/Math Barn
Teacher Planning Center

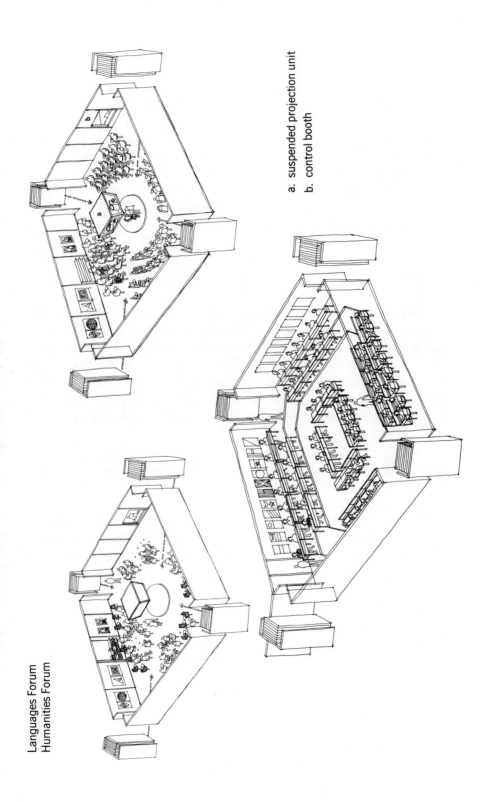

Languages Forum
Humanities Forum

a. suspended projection unit
b. control booth

tral spaces are rimmed by small special-purpose rooms—for listening, for conferring, for testing, for seminars, and for recording. Nearby is an area for instruction in typing—an almost essential skill (for which preadolescents show a special aptitude), which is easy to learn with a minimum of formal instruction. The typing room is especially equipped with audio-visual aids for instruction with large groups. The room is augmented with small booths where students can work in comparatively isolated surroundings on assigned papers.

In the upper right-hand corner of the diagram are two areas labeled "Humanities Forum" and "Languages Forum." These are highly flexible spaces to provide instruction for groups of different sizes. The arena for languages is step-tiered and wired for sound to each student station. Operable partitions make possible four separate sections for 14 students each. Mobile control consoles can be plugged in at the front of each quarter section. With all partitions retracted, the large space doubles as a place for debate or a lecture room. The humanities forum is likewise divisible by four. Thrown open, it constitutes a small theater-in-the-round or conference center. Its utility is enhanced by seats that pivot in a complete circle, so that each quarter-section can turn itself into a buzz session after the group as a whole has received a presentation.

The library-resource center is the heart of the building, physically and philosophically. It is situated so that students naturally pass through it many times a day, entering, leaving, or moving around the school. Readily accessible books, magazines, and audio-visual and electronic resources, dictionaries in which to look up words that have just come up in class, visual displays—everything the library has to offer should be represented out in the open, inviting students to partake at any time, all the time. It is an intellectual supermarket.

Note the diverse furnishings including carrels which students can use as their independent study HQ.

A living room or study atmosphere is achieved in the library through the use of informal and comfortable materials and fabrics on walls and floors, deployment of lounge chairs and work tables in open arrangements and variety in atmosphere.

Display space in the library is used to help make the school a nexus of the best works of other men's minds and hands as well as projects by the school's students.

Live television coverage of momentous events can be turned into potent instruction if auxiliary means are used to get the fullest meaning out of the experience. The school shouldn't be a place cut off from the events in the outside world; it should be electronically plugged into the world community.

4

George E. Mills

The How and Why of the "Middle" School

The reasons for the "middle school" are not simple. They consist of a complex, interrelated series of observations and studies. In an application of these reasons to the needs of a newly created school district, two new "middle" schools have been built and are in operation in Saginaw Township Community School District, adjacent to Saginaw, Mich.

For some time the junior high school concept has been under scrutiny. Many educators believe that while the theory of the junior high school is excellent, in practice it has resulted in junior high schools becoming miniature senior high schools, with the social activities, the athletic programs, and the instructional programs of the senior high school moving into the lower educational level. To some it has been apparent that this movement downward of the patterns of the senior high school has not solved the problem of educating boys and girls at lower age levels. Rather, it has multiplied and intensified the problems of their normal growth and development.

There are those who advocate that the perfect school would be that in which all students, kindergarten through the 12th grade, are present. This theory has obvious merit. Nonetheless, it has certain obstacles. Most school communities must break the 13 year sequence in terms of their ability to finance school facilities in the face of exploding populations.

As we studied the 320 physical, mental, emotional and social

From *The Nation's Schools* (December, 1961): 43–52 and 72–74.

growth characteristics and teaching implications for boys and girls, from kindergarten through the 12th grade, we concluded that there were centers of similarity in this 13 year span that merited close study. We observed that the kindergarten youngster and the first, second, third and fourth grade youngsters had more of these growth characteristics in common. We noted further that the growth characteristics of boys and girls at the age levels represented in the fifth, sixth, seventh and eighth grades also had great areas of similarity. We felt, too, that the age level represented by the ninth, tenth, eleventh and twelfth graders in terms of those growth characteristics had large areas of similarity.

In addition, there were strong indications from the Edsel Ford Foundation Curriculum Study in Dearborn that the four-year high school (since tradition forces these four years to be considered for college entrance) ought to be under one hat or in one institution, rather than having the ninth grade in a separate institution. These conclusions led us to establish the *primary school*, which includes kindergarten through Grade 4, the *middle school* with Grades 5 through 8, and the *four-year high school* with Grades 9 through 12.

We are convinced that a school society and environment for boys and girls at the middle school level of growth can be managed better in terms of their development than at any other breaking point in the 13 years of their school experience. This is the kind of school society in which dating, dinner dances, and so forth are not considered appropriate experiences.

We believe that the *primary* schools should be devoted to the development of basic skills and the extension of interests and appreciations. The *middle school* also must be concerned with the development of basic skills but, equally important, with the reinforcement and extension of those basic skills through their application in meaningful situations where students have the opportunity to become increasingly *self-directing.*

The primary schools are considered neighborhood schools, where boys and girls from a given community area assemble for the purpose of learning. The middle school is the kind of situation in which several of these primary communities come together for the expansion of the learning environment, the rubbing of shoulders with peer groups from other neighborhood communities, and the stimulation of an expanding

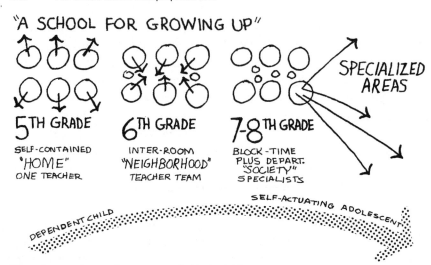

"A SCHOOL FOR GROWING UP"

SPECIALIZED AREAS

5TH GRADE
SELF-CONTAINED
"HOME"
ONE TEACHER

6TH GRADE
INTER-ROOM
"NEIGHBORHOOD"
TEACHER TEAM

7-8TH GRADE
BLOCK-TIME
PLUS DEPART.
"SOCIETY"
SPECIALISTS

SELF-ACTUATING ADOLESCENT

DEPENDENT CHILD

Place for growing up is a concept behind middle schools in Saginaw, Mich. Idea is to provide a "transition school" to facilitate growth and development of pupil from dependent child to self-actuating adolescent.

world. This is a part of the "growing up process"—the moving into the larger "environment."

In the middle schools, the fifth and sixth grade youngsters are in self-contained classrooms, but there is a significant difference, best illustrated by the fact that the fifth grade classroom is a different kind of physical facility than the fourth grade classroom. The sixth grade classroom is different from the fifth grade classroom, and the seventh and eighth grade classrooms are different kinds of physical facilities than the fifth and sixth grade classrooms.

Whereas in the primary school the classroom unit is largely self-sufficient and unrelated to other similar classroom units, in the fifth grade classroom in the middle school the pupil activities are related to those in the other classes in the fifth grade "house." This concept is broadened in the sixth grade "house," and is broadened still further in the seventh and eighth grade "house."

The *physical facilities* in terms of building and equipment as well as *program* are tailored for a particular grade level.

As these pupils move through the middle school, in terms of the fifth and sixth grade "houses," and in terms of the seventh and eighth grade block-of-time programs, they retain a "home base" which diminishes as they move through these grade levels, and as their specialized interests areas develop correspondingly and are stimulated. Thus this "school for growing up" really consists of three transition schools, each one leading the pupil on to a deeper and wider learning environment.

The Saginaw Township Community School Concept. The new Saginaw Township Community School District presented these exciting challenges and opportunities: (1) to consolidate the existing educational programs of five separate primary school districts into one program, making the improvements that such an opportunity afforded; (2) to develop new instructional programs for children in Grades 7 through 12, who previous to this time had been attending the Saginaw city schools; (3) to build new buildings (to house an exploding enrollment) that would be of maximum educational use and for a reasonable cost; and (4) to acquire a new staff of teachers—a staff which would be interested in and enthusiastic about the kinds of opportunities and the kinds of challenges that have just been mentioned.

Beyond these challenges was an overwhelming desire on the part of the first (and new) board of education and the first (and new) superintendent to build a school system in a community which presently ranked as one of the wealthier school communities in the state. But when the full 12 grades were housed within the school district, an average tax base (for the state of Michigan) for each student would then be established.

The total staff launched a massive in-service education program. For a short three months, utilizing large amounts of "released time from school," after-school and Saturday meetings, the total staff studied the various systems of educational philosophy, ranging from Dewey to Adler. An intensive look was taken at the various schools of educational psychology, theories of learning, and theory of personality development. Also studied intensively were the nature of society today, characteristics of our community, and the characteristics of boys and girls in terms of their emotional, intellectual, social and physical development. Out of this matrix of activity, the staff, together with the board of education and subsequent involvement of the community, established three major purposes for education in our community.

The first major purpose was to develop within the pupils a system of values for citizenship in our democratic society. It was felt that with the tremendous change in all aspects of our way of life, the one thing that must be done for and with boys and girls is to help them achieve a set of ethical values, mores and standards by which to face the changing world—and to face this changing world successfully and securely.

The second major purpose was the well known one of developing the ability to think clearly and objectively. This objective or purpose should need no further explanation.

The third major purpose was to develop mature, self-actuating individuals who are competent, self-sufficient, cooperative and who find satisfaction in giving as well as in receiving.

Supporting these three major purposes, the staff, the board of education, and the community agreed upon 24 general statements of specific purposes which support the three major purposes. Here are five examples:

1. To encourage respect for the dignity and worth of each person and to treat him accordingly.

2. To help each individual understand himself and his unique potentialities for leadership as well as for "followership," and to help him understand the contribution of each role to himself and his society.

3. To help each individual attain competence with the basic skills of reading, writing, spelling, speaking and the use of numbers.

4. To accept and encourage each person's spark of constructive creativity.

5. To provide children with experiences in democratic living and learning, which include experiences with the exercise of authority that originates sometimes outside the classroom, sometimes with the teacher, and whenever possible with a group.

What kind of educational arrangements could be made in terms of buildings, in terms of program, in terms of instructional materials, in terms of learning experiences that would develop these 24 specific objectives that supported the overarching three major purposes? This was the task.

Designing the School Plant. The board of education and the school administration conducted a nationwide search for an architectural firm to design the two new middle schools and the first of two new high schools—now named the Douglas MacArthur High School. This intensive search resulted in their selecting the firm of Caudill, Rowlett and Scott of Houston, Tex., as the prime architect, to design three new school buildings and to develop a long-range school site study for this new school district. Two local associate architects were appointed.

Daniel W. Toshach was chosen as the associate architect for the Chippewa Middle School (the centralized school) and Spears and Prine as the associate architects for the Mackinaw Middle School (the decentralized school). These architectural firms were handed the education specifications for the Middle School in September 1959, and the schools were in use the following year.

To dictate an architectural style is to restrict the creativeness of the architect. It would seem that each building should present a significant architecture—where the day-to-day awareness of the building, its vistas, its genius, its beauty and imagination would develop in the student body and the community a sensitivity to, and an education in, architecture.

In addition to program needs, the architects were instructed to spend money for school facilities in those areas of the school in which the pupils would spend most of their time—the classroom instructional areas.

The decision was made to build a centralized and a decentralized school with identical facilities so that the actual cost of each might be known. But more important, since many more schools would be built in the community during the next 20 years, data as to which is the better educational plant would be available to successive boards of education and school administrations.

Each middle school can house 650 pupils at optimum. The cost per pupil for the decentralized school was $1352; the cost for the centralized school was $1309. The total area per school is as follows: 62,441 square feet in the decentralized school, and 63,657 square feet in the centralized. The square foot cost in the decentralized school was $14.07, and in the centralized school, $13.37. These are costs as computed by A.I.A. formula and represent the architectural, mechanical and electrical contracts.

In both schools, the fifth grade classrooms are built three to a side

Mackinaw (decentralized) School

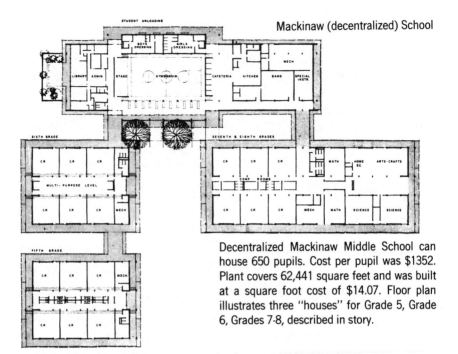

Decentralized Mackinaw Middle School can house 650 pupils. Cost per pupil was $1352. Plant covers 62,441 square feet and was built at a square foot cost of $14.07. Floor plan illustrates three "houses" for Grade 5, Grade 6, Grades 7-8, described in story.

Chippewa (centralized) School

Centralized Chippewa Middle School also can house 650 pupils. Per pupil cost was $1309, about 3 per cent less than Mackinaw.

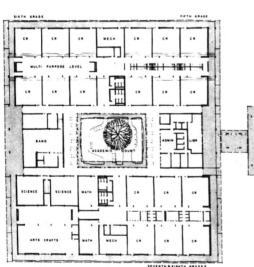

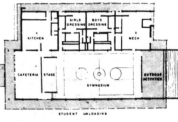

Square foot cost amounted to $13.37, with plant covering 63,657 square feet. Costs represent architectural, mechanical and electrical contracts.

Architects: Caudill, Rowlett & Scott, Houston, Tex.
Associate architects:
    (for Mackinaw): Spears & Prine, Saginaw, Mich.
    (for Chippewa): Daniel W. Toshach, Saginaw, Mich.

along a raised mall which houses sinks, storage space, and toilet facilities. The sixth grade classrooms are built three to a side along a raised mall, which is used as a long group instruction space. Each house, whether fifth or sixth grade, has storage space for science tables, handicraft tables, science equipment, and so forth. The sixth grade house uses gang toilets.

The three seventh grade block-of-time classrooms face the three eighth grade block-of-time classrooms. Between these classrooms is a series of various sized conference rooms and individual study carrels. The remainder of the seventh and eighth grade building consists of two mathematics classrooms, two science classrooms, and the unified arts area, consisting of three distinct areas and a large space for common use.

While the centralized building and the decentralized facility contain administrative offices, a teachers lounge, conference rooms, the instructional materials center, dining room, and the gym-auditorium space, they are arranged differently in each of the two plans. However, the spaces are virtually identical.

No classroom cells are found in middle school. The architects used the three-sided classroom concept so that classrooms no longer can be thought of as "cells." This openness, the use of glass, and the see-through possibilities have intrigued both teachers and pupils. We have found that it is much more difficult for adults (the public) to adjust to this type of space than it has been for the boys and girls. In fact, discussions and surveys have revealed that the pupils do not wish to go back to the "cells." The freedom and the spatial view have appealed greatly to them.

The availability of quiet spaces, either the individual study carrels or the conference rooms, incorporated with the use of house planning has solved the problem of quiet and noisy activity going on simultaneously within a given house. It is likely that some further acoustical treatment will be done to minimize the transfer of sound across the mall space and the conference and carrel spaces. The three walls of each classroom are utilized as teaching spaces, with chalkboard and tackboard extending from the ceiling to the floor. Each classroom has an outside entrance as well as access through the corridor or mall.

The provision of movable storage cabinets, movable cloak cabinets, book carts, tables and chairs results in the arrangement of the classroom to fit the instructional activity under way. The patterns of arrangement change often.

The classroom in the middle school must serve many purposes. It is a place where boys and girls, in their efforts to acquire information and perfect skills, study, read, write, organize, evaluate and drill. It is a laboratory for physical sciences, in which they study plants and animals, rocks and rockets, and the rest of their physical world. It is a workshop in which pupils build models, apparatus and other objects. It is a place to see motion pictures and television when these contribute to learning. It is a place for social learning, formal and informal. Committees, individual pupils, and the class as a whole work together on problems. It is a studio where children paint, paste, cut and model. It is room where children sing and listen to music. Also provided is a sufficient number of individual small group and large group work stations to accommodate all the pupils at any one time in a variety of activities.

The persistent problem of grouping has been faced. "Performance level grouping" is used. Reading ability is the primary determinant for inclusion in a verbal or nonverbal class group. The Iowa Test of Basic Skills is used. The reading scores are converted into percentiles, and, thus, class groups are established by taking a range of reading ability wherever such is possible.

"House" planning for fifth and sixth grades. A typical program for either a fifth or sixth grade proceeds on the basis of "house planning." The teachers in the fifth grade "house" will, in a general way, plan together the language arts program for the week, or the science, social studies, music program, or any given program. This "house" (or team) planning results in strengthening the skills and technics of all involved. Teachers report excellent results. At times, each teacher works with his or her own assigned class group, or the classes are put together in groups of two, three, four or more classes. On other occasions groups are divided into subgroups for specific skill development.

Grades 7 and 8 are housed in a combination of self-contained classrooms for language arts, social studies, group guidance, and foreign language, and in specialized classrooms for mathematics, science, music, unified arts (arts and crafts, homemaking and industrial arts), and physical and health education.

The block-of-time teachers, as they are called, have use of several small conference rooms of different size and student study carrels for all kinds of individual activities. Students have readily accepted self-disciplining responsibilities in the use of individual, small group, and class size activity.

The science program is a program in the development of science concepts, scientific attitudes, scientific methods and scientific inquiry. It is a "do" program. In the centralized middle school, Chippewa, which is built around a court, the court is used by the science classes for all kinds of projects and activities. In the decentralized school an outdoor science area is under development.

The mathematics classrooms are plentifully supplied with various kinds of mathematical apparatus, which are extensively used by teachers. The Yale school study mathematics program has been used rather extensively in Grades 7 and 8. The results are heartening.

Music program attracts many. The music program for the fifth and sixth grade pupils is handled by the classroom teacher with some consultative help from the music teachers for the seventh and eighth grades. The general music program for the seventh and eighth grade pupils is handled by a specialized music teacher. This program alternates with physical education once or twice a week, dependent upon the school.

After three semesters of operation we find that nearly 35 per cent of the pupils are involved in *instrumental music.* This means that the music facilities are taxed to capacity. It will be interesting to know if this high level of participation in instrumental music maintains itself over the coming years. It well may be that this is (1) the effect of deprivation from previous years, or (2) the halo effect of a new and exciting venture. Many teachers and parents suspect that this high level of participation in the instrumental program will be maintained.

The instructional materials center is a storehouse for all kinds of instructional materials. Library books, reference books, textbooks of various difficulties, magazines, newspapers, films, filmstrips, other kinds of audio-visual materials and equipment are available from the center. Teachers and pupils alike select materials from the instructional materials center. This program hypothesizes that book carts are taken to the center and the librarian and pupils select materials to be taken to the classroom. Or such materials may be used in the center.

5

Walter F. Fogg &
Hugh J. Diamond

Two Versions of
the "House" Plan

There no longer is anything new about the "school within a school" approach as a means of correcting the shortcomings of a jumbo-sized school. Yet *the* plan for "humanizing" mass enrollments has not been perfected. Meanwhile, variations of the "small schools within a large school" continue to appear. In the articles on the following pages, two successful versions of the "house" plan, as utilized at Scarsdale and Niskayuna, N.Y., are described. Both junior high schools embrace Grades 6, 7 and 8. Despite differences in organization, both districts report this common benefit: increased attention to individual pupils without loss of large-school facilities. Scarsdale's program is in its fourth year; Niskayuna's is in its second.

Scarsdale Plan Is Flexible and Relaxed
Walter F. Fogg

When our seventh and eighth graders still were part of a large, six-year high school, they were programed in all parts of a rambling building. Both the 1000 children and the teachers seemed to develop unnecessary tensions, and the children had little "sense of belonging."

This situation was changed completely with the opening of Scarsdale's $4 million junior high school. The building was designed as a "house plan" form of organization, the first in our area. Planning for

From *The Nation's Schools* (June, 1961): 65–69 and 94.

House plan forms the center of the school program at Scarsdale Junior High School in Scarsdale, N.Y. In each house (Popham, Butler and Cooper), provisions are made for teaching art, general music, science, mathematics, English and related subjects, and social studies. Shared areas include general administration, library, auditorium, and specialized music facilities, gymnasia, dining rooms, shop and homemaking spaces. The school was designed to bring together economically 1000 or more pupils and yet to preserve the values inherent in small schools. The school, located on a steep side-hill site, suits both the topography and educational program.

an enrollment of 1000 pupils in Grades 6, 7, and 8, the staff committee devised an organizational framework that guaranteed knowable-size groups of children without surrendering the specialized facilities appropriate to a large school—a school-within-a-school concept.

The present structure consists of two building masses connected by enclosed ramps or bridges. One of these masses accommodates two house units. The other incorporates one house, and many of the shared spaces (auditorium, cafeteria, gymnasium, shop and homemaking rooms) also are incorporated here.

How is the school organized? About 340 pupils from all three grades are assigned to a house and remain there for three years.

Teachers are selected to instruct only the pupils in one house. Three groups of teachers are matched carefully for subject balance within a house and between houses. They teach everything in the usual junior high programs *except* physical education, shop, homemaking and some of the specialized music courses.

Each house has 14 classrooms, including art, science and general music rooms. Also, there is a large visual-aid room for projection, informal dramatics, house meetings, parent meetings, and similar activities. A dean's office in each house is the nerve center for both administration and guidance.

Is there any grouping? Pupils in the houses are organized by grade levels, typically with four classes in each of the three grades and about 25 pupils in each class.

Generally, classes are deliberately heterogenous—nearly all pupils expect to enter college and nearly all do—except where course election (and guidance) causes some homogeneity.

At the extremes of the ability scale, needs of pupils are met primarily by individual rather than group methods. However, there are remedial classes for the slow learners and several program provisions for the gifted.

Twice a week a special interest program aimed at enrichment involves the entire school population. It embraces 50 groups from all houses and grades, and is held in areas chosen by the pupils.

How do the teachers function? At the sixth grade level teachers are responsible for the total school program except physical education, art, music and shop. The latter subjects are taught on a departmentalized basis. Science teachers are occupied almost entirely with Grades 7 and 8, but serve as consultants and advisers to Grade 6 teachers.

At the seventh and eighth grade levels all teachers are "specialists." Also, one English teacher in each house has extensive training and experience in teaching reading; he acts as a consultant to the other teachers in his house.

What about administration? It is important that a house have as much autonomy as possible; for this reason the house dean is a key figure. Although he is certified as a guidance counselor, he spends much of his time on administrative matters. He leads, stimulates, evaluates his staff, and he programs his pupils. He also makes the countless daily arrangements and adjustments that are necessary for smooth operation. While running his own little school, he also must see that his program meshes with the over-all plan and organization. Thus, the deans work closely with each other and their principal.

Of a total staff of 60, there are 12 "shared" members, including the principal, whose activities are school-wide. Other "share" personnel are: four physical education teachers, two shop teachers, two home-making teachers, a librarian, a nurse, and a psychologist. Music teachers have a unique role: Each is assigned to a house but directs all-school groups in band, orchestra *or* choir.

How are classes scheduled? Class periods are of uniform length (42 minutes). Most subjects are scheduled for a single period, but classes in art, shop and homemaking use two consecutive periods, to save cleanup time.

English and social studies at the seventh grade level are scheduled in a block of time with one teacher for two or three consecutive periods a day. Since sixth graders are taught special subjects by teachers on a departmental schedule, they must mesh with the total school program for these classes. The rest of the time the sixth grade teacher and pupils simply ignore the class bells.

What are the advantages of the house plan? After more than three years of experience with the house plan, we could not think of running our school without it. Some of the important gains are as follows:

1. Children have developed a sense of identity and belonging far stronger than is usual in a school of 1000. It is almost impossible for any child to become "lost."

2. Teachers know the children and other teachers better. One of the pleasant surprises has been the obvious pride and loyalty that teachers developed toward their houses.

3. Loyalty to the house has supported, rather than undermined, loyalty to the whole school.

4. Communication—teacher to child, teacher to teacher, and teacher to administrator—is greatly facilitated. Projects involving teamwork by several teachers grow easily out of physical proximity and a "knowable" group.

5. Flexibility is greater. Somehow we find it easier to start, stop and change direction in a school of 340 than in one of a thousand or more.

6. Traffic is reduced to a minimum, and there is less congestion. A pupil needs to walk only the length of two or three classrooms for at least 80 per cent of his school program. For this and other reasons tensions are reduced, and the general tone of the school is purposeful but relaxed. It is significant that the referral of behavior problems to house deans has almost been eliminated.

What are the special problems? We have discovered no serious difficulties, but for those who are considering such a plan the following observations may be helpful.

1. The principal is extremely busy coordinating. He is holding the reins on three spirited horses, not one, and he must see that they run together in the same direction and at their best speed.

2. There had been concern that the plan might be divisive (lead to unhealthy competition between houses) and might undermine loyalties to the school. In practice this has been no problem. In the shared classes, in the dining rooms, and in our activity program we deliberately mix the pupils from the three houses. The physical education teachers have carefully avoided setting up a sports program based on house competition.

3. Once the houses are set up and staffed, any rapid enrollment growth must be handled carefully in order to keep a reasonable balance in size and, more important, in staff utilization. It is not essential, of course, that the houses be exactly the same size, but they must have identical programs. Since the beginning of this program no teacher has requested a transfer from one house to another, and no teacher has been moved. Only two such changes have been made among pupils.

Is a house plan expensive? If Scarsdale Junior High School were to offer its present program in the framework of a conventional organization, it is difficult to see how any significant savings could be realized in either plant or staff costs. At the same time no increased costs have resulted from the operation of the house plan, and the teacher-pupil ratio in this school is no higher than in any of the other five schools in the district.

We seem to have remarkable support for our house plan among the teachers, the pupils, and the community. A principal can't ask for much more. Of course, we could easily think of one or two places where additional staffing would be advantegeous. An assistant principal chiefly concerned with pupil activities and some of the shared areas would be helpful, but doesn't every administrator yearn for additional help?

In Niskayuna, a 'House' Fits Into an Existing School
Hugh J. Diamond

Another version of the junior high school "house plan" is in its second year of operation at Van Antwerp Junior High School in Niskayuna, N.Y. At present, the special house arrangement is in operation for the sixth grade only, but future plans call for a house type organization with teacher teams staffing Grades 6, 7 and 8.

In this instance no new school was built; the organization plan had to be fitted into existing facilities. The decisive move involved a centralization of all sixth graders from five elementary schools with the seventh and eighth graders; this followed the separation of the ninth grade from the four-year high school program.

The Niskayuna plan of organization "balances" the following: the advantages of the self-contained elementary classroom with departmentalized team teaching; homeroom closeness with specialized teaching; the efficiency and economy of large groups with the intimacy of small groups; identification ("belonging") with stimulation (wider social and academic contacts); provision for progress of the academically talented and the handicapped children with a program for regular class groups, and the economy of teacher instruction for classes of a maximum 80 pupils with group and individual counseling.

The following explanation of the Niskayuna house plan offers a description of a new kind of sixth grade.

At Van Antwerp Junior High School all house members are members of Grade 6. When the plan went into operation in the fall of 1959, the 240 Grade 6 pupils were assigned to three houses. Each house was divided into three sections of about 80 pupils, making a total of nine sections.

Before the house and section memberships were fixed, two special groups were separated: the academically talented pupils and those with extreme learning problems. Between these extremes three other classifications emerged: high average, average and low average.

Sectioning was done on the basis of ability, achievement, work habits, school history, teachers' judgments, and the scatter-gram relationship of students' academic achievement to I.Q. scores.

Since the typical I.Q. of Niskayuna sixth graders is quite high (118), and since academic motivation is well above normal expectations, we were not surprised to find three sections of pupils in the high average category, three sections in the average, and only one section in the low average.

Once grouping was complete, the pattern of the individual houses could be established quickly. One house was given the one academically talented group, along with one of the high average and one of the average sections. Another house was given the one section with extreme learning problems, together with one high average and one average section. Finally, the third house combined a high average, an average, and a low average section. Houses were designated north, east and west.

Most important in creating and maintaining the elementary school atmosphere has been the establishment of heterogeneous homeroom groups. From the very beginning these groups have been kept together as working units for a large portion of the school day for instruction in English and social studies and in special subjects (art, music, physical education, and French). The pupil can identify with a single class group during a large part of his school day since he is taught English and social studies—and either reading, mathematics or science—by one teacher who knows him well as an individual.

The nine homeroom teachers are the same staff members who worked as a committee to plan the Grade 6 program. They are experienced sixth grade teachers from the elementary schools who moved into the junior high school building.

Before the change was made, these nine teachers were polled on their preference for teaching either reading, mathematics or science. Once the staff preferences were identified, the faculty organization of the houses got under way.

To each house there was assigned a team of three teachers which was responsible for teaching English and social studies to the *homeroom* group. In addition, each member of the team was assigned to the entire 80 pupil house for instructing homogeneous classes in his or her field of special strength and interest (reading, mathematics or science).

Within each three-teacher team, one teacher acts as chairman. He is responsible for planning and coordinating his house with the other two houses. Also, he represents his unit in planning with the administration and the consultants. (The consultants include five secondary department heads who are responsible for the coordination of the curriculum in Grades 6 to 12).

The three house chairmen, in turn, meet regularly with the principal to discuss common problems and to seek important decisions affecting the operation of the program. Each house chairman also crosses house lines to work with other chairmen for curriculum coordination either in reading, mathematics or science.

Opportunity is afforded members of each of the three-teacher teams to plan their activities and to lay out their schedules together. A great amount of sharing is necessary, for these teachers must know 80 pupils instead of 27, as in previous years. Each teacher now operates not in a single classroom situation but as a member of a professional team which develops and nurtures original ideas and which inaugurates more imaginative and creative approaches to subject matter.

In developing the English and social studies program the nine Grade 6 teachers work together as a group with the subject consultants. In the case of reading, mathematics and science, teachers of the respective subjects cross house lines to work with the teachers who instruct in the same specialty in the other houses.

The dual approach to teaching assures balanced instruction. While the *heterogeneous* homeroom group and the homeroom teacher assure warmth and security for the individual child, the *homogeneous* reading, mathematics and science classes provide special stimulation and challenge. In these three fields the subject content is covered as quickly or as slowly as the children can move.

Occasionally, a sixth grader who would benefit from an activity course is assigned to one. Likewise, a pupil who is advanced enough to be placed in a seventh or eighth grade mathematics class is moved ahead. These are exceptions, but our program is flexible enough to handle the unusual.

Important in the Niskayuna program is the activity period. This is the time when the sixth grader has the opportunity to meet with junior high school pupils outside his own house. Orchestra, band, chorus, student council, special interest clubs, and intramural sports programs receive attention at this time. Group study, too, is scheduled, and time is provided for individual groups to join together for enrichment, for special help, or for out-of-class preparation.

School people have seen in this new junior high school house program, including the new kind of sixth grade (our district has a K-5-3-4 organization), answers to two pressing needs: higher quality of education and adequate school housing for a rapidly growing school population. For parents it has held the promise of enriched educational offerings for their children. Pupils have been pleased with their early promotion to the junior high school. Taxpayers have seen the plan as a means of reducing immediate school housing needs by more efficient building utilization.

Even now, the "forgotten" fifth and eighth graders are taking over responsibilities in activities formerly reserved for the sixth and ninth graders. The effect of bringing elementary and secondary school teachers and elementary and secondary school programs together in the junior high school seems to be making itself felt, says Arthur Putman, principal of Van Antwerp Junior High School.

The children have made a wonderful adjustment to this new way of school life. They like the amount of individual responsibility given to them. The belonging to a house and the close association with the same group of children and teachers are especially attractive features for them.

Our teachers have reacted favorably. The first year is always the most difficult; now that most of the operating procedures have been smoothed out, the teachers are more than satisfied. They are particularly happy in being able to exploit their teaching strength. They enjoy working together with other teachers in the small team groups.

The entire program is based on good educational practices that have been put into use in many places, but rarely combined as we employ them. The junior high school plan for Grades 6, 7 and 8 is here to stay in Niskayuna.

6

"Middle School" for Tomorrow—Successor to the Junior High School

How should you house a junior high school? Following the White Plains conference, Architect Brubaker and Consultant Leggett drew up their idea of a "middle school" that would make everyone happy. Their sketches are presented on this and the following pages.

Building Blocks

Here are the components that make up your middle school. They can be arranged in any way that best suits your needs, your program,

Building blocks

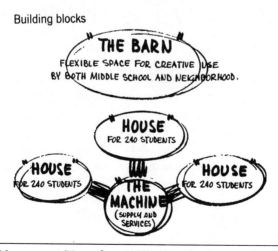

From *School Management* (November, 1960): 101-07.   Reprinted with permission of the publisher. This article is copyrighted © 1960 by CCM Professional Magazines, Inc. All rights reserved.

your community, the shape of your land, your local building codes and your budget.

The key to middle school design is flexibility. As needs change, so do programs. Enrollments vary, too, and groupings change with them. Adaptable facilities, therefore, are essential. Rigid schedules have no place here. Emphasis is placed, instead, on the individual. The components are designed with this in mind.

Each "house" consists of 240 students of middle school age, plus a team of teachers. The three houses share common facilities: "the barn," an adaptable shelter (theatre space and swimming pool) to encourage the natural creativity of pupils; and "the machine," to provide supplies and services. Mechanical and electrical aids will be used liberally in order to free teachers for program planning and individual student contact.

Program. Each middle school provides for the social and academic needs, interests and desires of 720 students.

Organization. Three "houses," each with 240 seventh, eighth and ninth grade students, plus common facilities.

Design components. A "house" of varied, flexible classrooms. A "machine" for service and supply functions. A "barn" for creative assembly and exercise.

Component 1 "The House"

Each house provides spaces adaptable to large and small group work as well as individual study. While details can vary with the particular school, these are the general space and facility requirements:

Homeroom area. Seventh graders will spend about 75% of their time here. Space allowances should be made for about 80 students in the typical house.

Seminar and classroom space. Eighth and ninth graders, in sections of various sizes and class hours, will need flexible learning areas.

Work space. Two areas are allotted for this purpose: a combined science and unified arts work space and a smaller, combined science

"The house"

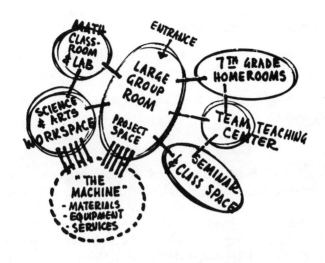

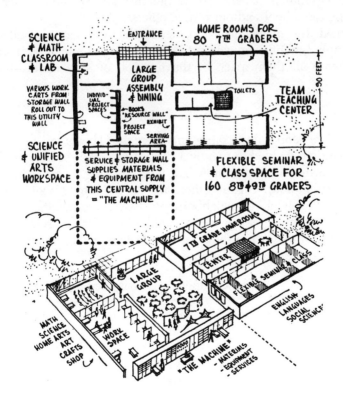

and math classroom and laboratory. Emphasis here is on small group and individual study, experiment and project work.

Large group meeting room. Assembly, dining, lectures, films, group projects and social affairs are carried on here.

Team teaching center. A headquarters for teachers and a place for their equipment.

Component 2 "The Machine"

One side of each house is attached to "the machine." the school's storage, supply, maintenance and control center. The house is serviced through this common wall separating its work space and large group meeting areas from the machine. Teaching aids, electronic equipment and learning materials are passed over as needed. Food, prepared in central kitchens, is delivered to the machine and rolled on carts into the dining areas of each house at lunch time. Heating and cooling equipment is located in the machine. Centered here, too, might be the school's adminstrative offices.

With all the mechanical and electrical equipment and all service and supply functions concentrated in the central machine, the houses can devote all their space to the first job of any school—teaching youngsters.

Component 3 "The Barn"

The middle school and community center. "The barn" is actually a large building divided in two by a central, covered social area. On one side is the theatre and exhibit hall with dressing rooms, work spaces and a flexible floor. On the other, are the swimming pool and locker rooms. Both school and neighborhood share these facilities. Space for community parking is provided near the barn for the convenience of the public. Students use the pool area lockers before going out to the playing fields next to the building.

The Components Assembled

Suburban Middle School

This example of a typical, available, flat suburban site presents one way a middle school can be laid out. The arrangement of its elements can vary with your needs and desires and the limitations imposed by the shape and location of your site. The houses, however, must sur-

"The machine". Three houses around the machine create a middle school for 720 students.

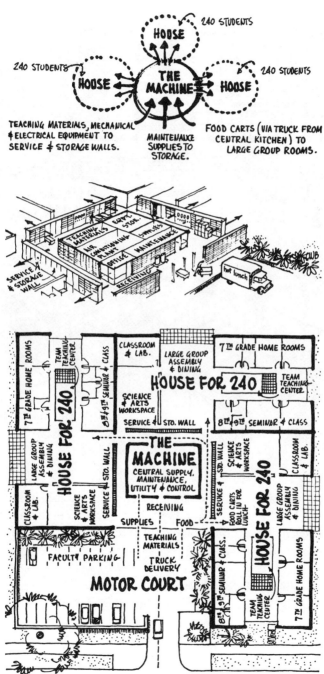

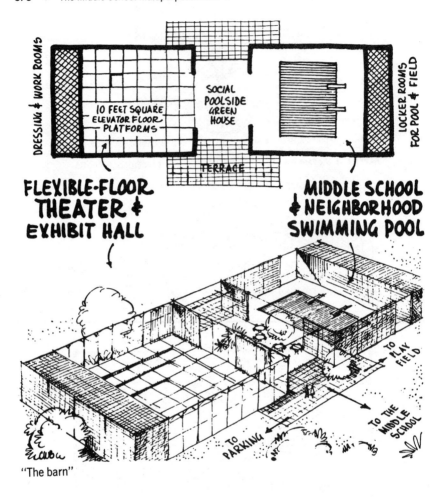

"The barn"

round the machine on three sides. In effect, they are treated as one large unit. In the plan given here, the barn faces a major street, making it easily accessible to residents who needn't pass through the rest of the school to reach it.

In the city, the components create a multi-floor Urban Middle School

Restricted by a small gridiron site in a crowded city area, the urban middle school expands upward rather than outward. Components still have the same relationship to each other, but the two house-machine units, built on separate levels, serve twice as many students. The

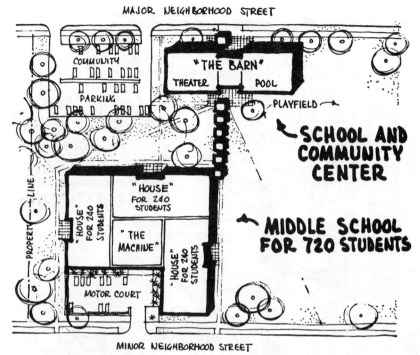

A suburban middle school

larger barn is necessary for the same reason. In this case, it has been extended to include a gymnasium, since climate and site limitations restrict the size and number of outdoor playing fields. School and community parking space is underground.

And in the country, an Exurban Middle School

Unhampered by a cramped site, the middle school of the exurbs spreads over an ample, wooded, rolling area set beside a lake. More freedom is possible here in the design, size and location of the school's components to take advantage of natural features. But whatever the geography, the inter-relationship of the middle school's components remains the same. Staffed by teaching teams, these units can provide the flexible, adaptable schools you will require for tomorrow's changing educational needs.

An urban middle school

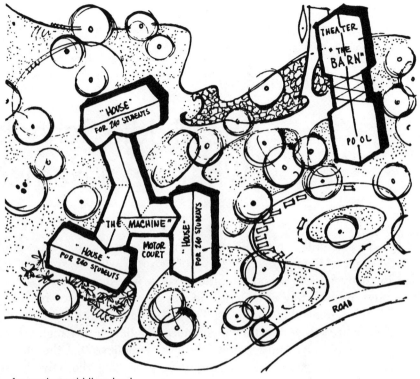

An exurban middle school

7

Carl L. Midjaas

The Middle School:
What's in a Name?

If a rose is still a rose by any other name, is the middle school anything more than a junior high school? Not if we believe what we see in many middle school facilities. Not a few new middle school buildings are indistinguishable in the way they utilize space from the junior high schools they replaced. They may be brighter and cosmetically more attractive, but they could accommodate junior high school programs equitably. And many would have us believe that the middle school is really a junior high school in disguise, that the only significant difference between the two is the inclusion of grade six (and perhaps grade five) into the usual junior high grade span. For some educators in search of instant innovation, the shift from junior high to middle school has taken no longer than the time required to put new letters on the building and change the office stationery.

If, on the other hand, we believe that the concept of the middle school recognizes the unique physical and emotional changes characteristic of transescent young people, the dangers of excessively competitive school activities, the need for an optimal balance between individual security and exploratory freedom, and the equal importance of effective as well as cognitive learning, then the middle school environment must not be a replica of what the junior high school has been.

More than anything else, what is required of educators in planning meaningful middle school facilities is that they (1) evaluate learning

From *Michigan Journal of Secondary Education* (Summer, 1971): 55–61.

program criteria carefully, (2) establish priorities for those criteria, and (3) insist that both program criteria and priorities be adhered to in the physical design of the middle school facility. Only by questioning the appropriateness of learning activities suggested for the middle school and establishing priorities for those program elements important in fulfilling its purposes can educators design a consistent and meaningful learning program. Only by insisting that building design follow program requirements can they develop an environment which promotes desired learning activites and behaviors. An important element in this process is carefully formulating written educational specifications, subsequently to be used by the architect as a planning guide and by the educator as a review of architectural design.

The heart of the problem in middle school design is evaluating learning program criteria.

> Big criteria have little criteria
>   upon their backs to bite 'em.
> The small ones have still smaller,
>   and so on *ad infinitum.*[1]

For every assumption which goes unrecognized and unexamined, the design of the middle school suffers. It risks becoming more and more like what we know, what we are familiar and comfortable with, but less and less like what we should have if the concept of the middle school is to be meaningful for young people. When programs in music or physical education or home economics are transferred intact and unchanged from the high school (via the junior high school) to the middle school, there has been a failure to examine the big criteria and "little criteria upon their backs." When learners are subjected to the same depersonalization which all too frequently characterizes junior high school or the same rigidly departmental approach to compartmental learning which permeates most upper-grade education, the purposes of the middle school have lost out to an acceptance of mindless tradition.

What characteristics are desirable in the design of the middle school? Whether the instructional strategy involves team teaching, differentiated staffing, non-grading, the traditional 1-to-30 classroom grouping, or a combination of these and other approaches, certain common elements seem essential for achieving the middle school's purposes. Any middle school must provide for accommodating that mix of security and freedom middle school learners need. Assuming the program provides ways for students to retain a sense of identity and group cohesiveness, while it permits increased degrees of exploration, the middle school facility should reflect this subtle combination: for instance, by containing team clusters or pods where the learner may spend a block of time each day with the same teachers, by providing for him a group learning activity space where he interacts with a common group of young people at fixed times during the day or week, or by establishing a "territory" which remains his for personal use during any unscheduled time and serves as office, study area, experiment station, project space, or whatever else he wishes to define. The exploratory aspect of the security-freedom mix suggests developing open labs where the learner can go at any time to work independently, or "mini-course" space where studies of mutual interest to learner and instructor can take place for periods ranging perhaps from one week to several months. It might involve a "general store" approach wherein materials which appeal to middle school students (e.g., cameras, books, cassettes, models) are displayed in a supermarket setting and are leased or sold to the learner at cost.

Second, the successful middle school facility avoids over-developed, elaborately equipped exploratory learning areas. The temptation exists to make the middle school science program as much like a high school program as possible or to provide an industrial arts program which would do justice to a small high school. But the rationale behind the middle school exploratory program is to introduce young people to a broad range of studies, not necessarily produce licensable craftsmen or fledgling physicists.[2] Some of the most successful middle schools in the nation provide what many would consider very limited physical facilities in science, art, home economics, physical education, and industrial arts. (One jig-saw comprises the extent of fixed power equipment in one school!) The middle school student can develop interest and achieve a sophisticated level of learning without retracing the mistakes of the high school. The elaborate provisioning of the middle school both results from, and further contributes to, the subject-centered approach to education.

Related to this desirability to avoid over-kill in equipping the middle school is the importance of interfacing program elements which traditionally have been segmental. When middle school philosophy talks about turning out learners who can see the relationships between art and music and language, the environment of the middle school needs to promote these interrelationships. A related arts complex combining the functions of art, crafts, family life education (or home economics), and music is not uncommon in the middle school. The interface between programs may also be encouraged by providing team instruction space or combined function labs where the sciences join with mathematics or the arts with industrial skills. As essential as any single approach in bringing this interdisciplinary element to reality is providing shared staff office/planning space. This may take the form of interdisciplinary team planning areas or simply a common office where non-team teachers in a variety of subject areas work side by side. Probably nothing contributes more to cooperation than physical contiguity.

Beyond facilitating the important task of helping learners understand the interconnectedness of knowledge, the middle school facility should reflect those program elements and instructional approaches which promise to be most meaningful to the middle school learner. Relevance is an overworked word in the lexicon of education but the lack of it is a very real fact of life in most school programs. If we examine music education for the middle school, we can glimpse what might be required in the middle school facility to make music truly relevant to young people. Most band and choral music programs appeal to a talented few.[3] Junior high school music education has traditionally emphasized the playing of only certain instruments (not guitars or recorders), the performance of "high culture" music (not current popular music), the "getting ready for concerts" syndrome (not the personal enjoyment of performing), and the performance of music (not the writing of music). Music appreciation simply as a course or activity is usually not available for those who do not wish to play in the band or sing in the chorus. With rock music, electronic music, and a broad spectrum of truly sophisticated popular music now in existence, it would seem evident that music teachers can no longer afford to ignore these developments while continuing to serve a very narrow range of interests. Music facilities in future middle schools could well include an electronic music laboratory for student compositions as well as the study of harmonics and music theory. Many more individual and ensemble practice areas might replace the larger band and choral rooms, or at least modify their size. Perhaps more important, music activities might pervade many parts of the building rather than be limited to an area next to the industrial arts shops or gymnasium. The student commons could provide areas for informal student performance, and practice areas need not be confined to a single part of the building.

No element of the curriculum should be immune from this kind of re-thinking. The study of man's ecology may require science areas very different from the usual biology laboratory designed for frog dissection. The use of math tapes with related self-instructional materials requires instructional areas unlike the traditional classroom chalkboard environment. The trend toward consumerism in home economics instruction suggests a de-emphasis of cooking and sewing as meaningful activities for most middle school learners. What passes for the social sciences in most schools is really history, and probably not very good history at that; a social science approach stressing concepts of psychology, anthropology, and economics might require a social science laboratory for experiments and projects. A physical education program which focuses upon the needs of young people rather than the needs of their parents might wisely avoid the trap of interscholastic athletic competition in favor of a very broad intramural and individual sports curriculum. In these and countless other instances, the middle school facility should be designed to encourage more meaningful learning programs, not necessarily more of the same.

An important element in the rationale of the middle school is the social development of the individual. The design of the middle school can contribute to this purpose by providing common areas for informal student interaction, small group activity and discussion areas, a variety of intramural and individual athletic areas developed around the life-time sports concept, and site development which provides environmental study areas (ponds, wooded plots, creeks) as well as student activity features (ski slope, sliding hill, ice rink, golf range, playing fields). Through skillful control of light, color, texture, and scale in the design of the building, the architect can create an environment in which young people like to be; he can provide intriguing perspectives and vistas which add interest and set mood. The use of carpeting, seating pits, and raised seating steps in learning centers, student commons, and some instructional areas serve as adequate and, from the viewpoint of many students, desirable substitutes for the conventional tablet-arm chair or desk and chair. A variety of architectural techniques can be applied to middle school design to create a warm, inviting structure which young people can enjoy.

Finally, the middle school facility should be planned with as much built-in flexibility as possible. The middle school is still an evolving concept limited only by the creativity of educators and their willingness to work. Using non-bearing wall construction at critical locations permits a limited degree of future change through removal or relocation. Demountable and operable wall systems are now familiar components in many educational designs, but they are relatively expensive solutions which leave much to be desired. The open-plan concept in school facility planning is an increasingly popular way of achieving flexibility through minimal use of interior walls and greater reliance upon an acoustically controlled environment. A related approach is the creation of uncommitted territory, space which lends itself to a variety of learning activities. General instructional area can be converted into science labs by using totally portable sink and work surface units which permit lab relocation at relatively short notice. The wisdom of avoiding excessively specialized, over-committed space in the middle school should be clear.

These, then, are characteristics often missing in the design of the middle school. When one visits a new "middle school" which features a competition gymnasium with extensive spectator seating, 900-square-foot classrooms which make no provision for the integration of knowledge, specialized facilities which ape the excessive specialization of the high school, or libraries and instructional material centers which reflect the needs of librarians rather than students, he can legitimately question whether this facility supports a middle school program. When the middle school gives slight attention to space for the social development of young people and provides little freedom for them to accept responsibility and learn from their mistakes, I question whether those who planned it understand what the middle school is all about.

Many of the elements I have described for the middle school will be considered nonessential by those who fail to understand the concept. But these features need not require a more expansive building if we are willing to accept a trade-off between those features we have unthinkingly assumed we must have and those which are essential to the middle school concept. Some of the most expensive elements in school design are, in their present format, questionable for the middle school: the over-equipped industrial arts shops and science laboratories, the large gymnasium, many home economics laboratories with their rows of stoves and sewing machines, music suites which reflect the interests of a minority of students.

The planning struggle will not be easy, for one of the middle school's greatest problems is that most middle school teachers were, and would perhaps like to remain, junior high teachers. But if we constantly examine our program criteria and the priorities we assign to these criteria we can have the more adequate facility for the middle school. Well-designed middle school facilities which reflect well-planned programs are far more than simply neutral vessels for the curriculum. They are causative agents for positive behavioral change among students and staff, promoting the integration of instructional effort and the establishment of learning programs more meaningful to middle school students.

Notes

1. Herzog, Elizabeth. *Some Guide Lines for Evaluative Research.* Washington, D. C.: U.S. Department of Health, Education, and Welfare, Children's Bureau, 1959.

2. Curtis, Thomas E. and Bidwell, Wilma W. "Rationale for Instruction in the Middle School." *Educational Leadership,* March, 1970, p. 579.

3. Gary, Charles L. "New Sound Waves in the Music Curriculum." *I/D/E/A Reporter,* Spring, 1970, p. 11.

8

Donald E. Overly

The Nation's School of the Month: Hithergreen School, Centerville, Ohio

The one-room school has gone full circle at Centerville, Ohio. But any resemblance between Hithergreen Middle School in suburban Dayton and its rural predecessor of 50 or 75 years ago stops before a superintendent can say "ungraded classes."

Instead of separate classrooms the interior of this Grade 6–8 school is entirely open. To provide the flexibility needed for a nongraded team-teaching program, Architect Eugene Betz divided the main space, functionally not physically, into three learning centers, a practical arts area, and an administration section. In the center is a circular commons area with a curbed arc at one end. Flexible partitions running along the arc of the circle close off the commons for large classes and band rehearsals. A circular gym curves into the commons, while its brick exterior wall continues as an interior separation.

Mobile storage bins backed with gray chalkboards double as dividers to separate teaching areas. They are positioned as the type and size of a group demands. Teachers rearrange other furniture as needed. Subject schedules are arranged in time modules. Areas for large group instruction, or individual study carrels can be accommodated at various times during the day.

"It takes a special kind of teacher to work here," commented Principal Tom Chambers. "To see students wandering around in one

---

big area would come as a shock to many, a nightmare to some, a challenge to others. We're lucky to have the teachers we do."

"I like this attempt to try a promising concept," said one school building consultant. He referred to Hithergreen's approach to architecture, learning and teaching.

Noise from various groups is no problem. With a minimum of distraction, five or six classes meet simultaneously in the same learning center area. Carpeting throughout Hithergreen, including shop and art areas, helps absorb noise. Acoustic baffles reduce sound spill-over. Each of the three learning center sections has its own domed room with a stepped ceiling following up to the dome. This not only relieves the visual monotony of a flat ceiling, but also serves as a sound and temperature barrier. Concrete bearing piers that support the roof and separate interior spaces are covered with rough gray boards for texture and interest.

Colors at Hithergreen are courageous. Purple brick walls contrast with white ceilings and vivid red carpeting. The gym almost gyrates with brilliant yellow ceiling girders that stretch up to a circle at the center of the domed roof to contrast with a charcoal gray ceiling. Off-white walls become dark gray at the second level, then merge to the charcoal ceiling. The floor is gray-green; yellow guard rails separate the floor from red-violet exit doors.

A satellite kitchen serves the school. Food is prepared at a nearby elementary school which has full kitchen facilities. Then it is put into hot and cold food carts and delivered to Hithergreen. These carts are set up in a cafeteria line anywhere in the school as required.

Hithergreen has no windows. Pupils, lights, gas and electricity combine to keep the school warm in winter; mechanical air conditioning keeps it cool in warm weather. By extracting excess heat from the

Hithergreen's interior layout:

1. Learning center	8. Storage	15. Clinic
2. Material center	9. Toilets	16. Dishwashing
3. Material storage	10. Conference	17. Music
4. Teacher lounge	11. Speech and hearing	18. Mechanical equipm't
5. Teacher workroom	12. Audiovisual equipm't	19. Gymnasium
6. Commons	13. Clerical	20. Shower
7. Practical arts	14. Principal	21. Lockers

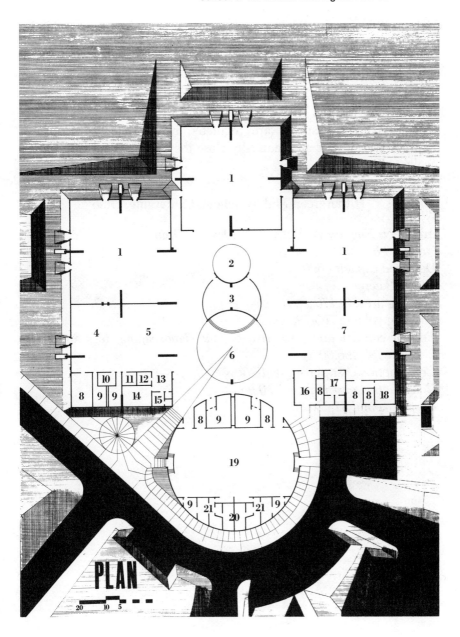

PLAN

high level fluorescent lighting and from heat generated by people, the school retrieves heat energy. When the heat from these sources isn't enough, electric heating panels in ceilings go on automatically. Fans in cupolas above each learning center pull interior air up past light fixtures and into a plenum; dampers either dump this warm air outside on mild days or mix it with outdoor air and pump it back into the school. Damper positions are regulated by thermostats. In warm weather thermostats automatically close the dampers and turn on the cooling system.

Hithergreen Middle School, Centerville, Ohio

Architect: Eugene W. Betz, AIA, Dayton, Ohio
Grades 6-8
Designed capacity 600
Site 15.3 acres
Building area 48,176 sq. ft.
Building volume 765,796 cu. ft.
Cost of construction (exclusive of land, landscaping, fees and furniture) $733,496.00
Construction cost per sq. ft. 15.30
Construction cost per cu. ft. 0.96
Cost per pupil $1,220.00

9

The Nation's School of the Month: Barrington, Illinois

The middle school (6–8 grades) in Barrington, Ill., was designed to make learning attractive for pupils and teaching challenging for teachers. But what sets the school a bit apart from other new schools are some of its other goals.

In a way, the school was planned by Supt. Robert Finley for the staff that will someday succeed his staff. And for the staff after that.

Moreover, the school was planned to accommodate virtually any kind of teaching arrangement that coming years make preferable or popular.

"I believe in the team approach to teaching," explained Finley, who has earned a reputation as an educational innovator, if not an iconoclast, for his firm, *avant garde* views on hiring teachers (the stress interview technic), rating them (no salary steps; raises strictly on merit), and leading them ("let them make mistakes—as long as they profit from them; that's what learning's all about").

"When I came to Barrington with my team-teaching ideas," said Finley, "and looked at a building that was 60 or 70 years old, I thought: 'Gee, team teaching just can't be made to work in this building.' I had myself a built-in excuse."

That excuse has been built out of Barrington's middle school.

"If the superintendent who succeeds me likes double-loaded corridors with egg crate classrooms—fine," Finley said. "The interior of

From *The Nation's Schools* (November, 1965): 61–68.

THESE FEATURES GIVE BARRINGTON MIDDLE

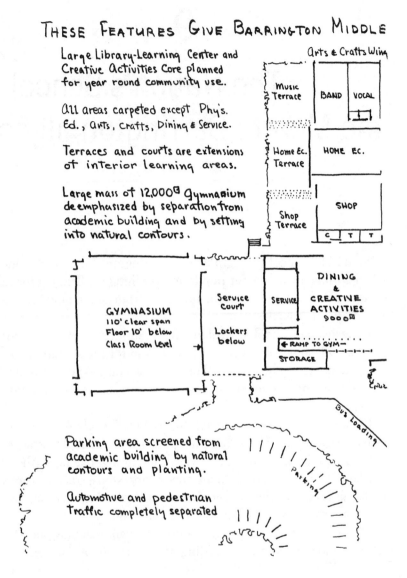

Large Library-Learning Center and Creative Activities Core planned for year round community use.

All areas carpeted except Phys. Ed., Arts, Crafts, Dining & Service.

Terraces and courts are extensions of interior learning areas.

Large mass of 12,000☐ Gymnasium deemphasized by separation from academic building and by setting into natural contours.

Arts & Crafts Wing

Music Terrace

BAND | VOCAL

Home Ec. Terrace

HOME EC.

Shop Terrace

SHOP

C | T | T

GYMNASIUM
110' clear span
Floor 10' below
Class Room Level

Service Court

SERVICE

Lockers below

DINING & CREATIVE ACTIVITIES 9000☐

← RAMP TO GYM

STORAGE

Bus Loading

Parking area screened from academic building by natural contours and planting.

Automotive and pedestrian Traffic completely separated

Parking

SCHOOL A DISTINCTION ALL ITS OWN

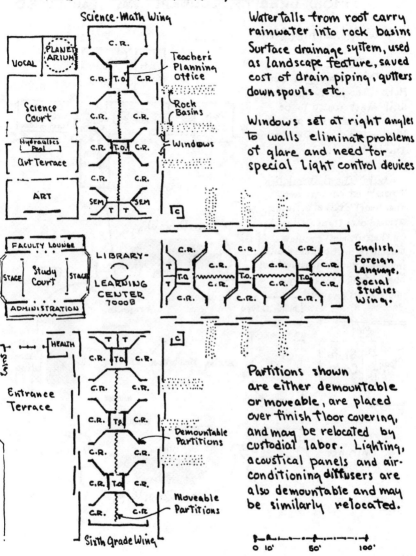

Waterfalls from roof carry rainwater into rock basins Surface drainage system, used as landscape feature, saved cost of drain piping, gutters downspouts etc.

Windows set at right angles to walls eliminate problems of glare and need for special light control devices

Partitions shown are either demountable or moveable, are placed over finish floor covering, and may be relocated by custodial labor. Lighting, acoustical panels and air-conditioning diffusers are also demountable and may be similarly relocated.

Science-Math Wing

English, Foreign Language, Social Studies Wing.

Sixth Grade Wing

0   10'   50'   100'

How "Freedom Concept" was Translated

Library·Learning Center

Educational Spec.

Make this area really count.
Make it a place where kids
will most want to be.
Learning materials are useless on the shelf. Architecture
should help us push the
books to the kids.

Architectural Translation

7000□ of central area,
the heart of the building,
around and through which
all students must circulate.
Emphasis on openness and
inviting areas for individual study.
Special features to intrigue,
interest and excite.

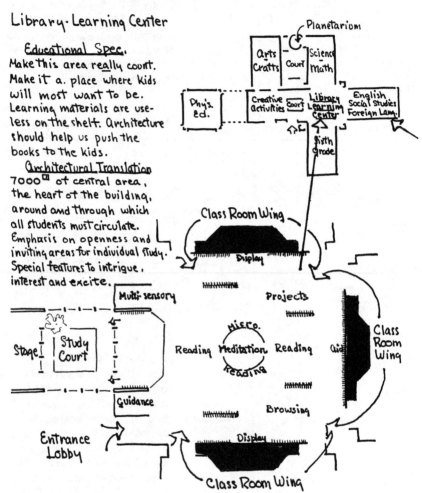

INTO DESIGN

BARRINGTON MIDDLE SCHOOL
CONE & DORNBUSCH ARCHITECTS CHICAGO

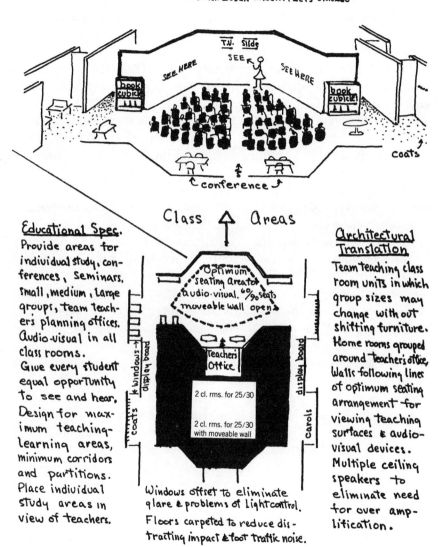

Class △ Areas

Educational Spec.
Provide areas for
individual study, con-
ferences, seminars,
small, medium, large
groups, team teach-
ers' planning offices.
Audio-visual in all
class rooms.
Give every student
equal opportunity
to see and hear,
Design for max-
imum teaching-
learning areas,
minimum corridors
and partitions.
Place individual
study areas in
view of teachers.

Windows offset to eliminate
glare & problems of light control.
Floors carpeted to reduce distracting impact & foot traffic noise.

**Architectural
Translation**
Team teaching class
room units in which
group sizes may
change without
shitting furniture.
Home rooms grouped
around teacher's office.
Walls following lines
of optimum seating
arrangement for
viewing teaching
surfaces & audio-
visual devices.
Multiple ceiling
speakers to
eliminate need
for over amp-
lification.

this building can be changed to that arrangement in a jiffy. That's protection for the community," he stressed.

Architect Spencer Cone of Cone & Dornbusch, Chicago, responded to Finley's plea for flexibility by using the system of components that emerged from the School Construction Systems Development project. Sponsored by Educational Facilities Laboratories, the project has been heralded as the base of a new tradition in American school architecture. The four S.C.S.D. components (structural system, ceiling-lighting system, air-conditioning system, movable and operable partitions—all described in box on page 395) are compatible. They can be easily divided by maintenance staff into rectangular chunks of almost any size.

Barrington could be classified as a comfortable conservative community (just northwest of Chicago), but its educational program is plainly progressive with emphasis on team teaching and a leaning toward the ungraded concept at all age levels. This attitude, accepted by the community, was a powerful factor in planning the new middle school. "For Barrington," said Architect Cone, "this is not just another school. There are doubters and in-betweeners, but the community is excited about the school rather than critical of it. I have heard no resentment of the cost, the concept, or of spending tax funds for items that could stir up a storm."

Said Supt. Finley: "I suppose some board members still have doubts about the building, but they had courage and faith enough in the people they hired to go along with them. I would be astounded if seven intelligent people didn't have doubts about something relatively new. But they investigated the project thoroughly, and once they were convinced of its possibilities, they stuck by their guns."

The administrative staff—the superintendent, two assistant superintendents, several principals in the system—worked with the architect during the planning stage. Although in some specialized areas, such as home economics, industrial arts, physical education and music, teacher suggestions were solicited, teachers for the most part were not involved in the planning, and for reasons that make sense to Finley and his associates.

"Educators," Finley pointed out, "are fond of saying, 'let teachers teach.' They want to eliminate the clerical work teachers do—the Mickey Mouse kind of details that don't relate to their prime function. Then often, and inconsistently, teachers are saddled with elaborate building committee assignments that take a lot of time, and produce more panic than progress. Ask a teacher, almost any teacher, what she'd like, and she'll say, 'built-ins, lots of built-ins.' Trouble is, by the time the building is up and in use, the teachers who helped plan it are working someplace else."

Barrington teachers understand this approach to building, Finley maintained. "I think many of them were relieved that they didn't have to make suggestions that probably wouldn't appear in the building anyway. When the building was at the point we could talk educationally with teachers, we did. In effect, we said: 'Look friends, this is the way it is planned, now how do we make it work best?' We then spent hours with teachers, exchanging views and ideas. We were talking their language; we weren't asking them where to put a wall or where to put an outlet for a phonograph."

Finley unmincingly condemns the committee process for building. "Building a school by committee is a stupid concept," he argued.

Finley and his associates tend to scowl when the middle school is used as a substitute name for a conventional junior high. "This is not a 'junior' high school," Finley stressed. "It's a school with a curriculum built for specific groups of kids at a specific learning stage. Sure it's a transitional school, but the high school probably is going to have to change as a result of what's happening in the schools that feed it. We don't think of 12 year olds as 'little gentlemen.' They're not little gentlemen. They're 12 year old kids, entities in themselves."

Although the middle school ultimately will be ungraded, pupils at the start are separated into sixth, seventh and eighth grades. The sixth grade has its own wing and has self-contained team-teaching units. The seventh and eighth grades are on a department system.

For grades seven and eight, the week is divided into 70 modules— 14 each day. Two modules are used for lunch and for extracurricular noon hour activities; individual class periods vary in length from one to three modules. English, for example, rates eight modules per week. Because aural-oral foreign language retention is believed to fall off after 30 minutes or so, single modules are used for repetitive exercises. The time modules can be divided into smaller units within team-teaching units.

The literal center of the school is in the learning center (7,000 sq. ft.) where all children spend some time every week. All students must pass through the learning center from their wing to enter the dining area or gym or the arts-and-crafts wing. "Our traffic patterns," said Finley, "deliberately placed this unit at the hub of the radiating wings. We've arranged the area—by placement of furniture and equipment—so that people won't necessarily go through the center in a straight line, but in such a way as to make it difficult for them to avoid seeing something in the learning center that will interest them and, hopefully, lead them to further study.

"In planning the center," Finley added, "We tried to eliminate barriers and walls—physical ones and psychological ones. We wanted a sense of freedom. But this sense of freedom must permeate the whole school, including teachers, if it is to work. If, in individual classrooms, pupils adopt a careless posture—an attitude that the school will provide for them—this posture will show up in the learning center. It's up to them to do their own digging. We're trying to have children say: 'This is our building, and we want to take care of it.'"

"We expect," said Assistant Supt. Fred Dippel, "that some kids are going to make mistakes and do some things wrong in the center. But there's nothing wrong with making mistakes. Maybe children should make some; the professional staff is there to help correct them."

Added Assistant Supt. Tom Hasenpflug: "We hope the school's teachers are showing the way by trying out some new concepts even if mistakes are involved in reaching them."

Summarized Finley: "We don't condone misbehavior. There's a difference between making mistakes and making mischief. That's a difference we stress."

"In the conventional library," Finley continued, "with four walls and usually one door out, someone is there to check you. This gives the impression that things are 'kept in there.' In our open environment, we try to give the impression that things should be 'taken out' of there. That is what we want. We're relying on our boys and girls to use this freedom wisely, but if controls are necessary, and I hope they're not, we probably will fall back on a monitor system of some kind."

As things stand now, the middle school will open late in 1965. The delay was caused by some trouble in fabricating the new components, a difficulty that is almost inevitable when new ideas are tried out. But suppliers report that these difficulties have been overcome, and other school districts interested in using all or some of the S.C.S.D. components will have a much easier time of it from the lessons learned at Barrington and at schools using many of the same components being built in Las Vegas, Nev. and in California.

Heading the school adminstratively is Principal Walter Pagels, who is really one of a triumvirate. Assisting him are two specialists: a director of pupil personnel concerned with counseling and deportment, and a director of instruction concerned almost exclusively with teachers and what and how they teach.

Barrington Middle School, Barrington, Ill.

Grades 6-8
Designed capacity 1,200
Initial enrollment 880
Site 25 acres
Building area (A.I.A.) 97,000 sq. ft.
Cost of construction (exclusive of land, landscaping, fees and furniture) $1,200,000.00
Construction cost per sq. ft. $12.37
Construction cost per pupil (capacity) $1,000.00
Barrington Middle School was selected as the Nation's School of the Month by a committee representing the National Council on Schoolhouse Construction. Award certificates have been presented to the school, the school district, and the architects. A similar award is made monthly.

Boom in S.C.S.D. Schools May Be Coming

"A very exciting plan which takes full advantage of the S.C.S.D. system," is the reaction of Ezra Ehrenkrantz, project architect for the School Construction Systems Development project at Stanford University, to the new school in Barrington, Ill., in which all S.C.S.D. components except cabinets are used.

The school district and Supt. Robert Finley, by being willing to participate even though there are experimental aspects in the system, will get something new for education, Ehrenkrantz said.

"The key thing the district has is space which is not locked in. It can be a laboratory for the use of the people teaching in it. Since the interior partitions are completely demountable, space can be rearranged for any kind of evolving educational system the district wants."

The Barrington school, with its open plan, angular arrangement of classrooms, and interior courtyards, is completely different from other S.C.S.D. schools for which designs have been completed. The other schools reflect a wide variety of approach, ranging from very large buildings to cluster plans.

"In all these, use of the S.C.S.D. system obviously did not limit the architects or prevent them from producing different kinds of schools to meet the varying needs of school boards. There is more variety of architecture than you would find in plans with fixed space from an equally able group of architects."

Ehrenkrantz believes the only esthetic limitation is the flat roof, which is essential for long spans.

"We're meeting the basic requirement that this should be a standard component approach and not a standard building approach," the architect said.

The Barrington project, besides being a good school building, will give some of the component manufacturers a chance to field-test their components closer to home.

It is too early to know how many schools using the components will be built in the next year or two. Ehrenkrantz estimates that 10 to 15, including S.C.S.D. schools, will be completed by the opening of school in 1966. Schools using some, but not all of the components, may number nearly 50. Much depends on the delivery schedule of the manufacturers, but all should be ready to start selling for schools which open in 1967. If the S.C.S.D. system has a big impact, it will start to show up in the fall of 1968, Ehrenkrantz believes.

Bids for three of the California schools came in at figures within the allowance of the California State Aid Formula. These are the Fountain Valley High School of the Huntington Beach Union High School District, $4.5 million; and the El Dorado High School, Placentia Unified School District, $2 million, both under construction; and the Fullerton High School No. 7 for the Fullerton Joint Union High School District, for which bids have just been opened, $3.5 million. Bids for a high school to be built by the San Juan Unified School District were rejected. Plans are being modified; the job will be rebid soon. —*McGraw-Hill World News.*

How the S.C.S.D. Components Work

Structural-Roof System. Using a 5 by 5 horizontal module and a 2 foot vertical module, the selected system provides column-free roof spans of more than 60 feet. The system uses one member to do the work of two. The roof deck is not merely supported by the trusses but put to work carrying the compressive loads ordinarily taken by their top members. This is the first use of orthotropic structural design for conventional building. Such technics, in which all parts contribute directly to structure, have been used for bridge building.

Air Conditioning System. The project's system houses in a self-contained rooftop unit air-handling and air-treating equipment for each 3,600 sq. ft. service module. To obtain the necessary flexibility, a multizone system is used, with warm air supplied by a gas-fired heater, and cool air supplied by direct expansion refrigeration.

Air distribution is through a multizone area incorporating eight mixing boxes, one for each 450 square foot zone. Conditioned air is carried from the mixing boxes to individual control zones by fixed fiber glass ducts. Flexible ducts then carry the air to strip diffusers, which are part of the ceiling system and can be moved as needed. Additional diffusers return air to the plenum space formed by roof and ceiling, from which it goes back to the unit. In Barrington, the unit is complete except for the condensers for air conditioning, which will be installed later.

Ceiling-Lighting System. In addition to light sources, finished ceiling, ceiling sound absorption, and sound attenuation between rooms, the selected lighting-ceiling component provides fire protection for the structure, air-distribution devices for the mechanical system, and support for demountable partitions.

The system is based on a 5 foot square metal grid suspended from the structure. Within this square grid goes a flat ceiling panel or a lighting coffer. Both are of prefinished sheet steel; both are available with perforated surfaces for increased sound absorption; both can be backed with mineral wool batts to provide necessary fireproofing.

The three types of lighting required—semi-indirect, direct, and luminous ceiling—are all provided by varying the number of two-lamp strip fixtures used and their placement in the coffer.

Interior Partitions System. This system of fixed and demountable partitions permits panels on one side of the walls to be changed independently.

The 3 inch thick partitions consist of steel studs faced on both sides with gypsum panels sandwiched between prefinished steel sheets. Snap joints make it easy to remove the panels, which can be placed anywhere under the ceiling on a 4 inch module.

Both types of folding partitions selected, panel and accordion, are supported by their own demountable structural frames to make them movable as well as operable and to avoid added loads on the structure.—*Adapted from material prepared by Educational Facilities Laboratories.*

10

Warren Holmes Company

28 Ways to Build Mistakes Out of Your Middle School

A lot of people think that the middle school is just a fancy title for a junior high.

They're right—and they're wrong.

Right, because if you make the grade levels comparable—sixth through eighth grade, let us say—a good junior high probably can do anything that a middle school can.

Wrong, because the words junior high generate a kind of ho-hum attitude on the part of teachers, students and the community. This kind of attitude discourages innovation and restricts the effectiveness of the best of school programs.

A new name—middle school—encourages everyone involved to take a fresh look at his own performance and at his role. It says in effect: we expect something different, something better from teachers, students and the community. It says: don't take us for granted. It says: shape up. It says: we're really trying to bring a new look and style to education.

If nothing else, the middle school offers a good excuse to rethink the purposes of education for young people at these ages and to develop imaginative new approaches. The design of a new middle school, or the conversion of an existing structure into a middle school facility, permits the development of new physical environments for teachers and students that can accelerate changes in the ways they behave.

From *The American School Board Journal* (July, 1970): 17-24. Reprinted with permission. Copyright 1970, the National School Boards Association. All rights reserved.

How functions within a building are grouped, the use of carpet in a student dining area, or the configuration of group instructional space should play an important role in changing how people act. If change for the better is the name of the game, then the design of the middle school facility becomes a critical element in the success of the middle school concept.

In the pages that follow, the staff of The Warren Holmes Company, a firm of architects, engineers, and planners based in Lansing, Mich., and the editors of The American School Board Journal suggest 28 ways to build out mistakes and help your district avoid some of the common and not-so-common errors in middle school design.

1. Put Counselors Where The Action Is

Given the highly unsettled nature of most middle school students, the counseling function emerges as vitally important. Put counseling facilities where students are most likely to use the service—near or in the learning center or, possibly, near the commons area. Student reception and waiting areas should be openly accessible to students and visually inviting.

2. Provide Dining Environments Where Food Is Fun

Avoid the barn effect in designing dining facilities for the middle school. Youngsters at these ages need a dining environment conducive to good manners and socialization. Several smaller dining rooms often are better than one large and forbidding cafeteria. Another suggestion: provide places where middle school youngsters can leave their books and other learning materials while they have lunch.

3. Don't Let a Problem Site Deter You from Creative Educational and Architectural Solutions

Turn hilly terrain, woods, water resources or other so-called site problems into assets. Sloping terrain can become a ski run for the middle school, while woods and water may be retained as outdoor learning areas.

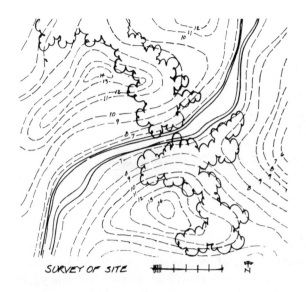

SURVEY OF SITE

4. Be Realistic about Folding Doors

Operable walls can be useful in certain applications, but don't expect folding doors to do more than they were designed to do. Flexibility of design is not achieved through flexible doors alone.

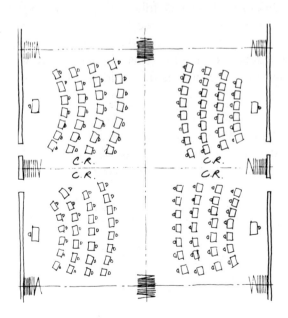

5. Consider Open Ceiling Grids for Art and Other Special Areas

The studio quality of an art space can be enhanced by the use of an open ceiling grid, and movable spotlights from such ceilings can accommodate a wide range of needs.

6. Tailor the Shape of the Building to the Site

Where special site conditions exist, the building design should take advantage of strong site characteristics while avoiding site disadvantages. The middle school can follow those elevations that are most desirable or make use of the most advantageous access routes for location of drives, parking areas, and building entrances. Preconceived notions about school design in terms of site characteristics are unwise. Consider burying a portion of the building to cut costs and increase usefulness.

7. Give Students a Place to Be Themselves

The middle school student needs places where he can develop social as well as intellectual interests and skills. A student commons

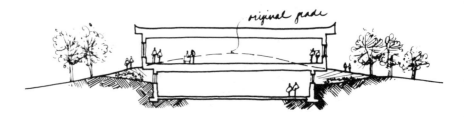

that is attractively designed with warm colors and intriguing spaces is an integral element of the middle school program, not a frill.

8. Consider Privacy

Small enclosed seminar, small group or tutorial space may be required by the middle school program for those special activities where privacy is desired. With such spaces provided, even the open plan achieves true privacy through differentiated design.

9. Encourage Independent Study through the Territory Concept

If independent study is to become a reality in the middle school, young people must have a place where they can work alone or in small groups. The independent learning territory approach gives each student a study space of his own. He may personalize his space by using a tackboard for photographs and other items of interest to him. He may use his space for meetings with two or three other students. Careful design can assure that these territories are under constant professional supervision.

10. Don't Be Locked in by Lockers

Lockers are a necessary fact of life, but the types of lockers and their placement can permit more functional integration into the school environment. Lockers can be of the newer, more silent design with insulated doors and special latches. They can be located as part of students' independent study spaces or in surge space close to instructional areas.

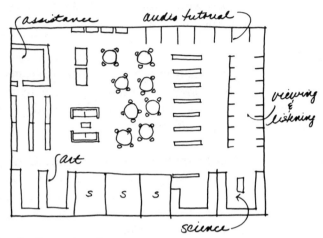

11. Make the Learning Center a Legitimate Learning Space

Make the learning center more than just a library or instructional media center. Plan it so a wide diversity of learning activities can take place within it. Consider incorporating into the learning center such features as a subject area assistance station, an audio learning laboratory, student science areas, a variety of small group conference spaces, auto-tutorial cubicles, and viewing and listening stations for young people.

12. Use Windows Wisely

Put windows where they are really needed. Don't let them monopolize valuable wall area or create light control and thermal environment problems. Windows make the most sense in smaller seminar and small-group spaces where a feeling of greater spaciousness may be desirable. They can serve useful functions at or near building entrances or where the outdoor environment can contribute to student activites. But as a general rule, each window should be justified in terms of expense, maintenance cost, and functionality in the learning environment.

13. Zone Vehicles within the Campus

Careful design of building and site can provide the necessary separation between bus loading and parental waiting areas. Road access to the building should be designed to prevent bus-car congestion, and

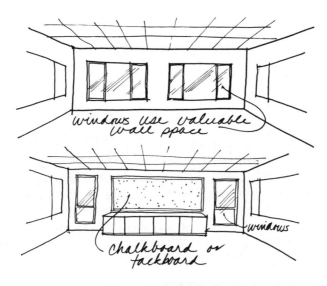

building entrances should be planned for separation of student transportation functions.

14. Plan a Small Assembly Area for the Middle School

The large auditorium is anachronistic in the middle school where learners will presumably receive more individualized and intimate

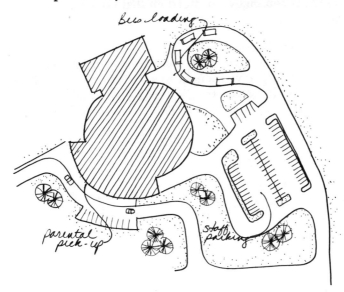

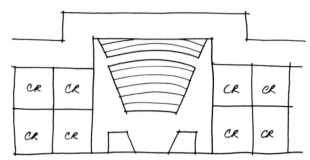

programming. But a small theater or assembly area for 300 or 400 students can serve for grade-level meetings (if there are still grade levels), team instructional efforts, or limited community use. The smaller assembly space will probably meet 90 percent of the needs of most middle school programs while providing a less overwhelming, more intimate setting for young people.

15. Keep Shop Areas Open and Free

With the exception of music, the specialized instruction areas within the middle school—industrial arts, home and family living, art—can be improved by more open facilities. Clean shop activities such as drafting, electronics, project planning might be grouped together for greater flexibility, while the noisier shop areas are clustered together for shared use of equipment and space. Even art and home economics areas can enjoy the freedom that comes with less conventional use of space.

16. Try a Variable Theater

Where an intimate theater is considered a desirable part of the middle school facility, give thought to a variable theater: one that can convert from thrust stage to theater-in-the-round to conventional proscenium stage in a few hours. This involves using movable stage

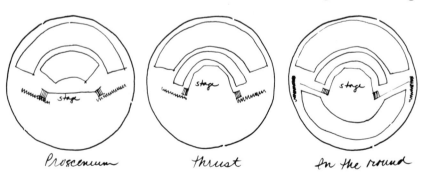

Proscenium   thrust   in the round

sections that can more than pay for the design effort by making the facility much more adaptable to future school and community needs.

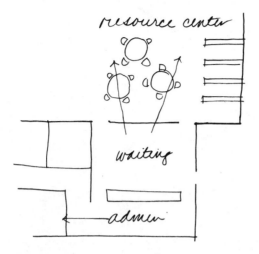

17 Give Visitors a First-Hand Look at the School in Action

Rather than isolate the community visitor in an adminstrative suite waiting room, design a segment of the learning center or other important element in the learning program to accommodate them. Let them see what is going on while they wait to see the principal or counselor.

18. Turn Kids on from Inside

Don't be misled by the "edifice complex" manifested when schools are prettily designed on the outside but nonfunctional on the inside. Keep in mind your purposes for the middle school. Insist that the interior design of the building and the site design reflect these purposes. The exterior shape of the building—round, square, volute, rectangular—means nothing as far as learning functionality is concerned. Don't allow superficial design features to override the significant purposes of the middle school.

19. Make Home Economics More Than a Cooking-Sewing Area

Today's middle school learners need more than cooking and sewing. They need to know how to budget family funds, buy a TV set, get a loan, make an investment. Facilities for home and family life education should include informal group discussion and individual activity areas for the important area of consumer education.

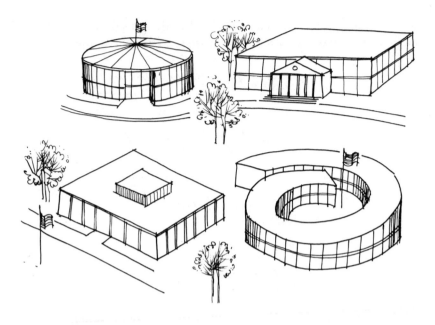

20. Don't Over-Furnish

Too many tables, chairs and desks can become obstacles to the flexible utilization of space. By designing the building to take into account a normal inventory of such equipment, greater freedom and functionality can be achieved. Seating pits are a demonstrated way to reduce the clutter of too much furniture while providing informal and appealing settings for learning.

21. Plan with Sex in Mind

The middle school concept strongly implies that girls should be introduced to the industrial arts while boys find out something about home and family life education. No instructional area of the middle school should exclude students on the basis of sex. Girls and boys need a broad exploratory learning program as well as the opportunity for indepth study of specialized areas.

22. Sound Condition Your Open-Plan Spaces

Carpet, acoustical ceilings and wall finishes are, of course, immediate solutions when open space is contemplated. But don't overlook the fact that the background masking sound can be introduced to improve

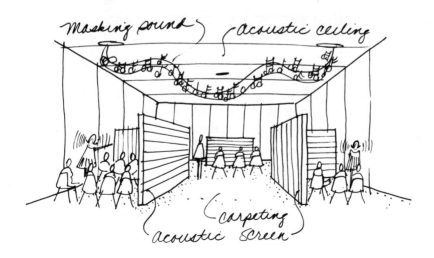

the sonic environment. Low level background noise (electronic "white" sound, air handling noise, or background music) can diminish what is being said in other parts of an open space. Voice amplification equipment sometimes is needed in the open plan because of the extreme deadness of open-space.

A ceiling speaker system with precise output controls can pinpoint the area of coverage through very low volume amplification.

23. If You're Unsure about Instructional Technology, Provide the Support Facilities

Not every school board is certain that instructional television dial access equipment, student response systems, or computer assisted instruction are feasible options for its schools. With an above-ceiling tray distribution system into which the cables and wiring for future

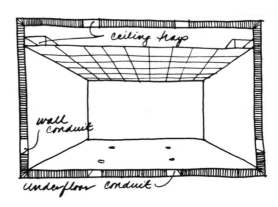

learning systems may be laid, as well as the in-wall and underfloor conduit with appropriate junction boxes, any middle school can have the potential for present and future developments.

24. Provide Multi-use Storage and Preparation Schemes

By grouping departments such as science and mathematics to-gether, shared preparation and storage facilities can effect economy in school design. Common prep-storage space between lecture rooms

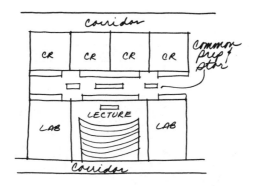

and a learning center, for example, can increase the utilization in both areas.

25. Provide Staff Offices That Improve Inter-Departmental Communication and Cooperation

The successful middle school program requires real cooperation among staff members. One way of providing the environment that promotes this cooperation is to group inter-disciplinary staff members in the same office area. Avoid design that perpetuates separated sectors within departmental organization.

26. Consider Use of Integral Furniture-Wall Systems

Interesting new concepts in modular wall-furniture systems permit visual screening to form "walls" in the open-space approach, while providing the vertical support for a variety of desk and storage units. The middle school can use such units to demarcate and furnish student study areas, teacher offices, counseling areas, or administrative office space.

27. Avoid Linear Corridors

Few school designs display a creative streak when it comes to making circulation space attractive. The tunnel effect in corridors can be avoided by designing circulation patterns that follow the natural shape of the learning spaces they connect.

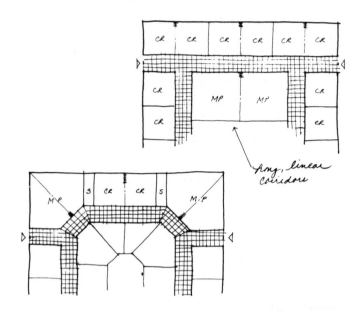

Any, linear corridore

28. Provide a Large Heated Slab for Outdoor Activities

Where weather conditions limit outdoor activities because of ice and snow, a large heated slab can assure an unobstructed space for games and classroom learning experiences.

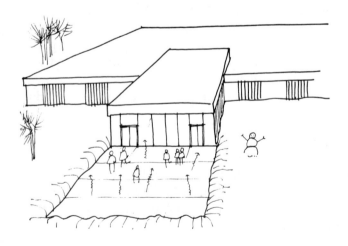

Bibliography:
The Middle School
Multipurpose Plant

"Armory Middle School." *Southern Educational Report*, November–December 1965.

Barrington Middle School: A Report. Barrington, Illinois: Barrington Public Schools, 1966.

"Berger Was Built to Blaze Trails—And It Has." *American School Board Journal*, February 1969, pp. 15–18.

Brown-Bridgewater Project, Section II. "A Study of the 4-4-4 Arrangement: The Middle School." Providence: Brown University, 1960.

"Caudill Builds Two Middle Schools." *Architectural Record*, January 1961, pp. 132–35.

Cordry, Vernon. "More Flexible Schedule at Fremont." *California Journal of Secondary Education*, February 1960, pp. 114–16.

Educational Facilities Laboratories. "Schools for Team Teaching." New York: Educational Facilities Laboratories, 1961.

"From the Top Down." New York: Educational Facilities Laboratories, February 1970, pp. 45–48.

Midjaas, Carl L. "Avoiding the Pitfalls of Middle School Planning." Address delivered to the National School Boards Association Convention, San Francisco, California, April 13, 1970.

"Northview Highlands Middle School." *Michigan Association of School Boards Journal*, April 1969, pp. 11–21.

"Planning and Operating the Middle School." *Overview*, March 1963, pp. 52-55.

"Teachers Designed This School." *School Management*, August 1968, pp. 30-35.

Zdanowicz, Paul J. "The Meredith G. Williams Middle School." *Educational Horizons*, Winter 1962, pp. 45-52.

Part V

Questions Facing
the Middle School

The middle School concept for early adolescents brought to the forefront many important and relevant issues about education and the youngsters it serves. Although little has been written about the early adolescent, this age group is certainly becoming a matter of growing interest and attention for many educational leaders, whether it be to promote or argue against this new structural and philosophical conception for middle schoolers of today.

Assuredly, the move toward the adoption of middle school proposal is not accepted blindly without raising questions about its real validity. This is, in part, a reaction movement against the stultifying junior high school and more positively a follow-up and a way to put into practice knowledge acquired about the transescents. The middle school is not yet a unified pattern or organization as many would prefer it to be. It would be so much easier and satisfying to have clear delimitations about what categories of children we are referring to, to place them into an already known grade structure, and to educate them to the best of our abilities and knowledge. But as might be inferred from previous chapters, such classification is diametrically opposed to the fundamental ideas of the middle school concept. Proponents of the middle school have greater concern for the philosophy underlying the middle school concept rather than for a formal classification system or structural change.

It poses a real challenge to educational leaders because of a growing recognition of the role education plays in enriching the quality of tomorrow's life. As a result there is a new commitment to educational improvement oriented to alter classroom practices, to develop significant curricula, to contribute to betterment and preparation of competent staff whose aims are geared to the development of personal values and standards of behavior adapted to our time.

Profiting from the "Hawthorne effect," leaving conventionality and conformity, the middle school philosophy puts back in question many data related to the educational system, problems that have for too long been overlooked or accepted at their face value. For instance, early adolescence, considered to be a period of turmoil, is now regarded as a formative stage. Curriculum planning and instruction for the "in-between" years—previously child-centered, subject-centered, or following the adjustment-to-life syndrome—are now conceived as

423

ones which should provide for the best utlization of actual knowledge synthesized into a workable framework. To be effective a program must provide for the child's continuing progress at each stage of his development according to his particular needs, interests, and abilities. Similarly, construction of school plant, utlization of available tools and techniques of instruction should provide maximum growth opportunities by satisfying the transescent's need to explore his world and assess his personality, to find his identity and inner stability. Traditionally organized elementary and junior high schools did not make sufficient provisions in terms of these changes.

We acknowledge the validity of the argument of the middle school opponents who raise the question: Is re-organization of grouping and grading practices and construction of new buildings sufficient to implement a new philosophy of teaching-learning experiences? But with careful analysis, it becomes obvious, especially when considering the junior high school's inability to promote change and adapt to innovations, that a new structure, namely the middle school, offers an opportunity to re-think and re-organize in such a manner as to offer children more appropriate education for present day needs. It calls for considerable redeployment of resources, building and facilities, staff, supplies, equipment, and other resources.

The middle school has been designed to provide educational programs and an environment to fit the needs and characteristics of the 11- to 14-year-old child. Since there is a wide variability in the student body, there could be no standard or uniform practice or curriculum to be followed. By utilizing an individual approach to learning, an unprecedented flexibility in planning, a deployment of creativity and imagination in teaching practices, a cognitive inquiry to the diversity of needs, the middle school concept provides for the growth characteristics of pre-adolescents to the greatest possible degree of attainment.

1

Fred Baruchin

Middle School for Elementary Youngsters?

Educationists love a band. But they must love a band wagon even more, for they're generally so eager to jump onto one. The lag between theory and its implementation in this profession has succumbed to the enticing strains of pipers. Never before have these "music men" been such a factor in influencing change in educational operations. And the pipers are as ubiquitous as they are loud.

The pliability of statistics to suit one's purposes is common knowledge. Now, with the refinement of communicative media, the mobility and interaction of professionals, and a fortune in funding, a peculiar new phenomenon is manifesting itself—that of hasty educational *change* based upon the unproven. This is a viable and pliable avenue through which one may twist academic contention to suit his purposes, to persuade laymen and professionals to discard standard practices. Certainly my concern is not a cry against innovation, for we exist in exciting times which bode well for education. Rather it is perhaps to guard against *premature innovation,* where communities may not be readily adaptable to change, and perhaps even the change itself may not yet be recommended in any scientific sense.

Such may be the situation with regard to the inclusion of elementary school youngsters in middle school arrangements. At a recent SUNY conference on the middle school, conducted in Albany, one of the key indications was that, thus far, there is a paucity of scientifically tested data justifying linking elementary youngsters with middle

From *New York State Education* (February, 1967): 44-47.

schools. Much theorizing has been done about the significance of advanced pubescence, departures from self-containment, cocurricular activities, social and emotional maturity, team approaches, non-gradedness, and individualization of instruction as these might relate to pre-adolescent youngsters. However, virtually no research has been cited to indicate specifically the effects of these modifications and innovations upon middle school fifth and sixth graders, and in their subsequent ramifications, upon the rest of the elementary grades. Indeed, let us remember that in making a transition as one involving the breaking apart of the elementary grades, attention must also be focused on the possible repercussions among the children of the remaining grades.

The impetus for the middle school activity right now emanates from three primary sources. (1) This organizational unit, in cities, will facilitate integration by gleaning groups of youngsters from neighborhood schools and feeding them into centrally located middle schools. (How long can society expect its schools *alone* to solve problems reflective of the much larger total *social* system?) (2) Overcrowded situations will be relieved by a realignment of grade levels. (Are we merely shipping overcrowdedness up the ladder?) (3) The junior high school is judged as falling short of its original purposes (though these weren't even defined until a decade after the first junior high school), and the panacea is considered to be the middle school.

Oddly enough, the nature of the shortcoming of the junior high school is not explored for corrective measures within the establishment itself. Rather it is assumed that a completely new entity must be the answer. (Does it not seem reasonable to anticipate that we might more easily be able to correct problems located within a going establishment, rather than expose ourselves to the myriad of difficulties certain to emanate from a new organizational unit?)

The fact that children are reaching puberty at least a year earlier than they were doing so in past generations seems to be a reality. Dr. Gilbert Forbes, a research pediatrician in Rochester, notes that the apex of spurt of adolescence occurs in girls at twelve years of age today, and in boys at fourteen years. A Maryland source indicates that "before age 11½, more than 20% of all girls reach menarche, 25% achieve an advanced stage of development of pubic hair, and 60% achieve marked breast development. Boys are slower to develop than the girls; but 30% of the boys begin their pubertal growth during

grade five." Time after time, proponents of middle schools for intermediate grade elementary pupils cite these pubescent criteria to
"prove" their point. I cannot believe, however, that the mere acquisition of menarche, pubic hair, and breasts constitutes sufficient reasons
for inclusion of fifth and sixth graders in middle schools. By the same
token, the point may very well negate the idea of middle schools for
pubescent elementary youngsters because of the implication inherent
in the socio-sexual rush which would consume youngsters (girls particularly) whose physical development has outraced the emotional.

Berman, a psychiatrist, expresses concern about the timing of the
present transition from the elementary to the junior high level, con-
tending that "during the highly volatile years of eleven through thirteen or fourteen, youngsters should have a familiar, secure background in which to operate." By the same token, Ilg and Ames see the
eleven year old as being at odds with his environment, while the child
at twelve is in a state of relative equilibrium both within himself and
his environment. Recognizing the socio-cultural, sometimes traumatic,
shock of a child's entering a new educational unit, be it called middle
or junior high, it seems in view of this, that the twelve year old would
be more receptive to the change than the eleven year old. And might
it not follow that the pattern of accomplishment and progress through
the completion of the eighth grade (and subsequent to it) would be
smoother were it to be built upon an entrance, foundational, transitional year of equilibrium (as at 12) and not disequilibrium (as at 11)?
What unique practices will be employed in the middle school to
orient relatively immature ten-year-olds and settle down eleven-year-
olds in disequilibrium with themselves and their environment? And
why will these practices necessarily be more successful than practices
which might otherwise be developed to stabilize the present junior
high school environment? In short, are we attempting to solve our
present junior high problems by building a new organizational entity
and developing procedures which may be suitable to it, simply because we've run dry imaginatively with regard to the present establishment?

In their study on *Cooperative Research on the Nongraded,* Di
Lorenzo and Salter defined the nongraded unit as a "pattern of
elementary-school organization designed to insure full recognition of
individual differences in the instructional setting by the elimination of
arbitrary grade classifications and grade expectations." The concern

for allowing youngsters to proceed at their individual rates is one of the assumptions upon which nongraded units are based. Grade placement in the past has been notorious for utilizing essentially chronological criteria. Middle schools, in ascribing entrance to grade level, therefore, indirectly endorse chronological bases for entrance. By doing so, they stand incompatibly with elementary nongraded programs. Nongraded children completing the first four years could be nine when going into a middle school fifth grade or ten when going into a middle school sixth grade.

Are youngsters this age ready to interact socially with early adolescents, and assume the self-direction characterizing much middle school theory? And should they be sheltered in this new environment, what impact will this have on them vis-a-vis the promise of the leadership roles they would abdicate at the elementary level? Will we be prematurely stuffing down elementary schoolchildren's throats the activities designed for middle school years, as we have forced high school activities upon junior high youngsters in the past? (Should it be said that we shall avoid this pitfall in particular within the middle school arrangement? Then, why can't we avoid it at the junior high school level right now, and thereby correct one of its shortcomings?) In the present arrangement, a child moving through elementary nongradedness a year in advance of some of his peers, at least, has the benefit of an additional year or two of maturation before going to the junior high.

The idea of a middle school entity has engendered much thought and action in its short-lived time thus far. It seems incredible, however, that so much implementation has already occurred—that debate of the pros and cons of middle schools is becoming heated—for in actuality there seems to be little consensus over what constitutes a middle school. The educational justification is debatable if we know what kind of unit we're discussing. However, the middle school presently takes many forms. The respective characteristics of middle school and junior high, so far as program, faculty (preparation and retraining), administration, supervision, curricula, methodological approaches, and the real behavioral needs of the children themselves are concerned, lie virtually unexplored. How can we possibly debate the issues before we isolate the characteristics of the different institutions?

The area of teacher preparation for middle schools portends all sorts of complications, since it may very well take many years for teacher preparation programs to relate their efforts to the uniqueness of the level, if indeed the level is unique.

This has been a cursory attempt to suggest that the argumentation for linking the elementary grades onto the middle school may not be as justified and as scientifically based as its proponents make it seem. Further, it is to suggest that a formal effort certainly is in order, upon which we shall be able to base our assertions in favor of, or against, this new organizational pattern. This study would have its purposes:

1. The isolation of the actual differences between middle and junior high schools, and the identification of the characteristics peculiar to each.

2. The determination of whether or not the middle school offers more promise to elementary youngsters in terms of improved academic achievement in the basic studies, improved social development, better self-concept, and more positive and sustained attitudes toward school—all of which should comprise the real justification for including these youngsters in the new organizational unit in the first place.

2

Alfred H. Skogsberg & Mauritz Johnson, Jr.

The Magic Numbers of 7-8-9

Alfred H. Skogsberg

Grades 7, 8, and 9 definitely belong in the junior high school. In large urban school systems, moreover, there is solid evidence in favor of placing grade 10 in this transitional unit.

Organizational structure determines operation. It sets the limits of functional specifications and defines how people work together in the organization. Axiomatically, a defensible organizational structure, one that is efficient and effective, must be functionally related to the purposes for which the school exists.

Specific educational goals are determined by these purposes laid down by our society. The means selected must be related to the goals to be achieved, but more important they must be created in terms of our knowledge about how pupils grow, develop, and learn, and in terms of their special developmental needs during each major phase of their progress toward full-fledged maturity in our society.

No one will deny that educational programs must provide the best environment for pupil progress. Recently we have begun to design our programs in terms of what pupils are like in their various stages of growth. Early adolescence is a critical period in growth and development. The junior high school was organized fifty years ago to provide better education for early adolescents, boys and girls twelve to fifteen

---

From *NEA Journal* (March, 1963): 50–51.

years of age. This is a well-defined group in terms of growth and acculturation.

These early adolescents need a broad curriculum to challenge the abilities of the most able and to provide a wide orientation to the world of work and to various cultures through exploratory experiences.

Emphasis must be on the continuance and extension of basic skills and the start of new ones. Because the junior high school is the beginning of secondary education, the program should provide for the beginning of special education and for the start of terminal education as well.

No longer need we be plagued with that confused bugaboo of whether "high school subjects" should be moved down. Research and experience indicate unmistakably that who takes what and when is better diagnosed through the application of the readiness principle than by digital computation of length of stay in school or accomplished span of life.

In addition, personal developmental needs of this early-adolescent age group require attention and time. This transitional education for our younger youth needs a minimum of three years for its accomplishment. The fact that some few youths will be ready for senior high school education in two years while others need four doesn't change the fact that the great majority will need three.

Ninth graders belong in the junior high school because they are early adolescents psychologically, physically, and culturally. Furthermore, placing grade 9 in the junior high school strengthens the senior high school program by freeing it from the need to stretch over disparate developmental phases.

When the total number of pupils in a district requires more than one building, there is then a forced subdivision of the student body. The basis of this subdivision must be educationally justifiable. We must take into account the nature of the pupils and how they grow in relation to the purposes to be achieved. This is the only intelligent way to plan an educational program. Not by happenstance did Japan, drawing on the best from the United States, reestablish its whole school system after the war on the 6-3-3 basis.

The phases of child development, society's vocational and avocational requirements, application of the readiness principle to subject matter, personal needs in our culture, time necessary for certain maturational changes, and relevancy of operation to purposes lead to an inescapable conclusion: Young people in what are commonly called grades 7, 8, and 9 belong in the junior high school.

Mauritz Johnson, Jr.

As far as I can determine, there is no reason to believe that the junior high school in all cases must be composed of grades 7, 8, and 9. Decisions regarding school organization must take into account both theoretical and practical considerations, and some of the latter are specific to a given community or school system.

If there are any theoretical bases for separate identification of a junior high school, the most important one certainly is to provide pupils during the early years of adolescence with an educational and social setting that separates them from young children on the one hand and mature youth on the other. From a practical standpoint it is difficult to administer a single program, including student activities and social life, that has to span six years from pre-adolescence to virtual adulthood.

If an individual approach were possible, pupils would enter junior high at different ages and remain for varying lengths of time. And if we based entrance on what we now know about child psychology and child growth, most girls would probably pass through this unit at a younger age than most boys.

However, since we do not seem to be able to adapt our organizational schemes to this extent, we are forced to select those grades in which the greatest proportion of boys and girls reach pubertal status. In the past, the greatest concentration of such pupils was found to be in grades 7, 8, and 9, which would seem to favor the argument for the present junior high school organization.

However, we now find that children in many communities reach pubescence before seventh grade. In these situations the beginning phase of adolescence may occur primarily in grades 6, 7, and 8. If so, this would lend support for a 3-4 secondary school division and a five-year elementary unit.

A second theoretical argument for a junior high school organization, whatever grades it encompasses, is the strong urge for independence among children in the early adolescent years. It would be undesirable to require students to wait until they are sixteen or seventeen to have responsibility for the conduct of their own affairs. The junior high school is valuable because it permits adolescents an earlier assumption of such responsibility and doubles the opportunity for leadership.

This second argument again brings us back to the question of where we are going to divide the elementary school organization from the secondary school organization. Most school systems divide the two organizations equally, with six grades alloted to each. If they further divide the secondary organization to provide for a junior high school, it is almost always a 3-3 split. Actually, this 3-3 division is very practical for administrative purposes because it is considered undesirable to have an administrative unit of only two grades, one of which is newly entering and one preparing to leave.

But then it may be asked whether secondary education should be limited to six years. If one more year is added, two acceptable divisions emerge, instead of one. These are 4-3 and 3-4. Either breakdown would be acceptable, depending on the average maturity of the youths in the given community.

It should be noted that none of the theoretical arguments advanced thus far relates to curriculum. The range of intellectual needs at the early adolescent level is too great to avoid considerable overlap with both the elementary and the senior high school. A desirable junior high school curriculum provides for this diversity and also for the gradual transition to the upper secondary school.

The decision as to form of organization will have to be made on practical grounds and on the basis of social and administrative viability. Any pattern is satisfactory that gives *identity* to youths during early adolescence, includes at least three grades for *stability,* and *brackets* those grades in which significant numbers of pupils reach pubescence.

3

Mauritz Johnson, Jr.

School in the Middle

Every so often some indignant or exasperated soul prescribes major surgery for the American educational enterprise, and more often than not the object of the incision and derision is the junior high school. While this operation has about as much chance of being pulled off as has the abolition of the income tax, such desperate proposals tend to divert attention from the very real needs for improvement at this school level. In an atmosphere of such dire threats, fervent supporters of the junior high school brook no criticism of their beloved institution, however valid it may be. But, while detractors who advocate decapitation to cure a headache are of scant help to the patient, neither are his well-intentioned friends who call the headache an illusion or a normal condition.

The junior high school is an American invention which dates from the first decade of this century. In 1920 there were fewer than 400 of them; in 1940 there were over 2,000; and now the number is probably close to 5,000. In quantitative terms the movement has been a distinct success.

Actually, it was an integral part of a larger movement which involved the downward extension of secondary education through the annexation of grades seven and eight from the elementary school. In large school systems, physically separate three-year junior and senior high schools were established, but in small ones a single six-year

From *Saturday Review* (July 21, 1962): 40-43, 56-57. Copyright © 1962 Saturday Review, Inc.

secondary school became the mode. In the latter, the old four-year high school usually persisted as a unit, with the two appended grades occupying an indefinite status. Rarely has the junior high school idea been a guiding force in the six-year high school.

What is the junior high school idea? In a word, asylum. The junior high school is supposed to be a bridge between the elementary school and the upper secondary level and, indeed, a bridge between childhood and that attenuated near-adult stage we call adolescence. Within this "transition school for early adolescence," a very special environment is to be created in which pubescence can be experienced without trauma or trepidation. The forbearance of understanding teachers and the comfortable camouflage of the "peer group" (all of whom are in the same boat), facilitate the rapprochement of the sexes, the learning of new social skills, the exploration of bodily changes, and tolerant acceptance of ambivalent vacillation between childish dependence and brash assertiveness. At the same time, the right combination of wide "exploration" and wise guidance would assure that, when the metamorphosis was complete, the physically healthy, emotionally stable, socially adjusted, civic-minded specimen which emerged from the cocoon would be well prepared to take advantage of whatever opportunities later adolescence might offer.

If this description appears to be a caricature, such is not the intent. Realistic or not, defensible or not, these are the goals that junior high schools have sought to achieve. It is easy to extend our overly sentimental view of childhood too far, but it cannot be gainsaid that in the contemporary American culture the phenomenon of adolescence is characterized by a quest for heterosexual social relationships and emancipation from adult control, and this phenomenon cannot be ignored. Apparently, the leap from childhood dependency to sophisticated individuality can rarely be accomplished in advanced Western societies without the intermediate use of the group of contemporaries as a transitory source of security. In a world in which adults expound one set of values and espouse another, in which schooling is prolonged and economic dependence is protracted, and in which social life is largely outside the family, the value of a haven the junior high school attempts to be is readily recognized by many parents of this in-between age group.

If this phase of development is often a difficult one for those passing through it, it is even more so for the adults around them. To establish and maintain a junior high school which fully exemplifies the idea underlying that institution is not easy, and many schools, it must be conceded, have been less than successful in this regard. And, as with the girl with the curl, a good junior high school can be very, very good, but a poor one can be horrid.

It is not difficult to find some teachers who view youngsters at this level as obnoxious nuisances, rather than as energetic, curious, fumbling individuals on the threshold of adulthood. Some junior high schools provide social activities as formal and sophisticated as those in which high school seniors engage. Some promote extensive interscholastic athletic programs which feature strenuous physical exertion, intense emotional involvement, and often late hours. In some, the break from grade six to seven is as abrupt as it ever was between grades eight and nine. But these are shortcomings in human performance and institutional arrangements, rather than inherent defects in the idea, which in many schools is faithfully and skilfully practiced.

But if the idea itself makes a certain amount of sense, it also gives disconcertingly little attention to the primary responsibility of any educational institution—intellectual development. Not that the intellectual aspect is completely ignored or that it is incompatible with the concern for transition, but simply that the emphasis on it is not explicit and its nature is not defined.

It was not ever thus. When the first junior high schools were established, there seems to have been greater concern about the downward extension of secondary education than about the separation of the secondary school into two components. The chief motive for extending downward stemmed from a dissatisfaction with the elementary school curriculum and methods in grades seven and eight. To a large extent these were "review" years, preparatory for eighth-grade graduation (or nongraduation). For many pupils this review was considered unnecessary, and it only delayed their beginning more advanced academic studies under teachers who were specialists in these subjects. For the many overage pupils who populated these grades, the steady diet of review of common branch subjects seemed, perhaps not entirely futile, but at least of less value for imminent entry into the world of work than one accompanied by some specific vocational training. It was through this combination of earlier academic instruction and terminal vocational training that the "needs" of the young (and not so young) adolescents were to be better met.

The separation of the junior high grades from the upper ones was not at that time so much for social and emotional reasons as to make the *academic* initiation at grade nine easier for pupils, since approximately half of all high school students were in the freshman classes of the conventional high schools, and that was as far as many of them ever got. It was *this* transition that was of greatest concern, not the one from grade six to seven or the one represented by pubescence. Indeed, if social and emotional considerations entered the picture at all, they revolved about protecting the younger children *from* the unwholesome influence of the young adolescents in the seventh and eighth grades within the elementary school, not providing a haven for the new junior high school group.

Again, this is not to deny the usefulness of a separate and special social setting for this transition period, but merely to emphasize that the early concern for more suitable intellectual fare has of late been obscured. We may grant that the earlier vocational emphasis is less appropriate today because of longer compulsory education, diminished overageness as a result of changed promotion policies, and increased importance of intellectual development in a technologically more complex economy. But precisely because more people do need to develop further than ever intellectually, it is all the more important that those who wish to improve the junior high schools again turn their attention to this central area of the school's responsibility.

It is in regard to intellectual training that those who are inclined toward abolition of the junior high school must also consider the consequences of such a step. To return grades seven and eight to an elementary school status is unthinkable. Pupils at this level must have the intellectual resources which a secondary school is better able to provide—teachers prepared in specific subject areas; laboratory, library, studio, and shop facilities; and a sufficient concentration of pupils for differentiation in the curriculum consistent with the extensive range of abilities among pupils at this level. The elementary school as we now know it cannot provide these conditions. If the junior high school were to be destroyed, the only other alternative would be to merge it with the senior high school in a single six-year unit. What advantage this would offer in strengthening the lower three grades intellectually is unclear.

Some communities, because of building considerations or sheer tradition, retain grade nine with the upper three and maintain a two-year middle unit. There is a feeling in some quarters that ninth graders fare better academically under such an arrangement. This is highly questionable, unless there is a great disparity in the qualifications of teachers at the two levels. Actually, when teachers are equally qualified, ninth graders in a junior high school setting appear to achieve as well or better than they do as freshmen in a four-year high school. Furthermore, a two-grade school lacks stability in that pupils enter one year and leave the next. Although it is better than no middle school at all, it has not been found to be as satisfactory as a three-year unit.

A legitimate question, however, is which three grades? While the seven-nine unit predominates today, there is increasing interest in a six-seven-eight combination, because it appeals to the four-year high school advocates, to the proponents of a three-year middle unit, and to those who want pupils introduced even earlier to teachers who are specialists in their subjects. It would be resisted by those who for several decades have introduced an elementary school philosophy into the junior high school to counteract what they consider to be too early departmentalization, too great an academic emphasis, and too much imitation of high school social and athletic practices. The wisdom of such a unit should not, however, be determined by how large a coalition can be mustered in its favor.

Since the middle school as a separate organization can be justified on social grounds only if it embraces the period during which the majority of pupils reach adolescence, the six-seven-eight unit would be valid only if it could be shown that large numbers of sixth graders are pubescent. There is some evidence that youngsters do mature earlier today than they did a generation or two ago, and certainly they acquire greater amounts of general information and social sophistication earlier. In some communities, however, this is not true, and it is senseless to argue for the same organizational pattern everywhere. But it does not follow that the matter of organization is, therefore, inconsequential. What is important is that we be clear as to *why* a middle school unit with identity of its own is desirable, and what it needs if it is to be a stable, viable unit.

Junior high schools can be eliminated or altered, but pupils of junior high school age will remain, and who will teach them and what they will be taught are the really significant questions. Their teachers need to be as well versed in their respective subject fields as possible, and in addition be cognizant and appreciative of the relative immaturity of these pupils, their transitional status, and their tremendous diversity. Junior high school teachers must be willing and able to help pupils become students, equipping them with the tools and procedures for a lifetime of study, rather than assuming that they are already so equipped or can acquire, on their own, the ability to study effectively and independently. If junior high schools would address themselves to this problem seriously, pupils, their parents, and all of their subsequent teachers would be grateful.

Good junior high school teachers are even harder to come by than good elementary or senior high school teachers. It would be an over-simplification to say that some teachers are attracted to the profession out of a desire to be with children and others from an urge to engage in the transmission of ideas, and that at the junior high school level the pupils aren't lovable enough for the one group and the ideas dealt with aren't complex enough for the other. Nevertheless, a recent study at Cornell showed that among some 600 teachers who were surveyed, those teaching grades seven and eight were markedly less satisfied with their level of assignment than were teachers in the grades below and above. When the reasons were analyzed, the nature of the curriculum (the ideas), rather than the nature of the pupils at this level, seemed to be predominant. Teachers who enjoy teaching many subject areas cannot do so in the junior high school, nor can those who enjoy teaching advanced content do that. Perhaps this is inevitable in an "in-between" school.

Yet, there is a clue here that the curriculum at this level needs some careful rethinking and perhaps a complete overhauling. Typically, all seventh and eighth graders are required to take some nine or ten subjects for the same length of time, despite considerable differences in their abilities, interests, and accomplishments. No matter that a pupil is tone deaf and has been taught music by a specialist through-out six elementary school years—he must still "explore" it, along with his friend who plays in both band and orchestra and practices an hour each evening. No matter that a pupil is weak in the fundamentals of arithmetic—his mathematics teacher, fresh from a course in partial differential equations, must teach him the types of life insurance and what enters into overhead in retailing, just as he must teach these topics to all the mathematically eager pupils awaiting the delights of algebra, geometry, and the infinity beyond.

In all fairness, it must be said that many program changes are currently being made in junior high schools—some eighth graders study algebra; foreign language, taught by the direct method, is offered in grade seven; set theory, Venn diagrams, and other modern mathematical topics have been introduced; and more science is being given. But these changes represent only creeping improvement, not the giant step that is needed. It is true that the quality of teaching makes or breaks any program, but a poor curriculum is a millstone around the neck of the best of teachers.

Take the bright young social studies teacher who did graduate work in comparative economics or American foreign policy. A complete stranger in the community, he must begin by teaching that one Silas Wright established the first local grist mill, and then recount for the nth time the story of the Indian tribes which inhabited the area and the great contribution they made to American culture, and spend the rest of the year in a provincial tribute to the greatness of the particular state. Or, consider the English teacher, a literature major, of course—primarily British literature, particularly poetry, especially the Lake poets—with no study of grammar since high school (the college English department didn't offer it) and only vaguely aware (from an education course) of the current controversy between proponents of structural linguistics and advocates of conventional grammar. What will be the major emphasis in her junior high school English classes? Grammar, of course, and what literature there is may consist of whatever novel is in the anthology, some short stories by Poe and O. Henry, and a long poem by Longfellow. The rest will be free reading of "adolescent literature" on romance and nursing for the girls, and war, sports, and automobiles for the boys.

Somewhere, at this very moment, an engineer, a doctor, and an AAUW member on a school board are doubtless fighting the good fight to employ a junior high school science teacher who has his master's degree in physics rather than education. The fact is, however, that most students who do graduate work in physics will be advised by their physics professors (and their common sense) to sell their valuable talents to some one other than a board of education. Those who actually become junior high school teachers may find that Ohm's law is the most advanced physics they teach, and that a large part of the time they must deal with such matters as testing food for starch with iodine, reading a weather map, and tracing the flow of blood through the heart.

Nevertheless, a curriculum must obviously be planned with the maturity and requirements of the learners in mind, not the strengths and desires of teachers. Yet, if the nature of the curriculum affects the availability and enthusiasm of teachers, so, too, the improvement of curriculum depends in the main upon the discontent and initiative of teachers. Administrators, laymen, and professors from both the scholarly disciplines and professional education can encourage and assist them, but in the final analysis, teachers, singly and in groups, must do the job. What deters them is not so much their own shortcomings as certain beliefs which are prevalent in many communities: that the problems in the junior high school are inevitable and unsolvable; that the junior high school must forever remain as it has been; that some outside authority really decides all the questions; that getting rid of the junior high school altogether will take care of the problems.

Many specific suggestions could be offered for the improvement of the curriculum at this level, but this is a matter on which those who are in a position to make the changes must work. It might be urged, though, that the changes be in the direction of greater emphasis on significant ideas as opposed to inert facts, greater continuity of intellectual development; greater flexibility of programming, particularly in the area of the "arts," for pupils who differ so greatly; and at least as much attention to independence in studying and thinking as in the social and emotional spheres. The fact that many junior high school pupils are so preoccupied with their adolescent developmental problems that they are distracted from learning may be, in part at least, of our own making. If we could provide a curriculum which would engross their attention more fully, they might then be distracted from many of their physical, social, and emotional problems.

One can insist that the curriculum of the middle school, and specifically its intellectual component, is in need of reexamination without implying that efforts to take into account the transition from childhood should be abandoned or neglected. Many problems, such as those relating to the grouping of pupils and the maintenance of standards, cannot be solved satisfactorily until the curriculum is reformed. For example, we currently form instructional groups, and then either fail to provide curricular differences or attempt to adapt the curriculum to each group. Instead, we should reverse the process by organizing the curriculum first and then forming the groups accordingly. We define junior high school courses in terms of grades, when we know there are greater differences among pupils *within* seventh grade than there are *between* an average seventh grader and an average senior. It is impossible to speak of standards without reference to relatively specific and stable curriculum elements, and the grade concept has lost its usefulness for this purpose.

To return to the opening metaphor, euthanasia is not the answer to the junior high school's malady, but a curricular lobotomy may be necessary. The present dosage of vitamins will not give us the kind of middle school we need.

4

Paul Gastwirth

Questions Facing the Middle School

Perhaps the most important problem facing the middle school is that of *definition*. What is a middle school? Sometimes the term "middle school" is mentioned with respect, and sometimes with scorn ("muddle school), but seldom with clear understanding. In a report issued by the Educational Facilities Laboratories and titled *Middle Schools*, six different types of grade organization are mentioned as middle schools: 7-8, 7-8-9, 6-7-8, 6-7-8-9, 5-6-7-8, 5-6-7-8-9.

The confusion is so flagrant that the author of this brochure, Miss Judith Murphy, boldly states, "Diversity is the keynote. Least important of all as suggested earlier, is the precise scheme of grades."[1] Miss Murphy presents an *ad hoc* definition of a middle school as one "in between elementary and high school, housed separately and, ideally, in a building freshly designed for its purpose and covering at least three of the middle school years, beginning with grade 5 or 6." The author then pulls the rug out from under the middle school by saying, "If the middle prschool is kept unfrozen in program as well as physical design, it can serve as a true expansion link in the school system, adding or subtracting grades to meet changing enrollment pressures."[2]

What should be the organizing principle of a middle school? Shall it be grade organization? Shall it be the chronological age of pupils? The social and pschological maturity of pupils? The logistics of building space within the system? The demands of political groups? The demands for desegregation? Administrative convenience? Economy?

From *The Clearing House* (April, 1967): 472–75.

The nub of the issue is, of course, the question: Is not the conventional junior high school, grades 7-8-9, the place in which the early adolescent can receive, most efficiently and economically, the kind of education most appropriate for him?

If the "precise scheme of grades" is not important, why are the proponents of the Middle School so insistent upon the particular scheme of grades that they favor? It appears to me that grade organization is a vital factor in the development of both curricular and cocurricular learning experiences. Of course, in a non-graded school of the future, the concept of grade organization will be replaced by the concept of age-level organization.

In my quest for a definition of the Middle School, I have found these items mentioned as characteristic features of a middle school:

a new building
effective use of school plant
home economics and industrial arts shops
use of television
foreign language instruction
language laboratories
divisible auditorium
large and small group activities
air conditioning
movable walls
carpets
imaginative architectural design
planned for the next superintendent, that is, for the future
instructional swimming pool
library carrels
audio-visual materials
programed learning
team teaching
specialization and departmentalization
individualization
flexible schedules
non-gradedness
a program based on 20 minute or 30 minute modules
a program based on 55 minute units
a program based on units of 1½ or 2 hours

As you examine these two dozen or so items, you will notice that not even one of them may be said to differentiate a 5-8 middle school from a conventional junior high school!

How can the problem of identification be solved? Certainly not on so-called "practical grounds," which vary from district to district throughout the country. The middle school, if it is to have meaning for us as educators, must have a unique philosophy and an organizing principle to implement it. It must be based on a pattern of organization that will help pre-adolescents develop into adolescents by enabling them to explore their aptitudes, to find themselves, and to achieve some measure of self-identification. Its pattern of organization should obviously bracket those age levels at which the vast majority of pupils enter and complete the period of pubescence. Its structure should also provide a stable educational environment designed to help pre-adolescents achieve an inner stability. The middle school must not be permitted to become a revolving door for pupils on the way from the elementary to the high school.

Unless these conditions are met, the middle school will be in constant flux and will resemble a race track where everything is in motion, including the judges' stands and spectators' stands. Can you picture that?

Since the middle school concept is being proposed as an alternative to the junior high school, perhaps we may be able to obtain a clearer image of the middle school first by considering what is allegedly wrong with the junior high school, and second, by focusing our attention on one type of middle school, that which has a grade 5-8 organization.

Some of the strictures leveled at the junior high school are the following:

(1) Rigid departmentalization
(2) Extracurricular fanfare
(3) Marching bands
(4) Elaborate graduation ceremonies
(5) Excessive emphasis on interscholastic athletics
(6) Sophisticated social events such as a Senior Prom

With one exception, rigid departmentalization, these criticisms are superficial and peripheral. In the schools to which these criticisms apply—and the number of such schools is small—the objectionable features named can be eliminated or mitigated without undue difficulty. It must be remembered that some of these features, e.g., elaborate graduation ceremonies, are the legacy of the obsolete K–8 school!

Further, what guarantee do we have that all the cocurricular and social hoop-la will not be present in a 5–8 middle school? We must guard against the logical fallacy committed by critics who believe that their valid criticism of an existing institution or policy somehow guarantees the validity of their own alternative proposals. However sound their criticism may be, their own suggestions for improvement may be just as inadequate as or even worse than the programs criticized. In attempting to mitigate the sophistication of the junior high school they may succeed only in extending it to the lower grades, thus making the Middle School a *junior* Junior High School.

With respect to rigid deparmentalization, many junior high school principals have for years sought to modify the departmental program of seventh graders by introducing a core of English and Social Studies, or by having the same instructor teach two subjects to the same class, or by other methods. It is interesting to note, however, that one of the main arguments used by proponents of the 5–8 middle school is that it would provide fifth and sixth graders with a departmentalized program in which the academic subjects would be taught by specialists! Also, in some middle schools, the most sophisticated form of departmentalization, namely, individual programming, is being planned for fifth graders.

In view of current trends toward the vertical organization of the curriculum in a K-12 program, and in view of the growing partial departmentalization of the 5th and 6th grades in the elementary school, there would seem to be less need than ever for a middle school to encompass grades 5 and 6. These trends indicate a desire to provide children with superior preparation both for the greater departmentalization that they will encounter in the junior high school and for the greater stress on the learning of organized subject matter at the hands of specialists. On the one hand, the vertical organization of the curriculum provides built-in continuity in the subject areas, thus easing the articulation among the three school divisions. On the other hand, the use of the dual progress plan, team teaching, partial departmentalization, and special teachers or coordinators in art, music, science, health education and other subjects, provides children with exposure to subject specialists in the elementary school.

In these ways, pupils become acquainted with several teachers and different groups of children while remaining attached to one teacher and a home base class and classroom. Thus elementary schools in progressive school systems are already providing the type of program for fifth and sixth graders that is being blueprinted for the grade 5-8 middle school.

However we define the middle school, it would be a catastrophe to accept the concept of the middle school as an expansion link between the elementary and high schools, "adding or subtracting grades to meet enrollment pressures." The middle school must be defined on the basis of educational philosophy and psychology. It must be developed as a distinctive educational institution, uniquely designed to serve the needs of early adolescents. It must be established as a school with a status and integrity of its own, strong enough to withstand the pressures of economic and political opportunism.

The second basic problem that will face the 5-8 middle school is that of *personnel.* The junior high schools have also been criticized for their personnel shortage and for the high percentage of provisional teachers employed. Is there any prospect, much less guarantee, that the middle school will be able to solve the problem of teacher shortage?

Teachers in the junior high school are subject specialists. They naturally tend to gravitate toward the senior high school where they will have the opportunity to teach their subjects in greater depth and at a more advanced level. The presence of the ninth grade in the junior high schools helps it retain these subject-oriented teachers. The removal of the ninth grade would simply hasten the exodus of these teachers from the middle school.

A third basic problem that will confront the middle school is that of *pre-service and in-service training of teachers.* It took years for the junior high school to gain the status, the stability, and the funded experience that, in the eyes of teacher colleges, warranted the establishment of separate courses in the many areas of junior high school teaching and administration. During this long period, college students continued to exercise their option between elementary and secondary school education. Preparation for junior high school teaching was included in the courses in secondary school education.

With the middle school, we face an entirely different problem. Will students who are interested in the 5-8 middle school specialize in elementary, junior high, or secondary school education? Who has the experience to give courses in middle school technique? Who, indeed, knows how to organize such a course in view of the fluidity of the concept of middle school?

There are, of course, many other problems that confront the 5-8 middle school—questions concerning the internal organization of the curriculum, the subjects to be included, methods of grouping, techniques of individualizing instruction, deployment of teacher personnel. I do not see how we can even begin to grapple with these problems unless and until we have a clean-cut operational definition of the Middle School.

Postscript: In NYC, civil rights groups had been led to believe that the middle or intermediate school, organized on the 4-4-4 plan, was the key to school desegregation. When the Board of Education prepared to open the new Intermediate School 201 in East Harlem in the fall of 1966, the parents and community were shocked to find that I.S. 201 was a segregated school. The whole controversy over community control of curriculum and personnel of I.S. 201 stemmed from the feeling of the civil rights leaders that they had been "betrayed" by the Board of Education.

Two years earlier, when the Allen Committee[3] had recommended the establishment of intermediate schools to facilitate desegregation, I had warned that the middle school would not achieve the desired objective. A middle school built in a ghetto would be fed by segregated elementary schools. An intermediate school built in a middle-class area would be fed by white segregated schools. As far as peripheral areas are concerned, a three-grade junior high school (7-8-9) would embrace wider boundaries than a four-grade middle school (5-6-7-8)!

Civil rights leaders in the big cities now realize that the middle school idea will not give them integrated schools in the ghettos; that it is not a symbol of hope, but a snare and a delusion; and that the emphasis must now be placed on *quality education* within the present framework, rather than on untried, unproven, expensive, and ill-defined innovations.

Notes

1. Murphy, Judith. *Middle Schools.* New York: Educational Facilities Laboratories, 1965, p. 9.

2. *Ibid.,* p. 6.

3. A committee appointed by New York State Commissioner of Education, Dr. James Allen.

5

Richard L. Post

Middle School:
A Questionable Innovation

Mr. Eugene Regan's article "The Junior High School is Dead" in the November 1967 issues of *The Clearing House* contains many statements which seem to be no more than questionable opinions. Permit me to offer a few "questionable" opinions of my own based upon 18 years experience as a teacher and principal in seventh, eight, and ninth grade junior high schools.

Possibly my greatest misgivings concerning the current interest in the middle school stem from a feeling that educational gimmickry is being substituted for genuine innovation. The innovations which intrigue me are those offering an opportunity to stimulate the individualization of instruction. Independent study, continuous progress curricula, team teaching, and flexible scheduling seem to be the issues worthy of our serious consideration. I fail to see how the transfer of the ninth grade to the senior high and the fifth and sixth grades to the middle school can help us move in this direction. In fact, if the ninth grade students are moved into a more subject-centered school, and if the fifth and sixth grade students are subjected to increased departmentalization, we may set education back 50 years. Our energies may be directed toward an innovation which does not really merit serious consideration, and the important new ideas in education may be ignored.

The grade organization adopted by a district may be 6-3-3, 5-3-4, 4-4-4 or 6-6, with little real difference in the quality of the education

From *The Clearing House* (April, 1968): 484–86.

offered. The program and staff within each institution determine its quality, and it is improvement in these areas that should occupy our interests.

It is generally agreed that a comprehensive senior high school should have at least 1000 students in order to offer needed laboratories and special facilities and to utilize its staff in areas of their major strengths. If to achieve this size the district must include grade nine, then the four year school would obviously be desirable. However, if size is not a problem, prime consideration should be given to where the ninth grade student might get the most appropriate program.

Mr. Regan has evidently experienced far greater control by the senior high over the junior high curriculum than has been my lot. High school graduation requirements have been expressed as a number of credits earned in grades 10, 11, and 12. Some subjects required for graduation may be taken in junior high, but these are not limited to the ninth grade. We have offered for the past seven years a six-year sequence in each of three modern languages. This is a 7–12 sequence and is listed upon the transcript as such. Our transcript must include grades 7–12, also, since some students take algebra in grade eight and colleges are usually interested in this credit. The state requires physical education in grades 7, 8, 9, and 10 and this is also shown on the transcript. I have never felt that these requirements inhibited the development of a sound junior high program, and certainly the moving of the ninth grade to the senior high would solve no problems if they existed.

It has been my experience that teachers whose interests are more subject-centered than child-centered gravitate to the senior high. As a result I have felt that senior high schools are more inclined to set arbitrary standards and utilize more impersonal teaching methods than junior high schools. It seems unwise to place these ninth grade students in this environment until sufficient changes have been made in program and practice to insure that their needs will be met.

At age 14 decisions about continuing in school, about value systems, and about social attitudes are of prime importance to students, and a school whose primary concern is with needs of these individuals is necessary. In our junior high we utilize the block-of-time, attempt to give continuous instruction in reading, offer alternate courses for the gifted and the handicapped, and in other ways attempt to center our interest on the individual student. I'm not certain that the ninth grade student could get any better program than this if he were moved into a senior high school.

My feelings are even stronger when we discuss the social aspects of such a move. We have no night activities and our ninth grade students do not attend senior high social events. We do not permit students to drive cars to school. I do not see what useful purpose can be served by having 14-year-old girls going to the junior prom and riding home from school in cars with 18-year-old boys. Even if it were granted that ninth graders are more mature than they were 30 years ago, this maturity should be directed toward worthwhile junior high projects such as adopting a foster child, community beautification, or planning assemblies and programs. I feel that in the four year high school the few social opportunities available might encourage the wrong sort of development. The fact that students mature earlier should not lead one to the conclusion that we should encourage earlier sophistication of their social activities, since early marriage is still an economic mistake and dating activities should be deferred as long as possible.

The elimination of interscholastic athletics and its accompanying activities are often given as the major gain resulting from the transfer of the ninth grade to the senior high. I'm afraid that if the community wants a competitive athletic program for 12-, 13-, and 14-year-olds, it's going to have one regardless of the school organization. Little Leagues, Pee Wees, and Boys Clubs will fill the gap. I happen to feel that educators can do a better job administering such a program for the good of the child than the alternate leadership usually available in the communities. Moreover, junior high regulations are usually sounder than senior high regulations and superior to community sponsored substitutes.

In our state, a 9th grade boy in a 4 year school could play in 10 football games with 12 minute quarters. The same boy in a junior high can play in only 6 games with 8 minute quarters and he cannot scrimmage with any 10th, 11th, or 12th grade students. Junior highs in our league do not permit rooter buses, tournaments, or other practices available to senior high students. There are many values both to the individual and to the student body accruing from a sound athletic program, and the junior high faculty can control this program if it chooses. If practices aping the senior high are undesirable—stop them. But needs of the junior high students should determine the practices.

There are many real challenges facing educational leaders today. Because of a growing recognition of the role education plays in improving the quality of life, there is a new commitment to educational improvement. A move to shift grades from one institution to another hardly seems worthy of consideration when we are on the verge of beginning to understand the teacher-learner relationship, and when fundamental changes in the nature of teaching could result. Another realignment of grades seems ridiculous when the graded school itself may be on its way out.

We are presently completing the plans for a new junior high school in our district. Its instructional materials center will occupy one-quarter of the floor space, its classrooms will not be divided by partitions, and I hope its staff will be dedicated to the individualization of instruction. It will include grades seven, eight, *and nine,* as we have yet to see any sound educational reason for depriving the ninth grade students of the opportunity to develop in this environment. The time may come when we will need to build another senior high. The issue of what grades to include will again arise. If the proper educational plan is devised, placing the individual learner in his rightful role, even those of us who "cling loyally to the JHS banner" might recommend a four year senior high.

6

Wayne Jennings

The Middle School? No!

In the November, 1966, issue of the Minnesota *Journal* of Education, Neal Nickerson, Glenn Darling, David Meade, and Josephine Kremer ride another educational hobby horse that is going nowhere. They are pushing to have the middle school replace the present junior high school. Of all the concerns in junior high school education this approach is about the most unproductive we've encountered. It almost seems as if the authors had read about the middle school and have seized upon the idea as a solution to something—something never really defined in their articles.

To be sure, they mean to improve our schools; but their plan will, in fact, inflict harm. It is the typical schoolmen's penchant for manipulating quantitative things like grades, rooms, buildings, and materials and for failing to work on qualitative measures like teacher attitudes, classroom methods, and curriculum. Anyone who has read in the field of educational psychology, educational goals, recent NASSP *Bulletins,* or ASDC materials like *The Junior High School We Saw; The Elementary School We Need; Perceiving, Behaving, Becoming: A New Focus; Individualizing Instruction;* and such works knows that the foremost educational problems we face are centered about developing in youngsters a healthy self concept, a mature personality, effective citizenship skills and attitudes, and knowledge significant for living.

There is much agreement that the schools could do much more in these areas where, in truth, we are doing rather poorly. To turn from

From *Minnesota Journal of Education* (Janurary, 1967): 73-74.

fundamental problems to reshuffling of grades five through nine is to detract needed attention and to postpone study on long-delayed matters. The authors must see classroom and curriculum as the schools' heart. Then why not make proposals to diminish inefficient lesson hearing, sitting, and passive student roles so common in nearly every classroom?

Argument Supports Present Plan

The writers have tried to justify a grade five through nine middle school on psychological and physiological grounds. As good an argument can be made for keeping the junior high school at grades seven through nine. To prove their case some arguments became extended to the breaking point. For instance, it was said that, ". . . the least differences were found between pupils in grades six and seven and between pupils in grades nine and ten. Yet it is between these grades that our present 6-3-3 plan divides children." Actually this turns out to be an argument for retaining the present junior high instead of a middle school!

Of course, beginning seventh graders are like sixth graders; they haven't begun to change yet. If the junior high school is for that turbulent age period beginning somewhere in grade seven and ending somewhere in grade nine, why include sixth graders who won't even enter the turbulent period? Most beginning seventh graders are like elementary pupils, it's true. But in a few months the behavioral, academic, and emotional syndrome hits. Seventh grade teachers see this happen, first in a few scattered individuals early in the year and finally spreading through the entire class as the year progresses.

At the other end, every junior high teacher is tremendously impressed with the difference between ninth graders at the beginning and end of the year. At the beginning they are much like eighth graders and so belong in the same school. A lot of maturing occurs during the year. The boys settle down, the girls get their boy-crazy attitudes in perspective, and both are ready to pursue their studies more seriously. Only then are they like tenth graders and ready for high school. Certainly there is a big difference between the beginning seventh grader and the finishing ninth grader. That's just exactly what the junior high school is for—to bridge this great change of life.

Quite a number of authorities agree that the junior high school is rightly placed to handle this period. A stronger case is made for the junior high with grades seven, eight, and nine than the fantastic confusion, expense, and additional problems of a new organization.

Name Not a Vital Issue

Why should we rename the junior high school? Most junior high teachers are not embarrassed by the name. Would it really help to call it Northeast Middle School instead of Northeast Junior High? Even if we changed the name and the grades, everything else would remain the same. The other needed changes won't come without hard work. We will solve school problems when we decide to face them in an all-out fashion and when we get real support from those persons who tend to dissipate our energies and confuse our efforts by nit-picking aruguments.

Well-intentioned educators can help in many areas. For example, one severe problem is getting staff with training and inclination to work with the rather squirmy 12 to 14-year old. We could solve this problem if all of us got to work on it. But the U of M and virtually every other teacher training institution in Minnesota excepting St. Cloud SC and Mankato SC have refused the junior high school's administrator's plea for teachers trained at this level. The institutions have been too busy training subject matter specialists or proposing the juggling of numbers, grade levels, and schedules. Why hasn't even one program been advanced to fulfill the desperate need for skilled junior high teachers? Or where has support been during the current struggle to change the state certification requirements for training teachers of early adolescents?

Address the Real Problem

Those of us working in junior high know the tough problems of building effective instructional programs. We do not have all the answers and we welcome help. Some of us do react strongly to the unnecessary and specious suggestion of a middle school which doesn't address itself to the problem. The middle school offers no real merit over the present well-established junior high school system. There is much important work to be done in making our present schools for young adolescents effective without setting up another school organization, only slightly different. This would be a diversion.

The key to better education is not in slicing the pie differently but in altering classroom practices, developing a curriculum significant for life and preparing competent staff. We invite readers—and writers—to think along with us on more fundamental issues.

7

William T. Gruhn

What Do Principals Believe about Grade Organization?

1. Purpose of the Study

There is more interest today in the grades that should be included in the junior high school than at any time since the beginning of the reorganization movement before 1900. This is due largely to the rapidly increasing enrollments in the elementary and secondary schools, leading to an unprecedented demand for new school buildings. The purpose of the present study was to find out what principals of junior high schools and representatives of state departments of education responsible for secondary education believe to be the best grade organization for junior high schools.

This study was part of a comprehensive survey of junior high school education in the United States which included all schools listed in the most recent state directory available for each of the 50 states and the District of Columbia. Schools were included only if they had a separate administrative organization, an enrollment of 300 or more pupils, and consisted of grades 6-7-8, grades 7-8, or grades 7-8-9. This study included "junior high schools," "middle schools," "intermediate schools," and any other schools which consisted of grades 6-7-8, grades 7-8, or grades 7-8-9.

The study was made through questionnaires sent to principals of the schools. For part of the study, questionnaires requesting opinions about grade organization were sent to the person responsible for secondary education in each of the state departments of education.

From *Journal of Secondary Education* (April, 1967): 169–74.

2. Grades and Buildings

Questionnaires sent to principals of junior high schools in the spring semester, 1964, requested information about the grade organization of schools as follows: (1) the numbers of schools of three types—grades 6-7-8, grades 7-8, and grades 7-8-9; (2) the year the schools were established; (3) the types of schools for which the buildings presently occupied were originally built; (4) plans to continue their present grade organization; and (5) reasons for establishing schools with their present grade organization. Questionnaires which included questions (1) and (2) were sent to principals of all schools in the state directories which met criteria for the study given above. Replies were received from 3368 schools as follows: (1) schools with grades 6-7-8—92% replied, 138 usable; (2) grades 7-8—91% replied, 442 usable; and (3) grades 7-8-9—84% replied, 2788 usable. Questionnaires which included questions (3), (4), and (5) were likewise sent to all schools with grades 6-7-8 or grades 7-8, with the replies as indicated above, but these questions were sent to only one in seven of the schools with grades 7-8-9, selected at random from the total file, with replies from 87%, with 402 usable. Information about the grades included in these schools, the year when the schools were established, the buildings in which they were housed, and their plans to continue with their present organization is summarized as follows:

1. The most common of the three types of schools in 1964 among the 3368 from which replies were received were those with grades 7-8-9. For the 3368 schools in the study, the percentage of each type was as follows: (1) grades 7-8-9—83%; (2) grades 7-8—13%; and (3) grades 6-7-8—4%. More than half the schools with grades 6-7-8 were in three states—Illinois, Michigan, and Texas. More than half the schools with grades 7-8 were in six states—California, Illinois, Indiana, Massachusetts, Michigan, and Texas.

2. The numbers of new schools of all three types established each year has been increasing, with more new schools established during the three years 1961-1964 than during any similar previous period. Among the 3368 schools in the study, the percentage of the total established by years was as follows: Before 1951—32%; from 1951-1961—45%; from 1961-1964—16%; no reply—7%.

3. Most of the schools were located in buildings originally intended for junior high schools. Only a small percentage of the schools were

located in former senior or four-year high school buildings. For example, schools with grades 7-8-9 were located in buildings originally built for use as follows: (1) for junior high schools—69%; (2) for combined elementary-junior or junior-senior high schools—4%; (3) for senior high or high schools—16%; (4) for elementary schools—6%; (5) for other schools or no reply—5%. Schools with grades 7-8, as compared with grades 7-8-9, were less frequently located in buildings originally built for junior high schools, as indicated by the following: (1) for junior high schools—51%; (2) for senior high and high schools—24%; (3) for other schools or no reply—25%. Schools with grades 6-7-8, as compared with the other two types, were least often located in building originally intended for junior high schools, as the following reveals: (1) for junior high schools—41%; (2) for senior high and high schools—33%; (3) for other schools or no reply—26%.

4. Schools with grades 7-8-9 more often than the other types of schools had plans to continue indefinitely with their present grade organization, while quite a few schools with grades 7-8 or 6-7-8 had plans to change to another grade organization, most frequently to grades 7-8-9. The percentages of the three types of schools planning to continue indefinitely with their present grades were: (1) grades 7-8-9—91%; (2) grades 6-7-8—64%; and (3) grades 7-8—51%.

5. More than half the schools with grades 6-7-8 and those with grades 7-8 were established with their present grade plan primarily because of school buildings or the school district organization. The percentage of each type of schools established with their present grade plan for these reasons was as follows: (1) grades 6-7-8—54%; (2) grades 7-8—57%. Only a few schools with grades 6-7-8 or grades 7-8 were established with these plans, rather than with grades 7-8-9, primarily because it was considered to be better for the educational program, with the percentages of schools giving this reason as follows: (1) grades 6-7-8—14%; (2) grades 7-8—12%. The principals of quite a few schools, however, replied that there was a combination of reasons for having their present grade organization, with almost all of them indicating that administrative reasons were among them.

3. Best Grades for the Junior High School

Opinions were requested through questionnaires in the spring semester, 1964, from principals of the three types of schools and from representatives of state departments of education on the grades that they considered best for the junior high school to achieve each of the following: (1) to provide the best total school program, (2) to attract and retain competent counselors, (3) to attract and retain competent teachers of science, mathematics, and foreign languages, (4) to develop a superior acadmic program, (5) to develop a superior program in industrial arts, music, home economics, art, and physical education, (6) to develop programs of sports and other extra-class activities, (7) to provide experiences in leadership, and (8) to provide the best age group.

Questionnaires were sent to all principals of two types of junior high schools, those with grades 6-7-8 and those with grades 7-8. Questionnaires were also sent to principals of one in seven of the schools with grades 7-8-9. Replies were received as follows: (1) grades 6-7-8—92% replied, 138 usable; (2) grades 7-8—91% replied, 442 usable; and (3) grades 7-8-9—87% replied, 402 usable. Similar questionnaires were sent in the summer of 1963 to directors of secondary education in the 50 state departments of education, with 100% replies from the director of some other state department representative. The opinions of principals and representatives of state departments of education concerning the grades that are best for the junior high school may be summarized as follows:

1. The "total program" for the junior high school can be provided best with grades 7-8-9, in the opinion of most of the principals (80%) of schools with grades 7-8-9, most of the principals (62%) with experience as principal of more than one type of school, and almost all (92%) of the state department representatives.

   Principals of schools with grade 6-7-8 and those with grades 7-8 were divided in their preferences for the grades they considered best for the "total program." Principals with grades 6-7-8 indicated the grades best for the "total program" as follows: (1) grades 6-7-8—40%; (2) grades 7-8-9—39%; (3) grades 7-8—16%; (4) no difference or no reply—5%. Principals with grades 7-8 indicated these preferences: (1) grades 7-8-9—43%; (2) grades 7-8—35%; (3) grades 6-7-8—11%; (4) no difference or no reply—11%.

2. Competent counselors and teachers of foreign languages, mathematics, and science can best be attracted and retained by schools with grades 7-8-9, according to a high percentage of the principals of all three types of schools and state department representatives. Only a few principals considered grades 6-7-8 or grades 7-8 to be best to attract and retain competent counselors and teachers of these subjects. Quite a few principals indicated that, in their opinion, the grades made "no difference" in attracting and retaining such staff members.

3. A superior program in industrial arts, home economics, music, art, and physical education can be best developed in a school with grades 7-8-9, in the opinion of a substantial percentage of principals of the three types of schools and state department representatives. Only a few principals of any group considered either grades 6-7-8 or grades 7-8 best for developing programs in these subjects, although quite a few principals indicated that the grades made "no difference."

4. Leadership experiences for early adolescents can be best provided with grades 7-8-9, according to a high percentage of principals of schools with grades 7-8-9, those with grades 7-8, those with experience as principal of more than one type of school, and state department representatives. Only principals of schools with grades 6-7-8 were substantially divided on this question, with preferences as follows: (1) grades 7-8-9—38%; (2) grades 6-7-8—36%; (3) grades 7-8—9%; (4) no difference or no reply—17%.

5. A sports program and other extra-class activities can be developed best with grades 7-8-9, according to a substantial percentage of principals of all three types of schools and state department representatives. In fact, only a few of the principals of any group replied that, in their opinion, schools with either grades 6-7-8 or grades 7-8 were best for developing such programs.

6. A superior academic program can be developed best with grades 7-8-9, in the opinion of a substantial percentage of the following: (1) principals of schools with grades 7-8-9 (74%); (2) principals with experience as principal of more than one type of school (53%); and (3) representatives of state departments of education (82%). Principals of schools with grades 6-7-8 were quite divided on this question as follows: (1) grades 6-7-8—33%; (2) grades 7-8-9—29%; (3) grades

7-8—11%; (4) no difference or no reply—27%. Principals with grades 7-8 likewise were divided on the best grades for a superior academic programs as follows: (1) grades 7-8-9—38%; (2) grades 7-8—22%; (3) grades 6-7-8—8%; (4) no difference or no reply—32%.

7. Principals differed more on the grades that "provide the best age group" for the junior high school than on any other question. Grades 7-8-9 were considered to provide the best age group by most of the principals of schools with grades 7-8-9 (71%), those with experience as principal of more than one type of school (57%), and state department representatives (86%). Principals of schools with grades 7-8 were divided on this question as follows: (1) grades 7-8-9—39%; (2) grades 7-8—38%; (3) grades 6-7-8—13%; (4) no difference or no reply—10%. Principals with grades 6-7-8 were likewise divided as follows: (1) grades 6-7-8—40%; (2) grades 7-8-9—32%; (3) grades 7-8—19%; (4) no difference or no reply—9%.

4. Best Place for the Ninth Grade

Opinions were requested in the spring semester 1965 from principals concerning the best place for the ninth grade—the junior high school (grades 7-8-9), the four-year high school (grades 9-12), or the six-year high school (grades 7-12)—to provide for each of the following: (1) the best experience in leadership and citizenship, (2) the best opportunity to develop wholesome boy-girl relationships, (3) the least likely to lead to undesirable early social sophistication for ninth grade girls and boys, (4) the least likely to lead to steady dating by ninth grade pupils, (5) the least likely to lead to dating by ninth grade girls and older boys (grades 11-12), (6) the best opportunity for the ninth grade in academic studies, and (7) the best total educational experience for ninth grade pupils.

Questionnaires were sent to all principals of two types of schools—those with grades 6-7-8 and those with grades 7-8, and to principals of one in seven of the schools with grades 7-8-9. Replies were received from principals, by types of schools, as follows: (1) grades 6-7-8—72% replied, 148 usable; (2) grades 7-8—91% replied, 493 usable; and (3) grades 7-8-9—85% replied, 399 usable. Replies were tabulated separately for those principals who had previous experience as principal of a four-year high school. There were 91 principals with such experience. The opinions of principals concerning the best place for the ninth grade were summarized as follows:

1. The best experience in leadership and citizenship for ninth grade pupils can be provided in the junior high school, in the opinion of most principals of all three types of schools, as well as those with experience as principal of a four-year high school. The percentage of principals of each group who indicated that the junior high school is the best place for such experience was: (1) principals with grades 7-8-9—91%; (2) principals with grades 7-8—65%; (3) principals with grades 6-7-8—55%; (4) principals with experience as principal of a four-year high school—76%.

2. The best opportunity to develop wholesome boy-girl relationships among ninth grade pupils is in the junior high school, according to most principals in these groups: (1) principals with grades 7-8-9—81%; (2) principals with experience as principal of a four-year high school—72%. Principals of schools with grades 6-7-8 were quite divided in their opinions concerning the best place for ninth grade pupils to develop wholesome boy-girl relationships as follows: (1) four-year high school—50%; (2) junior high school—43%; (3) others or no reply—7%.

3. Both ninth grade boys and girls are least likely to develop undesirable attitudes of social sophistication if the ninth grade is in the junior high school, in the opinion of a substantial majority of the principals of schools with grades 7-8-9, those with grades 7-8, and those who have also been principal of a four-year high school. Principals of schools with grades 6-7-8, however, were more divided in their opinions on this question. For ninth grade girls, principals with grades 6-7-8 indicated the least likely place to develop undesirable social sophistication was as follows: (1) junior high school—44%; (2) four-year high school—38%; (3) others or no reply—18%. For ninth grade boys, principals with grades 6-7-8 indicated the place they were least likely to develop such undesirable attitudes was: (1) junior high school—40%; (2) four-year high school—41%; (3) others—19%.

4. Steady dating is least likely to begin among ninth grade pupils if the ninth grade is in the junior high school, according to a substantial majority of three groups of principals, as follows: (1) principals with grades 7-8-9—75%; (2) principals with grades 7-8—61%; (3) principals with experience as principal of a four-year high school—

68%. Principals of schools with grades 6-7-8 likewise considered the junior high school the least likely place to lead to steady dating by ninth grade pupils, though they were more divided, as follows: (1) junior high school—49%; (2) four-year high school—24%; (3) no difference—18%; (4) others or no reply—9%.

5. The junior high school is least likely to lead to dating by ninth grade girls and older boys (grades 11-12), in the opinion of a substantial majority of all groups of principals, as follows: (1) principals with grades 7-8-9—85%; (2) principals with grades 7-8—72%; (3) principals with grades 6-7-8—68%; (4) those with experience as principal of a four-year high school—85%. In fact, on no other question did such a high percentage of principals of all groups indicate that the junior high school is the best place for the ninth grade.

6. The junior high school was considered to be the best place for the ninth grade academic studies by most principals (60%) of schools with grades 7-8-9 and by most principals (51%) who had previous experience as principal of a four-year high school. Principals of schools with grades 7-8 were divided, however, on this question as follows: (1) four-year high school—43%; (2) junior high school—41%; (3) others or no reply—16%. Most principals (62%) of schools with grades 6-7-8 considered the four-year high school to be the best place for ninth grade academic studies.

7. The junior high school is the best place for the "total education experience" of the ninth grade, in the opinion of a majority of three groups of principals, with the percentage of each group expressing this opinion as follows: (1) principals of schools with grades 7-8-9—79%; (2) principals with grades 7-8—53%; (3) principals with experience as principal of a four-year high school—71%. Principals of schools with grades 6-7-8 were the only group which indicated that the ninth grade would have the best "total educational experience" in the four-year high school, with a small majority expressing this opinion—51%.

5. General Conclusion

The junior high school with grades 7-8-9 therefore had more support from the principals and state department representatives included in this study than either of the other two types of schools. Grades 7-8-9 were considered to be the best grades for the junior high school on the questions raised in the study, as compared with grades 7-8 and grades 6-7-8, and junior high school was considered to be the best place for the ninth grade. Support for a junior high school with grades 7-8-9 was especially strong among principals of schools with grades 7-8-9, principals with experience as principal of more than one type of school, and state department representatives. Even principals of schools with grades 6-7-8 and grades 7-8, however, showed more support for a junior high school with grades 7-8-9 than for either of the other plans. Finally, there was little support from any group of principals on any of the questions raised in the study for schools with either grades 6-7-8 or grades 7-8, except from the principals of those schools. Even these principals, however, showed only limited support for these types of schools.

8

Nicholas P. Georgiady &
Louis G. Romano

The Middle School—
Is It a Threat to
the Elementary School?

In the mass media as well as in the literature of our profession there has been repeated reference to the "lost generation"—the pre-teenagers and teenagers of our time. These are the children who have failed to find significance and meaning in their educational experiences or in life itself. This has set in motion a search for a more appropriate program of educational experiences for these young people.

Definition of a Middle School

One promising idea has been the concept of the middle school. The literature varies in identifying the scope of such a program. Some writers include grades 5, 6, 7 and 8[1] while others limit it to grades 6, 7 and 8.[2] There appears to be general agreement that it should not include grade 9.

The authors prefer to define the middle or intermediate school as a new school organizational arrangement encompassing what are traditionally grades 5, 6, 7 and 8 for purposes of planning and conducting a unique set of educational experiences for early adolescent or transecent students.

From *Impact,* New York Association for Supervision and Curriculum Development (Winter, 1967-68): 14-18.

Failure of the Present Junior High School

In its first conception, the junior high school was intended to be a unique organization to meet the needs of children between the ages of 10 and 13. The passage of time has disillusioned many early advocates of this structural pattern as they have viewed the gradual but unmistakable emulation of the high school program in the junior high school. The result has largely been a watered-down high school program conducted in the junior high school. Teachers and administrators in the junior high school have tended to keep their eyes focused on the high school and have often regarded their positions at the junior high school level as hopefully leading to ultimate assignment to the senior high school.

Conditions Leading to Development of Middle School Concept

Several conditions have developed which have rendered obsolescent the earlier concept of the junior high school. For one, physical maturation of children has been accelerated. Accompanying such earlier maturation is a host of related emotional and social problems raised by the task of the child's recognizing the nature and significance of such changes and accepting and adjusting to them. Secondly, the junior high school of the past was concerned with providing an easier transition from the elementary school to the high school. The underlying reason was to increase the holding power of the schools—to retain students in school longer. The junior high school was designed for relatively unsophisticated students living in an unsophisticated society. However, the greatly accelerated pace of living in our society, increased pressures and more rapid communications have changed children into more socially oriented individuals at an age earlier than ever before. In short, students in this period are experiencing a major disorganization.[3]

Principles in the Middle School Concept

To meet and deal with the conditions cited above, the middle school concept will require the following important principles:
1. To recognize clearly the unique physical, emotional, social and psychological characteristics of children in this age group.

2. To utilize knowledge concerning characteristics of these children as major criteria for developing school programs for them.
3. To develop a curriculum not necessarily modeled after either the high school program or the elementary school program but articulated with both.
4. To provide greater opportunity for self-direction and responsibility for learning on the part of students.
5. To provide opportunities for students in the understanding and appreciation of democratic principles through the practice of democratic skills.

Other important considerations should be provided for in the middle school. There ought to be far greater opportunity for and encouragement of pupil-teacher planning.[4] Likewise, there ought to be recognition that individual differences among and between students become more pronounced as they grow and develop. This necessitates a lush environment of instructional materials, techniques and human resources to permit further individual growth and development according to the needs of each student. Related to this is the important recognition that the non-graded approach provides recognition of the individual and seeks to develop a program according to his pattern of growth.

Numerous other characteristics of the middle school concept can be cited as being important. However, essential to the planning carried on in the middle school concept is the recognition that the maximal development of students should be the ultimate goal.

Possible Negative Effects

A question raised frequently asks what effect the middle school concept will have on the elementary school. Some educators tend to view the middle school as a threat to the existence of the elementary school as it is presently constituted. If the middle school is viewed as being a renamed junior high school with the addition of one or two grades, the result would be a materialization of the threat expressed. This will probably result in pressure for departmentalization at lower grades than previously, a pressure to "get students ready" for the middle school, a pressure for scholastic achievement as measured by standardized tests, a pressure for counselors to assume roles and responsibility for total guidance of students, possible pressure for participation in inter-scholastic, highly competitive sports and pressure for more sophisticated social activities. The whole question of accreditation of schools below the high school level may well be advanced as a result. The elementary school could very well become a "junior middle school"!

Possible Positive Effects

Rather than posing a threat to the elementary school, the well-planned, soundly-based middle school concept could serve to improve the elementary school in several ways:

1. An important principle of the middle school concept is the fuller recognition of and provision for individual differences. To accomplish this, better records on each student will be needed. Counseling, guidance and planning will give rise to such important information. Additional counseling services provided by specially trained persons, including psychologists, will serve to supplement the important work of the classroom teacher in this regard. Use of such records and personnel may be extended to the elementary school.
2. The non-graded pattern, as an important characteristic of the effective middle school, may be extended to the earlier grades.
3. The middle school will have good programs in physical education, music and art utilizing the services of trained personnel in these areas. This should serve as an example to the elementary school in the lower grades where efforts of classroom teachers in these areas are often weak and can be supplemented.
4. The use of more specialized personnel, technicians and other aides, should be available to assist teachers in the middle school. The elementary school may also recognize that teachers can work more effectively with children when provided with such aid.
5. The technique of the inquiry method is a characteristic of a good middle school. This calls for a central learning center with materials in variety. A staff member in such a center should be competent to help children use a variety of materials and resources in dealing with individual study problems. The elementary school should benefit from the example.
6. With the inclusion of grades 5 and 6 in the intermediate or the middle school, the elementary school will be modified to permit 4th

graders to assume tasks in the safety patrol and other responsibilities which develop confidence and independence.

7. One of the objectives of the middle school is "to advance the children academically and intellectually and to slow them down socially."[5] The middle school could act as a buffer in the extension downward of social activities more appropriate to the mature students. Therefore, the elementary school would be in a better position to develop social activities commensurate with the social and emotional needs of younger children.

8. To accomplish the objectives of a sound middle school program, physical facilities will need to be appropriately provided. In the same way, the needs of lower elementary school children will be better met with physical facilities specifically designed for them.

While many of the characteristics of the middle school have implications for and application to the elementary school, these need to be carefully reviewed in light of the characteristics of elementary school children before such application is made.

Summary and Implications

As has been stated, a void exists in the educational continuum wherein the age group between ten and thirteen years is inadequately provided for. The early promise of the junior high school has failed to materialize. An acceleration of social and physical maturation on the part of children in this age group and rapid changes in our society have made necessary a re-examination of educational programs at this level. One area of promise lies in the middle school concept predicated on a knowledge of the unique characterisitics of pre-teenage children.

Though viewed by some as a threat to the elementary school, the middle school in reality affords promise through example to the elementary school. These not only coexist simultaneously but can substantially assist and supplement each other effectively.

While the comments up to this point have been confined to the possible effects of the middle school on the elementary school, it should be recognized that there are other implications that deserve attention.

There is a need for strong pre-service and in-service programs for both middle school personnel and elementary school personnel based on the unique characteristics of each of the schools and the relationship between them.

Thought should also be given to the development of an organization of middle school administrators, curriculum specialists, and teachers as well as a body of literature pertaining to the middle school curriculum. While this may appear to be divisive in nature, the underlying thought here is that the middle school concept should be regarded as unique if it is truly to meet the needs of the children in those grades involved. It cannot be regarded as part of the elementary program or the secondary program lest it become, for example, a downward extension of the secondary school program as exemplified by the junior high school. With the development of the middle school concept, there must be a re-definition of the role of the elementary school. The result should be positive change in the direction of maximizing learning experiences for boys and girls in each school.

Notes

1. Nickerson, N.C. "Regroup for Another Try." *Minnesota Journal of Education,* November, 1966.

2. Howard, A.W. "Which Years in Junior High?" *Clearing House,* December, 1966.

3. Eichkorn, Donald. *The Middle School.* New York: The Center for Applied Research Education, p. 9.

4. See discussion of pupil-teacher planning, Krug, E.A. *Curriculum Planning.* New York: Harper Bros., 1957.

5. Murphy, Judith. *Middle Schools.* New York: Educational Facilities Laboratories, 1965, p. 23.

9

Mary F. Compton

After the Middle School . . .?

During this latter half of the twentieth century, public education has entered a period of crisis. This is manifested in dropout statistics, student unrest, and an upsurge in the number of rapidly-established private institutions throughout the country. One can hardly peruse a newspaper or popular periodical without locating at least one article dealing with the woes of education. As never before, educators are beginning to realize that, in addition to putting their own houses in order, they need to view education as a continuous stream from nursery school through higher education—or, as someone has put it, "from womb to tomb." We can no longer isolate ourselves as specialists in early childhood, elementary, intermediate, secondary, or higher education, without regard to the levels which precede and follow our own specific interests. A change at any of these levels effects changes at all others.

What and Why of the Middle School

A major educational trend of the latter 1900's is the movement toward the middle school as an alternative to the junior high school. The tremendous growth of this organizational pattern is evidenced by at least two national surveys. William Alexander of the University of Florida using the following definition in locating middle schools during the 1967-68 school year: "a school which combines into one

From *Michigan Journal of Secondary Education* (Summer, 1971): 28-36.

organization and facility certain school years (usually grades 5-8 or 6-8) which have in the past usually been separated in elementary and secondary schools under such plans as the 6-3-3, 6-2-4, and 6-6."[1] Alexander located 1101 of these schools within the 48 contiguous states. In 1970 Ronald Kealy[2] of George Peabody College updated the previous survey and found 2298 in the 50 states. The schools vary greatly in internal organization and program, often within school districts. Many, unfortunately, are no more than watered-down versions of the junior high school.

A *true* middle school resembles neither the junior high with its departmental, subject-centered program nor the elementary school with its traditional self-contained organization. Real middle schools focus on the learner—not the subject disciplines. We are beginning to accumulate data on youngsters from ten to fourteen—physiological, psychological, and sociological data—which indicate that youngsters during these years are indeed in a period of transition between childhood and adolescence. They are unlike both the younger child and the full-fledged adolescent, and they need a program which differs from that of the elementary school and the high school. Implications can be drawn from the nature of these pre- and early adolescents for the kind of educational program needed. These include the following:

1. Youngsters during these years can benefit from instruction by specialists; they recognize competence and incompetence in teachers; they enjoy variety; and, they are capable of understanding the relationship between various subjects. Interdisciplinary team teaching and/or single-subject teaming would, therefore, seem appropriate.

2. Variation in developmental rate, academic ability, and interests indicates that youngsters need opportunities to work on their own. This could be implemented in several ways, including programs of independent study in which each youngster may utilize various media to explore questions of interest to them and through skills laboratories designed for remedial, developmental, and advanced work in reading, writing, listening, mathematics, science, foreign languages, art, music, and physical education.

3. The importance of the peer group during these years would indicate the need for the opportunity for youngsters to work in small groups of ten to fifteen. These small groups could supplement large-group instruction by providing opportunities for the exploration of ideas and questions and for the pursuit in greater depth of interests

germinated by large-group instruction. Another type of small group could replace the homeroom unit—but not assume its role. This would provide the opportunity for youngsters to explore questions of importance to them (and selected by them). The teacher's role in the small group would be that of consultant and director of verbal traffic—a facilitator of discussion rather than the leader. This teacher would be the primary guidance worker in the school, counseling youngsters who have individual problems not severe enough to be referred to a full-time professional guidance worker.

4. The wide range of development, ability, and interests calls for an activity program in which each youngster can participate—a program based on personal development rather than on enhancing the school's prestige or entertaining the public. There will be interest and hobby clubs as well as intramural sports, instead of high school clubs, marching bands, cheer leaders, and interscholastic sports.

5. A flexible schedule would be based on the uniqueness of each youngster and tailored for each individual. The absence of grade nine and the spectre of the Carnegie unit allows great flexibility in the program. *True* nongrading or continuous progress programs are possible without the dominance of six or seven neatly-tied packages of x number of minutes for y number of days per week.

6. Evaluation would be based on individual progress rather than on a punitive grading system which has been waved like a club over the heads of youngsters to control them.

7. True articulation between the middle school and the levels which precede and follow it is required to ease the transition from one educational level to the next.

The Middle School Graduate

Youngsters who have experienced a middle school program such as that described above will be unlike those from the traditional junior high school program. They may be younger for two reasons: (1) they will enter high school in grade nine instead of grade ten, and (2) if the middle school has employed a *true* non-graded approach rather than the traditional grade-a-year plan, they will enter high school when they have reached the academic and maturation levels which render high school matriculation appropriate. Greater numbers of these youngsters may also survive educationally to enter high school because they have been able to identify the middle school program as made for them. They will not, therefore, be as likely to be sitting and waiting for their sixteenth birthdays so they can officially drop out.

Even more significant than the age and number of these entering students are characteristics which may result from a middle school program based on the uniqueness of students during the middle years.

Greater Knowledge About Subject Areas

Instruction by specialists may result in students' acquiring greater depth and breadth of knowledge in the subject fields than the usual entering high school student. Interdisciplinary team teaching can help youngsters to see beyond the artificial barriers of subject areas and to understand the interrelatedness of knowledge. Flexible scheduling will permit the youngsters to pursue his interests instead of having to rush through a period with one eye on the clock, and such flexibility will also provide time for greater interchange of ideas with teachers and other students. He will be accustomed to working with teachers who stimulate his thinking rather than to providing "pat" answers to predetermined questions. He will have experienced a program not only centered around him, his needs, and interests, but also sufficiently flexible to have been tailored to him instead of attempting to fit him to the program. Most important, he will have been an active participant in the learning process rather than a passive absorber of facts.

Independent Learning

Through a program of independent study for all students—even the least able—the youngsters will be capable of assuming responsibility for realistic goals to be pursued on his own. This experience will have provided him the opportunity to learn to budget time. He will seek the advice and aid of specialists who are aware of his ability and the resources—print, non-print, technological, and human—to which he may turn for help in solving some problems. These resources may also serve to trigger other questions of which he may have been previously unaware. He will know and understand himself, his strengths, limitations, needs, and goals more fully than do students from the traditional program. Consequently, the range of differences among entering high school students will be much greater than it has been assumed to be in the past.

Personal and Social Adjustment

An emphasis on guidance in the middle school will help the youngster avoid many of the psychological difficulties experienced by his counterpart of today. Teachers prepared to help youngsters deal with personal and social problems will be complemented by professional guidance counselors who will be available to help with more severe problems. He will, then, have at least one adult at school to whom he can turn whenever he has a problem. Through small group discussions with his peers, he will find he is not alone in many of his problems. He will have been aided through the turbulent years of transition between childhood and adolescence during which many problems of adolescence take root. He will view school as an interesting and even an exciting place where someone cares about him as an individual and about the kinds of things about which he is interested and concerned. He will not be afraid to risk being inaccurate because every question, comment, or answer will be deemed worthy of consideration. He will be accustomed to being evaluated on the basis of his own abilities and goals rather than on that of some elusive "average." His self concept will be positive, and he will have developed tolerance for people who differ from himself through "rapping" with others in various kinds of group activities.

If the youngster has participated in such a middle school program, his positive view of himself, his classmates, his teachers, the school, and learning in general should result in fewer personal and social problems during adolescence; he should have good school attendance and be less likely to drop out during the high school years.

Creative Thinking

Empirical data[3] indicate that the ability to think creatively is usually less apparent during the years of late childhood and early adolescence than in the early elementary years. A middle school program tailored for the individual youngster, through which he can explore his interests and test hypotheses, should encourage creative thinking. Instead of focusing on a single approach to a single correct answer, he will be free to engage in divergent thinking and to explore various avenues to various possible answers. Experience in this kind of thinking will render him inquisitive, active, and creative.

Articulation

The youngster should be no stranger to the high school if his middle school has implemented a well-planned program of articulation. He will have had opportunities for sharing staff and facilities with the high school as well as the elementary school. Exchange teaching with these schools is one promising practice. Instructional staffs can ease the transition for students when they are able to form a more holistic view of the continuity of the program, and "Walking in the other fellow's moccasins" will tend to make teachers more tolerant of the problems encountered at each level. Other possible practices are joint special programs and activities as well as advanced instruction. Joint curriculum planning by elementary, middle school, and high school staffs will assure better articulation. If the youngster is no stranger to the high school, its staff, its program, its facilities, and its expectations, the usual period of adjustment may be virtually eliminated.

Changes in the High School

No one can guarantee that the middle school will bring about changes in the high school. One can only hope that sensitive, innovative high school staffs will take a critical look at the program they offer in light of the nature of the students they receive from the middle school. Changes will be necessary if the high school is to meet the needs of these students.

The High School in the Big Picture

The view of the high school as a separate and autonomous institution will give way to the concept of a broad continuum of public education—from the nursery school through the graduate school. It will seek to become a cooperative, functional part of the "big picture." It will no longer judge its entering students by the degree to which they are "ready for high school" and will begin to identify new ways of serving students. It will no longer seek to control those levels which precede it in matters concerning Carnegie-unit credit because it will be the sole institution granting such credit. The high school, in assuming its role in a much broader picture, may come to refute the control of university requirements and to plan a program *it* feels will be best for its students.

Disappearance of the "Track"

The practice of channeling students into one of four curricula—academic, vocational, commercial, and general—must disappear if the high school is to meet student needs. The narrow confines of a specific program of studies are far too restrictive for the youngster who has had the opportunity to explore a wide variety of subject areas. Instead, the high school may provide the opportunity for the student and his parents to design a tentative program of studies with a counselor prior to high school entrance, with many opportunities for periodic review and revision of the program throughout the high school years. Vocational alternatives (with emphasis on the plural) should be considered by all students, including those whose major goal is higher education. Unsuccessful experience in college would lose some of its trauma if students have explored alternative choices. The college student may also have more satisfying means of supplementing his income if he has vocational preparation beyond that of the common laborer.

Flexibility in Grouping and Scheduling

The flexibility of the middle school should produce a student who is not only capable of assuming responsibility for his own learning, but who is eager to do so. He will not be satisfied with the monotony of a rigid daily schedule when he is accustomed to pursuing work on his own in a variety of subject areas for at least part of the day. He will also be accustomed to variety in group size—large groups for general presentations, small groups for discussions, and the "non-group of one" when he is working on his own.

This kind of program is virtually impossible within the confines of the typical high school schedule. Block-of-time scheduling and the variation of classes throughout the week have been tested and proved successful in many high schools. These practices appear to be acceptable to both students and their teachers. It is interesting to note that these high schools have encountered little or no difficulty in helping students meet the requirements for college entrance.

The "Non-extra" Extra Curriculum

An expanded concept of curriculum will be required of the high school in light of the middle school. "Extra-curricular" activities will be considered important enough to be included within regular school hours, instead of relegated to an after-school status for those who can provide their own transportation.

The high school may also find that the usual activities program may no longer interest its students. True middle schools, for example, reject the incorporation of "farm teams" for the high school's interscholastic athletics program. Instead, the middle school will have recognized the need for youngsters of varying physical ability to participate in team sports and will provide intramural activities for not only the usual seasonal sports but for those which carry-over— such as bowling, swimming, tennis, boating, and gymnastics. Consequently, the high school may have to revamp its athletic program to include intramural and recreational activities.

Marching bands will be one of the accoutrements of interscholastic sports missing from the middle school. Instead, it will offer programs of instrumental music for all interested students. Some students will choose to join performing groups; others will learn to play for their own personal enjoyment. Choice of instruments will extend beyond those required for bands and orchestras to include the guitar, banjo, accordion, harp, organ, xylophone, marimba, bongo drums, and many others. This type of program will necessitate an expansion of musical experiences in the high school.

The activities program based on requests of middle school students will require a revamping of that of the high school. To meet the expanding interests of its students as they progress through high school, the program of the high school should be even more broad than that of the middle school. It may include hobby and special interest clubs, scenario writing and film production, barbershop quartet singing, book review groups, toastmaster clubs, choreography, orchestration of musical scores, skin diving, sailing, camping, and creative and interpretive dancing.

Evaluation of Pupil Progress

One of the imperative changes to be undertaken by the high school will be its system of evaluating and reporting pupil progress. If the student is to be evaluated in terms of individual progress, the high school must eliminate its system of letter grades, percentage scores, stanines, or coded numbers. It will turn to other means of evaluating progress which will be more meaningful to the student as well as to his parents—and to higher education. Performance-based programs and other individual curricular offerings will highlight self-evaluation by the student.

High school transcripts might indicate experiences successfully attempted and not those the student was unable to complete for various reasons. The student would not, therefore, be penalized in terms of time expended or failing grades for attempting something in which he felt he was interested but for which he was unprepared.

The Opportunity for the High School

The high school that designs its programs in light of the nature of students entering from the middle school will have a degree of flexibility never before evident in its history. It will find itself in a unique position to bring together all levels of education into a continuous educational stream—with programs designed for youngsters. It may well relieve the crisis in which American education presently finds itself. Few educators will deny it credit for such an enterprise!

References

1. Alexander, William M. "A Survey of Organizational Patterns of Reorganized Middle Schools," USOE Cooperative Research Project 7-D-026, 1968.

2. Kealy, Ronald P. "Middle Schools in the United States: 1969–70," Mimeographed, 1970.

3. Torrance, E. Paul. *Guiding Creative Talent.* Englewood Cliffs, N. J.: Prentice-Hall, 1962.

10

Gordon F. Vars

Teacher Preparation for Middle School

After 60 years of existence, the junior high is still largely a "school without teachers"—that is, without teachers prepared specifically for work at this level.[1] Will the situation improve if we re-juggle school organization and establish middle schools? Not likely. It is difficult to see how forming intermediate units with somewhat younger students will increase the supply of teachers, except perhaps to make it easier for administrators to hire teachers away from the already-shorthanded elementary schools.

Establishing special certificates or endorsements for junior high or middle school teachers will not solve the problem, either, judging from the experience of the few states that have tried it. Witness the excellent middle-grade teacher preparation program adopted in September, 1967, by the Nebraska Council on Teacher Education.[2] To date not one college or university in that state has a program to prepare teachers for certification under this plan. Even in states where both special certification and programs exist, college students stay away in droves. Why? Why has there been so little response to the need for especially-prepared teachers for the middle schools?

Is it because educators cannot make up their minds about the kind of teacher they want? This does not appear to be the case. From the very early days of the junior high school movement, a widespread

From *The High School Journal* (December, 1969): 172–77.

consensus has existed on both the personal qualities and the professional competencies needed. Teachers, administrators, curriculum specialists, and others working at this level agree that the effective middle school teacher is a reasonably cultured individual of good character who:

(1) understands and enjoys working with youngsters in this age range;
(2) knows something worth teaching to young people; and
(3) knows some effective ways to teach.

Of course, when stated in such general terms, these qualifications apply to teachers at any level. The uniqueness of junior high and middle school teaching stems in part from the diversity and rapid change that characterize young people as they approach and pass through puberty. It takes an especially resilient teacher to work with such a volatile age group. Harry Broudy puts it very well when he says the teacher should be "someone who has not yet fully incorporated the values of the middle aged, who shares the anxiety of the group in coping with elders and officials, and who still has some of the youthful rebel in him. In other words, he is still warm from the transitional state albeit indubitably a member of the adult community."[3] This calls for selective recruitment and careful screening of prospective teachers for the intermediate level.

A second source of uniqueness is the "in-between" status of the school itself. It receives students from an institution concerned primarily with common learnings, especially the basic skills, and passes them on to one that stresses specialization and at least the beginnings of vocational preparation. Also, the elementary school tends to be somewhat more child-centered, whereas subject matter mastery receives greater emphasis in high school. Blending these points of view and helping youngsters to make a smooth transition from one kind of institution to another imposes special demands upon all who work at the middle level. We shall see presently how these somewhat conflicting demands affect teacher preparation.[4]

If the need is obvious and there is at least general agreement on the kind of teacher required, why are not more colleges and universities preparing teachers for the middle schools? At least part of the difficulty appears to come from five false antitheses rampant in the field of teacher education.

1. Encounter vs. Professional Skill Training

Teachers at any level must have some affinity for the age group with which they deal, so ample opportunity to "encounter" and interact with students is essential in any teacher preparation program. Although difficult to prove through research, experience with young people would appear to be especially crucial in preparing junior high or middle school teachers.[5] Programs become distorted, however, when teacher educators emphasize these experiences to the neglect of others.

On the other hand, there are those who stress analysis of the teaching process, utilizing microteaching, interaction analysis, and various types of feedback—notably videotape—to help students learn the skills of teaching. Sometimes age-level differences and the uniqueness of each individual child are overlooked or minimized in this pursuit of a science of pedagogy.

Prospective teachers do need early and sustained association with boys and girls to find out if they really want to teach and to determine the age level with which they work best. But they also need all the skills they can master, both prior to and throughout full-time teaching. Teaching skills must be learned in realistic classroom situations and geared toward particular age groups, with ample allowance for individual differences in both teachers and students. Both "encounter" and skill training are essential.

2. Subject Matter vs. Method

Hardly anyone these days argues this in either-or terms, but some teacher preparation institutions emphasize one or the other. Secondary programs, especially in liberal arts colleges, tend to be heavy on courses in the teaching field, with perhaps only one course on teaching methods. Elementary programs usually include numerous methods courses and, consequently, less work in the substantive fields. Those who would prepare teachers for the middle school years will immediately find themselves pulled in both directions. Resolution of this conflict is related to the next antithesis.

3. Depth vs. Breadth

Should middle school teachers be specialists in one subject area or somewhat familiar with several? Here, again, the contrasts between typical elementary and secondary patterns create the need for compromise in programs for junior high and middle school teachers. Specialization may be desirable in fields like foreign languages, industrial arts, or physical education, but in the basic academic areas, "modest" depth in two related areas appears to be preferable. The many block-time, core, humanities, or interdisciplinary team teaching programs in the intermediate grades call for teachers familiar with both content and methods in related fields, such as English and social studies or science and mathematics.[6] The effective middle school teacher will know both content *and* methods and have reasonable depth *and* breadth of subject matter background.

4. Program vs. Certification

Which should come first, special teacher preparation programs or special state certification requirements? Unfortunately, most colleges and universities gear their programs to existing state regulations, despite frequent assertions by state officials that experimental programs are encouraged and will be granted special dispensation. As a result, reformers frequently concentrate on getting the rules changed. This is essentially a political process, and the compromises necessary to win acceptance may result in regulations that are so watered down as to require little real change in practice, or that are so permissive that they are largely ignored.

At the other extreme, college educators may fight valiantly to establish special teacher preparation programs in their institutions, only to find that students still prefer the conventional elementary or secondary programs. Why? Perhaps the new program aims at too narrow a range of teaching levels. For instance, a student who is unsure whether he wants to teach junior or senior high might better take a regular secondary program, rather than one that limits him to teaching in grades seven, eight, or nine. Sometimes the special program takes longer, or requires commitment too early in a student's college career. Or it may just be so new that few students have heard of it. To sum up, programs that are little known, that require extra work, or that restrict a graduate's chances of employment will not attract large numbers into junior high or middle school teaching, regardless of the certificate they lead to.

Clearly, both programs *and* certification requirements should be designed to encourage qualified young people to teach in the middle grades. State certification officials should work closely with interested college and university staff members, and also seek the advice of administrators and teachers in the field. If it seems desirable to revise certification grade levels, broad bands should be established, such as Nebraska's elementary (K-6), middle (5-9), and secondary (7-12). In any case, completion of a special middle school preparation program should be recognized in some way by certification officials, perhaps by endorsement on either an elementary or a secondary certificate.

5. Push vs. Pull

After 60 years in the doldrums, it will take a great deal of force to get middle school teacher preparation moving under full sail and headed in the right direction. At what point should the effort be applied? Should college educators push harder to get programs established? Should school administrators and hiring officials exert more pull on college administrators and certification officials? Is *anything* likely to be done as long as junior high and middle schools are permitted to employ just about anyone they can get, regardless of whether they have had any special preparation for this level?

Obviously it is going to take concerted effort by everyone to solve the problem. Interested individuals can have some impact, but action is more likely if organizations of teachers, administrators, curriculum supervisors, and others bombard the colleges and the state certification authorities with demands for change. In the meantime, interested college staff members should push from within to change existing teacher preparation programs or to establish new ones.

State education department officials, especially those concerned with teacher certification, should take the lead in bringing together representatives of all interested parties to plan over-all policies and to stimulate development of programs at teacher preparation institutions. At the national level it is hoped that leadership might come from two groups, the Committee on Junior High and Middle School Education of the National Association of Secondary-School principals and the newly-created Council on the Emergent Adolescent Learner of the Association for Supervision and Curriculum Development.

In the final analysis, the massive inaction on this vital problem reflects a serious lack of communication among teachers, administrators, teacher educators, and government officials concerned with improving education in the middle schools. It is time for action, for mobilizing our forces to see that middle school students are provided with the finest possible teachers.

Notes

1. Dixon, Norman R. "The Search for JHS Teachers." *Clearing House,* October, 1965, pp. 82–84.

2. Harlan, Hugh. "Preparing Teachers to Teach in the Middle Grades." *Creating the Environment for Learning,* pp. 36–42. Lincoln: Nebraska State Department of Education, 1969.

3. Broudy, Harry S. "The Junior High School: A Philosopher's View," from "Highlights of the Tenth Annual Conference for School Administrators . . .," p. 13. Ithaca, New York: School of Education, Cornell University, 1963.

4. Vars, Gordon F. "Preparing Junior High Teacher." *Clearing House,* October, 1965, pp. 77–81.

5. Vars, Gordon F. "An Examination of the Relationship between Success in Junior High School Practice Teaching and Prior Experience with Children," *Teachers College Journal,* November, 1967, pp. 64–67.

6. Vars, Gordon F., ed. *Common Learnings: Core and Interdisciplinary Team Approaches.* Scranton, Pennsylvania: International Textbook Company, 1969.

11

Jack E. Blackburn

The Junior High School
Teacher We Need

One recent Monday morning, a junior high school block-of-time class was having a current events discussion. Albert Schweitzer had passed away during the preceding weekend and much of the pupils' discussion dealt with Mr. Schweitzer. The teacher asked, "What stands out most in your mind when you think of Albert Schweitzer?"

There was a variety of responses from the class. One young adolescent said, "He was all for unfortunate people. I think he was real human. According to a news article I read, Mr. Schweitzer once said, 'You don't live in a world all your own. Your brothers are here, too.' "

The teacher responded, "What does being human mean? How do we distinguish between someone who acts human and someone who acts inhuman? Can you . . .?"

In one session of a college class in junior high school education, a student asked of the teacher, "Can you help us become more human in our dealings with kids?"

This past session of summer school, the writer attended a one-day conference at New York University. The main focus of the conference was an address centered around humanizing our schools.

The illustrations cited here are only three of many current happenings in which emphasis is on humanness. Concern with this is not

From *Educational Leadership* (December, 1965): 205–08. Reprinted with the permission of the Association for Supervision and Curriculum Development and Jack E. Blackburn. Copyright © 1972 by the Association for Supervision and Curriculum Development.

limited to educators. We could list numerous projects which are going on in our country and our world which show man's concern for his fellow man.

I, for one, am very pleased with the present emphasis in humanizing education. Never before in the history of American education has the climate been so appropriate for us to declare humanness as an educational goal. Some of us have often been reluctant, for one reason or another, to speak up for qualities which are uniquely human. I get the feeling that today, right now, this is the emphasis we need.

What does all of this talk about "humanizing" have to do with the junior high school teacher we need? To pose an answer to this question, we first need to turn attention to a concept of the purpose of education.

There is nearly unanimous agreement among our citizens that the general aim of education in a democracy is to contribute to the common good through aiding each individual in his process of becoming an intelligent, fully-functioning citizen. Each individual's unique self will determine the degree to which he becomes fully functioning. This is a very human goal.

If we accept this goal as a general aim for education, then what kind of teachers do we need to implement this objective in junior high schools?

Teachers Who Care

Some attributes of teachers who care have been described by a few people. Other perceptions, insights and skills have not been researched and discussed nearly enough. I would like to describe some qualities which, in my opinion, teachers need in order to aid pupils in their becoming process.

We need teachers who care about democracy.

In a country where citizens subscribe to a democratic way of life, we should not find it necessary to plead the case for democracy in school living. Yet, we are continually doing so. In fact, at least one person I know has raised the question—Is democracy indigenous to this country? When we visit schools and classrooms and see authoritarian practices being used, we might well raise such a question.

Teachers who care about democracy will know it and its opposing ideologies well. They will know that democratic living is learned. Their classroom organization will be such that it allows for pupils to engage in democratic practices.

From where I sit, academic freedom is a hot issue. From many states, teachers and lay citizens, we hear much about the subject of a teacher's freedom in the classroom. We need teachers who not only seek academic freedom for themselves but for pupils also.

Psychologists tell us that the most effective learning and personality development take place in democratic settings. To be democratic, we must have faith in others. Adlai Stevenson said so well:

> . . . I would . . . emphasize first that any discussion of educa-
> tion cannot be cast in terms of national needs . . . For
> education can serve the ends of democratic society only as
> it meets those of the individual human being. The essential
> condition of the system of free choice between conflicting
> ideas and leaders, which we call democracy, is that it be
> made up of all different kinds of people—which means that
> what we demand most of education is the development of
> informed people who are at the same time unique, differ-
> ent, unpatterned individuals.[1]

We need teachers who care about themselves.

In order for people to fully care about and have faith in others, they must view themselves in positive ways. To appreciate and respect the dignity and worth of another individual, a teacher must have looked within himself to know what is there.

We need teachers who care about helping pupils develop healthy self-concepts.

Seven years ago this writer participated in research designed to determine the relationship which exists between a nondirective drama technique and the development of reading skills and self-concept. This experience provided me with valuable insight. For example: How a person feels about himself ultimately determines his success or failure whether it be in reading, teaching, basketball, or any other endeavor.

Fortunately, we have available to us today some writings dealing with self-concept development. Teachers must continually strive to understand self and behavior. We need educators who take the time to understand their pupils; who will gather extensive information and use the data in the best interests of pupils.

To care about young adolescents one must understand them in their cultural setting. As Eric Hoffer puts it:

> The reasonable approach is to assume that the adolescents' behavior is induced largely by his mode of existence, by the situation in which he finds himself. This would imply that adults, too, when placed in a similar situation, would behave more or less like juveniles.[2]

The young adolescent is essentially a person in search of self in a complex world. He ponders the questions: "Who am I?" "Where am I going?" "What does all of this have to do with me anyway?"

What useful insights teachers can get when they turn directly to the learners themselves! One teacher asked his ninth grade classes the question, "What do you see as being the five biggest problems facing people your age?"

Representative responses were:

> We are being rushed along with the world to grow up and act our age.
> We need grades for college.
> We are worried over problems of the future.
> We worry about dropping out of school.
> We need to understand ourselves.
> We need more recreational activities.
> We live with grownups who think all teenagers are reckless.
> We are faced with the shortage of jobs because of automation.

The teachers we need for young adolescents realize that *values* and *self-concept* are almost, if not wholly, inseparable. These teachers cherish differences. They help pupils clarify their own values and respect the values of other persons.

We need teachers who care about making content meaningful in the lives of pupils.

"What is your class studying now Miss Bridges?"

"Oh, we're almost up to the Civil War. You see, it's almost the end of the year and we are supposed to cover American history from exploration to 1865 in the eighth grade."

"Do you mean uncover American history, Miss Bridges?"

"What? Oh, . . . it doesn't really matter. Students must have all of this for citizenship education anyhow."

How often we hear comments similar to these! And we must admit that teachers are not always at fault when they attempt to teach only what is in the book. Yet we know many teachers who use the excuse that a rigid structure is imposed upon them. They do not care whether or not the content has meaning to pupils.

One perceptive pupil, even from a school located in a "culturally deprived" area, said:

> My favorite kind of teacher is a scientist. My reason for liking scientists is that they are real intelligent and sensible. They are always discovering things. That's the way I want to be.

This youngster's insight should help some of us to sit up and take notice. In the past few years, teachers have continuously heard that learning by discovery can be most meaningful. Some teachers are so concerned about pouring knowledge into pupils they forget about helping pupils to discover. Teacher procedures might have more promise if we could somehow translate Rachel Carson's ideas into practice. She described experiences she had had with her nephew as they walked on the beach and in the woods in Maine. Mrs. Carson expressed her pleasure in plants and animals which they saw, much as she would share discoveries with an older person. Later, the nephew could easily identify what he and his aunt had seen. "I am sure no amount of drill would have implanted the names so firmly as just going through the woods in the spirit of two friends on an expedition of exciting discovery."[3]

For content to be meaningful to a pupil, he must see its importance to him. In order for pupils to learn skills most effectively, they must need them to get where they are going.

Pupils' opinions of what they need and their teachers' opinions are not always the same. A few educators propose what seems to be a sensible position about content selection. They say that the choice of content is not an either-or proposition; but rather that the learner as well as the world in which he finds himself must be considered in content decisions.

We need teachers who care about teaching in the junior high school.

A safe assumption seems to be that the most effective teachers of young adolescents are those who realize what junior high school education is all about. They are professional educators who understand goals of junior high schools and who work toward implementing these aims.

Because we cherish the dream of providing the best possible educational opportunities for each youth in our contemporary, democratic society, we continually must be involved in experimentation and innovation. The teachers we need have been and continue to be involved in rethinking and reconstructing educational practices for young adolescents.

Teachers who care about being in junior high school are teaching there because they so desire. These teachers are not simply "marking time" until they can be promoted to senior high school teaching. They value the goals of the school. They value the idea of teaching all children whatever their background.

Much needs to be said about changing the junior high school to better meet the educational needs of our young people. We must change the school when it is necessary. To change the school, we must have teachers who are willing to change. To change, we, as teachers, must *care.*

Notes

1. Stevenson, Adlai E. Quotation from *Teacher-Pupil Planning,* by Louise Parrish and Yvonne Waskin, pp. 155–56. New York: Harper & Brothers, 1958.

2. Hoffer, Eric. "A Time of Juveniles," *Harper's Magazine,* June 1965, p. 18.

3. Carson, Rachel. "Help Your Child to Wonder," *Woman's Home Companion,* July 1956.

Bibliography:
Questions Facing
the Middle School

Atkins, Thurston A. "It's Time for a Change—Or Is It?" *National Elementary Principal,* February 1969, pp. 46–48.

Bergstrom, L. H. "School Organization in Saskatchewan." *Canadian Education and Research Digest,* September 1965, pp. 248–57.

Boutwell, W. D. "What's Happening in Education? What Are the Middle Years?" *PTA Magazine,* December 1965, p. 14.

Brimm, R. P. "Middle School or Junior High?" *NASSP Bulletin,* March 1969, pp. 1–7.

Compton, Mary F. "The Middle School: Alternative to the Status Quo." *Theory Into Practice.* Columbus: The Ohio State University, June 1968, pp. 108–10.

Devita, Joseph C. "No Homework ... No Report Card Grades." *NASSP Bulletin,* October 1961, pp. 180–84.

Hedgecock, Laurie. "Eighth Grade Rebel." *NEA Journal,* September 1967, p. 19.

Howell, Bruce. "The Middle School—Is It Really Any Better?" *The North Central Association Quarterly,* Winter 1969, pp. 281–87.

Jameson, M. C. "A Candid Look at ... The Non-Graded School." *The Michigan School Board Journal,* October 1965, pp. 18–19.

Mass, Theodore C. "The Middle School Comes—And Takes Another Grade or Two." *The National Elementary Principal,* February 1969, pp. 36–41.

Nickerson, Neal C., Jr. "Regroup for Another Try." *Minnesota Journal of Education,* November 1966, pp. 14–15.

Pitkin, Victor E. "What Kind of Education for Early Adolescence?" *Nation's Schools,* March 1958, p. 113.

Rice, Arthur H. "What's Wrong with Junior Highs? Nearly Everything." *The Nation's Schools,* November 1964, pp. 30–32.

Rollins, Sidney P. "Are Middle Schools the Answer?" *Scholastic Teacher,* March 14, 1969, pp. 9–11.

Southworth, Horton C. "Teacher Education for the Middle School: A Framework." *Theory Into Practice.* Columbus: College of Education, The Ohio State University, June 1968, pp. 123–28.

The Times Educational Supplement. "Czech Nine-Year School." March 1965.

The Times Educational Supplement. "Middle School." May 1966, p. 1401.

Trump, J. L. "Whither the Middle School—or Whether." *NASSP Bulletin,* December 1967, pp. 42–44.

———. "Junior High Versus Middle School." *NASSP Bulletin,* February 1967, pp. 71–73.

Vars, Gordon F. "Junior High or Middle School? Which Is Best for the Education of Young Adolescents?" *The High School Journal,* December 1966, pp. 109–13.

———. "Core Curriculum in the Middle School." *Ideas Educational,* Winter 1967, pp. 25–28.

"While School Keeps." *Saturday Review,* August 18, 1962, pp. 56–57.

Whithey, Stephen B. "Critical Issues in Education." *The Michigan School Board Journal,* February 1963, p. 12.

Woodring, Paul. "The New Intermediate School." *Saturday Review,* October 16, 1965, pp. 77–78.

Selected References on Middle Schools

Books and Pamphlets

Ahlmann, J. Stanley, and Glock, Marvin D. *Evaluating Pupil Growth*. 2nd ed. Boston: Allyn and Bacon, Inc., 1963.

Alexander, William M. "New Organizational Patterns for the Middle School Years." *New Elementary School*. Washington, D.C.: Association for Superivision and Curriculum Development and Department of Elementary School Principals, National Education Association, 1968. pp. 52–67.

———. *A Survey of Organizational Patterns of Reorganized Middle Schools*. USOE Project No. 7-D-026. Gainesville: University of Florida, July 1968. 75 p.

Alexander, William M., and others. *The Emergent Middle School*. New York: Holt, Rinehart and Winston, 1968. 191 p.

Association for Childhood Education International. *The Transitional Years: Middle School Portfolio*. Washington, D.C.: The Association (3615 Wisconsin Avenue, N. W.), 1968.

Association for Supervision and Curriculum Development. *The Junior High School We Need*. Washington, D.C.: The Association, 1961. 37 p.

———. *The Elementary School We Need*. Washington, D.C.: The Association, 1965. 40 p.

———. *The New Elementary School*. Washington, D.C.: The Association, 1968.

Coleman, James S. *The Adolescent Society*. New York: Crowell-Collier Publishing Company, 1961.

494

Curtis, Thomas E., ed. *Middle School.* Albany: Center for Curriculum Research and Services, State University of New York, 1968. 270 p.

Eichhorn, Donald H. *Middle School.* The Library of Education. New York: Center for Applied Research in Education (70 Fifth Avenue), 1966. 116 p.

Erickson, Eric H. *Childhood and Society.* New York: W. W. Norton and Company, 1950.

Georgiady, Nicholas P.; Lewis, Robert; and Romano, Louis. *The Middle School: Guidelines for Educational Specifications.* Chicago, Illinois: The Chicago Board of Education, 1969. 89 p.

Gesell, Arnold, and others. *Youth—The Years from Ten to Sixteen.* New York: Harper and Row, Publishers, 1956. 542 p.

Grooms, M. Ann. *Perspectives on the Middle School.* Columbus: Charles E. Merrill Books, 1967. 152 p.

Havighurst, Robert J. *Developmental Tasks and Education.* New York: Longmans, Green and Company, 1952.

Henry, N. B., ed. *Individualizing Instruction.* Sixty-first Yearbook of the National Society for the Study of Education, Part I. Chicago: University of Chicago Press, 1962.

Howard, Alvin W. *Teaching in Middle Schools.* Scranton, Pa.: International Textbook Company, 1968. 161 p.

Howard, Eugene R., and Bardwell, Robert W. *How to Organize a Non-Graded School.* Englewood Cliffs, New Jersey: Prentice-Hall, Inc., 1966.

Jersild, Arthur T. *The Psychology of Adolescence.* New York: The Macmillan Company, 1963.

Kelly, Earl C. *In Defense of Youth.* Englewood Cliffs, New Jersey: Prentice-Hall, Inc., 1962.

Kindred, Leslie W., ed. *The Intermediate Schools.* Englewood Cliffs, New Jersey: Prentice-Hall, Inc., 1968. 531 p.

Kohl, John W., and Jones, Richard J. *The Middle School in Pennsylvania; a Status Study.* University Park: Pennsylvania School Study Council, Pennsylvania State University, College of Education, 1968. 35 p.

Loomis, Mary Jane. *How Children Develop.* The Faculty of the University School. Columbus, Ohio: The Ohio State University, 1964. 68 p.

Lounsbury, John H., and Marani, Jean. *The Junior High School We Saw: One Day in the Eighth Grade.* Washington, D.C.: Association for Supervision and Curriculum Development, 1964. 78 p.

McCarthy, Robert J. *How to Organize and Operate an Ungraded Middle School.* Englewood Cliffs, New Jersey: Prentice-Hall, Inc., 1967. 58 p.

Mills, George E. *The Middle School.* Ann Arbor: Michigan Association of School Boards, undated.

Murphy, Judith. *Middle Schools.* New York: Educational Facilities Laboratories, Inc. (477 Madison Avenue), 1965. 64 p.

National Education Association, Research Division, and American Association of School Administrators. *Middle Schools.* Educational Research Service Circular No. 3, 1965. Washington, D.C.: The Association, May 1965. 15 p.

————. *Grade Organization Patterns.* ERS Reporter. Washington, D.C.: Educational Research Service, National Education Association, November 1968. 25 p.

————. *Middle Schools in Action.* Educational Research Service Circular No. 2, 1969. Washington, D.C.: The Association, 1969. 80 p.

Nickerson, Neal C., Jr. *Junior High Schools Are on the Way Out.* Danville, Illinois: Interstate Printers and Publishers, 1966. 18 p.

Popper, Samuel H. *American Middle School.* Waltham, Mass. Blaisdell Publishing Company, 1967. 378 p.

Shaplin, Judson T., and Olds, Henry F., Jr., eds. *Team Teaching.* New York: Harper and Row, Publishers, 1965.

Shumsky, Abraham. *Creative Teaching in the Elementary School.* New York: Appleton-Century-Crofts, 1965.

Vars, Gordon F., ed. *Guidelines for Junior High and Middle School Education.* Washington, D.C.: National Association of Secondary School Principals, 1966.

Yates, Alfred, ed. *Grouping in Education.* New York: John Wiley and Sons, Inc., 1966.

About the authors—

Louis G. Romano is Professor of Education at Michigan State University. A former Superintendent of Schools in Wilmette, Illinois, he also has served as consultant to over 50 school systems in the U.S. and abroad.

Dr. Romano is author of three professional works, and also is co-author, with Dr. Georgiady, of a position paper on the middle school concept for the Chicago public school system. He is a founder and member of the Board of Directors of the Michigan Association of Middle School Educators.

Nicholas P. Georgiady is Professor of Education at Miami University at Oxford, Ohio. He has served as Deputy State Superintendent of Schools for Michigan. He also was visiting professor at the University of Wisconsin in Milwaukee, and Marquette and Michigan State Universities.

Dr. Georgiady is author or co-author of over 90 books and numerous articles for professional journals. He is active in research projects and is a member of many societies.

Dr. Georgiady was educated at Milwaukee State Teachers College, and at the University of Wisconsin, where he received his Ph.D.

James E. Heald is Dean, College of Education, at Northern Illinois University. Previously he was Director of University Planning at the University of North Carolina, and before that, Professor of Educational Administration at Michigan State University.

Dr. Heald has been a consultant on management and planning to many school districts, to the U.S. Department of Defense, the National Institutes of Health, and to foreign governments. He is co-author of three books, author of numerous articles, and a contributor in various capacities to state, regional, and national educational meetings.

Dr. Heald received his B.S. and M.S. degrees at Illinois State University, and his Ph.D. at Northwestern University.